CLASSIC YIDDISH

SUNY Series in Modern Jewish Literature and Culture
Sarah Blacher Cohen, Editor

CLASSIC YIDDISH FICTION

Abramovitsh, Sholem Aleichem, and Peretz

KEN FRIEDEN

State University
of New York
Press

Cover: Photograph of four Yiddish and Hebrew writers in Geneva, 1907, courtesy of Dvir Publishing Company. From left to right: S. Y. Abramovitsh, Sholem Aleichem, M. Ben-Ami, and H. N. Bialik.

Maps by Martin Gilbert

Published by
State University of New York Press, Albany

Production by Susan Geraghty
Marketing by Dana Yanulavich

Printed in the United States of America

For information, address State University of New York
Press, State University Plaza, Albany, N.Y., 12246

Library of Congress Cataloging-in-Publication Data

Frieden, Ken, 1955–
    Classic Yiddish Fiction : Abramovitsh, Sholem Aleichem, and Peretz
/ Ken Frieden.
        p.   cm. — (SUNY series in modern Jewish literature and
culture)
    Includes bibliographical references and index.
    ISBN 0-7914-2601-7 (hc). — ISBN 0-7914-2602-5 (pb)
    1. Mendele Moykher Sforim (S. Y. Abramovitsh), 1836–1917—Criticism
and interpretation.   2. Sholem Aleichem, 1859–1916—Criticism and
interpretation.   3. Peretz, Isaac Leib, 1852–1915—Criticism
and interpretation.   4. Social problems in literature.   5. Satire,
Yiddish—History and criticism.   6. Parody.   I. Title.   II. Series.
PJ5129.A2Z6725   1995
839'.0933—dc20
                                                              94-37692
                                                                CIP

CONTENTS

FIGURES

TABLES

PREFACE

Two or three generations ago, Yiddish was the primary language of the Jews in Eastern Europe and America. Today, following the Nazi genocide—and after half a century of vigorous assimilation—Yiddish is sinking into oblivion. By providing a bridge to the lost continent of Yiddish literature, this book resists a deepening estrangement from European traditions. The return to Ashkenazic origins also extends to broader horizons, since the development of Yiddish culture in Europe and America parallels the history of other ethnic traditions.

Yiddish writing in the late nineteenth century may be compared to postmodern architecture in the late twentieth century, because both Yiddish fiction and postmodern architecture make parody a dominant mode. Postmodern parody appropriates disparate styles and traditions while retaining ironic, critical distance. Some postmodern architects, for example, juxtapose Egyptian or Greek columns, Romanesque arches, and Gothic buttresses. By evoking precedents, postmodernism deliberately counters the ahistorical aesthetics of modern art. For entirely different reasons, classic Yiddish fiction relies heavily on parody and creates a patchwork of styles.

Few American readers understand that the Nobel-Prize winning stories by Isaac Bashevis Singer are only the tip of the iceberg; despite its remarkable accomplishments, Yiddish literature has never received the recognition it deserves. The present book remedies this neglect by interpreting the best Yiddish fiction of Sholem Yankev Abramovitsh, Sholem Aleichem, and Isaac Leybush Peretz.

Yiddish fiction uses the distinct forms represented by oral-style narrative, satire, and parody. At one extreme, oral monologues assume realistic conventions and appear to transcribe the colloquial speech of fictional characters; at the other extreme, parodies call attention to their fictionality by setting themselves in relation to prior literary models. Satires bring social criticism to bear on the reader's world. Given the character of Yiddish culture, orality was a guiding feature of nineteenth-century Yiddish fiction. This rhetoric of the spoken word differed from the predominant modes of modern Hebrew writing, which initially had only textual and liturgical exemplars.

As a result of their successive exiles, Jews neither integrated fully into European society nor remained completely rooted in origins; Yiddish literature expressed this double life by creating personae, fictional masks through which narrators speak. Yiddish authors frequently resorted to pseudonyms, which reflected their sense that they could not speak directly. Y. Y. Trunk shrewdly observed that as Jews "we do not appear in history as we are; we appear in disguise. Like the Jewish God, the Jewish people acts behind a cloud. . . . Who knows the true Jewish countenance? It appears like that of an actor, behind a mask." Much Yiddish writing speaks ironically, behind a mask.

While nineteenth-century Western European fiction typically revolves around heroic characters and their exploits, Yiddish writers employ irony, satire, and parody. Classic Yiddish authors seldom reveal the creation of a positive, new identity, but instead expose foibles that stand in the way. Often using irony, their satires of social norms go hand in hand with parodies of literary forms. Parody, in particular, was integral to the rise of Yiddish fiction. As latecomers to modern literature, Yiddish writers were obliged to rework prior traditions, from the Bible and rabbinic commentaries to contemporary Russian narrative. Unable to rely solely on the resources of ancient Hebrew Scripture or popular Yiddish storytelling, Yiddish writers also parodied—appropriated, incorporated, and modified—diverse elements from European novels and stories. For instance, both Abramovitsh and Sholem Aleichem wrote parodic versions of Cervantes' *Don Quixote,* set in a Jewish milieu. Twentieth-century British literature refers to centuries of writing in English; under the weight of past canons, implicit and explicit quotations become the general rule. In Yiddish literature, however, antecedent traditions could appear only in translation. Hebrew and Slavic words were embedded and altered in Yiddish, while biblical and talmudic quotations were embellished and revised.

Leaders of the nineteenth-century Jewish Enlightenment, following the program set by Moses Mendelssohn (1729–86) in Berlin, often shunned Yiddish or regarded it primarily as a means to educate the uneducated. This approach implied a "suicidal principle": as soon as the masses became sufficiently enlightened to speak French, German, Russian, and English, they and their benefactors would abandon Yiddish. Today, in light of prevailing ignorance of Yiddish culture, the time has come to reeducate the educated.

Scholars and other enthusiasts are contributing to a revival of interest in Yiddish. Many American universities offer courses on Yiddish language and literature, and intensive summer programs are sponsored by the YIVO (*Yidisher visnshaftlekher institut*) Institute for Jewish Research, by the Oxford Institute for Yiddish Studies, and by the Rothberg School at the Hebrew University of Jerusalem. Libraries around the world are building Yiddish collections, assisted by the National Yiddish Book Center. The Museum of Modern Art and the National Center for Jewish Film recently sponsored a retrospective of Yiddish cinema. Schocken Books has been issuing fresh translations in a series called "The Library of Yiddish Classics." The process of restoration and revival also has its pitfalls, fully evinced by popular books and films that appeal to nostalgic misconceptions of Jewish life in Eastern Europe. Yiddish literature need not serve a romanticized search for Jewish culture; in fact, Yiddish authors repeatedly criticized provincial life in the *shtetl*, attacking self-destructive practices and sweeping aside problematic identifications. Returning to classic Yiddish fiction, this study examines the pivotal role of satire and parody in social commentaries on Eastern European Jewish life.

Among the popular notions concerning Yiddish literature, one of the most pernicious is the idea that Yiddish writers were primitive artists who had little contact with European writing at large. Jewish culture has always benefited from its contact with other cultures, and Judaic literature is typical in this regard. I have indicated some of the debts Yiddish fiction owes to English, French, German, Russian, Polish, and Spanish fiction. To avoid provincialism, scholars of Hebrew and Yiddish writing must be aware of historical connections to world literature and contemporary methods of literary criticism.

Much more remains to be done to render the Yiddish tradition accessible to English-speaking readers, since most of the existing scholarship is in Yiddish and Hebrew. Moreover, few Yiddish critics in any language have employed the techniques of twentieth-century literary studies. Much of the best Yiddish criticism has been produced by scholars at the YIVO Institute for Jewish Research (in Vilna from 1925 to 1940 and in New York from 1940 to the present), by Soviet critics (especially in the 1920s and 1930s), and by Israeli academics (mainly in Jerusalem since the 1950s). Readers who desire a general introduction to the Yiddish language, which is beyond the scope of this book, may consult the reference works listed in the bibliography.

My readings draw eclectically from several methodologies. Taking a developmental approach to each author's work and to the relationships between them, I have concentrated on their early fiction. I emphasize the literary qualities of this tradition, and even where I sketch the biographies of the three major authors, I view their pertinent autobiographical writings as literary expressions. My goal is not to separate these authors, but to show the connections between them. Chronology is less determinative than are literary associations. Although Peretz was born before Sholem Aleichem, this study proceeds from Abramovitsh to Sholem Aleichem because this was the major line of influence in nineteenth-century Yiddish fiction. Peretz, in contrast, led a new group of writers into the twentieth century.

During the past decade several foundations and institutions have generously supported the writing of this study. I would like to thank the American Council of Learned Societies, the Emory University Research Committee, the Hebrew University of Jerusalem, the Lady Davis Trust, the Memorial Foundation for Jewish Culture, the National Endowment for the Humanities, the Yad Hanadiv/Barekha Foundation, and the YIVO Institute for Jewish Research. A grant from the Georgia Humanities Council enabled me to share a series of lectures on "Interpreting the Classics of Yiddish Fiction" with a Yiddish-speaking audience in Atlanta. Moreover, my students at Syracuse University and Emory University helped me to articulate much of what I have learned to say about Judaic literature. Parts of this book are based on papers delivered at conferences and previously published articles. I thank the editors of *The Jewish Book Annual* and *Modern Language Studies* for permission to reprint two of those discussions in modified form. For the photographs of Abramovitsh, Sholem Aleichem, and Peretz, and for the cover photo, I wish to thank the YIVO Institute for Jewish Research and Dvir Publishing Company.

My family and the late Joseph Glazer, as well as Dina Abramowicz, Zachary Baker, Benjamin Harshav, Avrom Novershtern, Chone Shmeruk, Vera Solomon, and Ruth Wisse provided assistance at several stages. I am especially indebted to Dan Miron for his oral and written guidance. His book *A Traveler Disguised,* the outstanding study of Abramovitsh's fiction, concludes: "This is the beginning of a new story. The story of the 'being' Sholem Aleichem, its development, its mode, or rather modes, of literary existence, its kinship with Mendele, and its points of departure from him—all this calls for a separate analysis and might be the subject of a sequel. Then there remains to chart the progress of the dramatic personae in modernistic Yiddish fiction. . . . Our present study must, however, end here." I have continued the story of Yiddish fiction where Miron leaves off.

Transliterations follow the YIVO guidelines, except in the case of names that have attained currency in another form. For the sake of consistency, I maintain the familiar spellings of the classic Yiddish authors' names throughout. When they occur in transcriptions of Yiddish or Hebrew titles, I have written Mendele Moykher Sforim (not Mendele Mocher Sfarim), Sholem Aleichem (instead of Sholem-Aleykhem or Shalom Aleichem), and I. L. Peretz (not Y. L. Perets). Phrases in Hebrew texts have been rendered by means of a straightforward system of transliteration based on current pronunciation. Less familiar Eastern European place names are spelled in accordance with Yiddish pronunciation, followed by other prominent spellings in parentheses. Chester Cohen's *Shtetl Finder* has been a helpful resource in this connection.

Much of Yiddish literature remains a closed book to today's readers; I have referred to available translations in my footnotes. An extensive list of classic Yiddish fiction in English may be found in the bibliography. Nevertheless, there is no substitute for the original works, and I have newly translated all of the passages that are discussed here. Often translation is a first interpretive gesture and an essential part of understanding. Because relatively few English translations are available—except in the case of Sholem Aleichem—one goal is simply to provide an overview of what is inaccessible to English readers. Ideally, this will inspire more people to read and translate Yiddish texts that would otherwise remain unknown.

Introduction

Sholem Yankev Abramovitsh, Sholem Aleichem (Rabinovitsh), and Isaac Leybush Peretz actively contributed to the invention of modern Jewish identity, as their satires reflected and provoked transformations of the Jewish experience. Between 1864 and 1916, Yiddish fiction traversed far-flung pathways of Jewish life and literary development. The three classic authors do not possess independent voices; their work resonates together in moments of harmony and dissonance.

S. Y. Abramovitsh (1836–1917) founded modern Yiddish writing, and his most important creation was Mendele Moykher Sforim—Mendele the Bookseller. The fictional Mendele became so popular that readers have often referred to the author under the name of his literary persona. When Abramovitsh invented this fictional personality in 1864, he generated an effective mouthpiece for the dissemination of his tales. Unlike the secularly educated Abramovitsh, Mendele has the narrower perspective of a traditionally versed Jewish man. Mendele's exposure to Western European letters is sporadic; his circle of acquaintances reaches only as far as the occasional German-Jew who has wandered into Poland and the Ukraine. Abramovitsh conceals his guiding intelligence behind the less obviously sophisticated Mendele.

Satire and parody gain prominence in Abramovitsh's Yiddish novels after 1869. Although Abramovitsh continues to employ the Mendele mask, during this phase he sets aside much of Mendele's earlier naiveté and his satires condemn corrupt religious and political institutions. As a consequence of the 1881 pogroms, however, Abramovitsh adopts a gentler tone in his revisions of the Yiddish novels and in his Hebrew stories of the 1890s.

Sholem Rabinovitsh (1859–1916), commonly known by his pseudonym Sholem Aleichem, was a self-appointed heir to Abramovitsh—whom he dubbed the "grandfather" of Yiddish literature. Sholem Aleichem gave expression to diverse fictional charac-

1

ters in a polyphony of colloquial monologues. The most famous of all Yiddish monologists is Tevye the Dairyman, whose renown in the United States owes much to the musical and film *Fiddler on the Roof*. While no fiddler appears in Sholem Aleichem's original stories written between 1894 and 1916, Tevye does play the lead role. In some ways similar to Abramovitsh's Mendele, Tevye combines simplicity and astute observation. He reports personal setbacks that typify the conditions of Eastern European Jewry, while his numerous quotations link him to biblical and rabbinic traditions.

Sholem Aleichem also produced socially critical fiction. His earliest novels show the influence of Gogol's and Abramovitsh's satires, and two of his later fictions from 1905 and 1907 attack the Jewish plutocracy of Kiev with its insidious exploitation of the poor. During his final years in the United States, Sholem Aleichem penned short stories criticizing ruthless business practices and empty religiosity in New York's Lower East Side. Sholem Aleichem critiqued what he saw as misguided directions in Yiddish life and letters. Sholem Aleichem broke from the Enlightenment tradition, however, as he developed a less polemical humor. He shifted his sights from social goals to a broader literary program of realism that renounced the European plots emulated by trashy Yiddish novels.

I. L. Peretz (1852–1915) is recognized as the first modernistic Yiddish writer. For nearly two decades he dominated the Yiddish literary scene in Warsaw, editing journals and producing varied works of short fiction, poetry, and drama. Although slightly older than Sholem Aleichem, he was more attuned to the demands and tactics of avant-garde European fiction. After Sholem Aleichem proclaimed himself Abramovitsh's "grandson," Peretz became the father of another literary family. Yet Peretz and Sholem Aleichem were never friends. The Abramovitsh–Sholem Aleichem literary pedigree was rooted in the Ukraine, while Peretz's writing cultivated a new literary landscape in Poland.

Starting in 1886 and concealed behind more than a dozen pseudonyms, Peretz experimented with narrative forms. Using the innovative technique of internal monologue, he was the first Yiddish writer to probe individual psychology. Peretz wrote social criticism in the 1890s and was active in the workers' movement until 1899, when he was arrested after delivering a lecture to striking workers. Later, as he produced his stories and folktales, Peretz moved away from the European realism sought by other authors. Instead he placed his stories in relation to internal Yiddish traditions, subtly employing traditional exemplars while distancing his texts from the folk versions of oral narrative. Peretz learned from popular traditions as profoundly as any other Yiddish writer, but he rewrote folktales in ways that delicately questioned superstitious beliefs. Some of Peretz's pious narrators themselves seem barely conscious of their own subtle hints at subversion. These critical works have, however, often been overshadowed by Peretz's simpler tales, which evoke a greater measure of sentimentality.

Satire and parody enable Jewish writers to present collective portraits and at the same time to situate their works in European literary history. Yiddish narrators frequently wield irony and—often posing as just one of the crowd—undermine their readers' assumptions. Through such personae, nineteenth-century Yiddish authors forge pathways for themselves while appropriating prior traditions.

Criticism of social hierarchies is implicit in most Yiddish satire, as when an ostensibly weak satirist questions the morals of those who are better placed. But Yiddish satire rarely presents an outright critique of powerful men and women. Instead it frequently employs strategies of self-satire, in which speakers lampoon themselves and their own social group. Sigmund Freud wrote in 1905 that self-criticism is typical of Jewish humor as a whole. This kind of self-scrutiny extended to Yiddish literary forms.

Intended for both general readers and scholars of literature, this book makes limited use of specialized technical terms. Several key words, however, require definition. *Parody* has a contemporary meaning associated with literary history; in that context, it refers to the appropriation of a prior form, or "repetition with a critical distance" (Linda Hutcheon, *A Theory of Parody*). Parody often employs irony but need not include the element of ridicule, since parodic appropriations frequently convey respect for their models. *Intertextuality* refers to any relationship between texts, ranging from quotation, allusion, or imitation to distortion, mockery, or repudiation. Yiddish fiction illustrates a wide range of parodic and intertextual modes by virtue of its unusual historical and cultural situation.

While parody places a text in relationship to its forerunners, *satire* sets the literary work in a politicized relationship to current events in the world. Hence it is sometimes useful to distinguish between fictional strategies that aim parodically at other texts and those that satirize current social situations. *Irony* is the central device for much parody and satire. The simplest definition of irony is "saying one thing and meaning another." The linguistic origins of irony—in ancient Greek, *eiron* refers to a dissembler in speech —indicate that conscious deception lies behind the ironic mask. Parodic works frequently use irony to mark their distance from the texts they parody, while satires employ irony to undermine the objects of their critique.

Skaz, or narration in an oral mode, was analyzed by the Russian formalists. They investigated the literary techniques that make possible this feigned orality. Nineteenth-century Russian and Yiddish fiction often used the device of *skaz* to create the impression of colloquial speech by a common, uneducated person. *Monologue* is related to the phenomenon of *skaz,* since both have recourse to first-person narration. In my earlier work *Genius and Monologue,* I define monologue as "solitary speech" in a variety of forms, of which dramatic soliloquy, conversational poetry, first-person narrative, and internal monologue are the most prominent. A more complex type of monologue creates another kind of isolation by deviation from the dialogical norms of speech. This latter sense of monologue somewhat resembles Mikhail Bakhtin's discussions of dialogue. Thus monologues are not necessarily monologic in Bakhtin's sense of being ideologically one-sided, dogmatic, or monolithic. On the contrary, Bakhtin's notion of *polyphony* applies to Yiddish monologues. The many masks and ironic personae of Yiddish literature bespeak a multivoiced fiction that may be compared to polyphonic music.

Yiddish literature has affinities to other writing in the margins of mainstream culture. "Literature in the Margins" might be another title for this study of a minority tradition, shaped and distorted by its marginal status. Yiddish literary styles evolved rapidly in the margins of Western literary history, when the leading authors explored successive styles; hence the case of Yiddish fiction might be a prototype for the stude of any minority (or colonized) culture that arises amid hostile surroundings.

No single theme unites this survey of Abramovitsh, Sholem Aleichem, and Peretz; one distinguishing feature is the intertextual evolution of Yiddish fiction. Prior critics, attempting to interpret these authors individually, have tended to focus on narrower phases in their work. *Classic Yiddish Fiction* underscores the process by which Abramovitsh, Sholem Aleichem, and Peretz matured as creative artists. Rather than isolate and classify rigid periods in their careers, it is helpful to recognize influences, throwbacks, rivalries, lacunae, overlaps, progressions, and regressions.

Yiddish writing in Eastern Europe differs from some other minority literatures because of its linguistic separation from the majority. It is incorrect to state that Yiddish is a dialect of German, since both modern Yiddish and modern German have their parentage in medieval German speech. As has been said, with an irony that contains much truth, the difference between a language and a dialect is that a language has an army and a navy. What began as a medieval variant of so-called Middle High German in the Rhine region became an independent and socially insular language for the Jews, when they migrated eastward into Poland and Lithuania, Belorussia and the Ukraine—later known as the Russian Pale of Settlement. The premodern Jews' linguistic and educational isolation meant that Yiddish writers were initially influenced by literary traditions in Hebrew and Aramaic that had been the focal point of Jewish scholarship since talmudic times. This dependent relationship added importance to Yiddish translations of Scripture and the prayer book, and gave rise to prayers that were composed for women who were seldom taught to read Hebrew.

For many Jewish intellectuals in late nineteenth-century Russia, the cultural language was Russian, the popular language was Yiddish, and the scholarly language was Hebrew. According to Simon Dubnov, members of the Odessa circle of Hebraists and Yiddishists (including Abramovitsh, M. Ben-Ami, and H. N. Bialik) spoke Russian among themselves. Following their traditional Jewish education, then, Yiddish writers were exposed to modern European literature in the original and in translation. All three classic Yiddish writers read several languages: Abramovitsh, who knew Yiddish and Hebrew from childhood, learned Russian and German; Sholem Aleichem, who knew Yiddish, Hebrew, and Russian from childhood, picked up some French, German, Italian, and English during his travels; Peretz knew Yiddish, Hebrew, and Polish from childhood and studied Russian, French, and German. This multilingualism left deep traces in their writing. Between the traditional world of elementary Jewish education in the *cheder* and the secular world of modern fiction, a polyglot culture assisted in the processes that were integral to the rise of Yiddish writing.

Yiddish writing has notable points of contact to women's studies. Until the late nineteenth century, Yiddish was predominantly a language read by women, not men. It was considered a "handmaid" to the nobler Hebrew, which was the domain of traditionally educated males. Yet Yiddish became a powerful instrument for Enlightenment secularization and a challenge to the prevailing traditionalism. Its aura was almost entirely worldly. As Hebrew suffused synagogue practices, Yiddish dominated the home and the Jewish marketplace, providing idioms of everyday life in a way that was impossible for Hebrew. Thus *leshon ha-kodesh* (the sacred Hebrew language) was male-dominated, while the *mame-loshn* (or the Yiddish mother tongue) reigned at home and in the secular world. The patriarchal/matriarchal implications of this situation have not been sufficiently explored, though a new generation of Yiddish scholars is beginning to examine these gender issues.

The Hebrew-Yiddish dichotomy may also be examined in connection with the relationship between writing and speech. According to Jacques Derrida's critique of Western metaphysics, philosophy since Plato has privileged the immediacy and presence of the spoken word, while suppressing the claims of writing. Derrida contends that writing is in fact a prerequisite to the supposed immediacy of vocalized speech. This tension is obvious in multilingual Jewish culture, since there is a prominent rift between the written Hebrew "Holy tongue" and the spoken Yiddish "mother tongue." Scripture, Talmud, rabbinic commentary, the prayer book, and medieval Hebrew poetry all stand as imposing textual monuments before any modern Jewish writer sets pen to paper. One obstacle for nineteenth-century Hebrew literati was precisely their inability to escape ancient prototypes, which led them to produce antiquated prose that seldom resembled everyday speech. The test came especially with the representation of dialogue, a virtually impossible task for an ancient written language such as Hebrew that had not been spoken in nearly two thousand years.

The challenge for modern Hebrew literature was unlike that of classic Yiddish fiction. Overburdened by an extensive corpus of erudite texts, Hebrew writers struggled to create the impression of orality. They could at best conjure up an illusion framed by elaborate conventions, since spontaneous Hebrew speech was unheard of until the end of the nineteenth century. In contrast, Yiddish writing had access to the language as it was spoken. This link was insufficient, however, to enable writers to produce effective prose. Transcription of actual speech makes poor literature even in the case of reported dialogue. Necessary prototypes for the Yiddish writers came from Scripture, Talmud, Midrash, and modern European fiction.

Whereas Hebrew writers were at pains to simulate oral discourse, Yiddish writers had to compose a new kind of fiction combining oral and literary modes. This was one accomplishment of Abramovitsh, Sholem Aleichem, and Peretz. They effectively recreated intonations of the spoken word, and yet their achievement is deceptively simple. Each author developed unique strategies by which he brought spoken Yiddish into the literary fold. This required appropriating literary forms from all available sources ranging from the Book of Genesis to contemporary Russian fiction by Nikolai Leskov.

Hebrew and Yiddish fiction in the late nineteenth century were complementary and moved toward synthesis at an elusive meeting point that was never attained. Hebrew writing needed the inflections of Yiddish speech, and Yiddish fiction needed the lineage of Hebrew scholarship. Both learned from nineteenth-century European realism, engaging in the transformation of literary forms. Actual translation played an obvious role. In spite of biblical and rabbinic forebears, the narrative genre remained largely foreign to modern Jewish culture until the beginning of the nineteenth century, when Rabbi Nachman of Bratslav told spiritualistic tales to his disciples. These stories were published posthumously in a bilingual Hebrew and Yiddish edition, which is an apt emblem for the symbiotic relationship between the two primary languages of Eastern European Judaic literature.

Classic Yiddish fiction inspired the Eastern European Jews' search for a modern identity that could replace outmoded forms. As increasing numbers of Jews renounced the ghetto of traditional Jewish learning, they turned to Western culture. Parody well describes their ambivalent relationship to a foreign culture they longed to emulate and yet held at a critical distance. Modern Yiddish fiction reflected that ambivalence, but it also furthered the process of cultural transfer—until the abrupt demise of the European Jews in the death camps.

PART ONE

Abramovitsh

FIGURE 1
S. Y. Abramovitsh

FIGURE 2
Abramovitsh's Eastern Europe

TABLE 1.
Chronology of Abramovitsh's Life

1836	Born in Kapolia (Kopyl), Minsk Province (date uncertain).
1850–52	Studied in yeshivot in Timkovitz (Timkovichi), Slutsk, and Vilna (Vilnius).
ca. 1853	Lived with his mother and stepfather in Melnik (Mielnik); traveled with Avreml Khromoy (the Lame) through Volin (Volhynia) and Podolia to Komenitz (Kamenets-Podolsk); became acquainted with Avraham-Ber Gottlober, whose daughters taught him Russian and German.
ca. 1854–55	Married and divorced his first wife.
1856	Passed examinations to become a teacher in Komenitz.
1857	First published in Hebrew: "A Letter on Education" ("Mikhtav ʿal dvar ha-chinukh").
1858	Moved to Berditchev (Berdichev) and married his second wife, Pessie Levin.
1860	Published a collection of essays in Hebrew, *The Judgment of Peace* (or *The Judgment of Shalom, Mishpat shalom*).
1862	Published his first Hebrew story, *Learn to Do Well (Limdu heitev)*, and edited the first volume of his Hebrew edition of the *Book of Natural History (Sefer toldot ha-tevaʿ)*, based on a German work by Harald Othmar Lenz.
1864–65	Serialized his first Yiddish novel, *The Little Man (Dos kleyne mentshele)*, in *Kol mevasser*, the Yiddish supplement to Alexander Tsederboym's Hebrew newspaper *Ha-melitz*.
1865	Published *The Magic Ring (Dos vintshfingerl)*.
1866	Published his second collection of Hebrew essays, *The Well of Judgment (ʿEin mishpat)*, and edited the second volume of the *Book of Natural History* in Hebrew translation.
1867	Published an expanded Russian version of his Hebrew work *Learn to Do Well* as *Fathers and Children*, alluding to Turgenev's 1862 work bearing the same name.

(continued)

TABLE 1. (*Continued*)

1868	Published *Fathers and Children (Ha-'avot ve-ha-banim*) in Hebrew.
1869	Published *The Tax (Di takse)* and *Fishke the Lame (Fishke der krumer)*; moved from Berditchev to Zhitomir, where he studied at the Rabbinical Institute but was refused ordination because of a radical sermon he delivered.
1872	Edited the third volume of the *Book of Natural History* in Hebrew translation.
1873	Published *The Nag* (or *The Mare; Di klyatshe*) in Yiddish.
1878	Published *Travels of Benjamin the Third (Kitser masoes Binyomin hashlishi)*.
1879	Published the expanded second edition of *The Little Man*.
1881	Moved to Odessa, where he became Director of the Jewish school (Talmud Torah), a position he retained until the end of his life (except 1906–8); pogroms after the assassination of Alexander II shook his confidence in reform.
ca. 1882	Suffered from a long period of depression and literary inactivity. His daughter Rashel died at the age of 19; his son Meir (Mikhail), a Russian-language poet, was exiled for political activities and later converted to Christianity.
1884	Published *The Tax* (1869) in Russian translation; celebrated his first 25 years of literary activity; honored in a biographical essay by L. Binshtok in the Russian-Jewish journal *Voskhod*.
1885	*Travels of Benjamin the Third* (1878) published in Polish translation.
1886	*The Nag* (1873) published in Polish translation and then suppressed by the censors.
1886–87	Returned to writing Hebrew fiction with "In the Secret Place of Thunder" ("Be-seter ra'am"; title from Psalms 81:8).
1888	Published expanded Yiddish versions of *Fishke the Lame* and *The Magic Ring*.
1889	Published the expanded Yiddish version of *The Nag* and printed an autobiographical essay in Hebrew.

(*continued*)

TABLE 1. *(Continued)*

1890–97	Published new Hebrew stories and Hebrew versions of the Yiddish novels *Travels of Benjamin the Third* and *The Magic Ring*.
1899	Serialized the beginning of his autobiographical novel in Yiddish as *Solomon, Son of Chaim* (*Shloyme reb Khaim's*), which first appeared in Hebrew under the title *In Those Days* (*Ba-yamim ha-hem*, 1894–).
1901–5	Revised his Yiddish and Hebrew works; deeply distressed by pogroms in 1903 and 1905.
1906	Moved to Geneva, Switzerland, following the Odessa pogrom of 1905.
1908	Returned to Odessa.
1909–13	Publication of Jubilee editions of his collected works in Hebrew and Yiddish.
1917	Death on 8 December.

Sources: Leon Binshtok, "A Celebration of Yiddish Literature," in *Voskhod*, 1884; S. Y. Abramovitsh, autobiographical essay in Nachum Sokolov's *Sefer zikharon*, 1889; Zalman Reyzen, *Leksikon fun der yidisher literatur, presse un filologie*, vol. 1, 1928; YIVO Pamphlet, "Di vikhtikste faktn un dates fun Mendeles lebn un shafn," 1936; *Mendele Moykher Sforim: reshimat ketavav ve-'iggrotav le-hatkanat mahaduratam ha-akademit*, 1965; Dan Miron, *A Traveler Disguised*, 1973; *Guide to Yiddish Classics on Microfiche*, ed. Chone Shmeruk, 1980.

CHAPTER 1

The Grandfather of Yiddish Literature

Modern Yiddish literature has its origins in the life and work of Sholem Yankev Abramovitsh (1836–1917). A follower of Abramovitsh once found him working at his desk and asked what he was writing. "I'm not writing, I'm driving away flies," he answered, and then explained his metaphor: "When I write Hebrew, all the prophets fall upon me: Isaiah, Jeremiah, the writers of the Song of Songs and Psalms, and each one of them proposes that I take a ready-made verse or an established phrase from him alone, for this expression. In order not to write in ready-made clichés, I first have to drive away all those flies."[1] This story illustrates the basic problem that confronted modern Yiddish and Hebrew writers. Abramovitsh required the literary models of the Bible and post-biblical Hebrew writing, but he was also compelled to resist their influence. While he appropriated prophetic and rabbinic modes, he retained a critical distance.

Abramovitsh himself wrote three accounts of his life: an essay in Nachum Sokolov's *Memorial Book* (*Sefer zikharon*, 1889); the two-part autobiographical novel *Solomon, Son of Chaim* (*Shloyme reb Khaim's*, 1894–1917), also known as *In Those Days* (*In yener tsayt* in Yiddish or *Ba-yamim ha-hem* in Hebrew); and his serialized memoirs entitled "From My Book of Memories" ("Fun mayn seyfer hazikhroynes," 1913–16). While these narratives should not be read as if they contained indisputable facts, they do command a privileged place in Abramovitsh's lifework. Numerous essayists have written about Abramovitsh in Yiddish and Hebrew, and his friend Lev Binshtok printed a significant memoir of his early years in Russian (1884).

Abramovitsh offered advice to those who interpret his work. After he read Y. H. Ravnitzky's introduction to a collection of his

---

[1]Simon Dubnov, *Fun "zhargon" tsu yidish un andere artiklen: literarishe zikhroynes* (Vilna: Kletzkin, 1929), p. 113; henceforth cited as "FZ" by page alone.

15

Hebrew stories in 1900, Abramovitsh objected: "you, as the editor, should have given an historical overview and an explanation of many issues and matters in the book, such as explaining the relationship of each story to the events of the time in which it was written."[2] By stressing the pertinence of historical background, Abramovitsh indicates that social contexts are essential to the meaning of his fiction.

Abramovitsh's first Yiddish novel (serialized in 1864–65) marked both the beginning of modern Yiddish fiction and a continuation of former trends. His work responds to three powerful movements that preceded him: Haskalah, Chassidism, and (for lack of a better term) Mitnagdism. The Haskalah, or the Jewish Enlightenment, was prominent in Western Europe roughly from 1750–1830, inspired by the rationalistic movement of the eighteenth century that was associated with Denis Diderot, François Voltaire, Gotthold Lessing, and Immanuel Kant. The leading Jewish member of the Enlightenment and founder of the Haskalah was Moses Mendelssohn (1729–86), who sought to educate Jews by translating the Bible into a German version written in Hebrew characters. Mendelssohn hoped that this Bible edition would assist Yiddish speakers in learning German. In Berlin at the end of the eighteenth century, proponents of the Jewish Enlightenment such as Aharon Wolfson (1754–1835) and Isaac Euchel (1756–1804) produced satiric plays. The modernizing influence of the Berlin Enlightenment prevailed over the Jews of Western Europe, and it then made inroads into Eastern Europe (ca. 1820–80). Abramovitsh took his first steps as a writer under the aegis of the Enlightenment and throughout his life shared its goals of education and progress. From 1881 until his death, Abramovitsh was employed as the principal of a Jewish school in Odessa.

Chassidism and Mitnagdism were equal and opposite forces that arose from the chassidic innovations of Israel Baal Shem Tov (1699–1761) and his disciples in Volin (Volhynia) and Podolia. Chassidic leaders emphasized the primacy of prayer, whereas their opponents placed greater weight on study. Mystical practices drawn

---

[2]Letter of 10 August 1900; translated from *Reshumot* 2 (1927), 428. A Yiddish translation is contained in *Dos Mendele bukh*, ed. Nachman Mayzel (New York: YKUF, 1959), p. 180; this volume is henceforth cited as "MB" by page alone.

from the esoteric *Book of Splendor* (*Sefer ha-zohar,* thirteenth century) were especially influential in chassidic circles. The mitnagdim (literally "opponents") rallied forcefully against the chassidim after the Vilna Gaon, Elijah ben Solomon Zalman, placed a ban on the chassidim in 1772. In the nineteenth century the chassidic strongholds stretched from Poland and Galicia to the Ukraine, while the mitnagdic center lay to the north in Lithuania. The exaggerated dichotomy between Polish Jews and Lithuanian Jews (or "Litvaks") derives from this religious split. According to the simplistic polarity, chassidim were known for their spiritual fervor and devotion to the mystical kabbalah, while mitnagdim distinguished themselves as rigorous talmudic scholars. Abramovitsh was familiar with both communities since he was raised in greater Lithuania and traveled south through Volin and Podolia, later settling in the strongly chassidic city of Berditchev. His early work was in part motivated by a wish to spread the Haskalah to Jews in both groups.

Among the chassidim, Rabbi Nachman's inspirational tales were printed in Hebrew and Yiddish (1815) after his death. At the same time, secular Jewish authors—influenced by the Enlightenment—fought what they saw as misguided enthusiasts and worked to improve the material conditions of Jewish life and education. For example, Joseph Perl (1774–1839) and Isaac Ber Levinsohn (1788–1860) used satire to oppose the chassidim (1819–30).[3] Another precursor from the mid-nineteenth century was Isaac Meir Dik (1814–93), whose story books, "in contrast to other Enlightenment works, did not frighten the pious readership."[4] Incorporating aspects of all these prior trends, Abramovitsh initially experimented with didactic essays and novels in Hebrew (1857–68). But his first genuine success came in Yiddish, with his synthesis of everyday scenes, traditional motifs, and subtle irony.

---

[3]See Israel Davidson, *Parody in Jewish Literature* (New York: Columbia University Press, 1907), pp. 61–73, for an early discussion, in English, of Perl's *Revealer of Secrets* (*Megale temirin*) and Levinsohn's *Words of the Righteous* (*Divrei tzadikim*).

[4]Shmuel Niger [Charney], "Yiddish Literature From the Mid-Eighteenth Cenrury Until 1942" ("Yidishe literatur fun mitn 18-tn yorhundert biz 1942"), in the *Algemeyne entsiklopedie,* vol. 3: *Yidn* (New York: CYCO, 1942), p. 101; henceforth cited as "YL" by page alone.

EARLY EDUCATION

Sholem Yankev Broyde, later Abramovitsh, was born in Kapolia (Kopyl, Minsk province) in 1836.[5] Jews called this region Lithuania (*Lite*), although it was then part of Czarist Russia (and now lies within the borders of Belarus). His father Chaim Moyshe Broyde was respected in the town and known for his linguistic talents. According to Abramovitsh, his father perceived a general weakness in Hebrew learning and "wanted to make an exception of Shloyme [the name denoting Sholem Yankev in his autobiographical novel *Shloyme reb Khaim's*], to try to teach him the entire Tanakh [Hebrew Bible] together with the translation, from beginning to end. Reb Chaim himself knew the Tanakh and wrote Hebrew. People used to delight in his letters."[6]

As a child Abramovitsh's perceptions of the world were, in large part, guided by biblical verses. Between the ages of about seven and ten, he was taught by a private tutor, Yosi Rubens, who placed special emphasis on the Hebrew language. During that time Abramovitsh memorized portions of the Bible, establishing the basis for his literary career in Hebrew. Since the revival of Hebrew as a spoken language did not begin until late in the nineteenth century, the Bible and Mishna were the main primers for Hebrew writers; in his youth Abramovitsh knew nothing of Enlightenment Hebrew literature.[7]

Yosi Rubens made a lasting impression on the boy. He was "a remarkable Hebraist and Talmudist . . . who was exceptionally skillful in carpentry, worked expertly in wood and stone and, in

---

[5]According to some sources, Abramovitsh was born in 1835. See also Max Weinreich, "Mendeles ershte 25 yor," *YIVO bleter* 10 (1936), 167–80. Weinreich reexamines the biographical information, gives Abramovitsh's birthdate as 1 January 1834, and contests a number of other established dates in Abramovitsh's life.

[6]*Solomon, Son of Chaim* (*Shloyme reb Khaim's*), in *Ale verk fun Mendele Moykher Sforim (S. Y. Abramovitsh)* (Cracow: Farlag Mendele, 1911), vol. 2, p. 26; henceforth cited as "SRK" by page alone.

[7]See Abramovitsh's autobiographical essay in *Sefer zikharon le-sofrei yisra'el hachaim 'itanu ka-yom,* ed. Nachum Sokolov (Warsaw: Halter, 1889), p. 118, henceforth cited as "SZ" by page alone. Lev Binshtok also recalls that, as a boy, Abramovitsh had little conception of European literature, which differentiates him from both Sholem Aleichem and Peretz.

addition, had an understanding of painting."[8] Apart from educating him in the Bible and Talmud, this teacher with his diverse talents made the young Abramovitsh aware of art, "awakened the boy's curiosity and drew him toward another, as yet unknown, dreamlike faraway place, a calling that was beyond the limits of the Talmud" (ibid.). Yosi Rubens specialized in making ceremonial art, but his artistry gave Abramovitsh an introduction to secular artistic pursuits.

Abramovitsh's description of his first talmudic studies echoes the multivoiced character of his fiction. He employs vivid imagery to describe his childhood encounters with the Talmud and Midrash, and he represents the textual world as a landscape. While studying the Hebrew Bible, "my teacher took me to the threshold of the Talmud, the primeval giant Og and Magog in the literature of all the inhabitants of the world. When I arrived there I was like a man who has come for the first time to a great market, astonished at the sight of all kinds of merchandise, business, and the many and various desirable objects, and I was struck mute by hearing the din, commotion, and shrieking from every side and corner. Buyers and sellers, agents and merchants, all running and pressing and rushing loudly, hastily, gripped by the lust for trade" (SZ 117). Abramovitsh's depiction elaborates on the folk saying, "Torah is the best merchandise." In contrast to the Talmud, which resembled a marketplace—with its exchanges between hundreds of rabbis across centuries—*aggadah* or legend seemed to him an orchard, an expansive field without an orderly plan. Abramovitsh remembered having been awakened on winter mornings and walking to the House of Study while it was still dark. The beauty of nature inspired him "to learn with all my heart. . . . My soul longed for God's Torah, to know all the secrets of the Talmud" (SZ 118). This sentimental, spiritualized recollection is at odds with the underlying thrust of Abramovitsh's fictional descriptions, in which he ob-

---

[8]Lev Binshtok, "A Celebration of Yiddish Literature: Solomon Moiseevitsh Abramovitsh and His Twenty-Fifth Year of Literary Activity," unpublished translation from the Russian by Jack Blanshei, p. 3. Modified slightly in consultation with Amy Mandelker and Nancy M. Frieden; henceforth cited as "CYL." The original essay is contained in *Voskhod* 12 (1884), 1–32; the cited passage occurs on page 2. Abramovitsh refers to his tutor as "Lippe" in his fictionalized autobiography, *Shloyme reb Khaim's*.

serves that nature enables Jewish children to counterbalance sti-
fling rabbinic customs.

Following his father's death in 1850, Abramovitsh studied in
traditional yeshivot in Timkovitz (Timkovichi), Slutsk, and Vilna
(Vilnius). He then lived for some time with his mother and step-
father in an isolated forest in Melnik (Mielnik), where he recalls
having felt the powerful attraction of nature. At the beginning of
his fictional autobiography, his mother indicates the change that
has come over him: no longer immersed in talmudic studies, he has
begun to occupy himself with scribbling and wandering through
the forest all day (SRK 7–8). As a mature writer, Abramovitsh contributed to the development of Yiddish fiction with his representations of nature. In *Fishke the Lame* (*Fishke der krumer*, 1869), his
persona Mendele the Bookseller mocks the Jewish habit of going
into mourning just as summer begins, on the seventeenth of Tammuz, in preparation for Tish'ah b'Av. Stories such as "The Calf"
("Dos toysefes-yontev-kelbl") express his childhood love of the
outdoors, but they also show the tension caused by his elders'
disapproval of what they viewed as a temptation of "the evil impulse."[9] Experiences of nature stood in direct contrast to rabbinic
textual study, and Abramovitsh's emphasis on natural beauty was
a threat to those who wished to maintain the insularity of "the
People of the Book." Everyday Yiddish contained limited vocabulary in which to discuss natural objects, as if the words "flower"
and "rose," "tree" and "oak" sufficed to name most local flora.
Influenced by the Jewish Enlightenment, Abramovitsh sought to
enhance Jewish awareness of the natural world both by including
vivid descriptions in his fiction and by printing a three-volume
Hebrew edition called the *Book of Natural History* (*Sefer toldot
ha-teva'*, 1862–72). This was Abramovitsh's reworking and translation of a German study by Harald Othmar Lenz; Abramovitsh
edited the preexisting book much as he later had his character
Mendele pretend to do. While he made no original contributions
to the natural sciences, Abramovitsh's depictions of nature set his
novels off from most prior Hebrew and Yiddish fiction.

---

[9]See *Seyfer habeheymes*, in MMS, vol. 1. The Hebrew version was published
during the same year in *Ha-'olam* 5 (1911), numbers 18–19, 23, 26, and 33. For
an English translation of "The Calf" by Jacob Sloan, see *A Treasury of Yiddish
Stories*, 2d ed., ed. Irving Howe and Eliezer Greenberg (New York: Penguin,
1990), pp. 97–111.

Abramovitsh recalls that he began to write poetry while surrounded by nature during the early 1850s. As a child in the small town of Kapolia (Kopyl), he had never read secular literature, and so when he experienced poetic feelings he thought, "this is Satan's work; the evil impulse is endangering me and through evil thoughts is leading me away from learning Torah" (SZ 119). According to his own account, Abramovitsh's first literary endeavors anticipated his later satiric style: "as soon as I began to write words of song, and the first fruits of my pen consecrated hymns to God, along came Satan—the angel of derision, who now rules over me in the figure of Mendele the Bookseller—and provoked me to mock human beings, to destroy their veils and tear their masks from them" (SZ 120). Thus Abramovitsh traces his use of satire to his earliest writing, and links it to "the figure of Mendele the Bookseller." Later, in the 1869–78 prefaces ascribed to Mendele, Abramovitsh mimics a traditional religious form—hymns in praise of God (*hillulim le-adonai*)—and enacts its parodic transformation. While Satan is known as "the angel of death" in the Talmud (Baba Batra 16a), Abramovitsh uses one of his typical literary devices and modifies this ancient phrase to "the angel of derision."

Abramovitsh possessed a precocious talent for impersonation, as was later true of Sholem Aleichem. As a child, Abramovitsh was "very popular because of his liveliness, his habit of asking foolish questions, and even more, for his mimes. By nature he had the ability to pick up, at first glance, a person's mannerisms and verbal peculiarities. He would imitate beautifully how any person spoke, stood, walked, until everyone held their sides, bursting with laughter" (SRK 24–25). This imitative gift advanced Abramovitsh's ability as a novelist with affinities to French and Russian realism. The example Abramovitsh gives, referring to himself in the third person, is relevant to his literary portraits of provincial Jews: "He especially liked to imitate *Gitel*, the prayer-leader [in the women's section], how she kissed the mezuzah on entering the house . . . ; how she pulled back her lips and said, 'God be with you!'" (SRK 25). This simple, pious woman always affirmed, in the language of the women's prayers, "Praised and revered be the Almighty, blessed be He and His name, who protects the People of Israel." Such blind faith later became the central object of Abramovitsh's satires, when he wrote in a manner that simultaneously "encourages and demasks" (MB 132). His example also shows how he combined satire of social forms with parody of textual precursors, in this case a prayer formula.

In the midst of creative work, when Abramovitsh wanted to capture the right word or expression for a folk character, he would address the common Jew within himself: "What do you say, little Jew?"[10] Thus he invoked the muse within, the everyday speech of typical Jews, which was far more accessible in Yiddish than in Hebrew. According to Y. D. Berkovitsh, Abramovitsh once commented on the difference between writing in Yiddish and Hebrew: with the former he could always consult his wife when he needed help with an elusive word, but with Hebrew he could only consult the Bible, Talmud, and Midrash.[11] In the term employed by Mikhail Bakhtin, the double reference to speech and literary exemplars facilitated his *dialogism,* his multivoiced fictions that convey diverse perspectives and linguistic levels through personae and narratives within narratives.

Much has been written about the persona of Mendele the Bookseller (Mendele Moykher Sforim), sometimes erroneously called Abramovitsh's pseudonym.[12] "Abramovitsh" was itself a fictitious name, since his father's name was Chaim Moyshe Broyde. Name changes were then a common ploy among Jews, as one means to avoid being impressed into a twenty-five-year military service in the Czar's army. To avoid falling prey to this system, Abramovitsh may have posed as the (exempt) eldest son of a (fictitious) family. Beyond such pragmatic considerations, Sholem Yankev possibly chose his alias to indicate that he was, figuratively speaking, "son of Abraham." The patriarch Abraham was not his role model, for he had a more immediate prototype.

TRAVELS

At the age of seventeen, three years after his father's death, Sholem Yankev wandered extensively through Eastern Europe together

---

[10]David Eynhorn, "Mendele at Work" ("Mendele bay der arbet"), in *Zikhroynes vegn Mendelen,* in *Ale verk fun Mendele Moykher-Sforim,* ed. Nachman Maysel (Warsaw: Farlag Mendele, 1928), vol. 20, p. 59.

[11]Y. D. Berkovitsh, *Ha-rish'onim ki-vnei-adam: sippurei zikharonot 'al Sholem-Aleichem u-vnei-doro,* 3d ed. (Tel Aviv: Dvir, 1976), p. 363.

[12]For a critique of this practice, see Dan Miron, *A Traveler Disguised: A Study in the Rise of Modern Yiddish Fiction in the Nineteenth Century* (New York: Schocken, 1973), chapter 5; henceforth cited as "TD" by page alone.

with a beggar named Abraham (or, in the diminutive, Avreml). Avreml Khromoy—which means Abraham the Lame—had returned from travels "with his wonderful tales and novelties about the fortunate Volin and Southern Russia, 'flowing with milk and honey.'" Evoking this biblical phrase, he "excited the imagination of the seventeen-year-old Abramovitsh, who decided to go out into the world with this Avreml."[13] These travels extended Abramovitsh's horizons far beyond the Lithuanian and Belorussian towns he had formerly seen.

More than a decade later, Avreml's makeshift horse-drawn cart found a literary counterpart in fictional renditions of Mendele the Bookseller's wagon. Moreover, Avreml inspired characterizations in Abramovitsh's seminal novels *Fishke the Lame* (*Fishke der krumer*, 1869) and *The Travels of Benjamin the Third* (*Kitser masoes Binyomin ha-shlishi*, 1878): "the memorable trip in the company of Avreml Khromoy subsequently provided our gifted folk writer with considerable material for his stories about everyday Jewish life. In these stories, replete with humor and good-natured sarcasm, and infused with truthful and unusual powers of observation, one meets places and scenes snatched directly from life, since he had the opportunity to scrutinize folk life closely with all its joys and sorrows, without any embellishment or disguise."[14] Their travels took them from Kapolia to Lutsk (Volin Province), and thence to Komenitz (Kamenets-Podolsk, Podolia). Along the way, Avreml tried to arrange for the marriage of Sholem Yankev so that he could pocket the matchmaker's fee, but Abramovitsh foiled this mercenary attempt. The journey became increasingly difficult as Avreml became resentful of his fellow traveler and threatened to confiscate his passport and abandon him. A choir boy introduced Abramovitsh to a cantor in Komenitz, who rescued him from Avreml and helped him become a yeshiva student at the House of Study. His strong biblical and talmudic training made a favorable impression in the community, and Abramovitsh was able to support himself as the private tutor for children in a number of

---

[13]Zalman Reyzn, *Leksikon fun der yidisher literatur, presse un filologie*, vol. 1 (Vilna: Kletzkin, 1926), p. 11. The ostensible reason for the trip, Binshtok recalls, was to help Abramovitsh's aunt find her long-lost husband. But Avreml had other ideas, and took his ward on a circuitous route.

[14]See Lev Binshtok's biographical essay, CYL, trans. Jack Blanshei, pp. 14–15; in the Russian original, p. 10.

wealthy families. In the mid-1850s Abramovitsh married and lived with his first wife in Komenitz, but they were divorced soon after.

Until this time, Abramovitsh had received a traditional Jewish education. In Komenitz he first encountered another kind of scholar, the Hebrew and Yiddish writer Avraham-Ber Gottlober (1810–99), who taught at the local government school for Jewish boys from 1852–54. This decisive encounter with a secular intellectual exposed Abramovitsh to the methods and contents of modern learning. Lev Binshtok recounts that he

> went over to Gottlober's apartment taking with him his single literary production—a drama already written during his childhood but left without a title—with the intention of hearing the opinion of the great poet and to receive his advice and direction for the future. Gottlober, as Sholem Yankev himself told me, could not keep from laughing as he read this work of childhood fantasy. He praised him anyway for his noble effort and predicted a brilliant literary future. From the very first, Gottlober recognized an uncommon talent hidden in this young Lithuanian, and therefore without waiting for Sholem Yankev's request, he offered his assistance and the use of his carefully selected library.[15]

Gottlober, with his "completely unfamiliar opinions," served as a new model for the aspiring author; Abramovitsh's first Yiddish novel presents a fictionalized representation of him in the character of Gutman. Under the tutelage of Gottlober's eldest daughter, Abramovitsh studied Russian, German, mathematics, and then passed a teacher's examination in 1854. His first publication, which Gottlober submitted to the Hebrew journal *The Preacher* (*Ha-maggid*) without the author's knowledge in 1857, was entitled "A Letter on Education" ("Mikhtav ʿal dvar ha-chinukh").

Abramovitsh taught in Komenitz from 1856–58, then moved with his second wife to Berditchev, where he continued his literary endeavors while supported by his new father-in-law. His earliest publications were in Hebrew. He wrote fiction, essays on scholarly issues, and his work of natural history designed to introduce Jewish readers to science. During the period of the "Great Reforms" in the 1860s, Abramovitsh was influenced by Russian liberal trends; in the 1870s his focus gradually broadened from efforts on behalf of social and educational reform among the Jews to a striving for

---

[15]Ibid., p. 24; in the Russian original, p. 16.

full-fledged political equality.[16] At that time, in conjunction with his populist leanings, Abramovitsh decided to devote himself to writing primarily in Yiddish.

Abramovitsh expressed his commitment to social reform in his autobiographical Hebrew essay written in 1889. An ironic undercurrent unsettles its superficially pious tone, as when he justifies his worldly difficulties by attributing them to divine providence: "in the heavens it was apparently decreed, before I left the womb, that I would be a writer for my people, a poor and impoverished people, and God willed that I would learn the ways of my people to the depths, and observe their deeds; thus He told my soul: wander like a bird in my world, and you will be wretched among the wretched and a Jew among Jews on earth" (SZ 120). These words echo familiar patterns of Jewish belief and expression in the Hebrew language. Nevertheless, the reader senses a tongue-in-cheek skepticism behind this facile acceptance of misfortune. Abramovitsh also makes an implicit social statement when he indicates that only through experiencing misfortunes has he been able to become a writer for his people. His avowed goals were those of the Jewish Enlightenment: "to teach the children of our people taste and discernment; to bring their worldly life and toil into a pact with our literature, so that the people would feel affection for it; and to enlighten and to be useful" (SZ 122).

YIDDISH FICTION

Abramovitsh explains the reason for his historic switch to Yiddish in a passage dating from 1889: "Then I said to myself, here I am observing the ways of our people and seeking to give them stories from a Jewish source in the Holy tongue, yet most of them do not even know this language and speak Yiddish [*yehudit ashkenazit*]. What good does a writer do with all his toil and ideas if he is not useful to his people? This question—For whom do I toil?—gave me no rest and brought me into great confusion" (SZ 122–23). The choice between Hebrew and Yiddish made an all-encompassing social statement, indicating the author's appeal either to an elite readership or to a wider audience. During the same period in

---

[16]See Max Weinreich, *Bilder fun der yidisher literaturgeshikhte: fun di onheybn biz Mendele Moykher Sforim* (Vilna: Tomor, 1928), p. 346.

Berditchev, Abramovitsh helped establish a charitable organization called "Enlightenment to the Poor" ("Maskil el dal").[17] This experience has an ironic literary correlate in *The Nag* (*Di klyatshe*, 1873), when the protagonist writes letters to an organization devoted to the well-being of animals.

Abramovitsh directed a great deal of energy to educating others; his main literary impulse was didactic, even though he satirized would-be enlighteners like himself. Because his professed goals were to enlighten and to be useful, his heavy-handed messages may obstruct our appreciation of his literary accomplishment. For instance, in spite of contemporary parallels, we may have difficulty responding to his satiric play *The Tax* (*Di takse*, 1869; not available in English translation) in which Abramovitsh exposes scandals associated with the distribution of kosher meat. His play is based on what he witnessed in Berditchev, and his outrage propelled him from light irony in the early 1860s to bitter satire in 1869. As early as 1864 he wrote that "at times I am filled with rage against the wealthy, and then one must not even mention the name of a rich man in front of me; I flare up like a volcano, I spew scorn and boiling anger, and my words turn into cries of protest."[18] His radicalization was furthered by community leaders' hostile response to his satiric play, *The Tax*, in 1869. He was compelled to relocate, and he continued his education at the rabbinical school in Zhitomir. Zalman Reyzn states that Abramovitsh "successfully passed his examinations, but his trial sermon in the synagogue was too radical, so that he did not receive a rabbinical degree."[19]

Yiddish was underdeveloped as a literary language when Abramovitsh turned to it in 1864. There were few exemplary works of fiction, the best of which were the Yiddish versions of Rabbi Nachman's chassidic tales and stories by Isaac Meir Dik. Yet chassidic lore and Yiddish fiction were entirely foreign to Abramovitsh's youthful interests. Thus he describes Yiddish in the 1860s as "an empty vessel" containing little more than idle words destined for

---

[17]See Max Weinreich, *Bilder fun der yidisher literaturgeshikhte*, pp. 331–34.

[18]Letter of 15 December 1864, in MB, p. 79.

[19]Zalman Reyzn, *Leksikon fun der yidisher literatur, presse un filologie*, vol. 1 (Vilna: Kletzkin, 1926), p. 18.

the uneducated (SZ 123). In general, Yiddish was associated with women's books that were scorned because they fell short of the merits associated with scholarly Hebrew. Yiddish held a subordinate role, and fiction was deemed frivolous, suitable only to women who could not read "higher" essays such as Abramovitsh's Hebrew edition of a work on natural history (*Sefer toldot ha-teva*ʿ).

Abramovitsh and several other writers prevailed upon Alexander Tsederboym, then editor of the Hebrew newspaper *The Advocate* (*Ha-melitz*), to print a Yiddish supplement. Thus began *A Voice of Tidings* (*Kol mevasser,* October 1862), and for this new Yiddish publication Abramovitsh wrote his first Yiddish book, *The Little Man* (*Dos kleyne mentshele*), in 1864–65. Serialized in those pages starting in November 1864, it was eagerly awaited by the readership. When an issue appeared without a new installment of *The Little Man*, "we heard a lot of people complain about it: 'What's this? Why isn't *The Little Man* there?'"[20] Shmuel Niger comments that as contemporary readers were increasingly prepared for Enlightenment ideas, they were "no longer frightened by the sharp opposition to Chassidism, and enjoyed the demasking of the community ring-leaders."[21] Abramovitsh attacked the corruption of wealthy and powerful Jews in books written primarily for the disenfranchised.

Abramovitsh expressed contradictory views about chassidic customs. In the first edition of one novel, *The Magic Ring* (*Dos vintshfingerl,* 1865), his persona Mendele mocks the chassidim of a certain town who cannot bear the thought of an enlightened man coming and sweeping away the filth in the House of Study: "The chassidim were not pleased, because Gutmann dressed like a German. And when the floor of the school was washed, they became furious. What's the meaning of this? To do such a thing in a school! What's this, washing off the mud that our ancestors left behind! . . . Only a non-Jew does something like that. But a Jew,

---

[20]Letter to *Kol mevasser* (1865), number 9, as quoted by Max Weinreich in *Bilder fun der yidisher literaturgeshikhte,* p. 342. A few years later, the same journal serialized Y. Y. Linetsky's important satiric novel, *The Polish Lad* (*Dos poylishe yingl,* 1867). Abramovitsh disclaimed any association with this author, whose work Sholem Aleichem admired, but the similarities deserve closer examination.

[21]Shmuel Niger, YL, p. 104.

who has a soul. . . . What does it mean? Is it befitting?"[22] Such
satiric portrayals led to Abramovitsh's unwilling departure from
Berditchev in 1869, after which he moved to Zhitomir.

Decades later, in the Hebrew versions of his Yiddish novels and
in his collected works, Abramovitsh softened his critiques. In the
second part of his fictional autobiography (ca. 1910) Abramovitsh
even praises the spirituality of the chassidim he met at an early age
in Timkovitz: "for the first time he saw chassidim, of whom there
was not a trace in K.[apolia], and about whom bitter mitnagdim
circulated sayings and ugly stories about sinners of Israel, wild
creatures, species of animals. . . . T.[imkovitz] was a new discovery
for Shloyme. . . . Chassidim are also Jews! But still there is a difference between them and mitnagdim, among whom he had until
then grown up in his town. A mitnaged has a frozen spirit; he has
only a head, for his heart is ice-cold."[23] Among the chassidim,
Abramovitsh recalls sentimentally, "prayer was a bright beam of
light that burst through the clouds of depression; they lit up the
orphan's gloomy spirit" (ibid., 8). Such nostalgic recollections contradict the satiric thrust of Abramovitsh's important early fiction.
Simon Dubnov more accurately refers to the youthful days when
Abramovitsh carried out "the Haskalah mission and the struggle
with chassidim in Komenitz and Berditchev."[24]

A major breakthrough came with Abramovitsh's play *The Tax*,
in which "for the first time in Yiddish literature, the socio-
economic antagonism that divides and disrupts the Jewish community is clearly and distinctly dramatized; for the first time the
question of the poor and the rich is sharply posed" (YL 105).
During the 1860s and 1870s, as Shmuel Niger asserts, Enlightenment writing moved beyond the issue of education and indicted
corruption within the upper echelons of the Jewish populace. This
social criticism made Abramovitsh a favorite author among Soviet Yiddishists in the 1930s, inspiring them to initiate the most

---

[22]Translated from *Dos vintshfingerl* (Warsaw: Joseph Levensohn, 1865), p. 7.

[23]Translated from *Shloyme reb Khaim's*, book 2, contained in *Ale verk fun Mendele Moykher Sforim* (Warsaw: Farlag Mendele, 1928), vol. 19, pp. 8–9. This
opposition between cool-headed mitnagdim and passionate chassidim had become a cliché by the time I. L. Peretz wrote his central chassidic stories in
1899–1901.

[24]Simon Dubnov, FZ 107.

ambitious critical edition of a Yiddish author ever attempted. Its completion was, however, rendered impossible by Stalin and the Second World War.

LATER WRITINGS

After the assassination of Alexander II in 1881, the Russian government adopted reactionary policies, and changing conditions provoked doubts about the adequacy of goals that had been set by the Enlightenment. As anti-semitic pogroms and reactionary politics rapidly altered the atmosphere surrounding Jewish writing, satire and social criticism were often replaced by neo-romanticism, idealized pietism, and nationalism (YL 110). Even Abramovitsh was less inclined to condemn the hapless Jews and, in the 1880s and 1890s, he limited himself to suggesting that passivity and quiet faith were not adequate "responses to catastrophe."[25]

In the midst of political turmoil between 1878 and 1884, Abramovitsh suffered from a depression that rendered him nearly inactive as an author. Simon Dubnov attributes this setback to the difficulties associated with his poverty in Zhitomir, followed by his demanding position as director of a Jewish school in Odessa. Lev Binshtok reported in 1884 that Abramovitsh "was suddenly somehow burned out, and his literary activity came to a complete halt" (CYL 47). The author himself described his inability to write in a letter to Binshtok dated 16 January 1880: "As soon as I take up the pen, I feel an overwhelming heaviness: my hands are bound as if by magical chains. The feelings strive to pour themselves onto the paper, but I am as if paralyzed and can't write!" (MB 107). Four years later, he wrote to another correspondent that "the misfortunes of the recent period have turned my heart into stone, so that my tongue has not allowed me to speak and my hands have not allowed me to write a word. This is the sort of silence that comes upon a person who suddenly experiences great suffering and it costs him health and life much more than groaning and crying with tears of blood" (MB 128).

---

[25] Compare David G. Roskies, *Against the Apocalypse: Responses to Catastrophe in Modern Jewish Culture* (Cambridge, Mass.: Harvard University Press, 1984), chapter 3. See also Alan Mintz, *Hurban: Responses to Catastrophe in Hebrew Literature* (New York: Columbia University Press, 1984), chapter 4.

Abramovitsh for the first time received a stable position in 1881, as the director of a Jewish school ("Talmud Torah") in Odessa. While his material conditions subsequently improved, his Yiddish creativity never regained the heights attained in the 1860s and 1870s. He became an educator in a more immediate sense than he had been as a Yiddish writer in earlier decades. Abramovitsh resided in Odessa for the rest of his life, with the exception of two years spent in Geneva, Switzerland, following the Odessa pogrom of 1905.

In light of anti-semitic incidents across Russia in 1881 (and later in 1903 and 1905), Abramovitsh reexamined his prior opinions, admitting that "the Jewish question has lately become unclear to me, and my view of many things has changed decisively." He continued, in a letter written to a friend in Russian: "this period of misfortunes for Jews, which has called forth so much literary and nationalistic activity, had the opposite effect on me, and stamped upon my lips the seal of silence" (MB 114). In another letter from 1882, Abramovitsh noted that the cultural climate was inimical to literary endeavors: "Almost our entire public from great to small, young and old, has worked itself into a talking frenzy; everyone is crying out with one voice. . . . This is the time to be silent and to remain silent until the public shouts itself out and then comes to its senses" (MB 115–16). Abramovitsh's silence, as a response to the turmoil of his milieu, articulates the interdependence between his fiction and the social context. Whereas earlier he had used satire to foster social reform, he later toned down his critical voice and attempted to preserve neutrality while surrounded by a turbulent political drama.

On one level, then, Abramovitsh's silence was his answer to the harsh conditions of Jewish life in Russia after 1881. Binshtok refrains from disclosing two more personal causes of his depression: in 1882 his daughter Rashel Abramovitsh died at the age of nineteen, and his son Meir (Mikhail) Abramovitsh (b. 1859), a Russian-language poet, was exiled as a result of political activities. Subsequently his son lived with a non-Jewish woman and converted to Christianity. Since Moses Mendelssohn, whose daughter Dorothea eloped with Friedrich von Schlegel and converted to Christianity, enlightened Jewish intellectuals had reason to fear the social consequences of their quest for political equality. The theme of intermarriage resurfaces most poignantly in Sholem Aleichem's 1906 story "Chava," as narrated by Tevye the Dairyman.

According to other accounts, Abramovitsh suffered from extreme duress at the hands of a ruthless man from Berditchev who blackmailed him to exact revenge for Abramovitsh's critical play, *The Tax*.[26] After these contretemps, the success of Russian and Polish editions of Abramovitsh's novels (1884–86) and celebrations of his literary jubilee encouraged him to return to literary projects. (Nevertheless, when a Polish journal began to print a translation of *The Nag* in 1886, its allegorical critique of the Czarist regime became obvious and this journal was shut down by the censors.) During the late 1880s, at the center of a vibrant literary circle in Odessa, Abramovitsh resumed writing in Hebrew, and his prose was charged with the dynamism of his intervening experiences with Yiddish fiction. Although Abramovitsh continued to produce fiction in Yiddish, the rise of modern Hebrew literature gave added impetus to his Hebrew writing.

Sholem Aleichem bestowed on Abramovitsh his honorific title, "the Grandfather of Yiddish Literature." In a 1910 essay written for the Jubilee edition of Abramovitsh's works (1911–13), Sholem Aleichem states: "I declare openly before the entire world that I was the one who crowned Reb Mendele Moykher Sforim with the name 'Grandfather.' That was a quarter century ago. Then I was still just a wag and a 'frivolous grandson,' as the Grandfather called me in one of his letters to me. From then on it was always 'Grandfather! Grandpa.'"[27] The word "crowned" (*gekroynt*) is significant: there are elements of prestige, as well as of familiarity and affection, in this name. But there is also a hint—never openly acknowledged by Sholem Aleichem or his contemporaries—of dismissal. To call Abramovitsh "Grandfather" was, for Sholem Aleichem, to relegate him to a remote age while still establishing a noble pedigree for himself. At the distance of two generations, Sholem Aleichem had less to fear from his precursor.

Abramovitsh and Sholem Aleichem were in fact just one generation apart, since Abramovitsh's prodigal son Mikhail was born in the same year as Sholem Aleichem. A Freudian might argue that

---

[26]See S. L. Tsitron, *Dray literarishe doyres: zikhroynes vegn yidishe shriftshteler* (Warsaw: Sreberk, 1920), vol. 1, pp. 109–13.

[27]Sholem Aleichem, "How Beautiful Is That Tree!" ("Vi sheyn iz der boym!"), in *Ale verk fun Mendele Moykher Sforim (S. Y. Abramovitsh)*, vol. 17: *Kritik iber Mendele Moykher Sforim* (Cracow: Farlag Mendele, 1911), p. 193n. Reprinted in SA 15:21–28.

Sholem Aleichem dissimulated his Oedipal rivalry with Abramovitsh by fictitiously situating him at a safe remove. Their dynamic
relationship evolved rapidly in 1888–90, when Sholem Aleichem
played a role in Abramovitsh's return to Yiddish literature by com-
missioning him to write for *The Jewish Popular Library* (*Di
yudishe folks-bibliotek*).[28] During that period, Sholem Aleichem
maintained a delicate balance between playing the part of an admiring disciple and acting as a critical editor.[29]

LITERARY RECEPTION

Abramovitsh published his first Hebrew essay in 1857 and remained part of the Yiddish and Hebrew literary world until his
death in 1917. But the zenith of his creativity was limited to 1864–
78 (in Yiddish) and 1886–96 (in Hebrew). He made his greatest
contributions to Yiddish fiction in the 1860s and 1870s, and he
later wrote Hebrew stories that assumed a seminal place in the
evolution of modern Hebrew literature. After working extensively
in Yiddish, Abramovitsh learned to create a more malleable Hebrew
prose.[30]

Abramovitsh is remembered as a Hebrew author for his *nusach*,
a particular Hebrew diction, style, or method. He wrote to Ravnitzky that "in your article you also should have set aside a section
on my style (*signon*) itself, because of its importance and because
of the benefit it has brought to literature and to our writers."[31] In a
letter of 1906 he lightly parodies Genesis 1 when he asserts that
"the style of my stories in Hebrew was a new creation. In the
beginning I took counsel with my heart and mind and said: 'Let us

---

[28]See MB 148–76 and Sholem Aleichem's response in the dedication to *Stempenyu*, contained in *Di yudishe folks-bibliotek* 1 (1888), v–viii; reprinted in SA
11: 123–26. The adjective "yudish" then referred to the Jewish people and was
not yet regularly used to designate the Yiddish language. In order to mark this
distinction, I refrain from transcribing the title as *Di yidishe folks-bibliotek*.

[29]Compare Dan Miron, *Der imazh fun shtetl: dray literarishe shtudies* (Tel Aviv:
Peretz farlag, 1981), p. 54.

[30]For a cogent statement of this view, see Robert Alter, *The Invention of Hebrew
Prose: Modern Fiction and the Language of Realism* (Seattle: University of
Washington Press, 1988).

[31]Letter to Ravnitzky of 10 August 1900, translated from the Hebrew original,
contained in *Reshumot* 2 (1927), 429. For a Yiddish translation, see MB 181.

make a Hebrew style that is lively and speaks *clearly and precisely* as people of our time and place speak, but the soul should be Jewish [*yisra'elit*] and should be worthy that one use it to write Hebrew stories for Jews. This was a very difficult thing to do, and praised be the Lord who came to my assistance so that I could create these stories; since that time Jewish writers have begun to use this new style, writing essays and stories—without praising or even mentioning the name of its creator."[32] In this characteristic mock-biblical passage, Abramovitsh figures himself as a creator who has been impiously neglected by mundane imitators.

H. N. Bialik was an admirer who did appreciate and acknowledge Abramovitsh's linguistic and literary accomplishments. Born in the Ukraine in 1873 and living in Odessa after 1891, Bialik received an informal education from the intellectual circle that included Abramovitsh, Ravnitzky, Ben-Ami (Mordecai Rabinovich), and Ahad Ha-Am (Asher Ginzberg). In the 1890s, as he was coming into his own as a Hebrew author, Bialik was accustomed to thinking of Abramovitsh as the literary leader of his age. Indeed, Bialik asserts that Abramovitsh went far beyond the individual creativity that characterizes all artists: he "created for literature a *nusach.* That is, he was the first to give us a literary style [or pattern, model—*shablon*]."[33] Bialik states that this *nusach* or *shablon* cannot be reduced to a "style, language, rhythm," nor is it a matter of "types, popular psychology, natural description, landscape." He recognizes Abramovitsh as a founder who made possible all future accomplishments, and he views Abramovitsh's *nusach* as the "stable ground" on which later artists created. Using an economic figure of speech, Bialik compares this *nusach* or *shablon* to coinage. He explains that "to create for literature a *nusach* means to provide, once and for all, fixed and enduring forms for the feelings and thoughts of the people and so, as a matter of course, to facilitate their expression; it means helping the people think and feel, disciplining its spirit, giving shape to what was

---

[32]Letter to Ravnitzky of 11 September 1906, translated from the Hebrew original contained in *Reshumot* 2 (1927), 431. A Yiddish translation is contained in MB 202.

[33]H. N. Bialik, "Mendele's *nusach,*" in *Ale verk Mendele Moykher Sforim (S. Y. Abramovitsh)*, vol. 17: *Kritik iber Mendele Moykher Sforim* (Cracow: Farlag Mendele, 1911), p. 151.

without form; bringing forth gold from the raw earth and melting it into current coinage" (ibid., 154). Bialik clearly valued Abramovitsh's Hebrew *nusach* because he appropriated it for his own poetic creations. As Abramovitsh's Hebrew fiction gained currency, Bialik's poetry became an equally compelling source of modern Hebrew verse.

Judaic literary history since Bialik has, for pragmatic reasons linked to the rise of Zionism, emphasized Abramovitsh's importance as a Hebrew author. Much as Sholem Aleichem dubbed Abramovitsh "the Grandfather" of Yiddish literature and in so doing accorded himself a venerable lineage, Bialik exalted modern Hebrew by extolling the virtues of Abramovitsh's influential style. In fact, other authors made equally remarkable advances in Hebrew style; I. L. Peretz adopted a more streamlined, modernistic narrative voice in his Hebrew stories of 1886–94. Abramovitsh's Hebrew, often spoken through his mouthpiece Mendele, is consciously archaic: it is baroque, reflective, slow-paced, descriptive, and brimming with recondite vocabulary drawn from disparate layers of biblical, talmudic, and post-talmudic writing.[34] He succeeded in reaching a general audience by capturing the oral intonations of Yiddish speech, whereas his highly allusive, literary Hebrew remains an acquired taste.

Abramovitsh encouraged a misreading of his early fiction through the lens of his final period. In his Odessa phase, he became more conservative and tried to preserve neutrality at a time when Jewish nationalists were engaged in a fierce struggle against assimilationists.[35] His own livelihood was at stake because the school he directed "was permeated by russifying tendencies" (FZ 122). During the 1860s and 1870s Abramovitsh continued the line of Enlightenment writing by opposing ignorance, superstition, and cor-

---

[34] In contrast, Peretz's prose is sparse, fast-paced, and written in a more accessible vocabulary. His Hebrew remains highly readable today, in part because the intervening development of Israeli fiction has followed Peretz more than it has emulated Abramovitsh. One may thus refer to Peretz's *nusach she-k'neged*, his "style in opposition" to that of Abramovitsh. See Gershon Shaked's section on Peretz in *Ha-sifrut ha-'ivrit 1880–1980*, vol. 1: *Ba-gola* (Tel Aviv: Keter, 1977), especially pp. 130–31. For a detailed discussion of Abramovitsh's use of language and satire, see Gershon Shaked's *Bein tzechok le-dema': 'iyyunim bi-yitzirato shel Mendele Moykher-Sforim* (Tel Aviv: Massada, 1965).

[35] See Simon Dubnov, FZ 109–10, 121–22.

ruption. But after the 1890s he ceased to aim at specific social ends, instead seeking to establish his fiction as a classical monument in Yiddish and Hebrew culture. To the extent that he remained an ideological writer, he was primarily committed to advancing the cause of Jewish cultural life.

Abramovitsh created alternatively in Hebrew and Yiddish, complementing the scholarly dignity of the Holy tongue with the oral fluidity of the mother tongue. He began in Hebrew, shifted to Yiddish for the benefit of a broader readership, and returned to Hebrew while continuing his Yiddish writing. For Abramovitsh, as for Peretz, creative translations between Hebrew and Yiddish comprised a part of his literary accomplishment. The first transition, in which Abramovitsh moved from Hebrew to Yiddish, was a highly successful period; he also exerted great influence on Hebrew writers in Odessa and elsewhere during his second Hebrew phase that began in 1886. The spoken language of Odessa intellectuals was Russian, while Hebrew and Yiddish served other purposes. Simon Dubnov recalls that in the 1890s Abramovitsh "spoke Russian with everyone, even with those writers who wrote Hebrew or Yiddish. That had become an accepted rule: one must write for the 'people,' who speak only the mother tongue, in Yiddish. But in life the intelligentsia needed to use only the state language. No one in our circle thought of speaking Hebrew" (FZ 44).

A particularly important instance of autotranslation occurred in the case of Abramovitsh's *The Magic Ring* (*Dos vintshfingerl*), written in 1865 and immensely expanded for Sholem Aleichem's two anthologies entitled *The Jewish Popular Library* (*Di yudishe folksbibliotek*, 1888–89). After this Yiddish publication folded, Abramovitsh had nowhere to print the planned continuation of *The Magic Ring*. Hence he translated the first part of the book into Hebrew and added further chapters in Hebrew. Simon Dubnov recalls, however, that when Abramovitsh "had the first part of the Yiddish original of the *Magic Ring* before his eyes, he made the Hebrew translation—or rather, the reworking—masterfully and without any difficulties. But when he came to write without the Yiddish original, he felt that it would not go smoothly" (FZ 46). Dubnov comments that a writer cannot simultaneously be creative in form and content. First Abramovitsh needed to "create the content in the language of that life which is depicted in the artwork." Even Hebrew fiction, Dubnov suggests, had to remain close to

Yiddish, the spoken vernacular of everyday Jewish life. Abramovitsh's Hebrew style owed a profound debt to Yiddish as well as to the multiple layers of ancient and medieval Hebrew.

Publishing practices have obscured readers' awareness of Abramovitsh's literary evolution. There are virtually no critical editions of classic Yiddish fiction, and material conditions have not been conducive to reliable printings. Most classic Yiddish fiction first appeared in newspapers or journals; to varying degrees, the authors oversaw the canonization of their works in collected editions. Yet even the seventeen-volume Jubilee edition of Abramovitsh's *Ale verk* (*Complete Works,* planned for 1907 but postponed until 1911–13) was marred by numerous misprints, as Abramovitsh himself complained bitterly to the publisher (MB 225–26). Ber Borokhov refers to the "general deficiency of all editions of our classics: they are provided by publishers who have no scrap of an idea about scientific demands, no hint of an historical sense, and have in mind no more than an exclusively commercial interest. Considering the primitive behavior of our ignorant publishers it is no surprise that their editions are full of the most foolish misprints."[36]

While textual philology often follows the principle of accepting the final version passed by an author, this approach is problematic in the case of Abramovitsh. The last edition of Abramovitsh's Yiddish works published in his lifetime is that of 1911–13, and the Hebrew canon was established by an edition from 1909–12. Yet the author's own assessment of his work was skewed because he consistently underestimated the significance of the early, short versions of his novels. As a result these first versions are seldom consulted. The Soviet critics alone, especially Meir Viner and Aharon Gurshteyn, attempted to restore the centrality of Abramovitsh's contribution in the 1860s and 1870s.[37] Abramovitsh's creative

---

[36]Ber Borokhov, "Di Peretz-bibliografie," in *I. L. Peretz: a zamlbukh tsu zayn ondenkn* (New York: Literarisher farlag, 1915), p. 108. This seminal essay has been reprinted in Ber Borokhov, *Shprakh-forshung un literatur-geshikhte,* ed. Nachman Mayzel (Tel Aviv: Peretz farlag, 1966), pp. 226–31.

[37]See Meir Viner, "Mendele in the 'Sixties and 'Seventies" ("Mendele in di zekhtsiker un zibetsiker yorn"), contained in his *Tsu der geshikhte fun der yidisher literatur in 19-tn yorhundert (etyudn un materialn)* (New York: YKUF, 1946), vol. 2, pp. 74–221, and Aharon Gurshteyn, "On *Solomon, Son of Chaim*" ("Vegn *Shloyme reb Khaims*"), in Abramovitsh's *Gezamlte verk* (Moscow: Der emes, 1935), vol. 6, pp. 7–45; see also Gurshteyn's "Der yunger Mendele in kontekst fun di zekhtsiker yorn: shtrikhn," *Shriftn* 1 (1928), 180–98.

impulse was strongest from 1864–78, after his shift from Hebrew to Yiddish made possible the future course of Yiddish fiction.

In a sense, the canonical image of Abramovitsh has been distorted by his success. Under the impression of celebrations, new editions, and translations, Abramovitsh extensively revised his works and sometimes weakened them in the process.[38] His greatest formal innovation, later emulated by a score of writers, was his parodic appropriation of a dignified, pseudo-religious tone combined with an undercurrent of satire. This attracted traditionally inclined readers through the mouthpiece of the folksy Mendele the Bookseller, while also offering critical observations of their milieu. As Abramovitsh tempered his critique and increased the sentimental dimension, his original social thrust faded from view. The popular reception turned a fiery reformer and innovative stylist into a doting grandfather.

---

[38]Compare FZ 117–18, in which Simon Dubnov recalls that Abramovitsh "ceaselessly polished" his works.

CHAPTER 2

S. Y. Abramovitsh: Mendele and the Origins of Modern Yiddish Fiction

The life of Sholem Yankev Abramovitsh cannot adequately explain what enabled him to change the course of Judaic literary history. He published the first modern Yiddish novel serially in 1864–65 and wrote four novels over the next thirteen years. These five works constitute the core of his creative achievement in Yiddish, yet few twentieth-century critics have read the earliest editions of his novels from the 1860s. Thus the true beginnings of modern Yiddish fiction have been obscured, because only the original versions of Abramovitsh's Yiddish novels show the development of his narrative voice.

Abramovitsh's work has become intimately associated with the persona of Mendele Moykher Sforim, or Mendele the Bookseller. This fictional character sells religious articles, sacred books, and secular literature to the Jews of Eastern Europe. By 1900, Mendele attained such renown that he virtually eclipsed the author's identity in popular awareness.[1] To understand this aspect of Abramovitsh's Yiddish writing, one must retrace Mendele's evolution during three distinct phases—1864–69, 1869–79, and 1886–96.[2]

---

[1]Compare Dan Miron's discussions of the Abramovitsh–Mendele dichotomy in "Sholem Aleykhem: Person, Persona, Presence," *The Uriel Weinreich Memorial Lecture* 1 (New York: YIVO Institute for Jewish Research, 1972), p. 10, and in *A Traveler Disguised: A Study in the Rise of Modern Yiddish Fiction in the Nineteenth Century* (New York: Schocken, 1973), pp. 92–94 and 148–68; henceforth cited as "TD" by page alone.

[2]These stages in Abramovitsh's literary development have been recognized by some scholars. See, for instance, Meir Viner, "Mendele in di zekhtsiker un zibetsiker yorn," in *Tsu der geshikhte fun der yidisher literatur in 19-tn yorhundert (etyudn un materialn)* (New York: YKUF, 1946), vol. 2, pp. 74–221; and compare Dan Miron and Anita Norich, "The Politics of Benjamin III: Intellectual Significance and Its Formal Correlatives in Sh. Y. Abramovitsh's *Masoes Benyomin Hashlishi*," in *The Field of Yiddish: Studies in Language, Folklore,*

Throughout his literary life, Abramovitsh employed the Mendele persona. For a time he created the second persona of Isrolik the madman, particularly in *The Nag* (1873), but he soon abandoned it.[3] Abramovitsh deliberately created the illusion that Mendele was a bookseller and editor who existed outside of the pages of his novels. This chapter returns to the earliest forms of the Mendele mask; the next chapter shows the metamorphoses that this persona underwent during subsequent decades. Later, when Abramovitsh switched back to writing Hebrew fiction, he drew from both of these earlier Yiddish periods.

The Mendele character gradually takes on new meaning in Abramovitsh's novels as he becomes an increasingly sophisticated critic of social ills. *The Little Man* opens as a first-person narrative by Mendele the Bookseller before it gives way to a long letter by another character. A year later, Mendele purports to have edited *The Magic Ring*, based on a story written by Hershl Roytman. In contrast, *Fishke the Lame* fully integrates Mendele into the novel as its first-person narrator.

THE LITTLE MAN

The Little Man (*Dos kleyne mentshele*, 1864–65) incorporates autobiographical elements in what is essentially a *Bildungsroman*, a novel of education. Framed by prefatory and concluding narratives by Mendele the Bookseller, it consists of Isaac-Abraham's letter recounting his life story. The fictional author of this epistolary autobiography tells a story of Jewish life in the small towns of Eastern Europe, as he moves from poverty through apprenticeships

---

and Literature, Fourth Collection, ed. Marvin I. Herzog, Barbara Kirshenblatt-Gimblett, Dan Miron, and Ruth Wisse (Philadelphia: Institute for the Study of Human Issues, 1980), pp. 3–19.

[3] Apart from the novel *The Nag*, Abramovitsh wrote a number of stories from the standpoint of Isrolik; several of them were published posthumously. See, for example: "Aderabe, ver iz meshuge?" in *Mendele un zayn tsayt: materialn tsu der geshikhte fun der yidisher literatur in XIX yorhundert* (Moscow: Der emes, 1940), pp. 5–8, and "Der baybak; a bletl funem dnievnik Isrolik dem meshugenems," *Shtern* 12, number 1 (1936), 6–12. During Abramovitsh's lifetime, the following Isrolik tales were published: "Yidishe kinder," *Isrolik*, number 8, 20 October 1875, 1–4, and "Isrolik der meshugener farflit in di hoykhe oylemes," *Der yud* 3, number 47 (1901), 50–52. Compare Dan Miron, *TD*, p. 238. See also Dan Miron and Anita Norich, "The Politics of Benjamin III," pp. 11–14.

and restless wanderings to illicit financial gains. By the conclusion of his narrative, Isaac-Abraham adopts Enlightenment ideas that undermine the bourgeois values he previously held, and the seemingly neutral self-presentation becomes a highly-charged social critique.

Abramovitsh wields literary devices centering around first-person narrative and satire. First-person narrative is present in most of Abramovitsh's work, and it is especially prominent in *The Little Man*. Both Mendele's frame narrative and Isaac-Abraham's story are told in the first-person form, bringing "polyphony"—Mikhail Bakhtin's word describing Dostoevsky's multivoiced novels—into Abramovitsh's fiction.[4] The richness of this novel derives in part from the interaction between the persona of Mendele the Bookseller and the character of Isaac-Abraham, the "little man" who achieves wealth.

The subtitle of *The Little Man* is *A Life Description by Isaac-Abraham Takif*; a *takif* is a powerful, influential person. Precisely this kind of power and influence comes under attack during the course of the narrative. Beneath the subtitle stand the Hebrew words "by a man" (*me'et 'ish*), prudently declining to claim authorship while encoding the author's initials (reversed) in the Hebrew word "man" (*'ish*), Aleph-Yud-Shin. The author's identity is present and at the same time concealed behind an ideal of universality; his popular appeal is embodied in the itinerant bookseller Mendele. Rather than speak in his own voice, as an author who had already expressed his Enlightenment views in Hebrew since 1857, he assumes a persona suited to his début in Yiddish; he dons the mask of an older, simpler man.

The opening words of the novel are Mendele the Bookseller's first self-presentation. His fictive name has not yet become a catchword and retains its original meaning when Mendele introduces himself as "the Bookseller" (*der moykher sforim*). By virtue of his tone, Mendele's account appears to be as spontaneous and circuitous as are his travels:

> I myself was born in Tsviatshitsh, and my name is Mendele the Bookseller. I'm underway most of the year, here and there. People know me everywhere, because I travel throughout Poland with

---

[4]A Bakhtinian critic could write a monograph about Abramovitsh's polyphonic style, on the model of Mikhail Bakhtin's *Problems of Dostoevsky's Poetics*, trans. Caryl Emerson (Minneapolis: University of Minnesota Press, 1984).

all kinds of books printed in Zhitomir—not to mention prayer shawls, *tales-kotns,* tassels, shofars, tefillin, amulets, *mezuzes,* wolves' teeth, and sometimes one can buy brass or copper utensils from me. In fact, since *Kol mevasser* appeared, I sometimes carry a few numbers of it. But that's not at all, not at all what I'm getting at; I want to tell about something else entirely.[5] (3)

Mendele's speech strikes us with its illusion of directness and immediacy. Although this is a written monologue, its rhythm and vocabulary suggest an oral delivery, using the technique Russian formalist critics later called *skaz.* Abramovitsh thus takes advantage of the intrinsic strengths of the Yiddish language, while borrowing from contemporary Russian fiction. Mendele describes himself as a seasoned traveler who brings traditional religious articles and sacred books to Jews in Poland; he is also aware of popular beliefs and stocks the desired amulets (*heyelekh* and *volftseyndlekh*). This opening narrator appears to speak from among the common Jews of Eastern Europe rather than as part of another social class or milieu. He also seems to speak or write spontaneously, frequently repeating "that's not what I'm getting at" (*nisht dos bin ikh oysn*)—as if he were impatiently brushing aside his unwitting digressions. As Dan Miron observes, Mendele creates "the impression that he is unable to concentrate on his story" (TD 160). At the same time, when Mendele later pretends to have digressed, he has sometimes made a pertinent critique: "Mendele always uses this kind of camouflage just after he has scored a particularly sharp point."[6]

In the foreground is Mendele's oral pretense. Breaking through this layer of folksy speech we feel Abramovitsh's presence, wherever the Mendele persona is laced with irony. The "implied author" —Abramovitsh's implicit presence, including his attitudes and

---

[5]*Dos kleyne mentshele oder a lebensbashraybung fun Yitskhok Avrom takif* (serialized in 1864–65; repr. Odessa: Nitzshe and Tsederboym, 1865); cited by page alone. Alternative translations are provided by Dan Miron, in connection with his analyses, in *A Traveler Disguised.* Abramovitsh's first Yiddish novel was reprinted with modernized spelling and a Hebrew translation in *Ha-'ishon ha-katan / Dos kleyne mentshele,* ed. Shalom Luria (Haifa: Haifa University Press, 1984). For an English translation of the later edition, by Gerald Stillman, see *The Little Man,* in *Selected Works of Mendele Moykher-Sforim,* ed. Marvin Zuckerman, Gerald Stillman, and Marion Herbst (Malibu, Calif.: Joseph Simon/Pangloss Press, 1991), pp. 53–167.

[6]Dan Miron and Anita Norich, "The Politics of Benjamin III," p. 24.

beliefs—hovers behind the Mendele mask.[7] An aura of irony surrounds the name of the town, "Tsviatshitsh," meaning "place of hypocrisy." Abramovitsh appropriates a convention of nineteenth-century Russian novels, which use comic place names that mock the foibles of each town's inhabitants.[8]

Amid the list of his humble wares, Mendele inserts a reference to *Kol mevasser* (*The Voice of Tidings*). This was the Yiddish supplement to the Hebrew newspaper *Ha-melitz*, in which *The Little Man* itself initially appeared, published in serial fashion starting on 24 November 1864. The narrator Mendele, who exists only in the pages of *Kol mevasser,* steps forward to announce that he carries the journal as part of his stock-in-trade. This detail momentarily breaks his grassroots aura. It expands Mendele's repertoire to include secular, Enlightenment writing, and creates a paradoxical situation of self-reflexivity that disturbs the realistic conventions of the fiction. Abramovitsh takes a bow as the real-life author hidden behind the Mendele persona.

After tossing aside the reference to *Kol mevasser* by commenting, "that's not what I'm getting at," Mendele begins his narrative. Mendele narrates an experience that supposedly occurred earlier in the year. There is a significant discrepancy between the aspiring young author, then in his late twenties, and this venerable bookseller:

> Last year (1863), around Chanukah, I traveled to Glupsk, where I reckoned on selling some candlesticks and wax candles. Well, that's not at all, not at all what I'm getting at. But Tuesday after prayers I arrived in Glupsk, and as is my custom I went straight to the House of Study. That's not what I'm getting at. When I rode up to the House of Study I saw circles of people standing around, arguing, chatting, laughing, and worrying. . . . Well, what do you say? I'm not made of wood, and besides, I'm also a Jew. I wanted to find out what was going on there. In this world

---

[7]Wayne Booth's notion of an "implied author" focuses attention on the author only insofar as his or her presence may be inferred from a text. See Wayne C. Booth, *The Rhetoric of Fiction* (Chicago: University of Chicago Press, 1961), pp. 74–76.

[8]Not only Russian authors set this pattern for later Yiddish novels. As Dan Miron notes, Peretz Smolenskin's Hebrew novels of the late 1860s used similar fictitious place names meaning "Dunghill," "Darkness," and "The Bereaved One." See Miron, "Sholem Aleykhem: Person, Persona, Presence," p. 3n.

one needs to know everything, hear everything. Sometimes it comes in handy. That's not what I'm getting at. (3)

Mendele combines traditionalism with practicality. He immediately heads for the House of Study, not out of piety but because his trade revolves around religious life. Moreover, his observation that "one needs to know everything" runs a fine line between Enlightenment universalism and the pragmatic advice of a merchant. For Russian speakers, the name of the town carries a humorous overtone: as "Tsviatshitsh" is a "place of hypocrisy," so "Glupsk" means "town of fools." Like the reference to *Kol mevasser*, these comic appellations run counter to the innocent pretenses of the work. At the same time, the connections to Russian fiction reveal Abramovitsh's appropriative, parodic relationship to prior literary models. Nevertheless, Mendele continues his story and emphasizes his share in *shtetl* life, drawn to and affected by all goings-on there. When he says that "in this world one needs to know everything," he implies that life is a collective effort, not an individual enterprise. He underscores his closeness to the life of the small towns and invites his readers to perceive him as a peer.[9]

The story within the story begins to unfold after the crowd welcomes Mendele and he learns that Isaac-Abraham, a wealthy man in town, has died. He reports a dialogue that conveys conflicting opinions about the deceased. One man expresses conventional regrets, but another questions his sincerity, saying bluntly that Isaac-Abraham was "an ignoramus, hard-hearted, and besides, a bit of a fool" (4). Finally the first man concurs with this verdict and the skeptic pronounces ironically: "That, Reb Avramtshe, is why I like you, because you always tell the truth" (5). Thus the presentation of Isaac-Abraham opens with an argument over his merits. By the end of his life story, the reader understands that Isaac-Abraham shared such doubts about himself, having recognized his substantial faults and missteps.

As Mendele begins to unpack his wares, the town rabbi summons him and greets him fervently. At this point Mendele boasts of his worldly wisdom, remarking that other booksellers might have assumed that the rabbi was interested in purchasing something.

---

[9]An excellent discussion of this dynamic relationship between Mendele and his readers is contained in Dan Miron's *A Traveler Disguised,* chapter 6.

Mendele concludes the reverse, since he knows that a seasoned buyer never shows enthusiasm.

> Another bookseller would surely have thought that they had waited anxiously for my coach with wares. But I'm no foolish, newly-born child, in the dark about what is going on; I didn't crawl out of the egg yesterday. You should know that as a rule the world consists of deception. A person who needs some necessary thing pretends that it is completely worthless to him, so that he can buy it for almost nothing. For example, if a person urgently needs a prayer book, for appearances he haggles over a book of penitential prayers, of lamentations, and a bundle of tassels. Meanwhile he blithely snatches up the prayer book, merely pretends to glance at it, then puts it down with a grimace and a smile: well, for a small sum I might also have bought this. Believe me, the entire world is a market. Everyone wants someone else to lose so that he can gain. Everyone is looking for bargains. But that's not what I'm getting at. I guessed from the rabbi's face that he didn't want to buy anything, otherwise he wouldn't have shown that he was waiting for me. It's true that the rabbi is a fine man—so should my fortunes go—but in this world one must deceive. (6)

Mendele prides himself on his down-to-earth wisdom, acutely describing business realities. At the same time, he is inclined to perceive all the world in these terms, generalizing the marketplace into a universal metaphor of greed and deception. Here Mendele possesses the unpretentious understanding of a careful observer; he describes mundane follies without condemning them outright. As Dan Miron comments, "Abramovitsh was not trying to reconstruct his own mentality and ideas in these conventional reflections" (TD 163). Rather, the gap widens between the flesh-and-blood author and his fictional speaker. Offering popular advice, Mendele says that "you should know a rule: the world consists of deception" (6). This skepticism, like the previous discussion of Isaac-Abraham, prepares for the story of a life. In this context, Mendele shows a glimmer of his traditionalism when he quotes Genesis 18:8 and refers to Midrash in support of his view: "Even the angels had to copy the way of the world, with our ancestor Abraham, when 'they ate'—that is, they pretended to eat" (6). The biblical reference anticipates the technique of quotation that, a generation later, characterizes Sholem Aleichem's Tevye. Mendele is at once worldly wise and quaintly traditional; Abramovitsh's greater awareness hovers nearby, behind such ironic intertextual allusions. In context, this allusion to Hebrew Scripture retains the critical distance needed to make this passage a parodic reworking rather than a naive imitation.

The rabbi leads Mendele into a room crowded with wealthy men, looking distracted and worried. His naive incomprehension creates humorous dissonance: "There sat the rabbi's assistants and all the wealthy men, apparently preoccupied, though wealthy people are always a little engrossed, worried. I myself don't know why, if one has money, there is so much to think about; it seems to me that to spend money one doesn't need to have any fancy ideas" (6–7). Beyond Mendele's level of presentation, the narrative ironically contrasts Mendele's simple discernment with the misguided ruminations of the rich. But according to the literary convention, the straightforward Mendele of 1864 remains unaware of this irony.

The implied author conveys a didactic message by means of the subsequent story within the story. Unlike Mendele, the other men who are present hope to profit from the proceedings. The rabbi produces a letter containing Isaac-Abraham's life-story and last will, and he begins to read aloud. Now the narrative resumes in a second, somewhat less folksy voice. With the reserved dignity of a powerful self-made man of the town, Isaac-Abraham portrays his humble origins. The son of a poor family, he has no recollection of his father, who died at an early age. His habit was to watch people closely as they spoke, looking into their eyes. Once he asked his mother: "What kind of little man is in your eyes?" Possibly he had seen his own reflection, but his mother answered: "That little man is the soul. That little man is not in everyone's eyes, not in animals' eyes, but only in Jewish eyes" (9).

This moment of self-perception is Isaac-Abraham's first encounter with questions of identity, viewed through his mother's eyes. On the one hand he is asking about himself, provoked by seeing his own image—a little man—in her eyes. On the other hand, he is finding out about the soul within his mother, which she says characterizes all Jews. In connection with this "mirror stage,"[10]

---

[10] See Jacques Lacan, "Le stade du miroir," in *Écrits* (Paris: Seuil, 1966), pp. 93–100.

her response also permits some freedom of interpretation. She may have said, "That little man is the soul," or she may have addressed her son: "That, little man, is the soul."[11] In the latter case Isaac-Abraham is himself the little man, and this ambiguity finds expression in his reaction: "From then on my imagination was engrossed by the little man. While sleeping I saw the little man; I dreamed of playing with the little man, of holding the little man, and of myself being a little man. . . . I longed to be a little man. It's no small matter, for a little man is a soul!" (9). This revelation sparks philosophical reflections about the soul, at the same time that it raises concrete issues of selfhood. Much of Isaac-Abraham's narrative deals with his efforts to understand "the little man"—the soul, himself, and his potential.

Isaac-Abraham continues his narrative by recalling his setbacks at the religious school and as an apprentice. He works for a tailor, a shoemaker, and then joins a boys' choir led by a cantor (*khazn*). While it seems to present a neutral memoir of events, the book implicitly critiques the prevailing system of apprenticeship. Abramovitsh makes Isaac-Abraham bear the brunt of the novel's social criticism, by having this character confess his wrongdoings. But Isaac-Abraham is a step above his wealthy contemporaries in the "town of fools," for he at least comes to acknowledge his failure to become an ethical, responsible person. He has remained a "little man" instead of becoming a true *mentsh.*

The novel suggests that questions of Jewish identity and education are inseparable from language, and that the Jews' speech has been corrupted by their ignorance. Isaac-Abraham meets a *maskil,* a proponent of the Jewish Enlightenment. This German-Jewish author, the enlightened Herr Gutmann, is the only person who treats him kindly and exposes him to higher ideals; Gutmann's prototype was apparently Abramovitsh's mentor and friend Avraham-Ber Gottlober. Herr Gutmann's first lesson concerns Isaac-Abraham's name and, in more general terms, his identity. When the *maskil* asks his name he finds himself unable to answer, having been variously called "Yitskhok Avramtshe," "Itshe Avremele," "Itsik-Avreml," "Itshiniu Avrominiu," and "Avromke" (23–24). Abramovitsh marks the linguistic predicament of many

---

[11]This significant, suggestive ambiguity was eliminated in later editions of *The Little Man.*

uneducated Yiddish speakers, unable to function beyond their narrow horizons. Illiterate, like many Eastern European Jews, the boy is caught between different dialects and diminutives that have been foisted upon him. The German-Jew clears up this confusion by telling him that his name is Isaac-Abraham, following the German pronunciation of the biblical names.

The problems of identity and language intensify, surrounding the ambiguous verbal phrase that is the title of the book, "the little man." Thus far it has referred to the soul and to the young Isaac-Abraham. Now it takes on a new meaning that unsettles the enlightened values he has begun to acquire from Herr Gutmann. Isaac-Abraham's difficulties stem from his inability to distinguish between conflicting usages of the phrase. Discussing a corrupt Dr. Steinhertz, Herr Gutmann comments that "he is really a little man, and so he's rich and everyone's favorite [*bay ale gor di neshome*]" (26). Gutmann's words reawaken Isaac-Abraham's interest in "the little man" and his longing to become one. He does not realize that Gutmann uses the phrase pejoratively to denote a petty spirit, a petit bourgeois, a small-minded person. Instead, Isaac-Abraham simply associates it with wealth, concluding that "if one is a little man, one is a rich, happy man," which leads him to the conclusion that he must become a little man. While asleep he dreams of being a little man, and he ineptly decides that the path to this goal is to "stop feeling and thinking" (28). Again Abramovitsh directs irony against the petit bourgeoisie through the mediation of his naive protagonist. The presentation of unhindered, confessional speech is balanced by an implicitly critical perspective of his narrative.

Further acquaintance with the dishonest Dr. Steinhertz leads Isaac-Abraham to conclude that being a little man means "drawing others' blood and getting money by deceit" (32). He then meets Iser, a teacher in the ways of corruption and exploitation, who explains that "a little man means flattering, being a hypocrite" (37). Thus Isaac-Abraham pursues his success story, but his real path to accomplishment does not end with wealth. Instead, after he ingratiates himself into the services of powerful men and becomes their "soul" (*neshome*), he finally realizes the error of his striving to be a "little man."

In the meantime, Isaac-Abraham's selfish strivings have pitted him directly against his former teacher, Herr Gutmann. Iser warns that "a little man must not envy such people as Gutmann, who make books. By no means! One must hate and persecute them because they're worse than fire, they sometimes make you sick with their truthful sayings" (45). The multivoiced quality of Abramovitsh's prose is evident in this passage that overtly attacks men like the author himself. Indeed, several scenes show that Gutmann values his impoverished life of truth above material wealth. Isaac-Abraham begins to feel pangs of conscience, dark thoughts, and he is tormented to the point of critical illness. He explains that this state has led him to write his life story as a confession.

Abramovitsh again has recourse to Hebrew, to liturgical models that counterbalance the colloquial tones of this narrative. Isaac-Abraham's voice modulates when he begins to confess his sins, employing the traditional formula: "For the sin which I have sinned . . ." (43–45). This locution reminds us that his story is actually his death-bed confession. At this point, the phrase "little man" recurs when Isaac-Abraham repents, using a Hebrew phrase: "For the sin I have sinned regarding impudence and the little man" (45)—through cheating and defrauding honest people.

In his will, Isaac-Abraham bequeaths part of his wealth to those who can correct his misdeeds. He asks the local rabbi to employ Gutmann—"a righteous man, a good man, even though he goes around without a headcovering"—to improve the Jewish school (48–49). Isaac-Abraham's transformation clearly serves Abramovitsh's enlightened ideals, showing the victory of education over greed. This is a *Bildungsroman* of material success and spiritual failure, in which education (*Bildung*) is the ultimate hero and Yiddish literature assumes a didactic role.

Isaac-Abraham's narrative ultimately explains the reason for the public reading. The audience consists of men who have all hoped for a share in his wealth, but instead they receive a moralistic lesson (*muser*): "Let the whole world know that wealth does not make one happy. One is happy only with a good heart and good deeds. It is better to suffer and be an honest man than to eat delicacies and be a little man" (50). The closing words also explain the reason for Mendele's presence at the meeting: "Please give this letter to Reb Mendele the Bookseller, because he knows the rules of printing, and besides, he travels all over Poland and will be able to sell it" (50).

When the public reading has ended, Mendele notes, those present are furious but remain silent. In some ways, Abramovitsh has written his contemporary readership into the book, anticipating a negative reaction to his critical social message. As the wealthy men of Glupsk could not know what to expect when called to hear Isaac-Abraham's narrative at the rabbi's house, the readers of *Kol mevasser* had no prior warning that Abramovitsh's serialized novel would contain a harsh critique of their world. One might view *The Little Man* in part as an allegory of Yiddish literature, containing depictions of the repentant writer Isaac-Abraham and his corrupt audience. The men of Glupsk are modeled after town leaders of Berditchev, where Abramovitsh had lived since 1858. Both the author and his readers are thus inscribed into the text, reflecting the situation of a young writer in relationship to a potentially hostile society; wealthy readers could only be silently aware of Abramovitsh's justice. Yet the book is primarily intended for the Jewish masses, and the rabbi entreats Mendele to "print the letter and sell it in all of Poland for a cheap price, so that the public will buy it more readily" (51). Aimed at the average Yiddish speaker, the text condemns the rich and affirms the greater merits of the exploited poor.

Mendele's frame narrative closes with his hasty departure for Tsviatshitsh in search of Gutmann. Unable to locate him, Mendele explains that he has printed the letter by Isaac-Abraham himself, and he requests that "Herr Gutmann should, as soon as he receives the letter, come to Glupsk, because the rabbi is expecting him; they are supposed to establish and improve the school and do other good things" (51–52). On one level, these closing words remain within the fictional pretense of fulfilling Isaac-Abraham's request. Beyond this fictional illusion, Mendele appeals to all of Abramovitsh's readers to come to the aid of their own towns by emulating the good Gutmann in his mission to reform Glupsk, the town of fools.

Instead of merely presenting the moralistic tale of Isaac-Abraham and his *crise de conscience*, Abramovitsh frames this account within a social situation that hints at his own aspirations and fears. The multivoiced style of the author's work may have been necessitated by the oppressive conditions set by rabbinic and czarist censorship. Abramovitsh's next novel confirms, in passing, that Isaac-Abraham's plan for Glupsk could only end in a failure for those people (like Gutmann or, on another plane, Abramovitsh) committed to reform.

The Little Man is both Mendele's literary début and Abramovitsh's first Yiddish novel. The main body of the text contains the life-story of Isaac-Abraham, and only momentarily returns to Mendele at the close of the work. Abramovitsh, the implied author, places his persona between himself and the internal narrative by Isaac-Abraham. At the same time, he justifies this pretense by having the latter ask that Mendele serve as the printer of his story. Hence he combines the conventions of a written form, the letter, with the oral tone in Mendele's frame narration.

THE MAGIC RING

Abramovitsh's second short novel, *The Magic Ring* (*Dos vintsh-fingerl*, 1865), expands the role of Mendele the Bookseller while retaining his basic image. Moving toward the convention of the preface (*hakdome*), this short work begins with a ten-page section called "A Story About a Story" (*A mayse iber a mayse*), purportedly explaining how the book came into Mendele's hands. As in *The Little Man*, Abramovitsh's speaker essentially respects the limitations appropriate to a conventional, pious Jew. He says he is traveling from Kabtsansk; that is, he's under way from Paupertown. *The Magic Ring* opens in the form of a pseudo-blessing:

> *Omar Mendele Moyker Sforim*—sayeth Mendele the Bookseller: Praised be the Creator, who in six days created heavens and earth with all the creatures—angels, animals, and birds; goats, sheep, ducks, and the human being, upon whom He bestowed the capacity to understand, to speak, and to write. I intend to describe here the miracle that God—may his name be blessed—performed for my sake a year ago (1865) during the summer.[12] (1)

Mendele combines traditional piety with unconventionality. His blessing begins as one might expect, but it reverts to a haphazard list of God's creations, and ends with a slightly ironic reference to a particular "miracle" God granted him. This supposed miracle turns out to be nothing more than a chance encounter with his

---

[12] Translated from *Dos vintshfingerl* (Warsaw: Levenzon, 1865); cited by page alone. As is the case with Abramovitsh's other early novels, no English translation of the first edition is available. Milton Himmelfarb has translated part one of the 1888 version for a forthcoming publication. In German, see Mendele Moicher Sfurim, *Der Wunschring*, trans. S. Birnbaum, in *Werke*, vol. 2 (Olten: Walter-Verlag, 1961).

friend Senderl, who trades him a German edition of the book we are about to read. This kind of pseudo-blessing recurs often in Mendele's prefaces, yet its significance gradually shifts. In all cases, the appropriation of Hebrew liturgy—in what the Russian formalists called a "refunctioning" of prior forms—was a critical feature in the emergence of Yiddish literature.

Mendele recalls his travels from Kabtsansk, employing naturalistic details that later become his forte. He describes his particular preoccupation in the coach:

> I sat in my prayer shawl and tefillin on the bench and said my morning prayers. The front wheel creaked a little, and my horse lifted its feet cheerfully, walking with a lordly gait. . . . In the middle of the eighteen benedictions—may I be forgiven for this—I took a snooze and my head swung hither and thither. Suddenly I drew myself up with a start and fell straight onto the ground. . . . I looked around, oho! and saw that the creaking wheel of my wagon was caught on the axle of another wagon that had been coming in my direction. (2)

This scene of prayer and collision, while deliberately comic, to some extent corresponds to the world in which pious Jews performed their ritual obligations wherever they found themselves. Abramovitsh thus retains the old-fashioned Mendele pretense, at the same time exaggerating his foibles to the limit of believability. There follows an enraged exchange between Mendele and the other driver, until they recognize each other as friends: "I looked the person straight in the face and also cried out: 'Oy, what's this? Reb Senderl!' A great joy and jubilation came upon me." The accident at once becomes a cause for celebration. The two men exclaim that "this is by God's providence, only because of our ancestors' merits were our coaches entangled, so that we not miss each other. Such a miracle is worth writing about" (3). Behind Mendele's back, or rather beneath the surface of his narrative, Abramovitsh mocks his simplistic belief in divine guidance.

Abramovitsh's choice of the name "Senderl" for his second bookseller was a jab at his first Yiddish editor. When Abramovitsh first wrote *The Little Man* for the journal *Kol mevasser,* his persona was not named Mendele, but instead Senderl. The editor of the newspaper *Ha-melitz,* Alexander Tsederboym, feared that his readers would identify this Senderl with him, since Sender was a common nickname for Alexander. Hence, without even consulting the author, he changed "Senderl" to Mendele—and played a part in creating the most prominent character in Yiddish literature. But Abramovitsh printed his second Yiddish novel independently, and he took this opportunity to reintroduce the name that had been excised. A collision occurs, then, between the two identities that had been split by an editor's hand. Abramovitsh sarcastically makes Senderl—now possibly a deliberate spoof on Alexander Tsederboym—into a far less sophisticated character than Mendele.

After Senderl comments on the sorry condition of Mendele's horse, Mendele displays a copy of *The Little Man*: "Here's a book for you. There you'll see that the young rascals of Glupsk tormented him. Don't think that my horse is an ordinary one, just any old horse; he's already been written up in a book, and on top of that, even in a newspaper" (4). Mendele adds to the humorous effect when he alludes to Abramovitsh's earlier book and to its earliest publication in *Kol mevasser*. Perhaps he even vies with his creator, Abramovitsh, for the notoriety his book brings. Mendele also prides himself on the literary fame of his ailing horse, implying that together they have risen beyond mere mundane existence. Senderl, with a confused sense of literary history, tells him not to boast:

> Throughout history one finds a lot of horses that are spoken about in books and newspapers. It's nothing! They say that a non-Jewish writer—one Lessing or Essing, what difference does it make? let it be Essenig—even wrote an ode to an ass. And a German-Jew whom I carried a year ago drove me crazy the whole way with Sancho Pancha's ass. It's written in a book *Don Scott* or *Kot* or *Quixote*. (4)

Mendele neither makes these malaprops, nor does he correct his friend Senderl; Abramovitsh disguises himself behind Sender's mask of ignorance that hides his broader European education. This disparity creates comic, incongruous situations at the same time that it satirizes Jewish culture and marks the parodic relationship to German and Spanish literature.

Enlightenment becomes an explicit issue when the two merchants start to trade books, and Reb Senderl explains that he has purchased a German book called *Dos vintshfingerl* (*The Magic Ring*). Mendele thinks that he has found something important:

> My heart skipped a beat when I heard the words "magic ring."
> That's real merchandise, I thought. That's just what Jews need,
> and it can become a big success, like the *Bovo mayse* or *A
> Thousand and One Nights.* So I pressed Reb Senderl until he let
> me have the book for a few Enlightenment books that had been
> lying around among my things. I tell you, Reb Senderl is no fool,
> either. He knows what's good and what's bad. One good story
> book, especially a magic ring, is worth all of the Enlightenment
> books put together. (5)

Abramovitsh's irony borders on burlesque. Since he himself was an
Enlightenment author, he cannot possibly agree with the pragmatic perspective of Mendele the Bookseller. Mendele, mainly concerned with the economic viability of a novel with a catchy title,
slights the tradition out of which he springs, again making light of
his creator. Self-irony of this kind is typical of Jewish humor, as
part of a process of critical reevaluation.

Like many subsequent Yiddish authors, Abramovitsh felt compelled to remain out of view. Apart from using the Mendele persona, Abramovitsh disclaims authorship by pretending that his
book is merely translated from a German work. On another plane,
an added irony linked to Mendele's editorial pretense derives from
the fact that for a decade Abramovitsh acted as editor and translator of an actual German work. In Hebrew translation, he brought
out three volumes of Harald Othmar Lenz' *Book of Natural History (Sefer toldot ha-teva`,* 1862–72). Sender's analogous merchan-
dise, a German book called *The Magic Ring,* is unearthed within
the narrative of Abramovitsh's Yiddish novel, *The Magic Ring.* It
turns out to be an Enlightenment book, camouflaged beneath the
claim to be a tale of miracles. The "magic ring" ultimately becomes a figure for education, since according to the fictitious author, Hershl, education enables one to satisfy every wish. The ring
presumably also alludes to Lessing's play *Nathan the Wise,* with its
story of a magic ring that is the centerpiece of this drama about
religious tolerance.[13] In the subsequent scene, Mendele unwit-
tingly and comically hints at a messianic motif. As he continues on
his way to Glupsk, he finishes his prayers and tries out the new
shofars he has received from Senderl. Although Mendele himself is
not an Enlightenment author, his shofar blasts indirectly announce

---

[13]See Gotthold Ephraim Lessing, *Nathan der Weise* (1779), act 3, scene 7.

that he is bringing salvation—in the form of the magic ring, education—to the Jews. The liturgical and biblical models again function as the basis for elements of a popular Yiddish tale.

Mendele reflects on the German book he has acquired. He reconsiders the needs of the Jewish people and contemplates the possible audience for an Enlightenment book:

> The German's book never left my mind. . . . May I be forgiven for becoming absorbed in thoughts. Because who knows what Jews need and like better than I do? Of what good to them are all books apart from penitential prayers and holiday prayer books? All of us are wise, all of us are clever, all of us know the Torah. That is, many people think that they are wise, handsome, fine creatures just because they are Jews. A Jew is born a sage, upright and pious, so why does he need to break his head with idle books? (6)

This is Mendele's own ironic commentary on Jewish pride and prejudice. In order to suggest that Jews have an exorbitantly high opinion of their learning, Mendele draws from Hebrew sources. He alludes to the liturgical formula, "All of us know . . . ," that is present in the morning blessing of the Torah. More specifically, he quotes from the Passover Haggadah, near the start of the Magid section: "Even if all of us are wise, all of us are clever, all of us are ripe in years, all of us know the Torah, we are still commanded to retell the exodus from Egypt." Relying heavily on such standard turns of phrase, Mendele counters the tradition by observing that "many people *think* that they are wise." He does not merely accept the tradition, but lightly questions it in a way that suggests Abramovitsh's enlightened views.

Mendele possesses enough education to scorn the familiar prejudices against secular learning, and he opposes those who have no use for secular narratives:

> You see, stories are really merchandise. Especially a short one. Jews, as soon as they start, want to know the end. This is just the Jew's character, to be curious and impatient. . . . But that's not what I'm getting at. The point is that stories are salable merchandise. And in short, a "magic ring" is certainly a fine tale. So I'll do good business if I speculate on printing the story in Yiddish. —Absorbed in such thoughts I traveled on in my prayer shawl and tefillin, with a shofar in my hand. (6; ellipses and dash in original)

While Mendele knows the usual prejudices against secular books, he is also aware that actual practices do not conform to these stricter attitudes. Mendele does not present himself as a scholar or educator, but essentially as an astute businessman. Abramovitsh keeps Mendele in the dark about his true function, yet the shofar in his hand hints at his social role as one destined to awaken the slumbering masses of uneducated Jews.

In Glupsk, after finishing his immediate business, Mendele explains that he goes in search of a translator for the German book. He seeks out a German-Jew whose Enlightenment ideology to some extent associates him with Abramovitsh:

> I first went to my old Herr Gutmann with the plan that he should translate the German's book for me. Yes, you should know that Gutmann came to Glupsk with his family a year ago, in accordance with Isaac-Abraham Takif's last will. So that for his money he should put things in order, improve the Jewish school, help orphans and poor children by teaching them good trades. But nothing came of all this order. Gutmann hadn't even completed his year in Glupsk when he was forced to flee, more dead than alive. (6–7)

This passage continues the fictional plot of *The Little Man*, according to which Gutmann was asked to reform Jewish education in Glupsk. At the close of the earlier book, Mendele mediates between the wealthy Isaac-Abraham, with his project of reform, and the enlightened Gutmann, who has been chosen to carry out these reforms. The present novel describes the failure of that plan, uncovering the depths of ignorance into which the town has sunk. In fact, Gutmann's story anticipates Abramovitsh's own later experience in Berditchev, when he fled after publishing the virulent satiric play *The Tax* (*Di takse*, 1869). In his account of Glupsk, Mendele maintains a certain distance from the tragi-comic events he describes. He employs irony, for example, when he paraphrases the general opinion of the townspeople:

> You want to make much of Jews?! And out of Jews from Glupsk, at that? The chassidim were not pleased, because Gutmann dressed like a German. And when the floor of the school was washed, they became furious. What's the meaning of this? To do such a thing in a school! What's this, washing off the mud that our ancestors left behind! . . . Only a non-Jew does something

like that. But a Jew, who has a soul (*a pintele yid*). . . . What does it mean? Is it befitting? (7; ellipses in original)

Here Abramovitsh's irony veers toward full-fledged satire of the chassidim. Later editions of *The Magic Ring* omitted this bitter caricature and critique.

Next Mendele explains what each faction had against Gutmann, before adding his own observations:

> One didn't like Gutmann's coat; another wasn't happy with his cane. A third disliked the fact that Gutmann knows Yiddish, and used to imitate him the way a non-Jew imitates a Jew. But one can't call this German-Jew a gentile because he doesn't know any non-Jewish languages, although when speaking he is full of hot air. Nor can one call him a Jew, because—God protect us—he's a bit weak in Hebrew. (7–8)

This is a central passage among those in which Abramovitsh deals directly with questions of Jewish identity. Gutmann and Mendele mediate between Abramovitsh the implied author and the common reader, representing different levels of education or stages of progress. Gutmann is unacceptable to the Jewish masses, while Mendele is known and liked by all. In his own way, Mendele appreciates enlightened efforts, but is well aware that they are seldom appreciated. Hence he comments, in a Russian folk tradition that resonates with Shakespeare's convention of depicting witty clowns, that "the truth is not to be had from anyone, except from fools and madmen. Doesn't one have to be a fool or a madman, these days, to tell the truth?" (8).

Since Gutmann has been driven out of Glupsk, Mendele turns to another acquaintance, also a poor German-Jew. He explains his rationale:

> You see, that German likes to tell the truth. He often sets me straight about the deceptions of Glupsk. Not long ago he told me about a fine creature of Glupsk who is leading the town by the nose and living like a king. . . . I made an arrangement with the German-Jew that he should translate the German's book into simple Yiddish. (Ibid.)

This new translator resembles Abramovitsh in his awareness of corruption in Glupsk. Mendele evidently respects this truthful German but cannot abandon his own more pragmatic business goals. Thus he asks the German-Jew to spice up his translation with erudite footnotes: "Indeed, it wouldn't hurt if you made a few notes to the story, because now that is all the rage" (9). Mendele says again that he understands the way Jews think:

> Believe me, Jews, I know about such things. One only needs to rack a Jew's brains; the words don't have to fit together. . . . The less one understands, the more you'll be admired. A thing that one understands is without importance to Jews, because what does it teach them? Only things one doesn't understand are matters of importance to a Jew. If one doesn't understand, obviously there must be something to it. (Ibid.)

Mendele ingenuously praises obscurantism as a selling point, behind a cloud of irony which we attribute to Abramovitsh. The editor of *Kol mevasser,* Alexander Tsederboym, was in fact known for adding elaborate notes.[14] The fictional Mendele is aware of popular tastes and misguidedly wishes to attain commercial success by means of ersatz erudition.

The German-Jew corrects him and hints at the far different commitments of the implied author. This exchange serves as a model of the educational function the work is designed to accomplish:

> No, Reb Mendele, the German-Jew responded. No. I'm not capable of wagging my tongue just so that people won't understand. I write only what I understand, what I feel, what is fitting, what one needs, what people can understand—even a boy, a simpleton, a rogue. . . . You want me, Reb Mendele, to take on the fashion of chattering, confusing people, talking nonsense. Why? So that I should please fools! Is there any sense (*seykhl*) in that? Is there any sense in saying that one should become a dunce for the sake of simpletons and fools? On the contrary, good sense tells us to scorn fools, and demands that we do what is necessary. (10)

The German-Jew expresses familiar Enlightenment ideas, repeatedly using the key word *seykhl*—sense, reason, or understanding. While Mendele shows a glimmer of understanding, insisting that he far prefers this man's work to that of the obscurantists, he adds: "I, too, am acquainted with the art of turning out notes and chat-

---

[14]Dan Miron comments that "as Tsederboym was notorious for adding his extensive notes to other writers' articles (in *Hamelits* and sometimes even in *Kol-mevasser*), this thrust was probably directed at him personally" (TD 298n. 39).

tering nonsense. Besides, I have written this long preface. I think that it is worth a hundred footnotes, and anyway one can also rack people's brains with it" (11). Mendele clings to his amiable, misguided goal of gaining repute by mystifying his readers. Yet the didactic message is clearer, in this multivoiced preface, than Mendele seems to realize.

"The Story Itself" follows Mendele's preface entitled "A Story About a Story." As in *The Little Man*, in *The Magic Ring* Mendele purports to relay a German text written by another person. Here the internal narrator is Hirsh Rothmann (or, in Yiddish, Hershl Roytman). In *The Little Man*, Mendele claimed to publish Isaac-Abraham's own deathbed letter, but here he presumably prints a translation of Hirsh Rothmann's book from German. In the 1860s, *maskilim* perceived German as the high road to education, a means of linking the Yiddish-speaking masses to Western culture. Hence the title page of Abramovitsh's second book boasts fictitiously that it has been translated from a German edition published the previous year by Brockhaus in Leipzig. The line between a literary pretense and a fraudulent claim is difficult to establish.

In pretending to translate the opening paragraph of a German narrative, Mendele's fictitious translator seems to draw from the style of interlinear Hebrew-Yiddish Bible translations. He begins by copying the German original, then supplying a corresponding Yiddish phrase.

> The author of *The Magic Ring* begins his book in the following manner: *Ich bitt' meine teuere Leser um Verzeihung*—that is, my readers should forgive me if, before acquainting them with the *tokhn*—that is, with the content—of *The Magic Ring* itself, I have *die Freiheit genommen*—that is, taken the liberty—to introduce myself, and to open before them a few pages of my lifestory. I hope that the readers will read these pages *mit viel Vergnügen*. (12)

The first clause and several subsequent phrases are German; incongruously, Mendele treats the Hebrew word *tokhn* in the same way. Mendele accords his translation with an air of authenticity, then, by including fragments of the imaginary original. This use of German has a precedent in Abramovitsh's *The Little Man*, where Gutmann speaks both German and a Germanic Yiddish. Mendele shows his traditional Jewish learning by following the format of *taytsh-khumesh,* the Pentateuch with a running Yiddish translation and commentary. A double parody is at work, drawing equally from prior German and Hebrew conventions.

The central part of *The Magic Ring* is a narrative attributed to Hirsh (Hershl). Much like Isaac-Abraham's story in *The Little Man,* Hershl's tale is dominated by a misconception. Isaac-Abraham grows up fascinated by the "little man" and mistakenly wants to become one; Hershl's childhood years are full of thoughts about a "magic ring" and he selfishly wants to possess one. To Isaac-Abraham, the little man first signifies the soul and later suggests wealth; similarly, Hershl seeks a magic ring in order to attain wealth and power. The difference is that Isaac-Abraham gives up his connection to Gutmann in order to become a bourgeois little man, while Hershl follows an enlightened Lithuanian-Jewish teacher in rejecting childish desires for a magic ring. Isaac-Abraham confesses his misguided ways and seeks to reform those like him; Hershl proposes a more exalted path to his readers.

The Magic Ring of 1865 has a flimsy plot that centers around Hershl's search for the "magic ring." When he attains his goal, the ring assumes another meaning that is subordinated entirely to Enlightenment ideas. Early on, Hershl conveys the superstitious beliefs concerning angels, demons, spirits, Paradise, and Hell which he learned from his father. His uncritical, youthful motto is "Father knows" (21). Without this principle, he asks, "What, God forbid, would have become of my little bit of Jewishness?" In any event, he believes wholeheartedly in the magic ring of which his father has spoken. Not until he meets a surrogate father, the enlightened Lithuanian Jew, does Hershl reach a new understanding of the magic ring. His wish has been to use the ring to become invisible and fulfill his desires with impunity, wanting to learn how "to see and not be seen." The Lithuanian points out that this invisibility is really just the façade that characterizes all hypocrites, flatterers, and thieves. In contrast, "a truly honest person must be the same in private as in public" (32).

Hershl's wish to become invisible resembles the desire of assimilating Jews to become virtually invisible by concealing their Jewish identities behind masks. Yet Hershl next learns about a truer "magic ring": wisdom. Through study, the Lithuanian promises, Hershl will get his magic ring, and Hershl affirms that "in the university I finally found the magic ring" (37). Only petty people (*kleyne mentshlekh*) expect miracles, for the wise are content with God's world and with wisdom, "the natural magic ring" (38–39). A skeptical, conventional reader might have objected to Abramovitsh's message by countering that the vaunted university education provided another form of magic invisibility: social acceptance among non-Jews.

The underlying purpose of *The Magic Ring* is to disseminate Abramovitsh's Enlightenment ideas. While "The Story Itself" is limited by its doctrinaire underpinnings, the preface entitled "A Story About a Story" enhances the literary role of Mendele the Bookseller. Abramovitsh innovates effectively in the frame narrative in spite of his didactic goals. The presentation of the story through the mediation of Mendele is, in some ways, more important than the story itself. Decades later, when Abramovitsh expanded and rewrote Hershl's narrative for the Jubilee editions of his collected works in Yiddish and Hebrew, he unfortunately suppressed the initial Mendele presentation.[15]

FISHKE THE LAME

Abramovitsh's early masterpiece, *Fishke the Lame* (*Fishke der krumer*, 1869), further develops the Mendele role and introduces new voices.[16] The original subtitle of this novella—*A Story About the Jewish Poor* (*A mayse fun yudishe oremelayt*)—reflects Abramovitsh's concern for the plight of the Jews; in Hebrew the title became *The Book of Beggars* (*Sefer ha-kabtzanim*).[17] But Abramovitsh describes the life of the poor using the perspective and voice of Mendele the Bookseller. The Mendele figure plays as active a part in the first edition of *Fishke the Lame* as in that of *The Little*

---

[15]Compare Dan Miron's thorough analysis of the expanded second edition from 1888, in TD, chapter 4.

[16]Dan Miron examines the role of Mendele in this novel, focusing on the expanded version of 1888, in his afterword to the Hebrew edition of *Fishke the Lame*. See *Sefer ha-kabtzanim* (Tel Aviv: Dvir, 1988), pp. 229–39.

[17]H. N. Bialik's translation of chapters 1–8, entitled *Sefer ha-kabtzanim*, was serialized in *Ha-dor* 1 (1901), numbers 25–27, 30, 34, 44. According to the editors of *Mendele Moykher Sforim: reshimat ketavav ve-'iggrotav le-hatkanat mahaduratam ha-akademit* (Jerusalem: Magnes, 1965), Bialik's translation influenced Abramovitsh's later Hebrew version that appeared in his complete works (1909–12).

Man. While there is no separate preface by Mendele, Abramovitsh does turn the narrative over to his fictional bookseller. Subsequently Mendele organizes multiple narrative voices in the text and coordinates diverse retellings as they begin to merge in a coherent whole.[18] If it were told by a distant, third-person narrator, the flimsy plot would lack dynamism. Abramovitsh's innovative use of first-person narrative enables him to present Fishke's story from a number of perspectives. This narrative strategy raises the novel above its explicit polemic against outdated marriage practices among the Jews of Eastern Europe.

The opening paragraph of *Fishke the Lame* resembles those of Abramovitsh's previous Yiddish stories. Within the same genre, Mendele provides a shorter self-presentation in a definite time frame:

> Last summer, in 1868, after I had acquired a fresh bit of merchandise and packed up my wagon with all kinds of books, I set out on my journey through all the places in which, thank God, Reb Mendele and his wares are still valued. You should see those Jews; they like it when the pages of a book are all different colors and sizes, when the letters are a little blurred and the pages are printed in all kinds of type—Rashi script, bold letters, miniature print, even Italian designs. Errors do no harm, since a Jew has brains and can guess at the meaning.[19] (1)

Once again Mendele presents himself as an unpretentious bookseller in the midst of his travels. The self-ascribed title "reb" (a term that indicates his humble dignity rather than rabbinic standing) emphasizes his share in the old world. Moreover, Mendele prides himself on knowing the Jews of Eastern Europe and their peculiar literary tastes.

Mendele next describes one of the hottest days of summer. Several details suggest Mendele's piety and his relationship to the Jews: he tells us, for example, that "people said psalms, cried, fasted, but for a long while God did not want to provide even a

---

[18]For a pertinent study, see Shalom Luria's "Ha-lashon ha-figurativit bi-yetzirato ha-du-leshonit shel Mendele Moykher Sforim," Ph.D. dissertation, Hebrew University of Jerusalem, 1977.

[19]Translations are based on *Fishke der krumer* (Zhitomir: Shadov, 1869); cited by page alone. For an English translation of the 1888 edition by Gerald Stillman, see *Selected Works of Mendele Moykher-Sforim*, pp. 171–312. An outstanding new translation was recently completed by Ted Gorelick for a forthcoming volume.

drop of rain" (2). This statement sounds reverent although it may contain an ironic, skeptical inflection. In his profuse sweating, moreover, Mendele humorously identifies himself with the Jewish people at large: "Sweating is a Jewish affair; who among all the world's people sweats as much as a Jew?" (3). Metaphorically, "to sweat" means "to work hard," and thus Mendele suggests his solidarity with Jewish toil. Finally, Mendele's description of his horse, which has "not changed at all," establishes continuity with Abramovitsh's earlier novels.

Mendele and his friend Alter, also a bookseller, stop to escape the heat of the day. Sitting under a tree in the forest near Glupsk, Mendele presses Alter to explain his sullen mood. The contrasts between the two friends further characterize Mendele: although they are partners in poverty, their outlooks differ. When Alter complains about having to feed a brood of children, Mendele shrewdly asks, "So why, in your old age, did you take a young wife who would bear so many children?" (7). When Alter answers that he needed a housekeeper, Mendele asks: "So why . . . did you divorce your first wife, who was a good housekeeper?" Although Mendele outwardly resembles other poor travelers of Poland, he possesses a greater share of wisdom. This enables him to act as a sympathetic observer who provides a structured account of all he sees, adding moralistic commentary to his retelling.

Mendele's conversation with Alter introduces a recurrent theme in *Fishke the Lame*: the degradation of marriage by antiquated social customs. Alter later illustrates the flaws in traditional marriage practices when he describes his attempt to arrange a match at a fair. His efforts are nearly successful until the two parties involved realize that both are trying to marry off boys. This error underscores the superficiality of the matchmaker's trade. Alter's own marital predicament reminds Mendele "of many things about Jewish matches [*shidukhim*]" (12). The most prominent mismatch is, however, that of Fishke; Mendele tells Fishke's tale to Alter in order to console him after his recent disappointment and humiliation. Fishke is an orphan and a lame bathhouse attendant. Mendele explains that, in Jewish circles, single men and women seldom remain single for long; if the usual matches do not materialize, the community arranges marriages between the poorest members of society. This practice has its seamy side, as when it is associated with superstitions surrounding a "cholera wedding." During periods of epidemic, small towns were known to resort to an old remedy. They set up the wedding canopy for a man and a woman at the cemetery, following a ritual that was supposed to counteract the disease.[20] The protagonist Fishke, it emerges, has been subjected to marriage in an equally demeaning manner—anticipating I. B. Singer's story "Gimpel the Fool" ("Gimpl tam," 1945).

Mendele reports Fishke's story as he has heard it from a coachman in the public bath. In turn, the coachman heard the story from three men who arrived at the bathhouse one day, looking for Fishke. The three strangers explained that after the town's blind orphan was widowed, she hastened to become engaged to a porter and promised money as a dowry. After the wedding canopy and feast were prepared, "Listen to what can happen! When everything was ready, the bride dressed, veiled, they went to bring the groom to the canopy. But the precious fellow wasn't home. They waited an hour, two hours, and still no sign of him; he was gone as if drowned. It turned out that the boy had misgivings" (19). At this juncture, the community apparently regretted this failed match because it meant that they would lose the festive meal. To avoid letting the feast go to waste, they hit upon an idea: "We thought and thought, discussed and discussed, and Fishke came to our minds. He should get everyone out of this mess; he should be the groom. What difference does it make to him!" (20). Hence they seek out Fishke so that "the bride will remain a bride, and the feast won't be spoiled." This is the story three strangers told the coachman, who told it to Mendele, who now tells it to Alter. When the three men had ended their account to the coachman, Fishke arrived and they quickly carried out their plan. Mendele concludes this story with a bitter remark: "Among us Jews they match up the lame with the blind, and on top of this just for a meal, so that the guests can eat and drink their fill!" (21). In the context of this corruption, Mendele jokes, Alter is well-suited to ply his trade in dubious matches.

Mendele and Alter then travel on their way together, and by chance they meet Fishke himself. Fishke climbs onto Mendele's wagon and begins to tell his own story, "lisping and in halting Yiddish" (24). He continues where Mendele has left off, telling about married life with the "blind orphan." They traveled to

---

[20]The 1939 Yiddish film based on *Fishke der krumer*, released in English as *The Light Ahead*, vividly enacts this "cholera wedding."

Odessa, where his wife found a suitor among a troop of beggars who treated him badly. During this internal narrative by Fishke, Abramovitsh's book portrays the life of beggars, as promised by its subtitle, *A Story About the Jewish Poor*. Abramovitsh shows deep sympathy for his character Fishke, who describes homeless wanderings and the beggars' hatred of the rich. Fishke also explains how the beggars deceived people: when they arrived at a city, all of them disguised themselves, "one as a lame person, another as a blind person, another as a mute" (28). Only Fishke and his wife were truly lame and blind. Hinting at the animosity between social classes, Fishke observes that "a wealthy man, the fatter and healthier he is, the more important and admirable. But one of us has to hide his health and be ashamed of it, like a thief" (31). In order to survive, the impoverished Jews are forced to deceive, to mask their true situation.

Fishke continues his story, which contains yet another imbedded narrative. As he was treated worse and worse by the band of beggars, he befriended a girl who had been abandoned by her divorced mother. He proceeds to tell her tale, meanwhile confessing his love for the girl. At the close, when Fishke says that her name is Beyle, it transpires that she is Alter's long-lost daughter, the child of his divorced wife. Thus the story within the story meets with the story itself, propelling Alter on a quest to recover his daughter. The book ends with the hope that Alter will transcend his mercenary practice of matchmaking, instead bringing together a suitable marriage between Fishke and Beyle.

Mendele remains in control of this narrative polyphony by asking Fishke questions and guiding his storytelling (24, 31). At the close, Mendele consoles Fishke as he earlier consoled Alter (43). With all of its sentimental excess, this novel places Mendele in the position of a traditional figure who uncovers human folly and seeks to set the world aright. Abramovitsh interweaves a somewhat far-fetched plot with an intricate system of narration, in which Mendele serves as the medium for the multivoiced telling of Fishke's story. He also serves as the medium by which Fishke and Alter are united in their search for Beyle. Abramovitsh uses Fishke's mismatch as a representative example of obsolete marriage practices. Successive first-person narrations present the perspectives of Mendele, Alter, Fishke, as well as that of the Jewish community that arranges marriages in a superstitious effort to combat cholera or for the sake of a meal. The genuine union of Fishke and Beyle will presumably occur beyond the boundaries of the narrative, now that Alter has been provoked to search for his neglected daughter.

Abramovitsh's fiction of the mid-1860s shows his concern for questions of Jewish identity and his endorsement of Enlightenment ideas. In *The Little Man,* Isaac-Abraham confesses his misguided life, dominated by selfishness and lust for wealth. The novel recounts his futile search for a more worthy path, uncovering the inadequacies of the apprenticeship system as well as of petit bourgeois habits. In *The Magic Ring,* Hershl takes the effort at disguise to its logical conclusion when he attempts to become invisible. Abramovitsh rejects this form of deception, which may be analogous to assimilation, and replaces it with educational goals. In *Fishke the Lame,* the problems of Jewish society are associated with poverty and antiquated marriage customs. *Fishke the Lame* focuses more closely on the life of the poor than on means to ameliorate their condition. While questioning Jewish marriage conventions, Mendele expresses his sympathy for the underprivileged members of Jewish society. First-person narratives by Mendele and Fishke enable Abramovitsh to convey both his perceptions of the poor and his hopes for a solution.

During the 1860s, the Mendele persona shifted almost imperceptibly. Initially, Mendele the Bookseller is a neutral intermediary who speaks to the audience as a familiar, amicable type. At the end of the decade, however, Mendele's ironies are far more pointed and indicate vigorous social criticism. Mendele is, increasingly, the voice through which Abramovitsh expresses his disapproval of traditional Jewish practices. This transformation of the Mendele persona is apparent in Abramovitsh's first dramatic work, contemporaneous with *Fishke the Lame,* and in his subsequent two novels.

The Little Man and *The Magic Ring* are in part narrated by anti-heroes, misguided strivers after wealth who eventually discover their errors. *Fishke the Lame,* in contrast, is partly narrated by a more positive, though impoverished, protagonist. Fishke, a man at the bottom of the social hierarchy who attempts to fulfull his innocent longings for a better life, is the hero of Abramovitsh's third Yiddish novel. But the true hero of all three works is Mendele, Abramovitsh's narrator, who is increasingly marked by his irony, satire, and parody.

CHAPTER 3

Satire and Parody in Abramovitsh's Later Fiction

Abramovitsh's writings exemplify the interdependence of political conditions and literary history. His early Yiddish novels express an optimism resulting from the wide-ranging reforms that freed the serfs in 1861 and liberated the Jews from other constraints. In the later years of this reformist period, from 1869 to 1878, Abramovitsh lambasted dishonest community leaders (in *The Tax*), counterprogressive elements on the Russian political stage (in *The Nag*), and provincial Jews who were oblivious to the modern world (in *The Travels of Benjamin the Third*).

Parody gains prominence in Abramovitsh's two novels of the 1870s. In *The Nag*, as in the preface to Abramovitsh's play *The Tax*, Mendele repeats liturgical formulae at the same time that he twists them out of their original contexts and turns them into subversive attacks on unexamined beliefs. Abramovitsh also satirizes Alexander II, when his allegory in *The Nag* likens the Czar to Ashmodai, the king of the demons in hell. Equally striking is Abramovitsh's appropriation of the *Don Quixote* story and of Hebrew precedents for his comic novel of adventure, *The Travels of Benjamin the Third*. These works combine parody of literary forebears with satire of social forms.

Abramovitsh's period of vigorous reformist writing was short-lived. The assassination of Alexander II in 1881 was followed by waves of anti-semitic violence and a harsher political climate. This turn of events led Abramovitsh to question the appropriateness of his former attacks on Jewish customs, and he essentially abandoned literature until 1886. When he returned to fiction, writing Hebrew stories and Hebrew versions of his Yiddish works in the late 1880s and 1890s, he toned down his satire. Mendele the Bookseller reappeared in a guise that was closer to that of Abramovitsh's earliest novels from the 1860s. From a pragmatic standpoint, given the more repressive political environment, satiric critiques of the Czarist regime were scarcely feasible in the 1880s.

During Abramovitsh's subsequent Hebrew phase from 1886–96, his message had less to do with striving for social advances than with means of survival in the face of persecution.

In the 1860s, Abramovitsh initially employs the figure of Mendele as a bridge between the Yiddish reader and himself. Rather than write from the standpoint of an educated *maskil,* as Abramovitsh had done in his early Hebrew works, his representative speaks in a manner that appears traditionally pious, untrained, improvised, and digressive. The Mendele persona undergoes a gradual transformation until it stabilizes in the 1890s as a controlled, self-confident, and ironic presence. Mendele becomes increasingly ironic over the years as he becomes associated with the author and the author's goals. But after passing through his radical satiric phase in the 1870s, Mendele retreats to a more moderate position —indicating Abramovitsh's awareness that Enlightenment ideals could not be realized as originally hoped.

THE TAX

During Abramovitsh's second period of creativity in Yiddish (1869–78), the earlier traces of irony give way to full-fledged social criticism. For example, Abramovitsh uses satire to attack the corruption associated with ritual slaughter and kosher meat distribution. The character Mendele becomes an ally in this battle, overtly sympathizing with the poor and righteous against the wealthy and corrupt. No longer a naive mouthpiece for Abramovitsh's ironic barbs, Mendele is a self-conscious reformer. The new Mendele imparts Abramovitsh's increasingly radical social message through honed literary devices.

Abramovitsh's first drama is *The Tax* (*Di takse,* 1869). This play is in fact contemporary with *Fishke the Lame,* yet its preface attributed to Mendele the Bookseller marks the beginning of a second phase in Abramovitsh's development. Since Abramovitsh's main accomplishments are in the area of prose fiction rather than drama, the present discussion concentrates on the distinctive preface. The play is a free-wheeling satire, and the preface employs a corresponding style. This text gives the impression of renouncing all prior inhibitions; where the original Mendele employed light humor, he now resorts to intensely sarcastic effects.

The Tax depicts the ills of the Jewish "town of fools" named

Glupsk. It transparently attacks the leaders of the Berditchev Jewish community, showing how these supposed "benefactors" (*baley toyves*) actually extort money from the poorest members of the community. In their chassidic town, they do this by exploiting religious practices and exacting a high tax for kosher meat.[1] When the two heroes Veker and Pikholtz attempt to counter the rampant evil, they are forced to leave Glupsk. One may surmise that Shloyme Veker is a self-portrait of Abramovitsh, whose name Sholem was often pronounced Shloyme.

The characters' names indicate their lack of moral fiber, as in medieval morality plays and in the long history of satires. One hypocrite pretends to be virtuous while stealing from the poor, and the play reveals his true character behind his props of virtue by referring to him as a wolf with a fur cap (*Yitskhok Volf Spodik*). Another character is a simpleton or fool (*Shmaya Tam*), while a third wants to leave things just as they are (*Yoysef Mekhteyse*). Their cohorts include a fleecer (*Shinder*) and a leech (*Piavke*). In contrast, the two honest and well-meaning characters, who strive to bring out the truth, are an awakener (*Shloyme Veker*) and a woodpecker (*Gedalia Pikholtz*). Evil prevails in the end, driving the would-be enlighteners out of town.

Mendele's preface to *The Tax* begins with a mock prayer that is far more vituperative than the corresponding first paragraph in *The Magic Ring* of 1865.[2] In the present case mockery prevails:

> *Omar Mendele Moykher Sforim*—sayeth Mendele the Bookseller: Praised be the Creator, who created vast seas and numerous rivers: the Nile, the Teterev, and the famous Gnilepiatke River; who created the dark regions, the deserts, wastelands, many wild places, and the great Jewish city of Glupsk. Praised be He, who chose the Jews from among all the peoples, and graced us with a tax, a collecting box, community leaders, synagogue directors, respectable men, attorneys, arbitrators, upright mediators, and very many beggars. Praised be the Creator for every-

---

[1] The 1939 Yiddish film entitled *Fishke der krumer* (released in English as *The Light Ahead*) adroitly incorporates this social background into its free adaptation of the Fishke story.

[2] Compare the discussion of this 1869 preface by Dan Miron in *A Traveler Disguised: A Study in the Rise of Modern Yiddish Fiction in the Nineteenth Century* (New York: Schocken, 1973), pp. 141–43; henceforth cited as "TD" by page alone.

thing He created: wild animals, lions, leopards, wolves, bears, and tax collectors. Praised be He for cows, oxen, horses, asses, for the fine women of Glupsk, and for the entire band of benefactors.[3] (5)

Mendele has traveled a great distance in the short five years separating the present passage from the preface to *The Little Man*. This ersatz blessing is laden with deliberate irony, particularly in its use of juxtapositions to characterize Glupsk and its inhabitants. First the city takes its proper place together with "the dark regions, the deserts, wastelands, many wild places." Next Mendele describes the powerful people of Glupsk and suggests the direct consequence of their activities when he adds to the list "very many beggars." Finally he places the tax collectors together with the most terrifying animals, and associates the women and insidious benefactors (*baley toyves*) of Glupsk with another series of animals. Again, the satire relies on a parodic appropriation of the inflections of Hebrew prayer.

Mendele goes on to explain how he discovered the play he is now introducing. Abramovitsh may have adopted this literary device in an effort to disguise his authorship of this subversive work: "Once, earlier this year after Sukkot, I received a parcel in the mail. At first I thought that it must contain tassles or children's headcoverings or the like. But when I opened it I found a whole bundle of papers, scribbled on in every which way, and among them was a letter" (5). Such pretenses were by now familiar to Yiddish readers, however, and the satire had reached a new level of intensity; Mendele had become an obvious pose rather than a viable pseudonym. Consequently, the men of Berditchev whom the play attacked saw through Abramovitsh's attempted disguise and ran him out of town.

The fictional letter from Glupsk reaffirms what we know of Mendele's character: "Since you have a reputation in these parts as an honest man, and since we know that you always travel through all the Yiddish places with books, and that you are occasionally eager to print stories at your own expense, we are sending herewith a very terrible story that took place in our city" (ibid.). Mendele

---

[3]Translations are based on *Di takse oder di bande shtot baley toyves* (1869; repr. Vilna: Fin and Rozenkrants, 1873); cited by page alone. No English translation is available.

claims to be merely the neutral editor of this manuscript, though he says it was in such poor condition that he has been obliged to make numerous improvements and to supply several missing pages. He even admits that "I haven't been able to restrain myself in some places, and have mixed in a few of my own words, based on what I have seen and heard during my travels" (5). Thus Abramovitsh clearly implicates Mendele in the editorial role and subversive thrust of this work.[4]

The new Mendele of *The Tax* is, then, radically altered. No longer does he seem to be an unobtrusive editor and traditional bookseller; rather, he claims to take a hand in rewriting the work, and he controls its satiric force. The preface concludes with a direct wish that Jews may rid themselves of the insidious "benefactors" who are the targets of the play's polemics (7). Hence Mendele's new image corresponds to the goals of the work he prefaces; this movement toward polemic continues in Abramovitsh's novels of the 1870s.

THE NAG

After Abramovitsh was forced to leave Berditchev in 1869 because of his satiric play *The Tax,* he settled in Zhitomir. His two novels of the 1870s continued the new satiric thrust that characterized *The Tax. The Nag* (or *The Mare; Di klyatshe,* 1873) is an all-encompassing social statement, refracting the condition of the Jews in Czarist Russia through a transparent allegory. The satire ridicules the indigent Jews and their oppressors, at the same time that it questions the motives of their would-be liberators. Like the subsequent novel, *The Travels of Benjamin the Third, The Nag* enacts a sweeping critique of backward Jewish life in the *shtetl.* These works thus recast the gentler message of Abramovitsh's early phase. Moreover, they employ parodic devices that extend beyond his initial uses of irony.

The Nag is the first of Abramovitsh's books to open with a preface that bears the title, "Preface of (*hakdomes*) Mendele the Bookseller." This indicates both the popularity of the fictional Mendele and his increasing centrality to Abramovitsh's writing. The prefaces in Abramovitsh's two main Yiddish works of the

---

[4]On Mendele's increasing editorial role, compare Dan Miron, TD 193–202.

1870s follow a pattern begun in the 1860s: they start with a prayer or mock blessing that ironically thanks God for the world's ills; next they explain how the fictional manuscripts reached Mendele; then they hint at Abramovitsh's artistic principles; and they close with another blessing that places in question the Hebraic tradition from which they draw. These are some of the most compelling instances of parody in Yiddish fiction.

The Nag combines the opening formula of The Magic Ring and the sharper tonality of The Tax in this as-if benediction:

> Omar Mendele Moykher Sforim—sayeth Mendele the Book-seller: Praised be the Creator, who after he created the wide world conferred with the divine retinue and finally made a small world, humanity, which He called the microcosm because it contains all kinds of creatures. You find in it all sorts of wild beasts and various species of domesticated animals; you find in it a lizard, a leech, a Spanish fly, a cockroach, and other such wretches, crawling things; you even find in it a spirit, a devil, a prosecuting Satan, a Jew-hating mocker, and other similar demons, plagues. You also see wondrous scenes like a cat playing with a mouse, or an animal that sneaks into a chicken coop and breaks their poor necks . . . , and other strange and wonderful things.[5] (3)

Abramovitsh parodies two of the richest resources at his command: the Hebrew prayer book and the popular Yiddish prayers (tekhines) for women. Evidently, the superficial imitation of these predecessors is undermined by the use to which it is put. The formula "Praised be the Creator . . . ," sometimes rendered as "Blessed art Thou, Lord . . ." (Gebentsht iz der borey . . . or Barukh atta . . . in Yiddish and Hebrew) is the cornerstone of Jewish prayer. The parody disrupts the traditional tenor, striking against the quietism that may ensue from uncritically praising God for everything that occurs.

Mendele is no longer the traditional bookseller of the mid-1860s. It is true that Mendele's bristling ironic tone is an extension

---

[5] Translations are based on Di klyatshe oder tsar baley khaim (Vilna: Rom, 1873); cited by page alone. For English translations of the expanded edition, see The Nag, trans. Moshe Spiegel (New York: Beechhurst, 1955), and The Mare, trans. Joachim Neugroschel, in The Great Works of Jewish Fantasy and the Occult (New York: Overlook, 1987), pp. 545–663. To interpret The Nag as a work of "fantasy and the occult" is, however, to miss its allegorical meanings.

of his satire that prefaces *The Tax*; but where the early drama is predominantly satiric, *The Nag* adds an allegorical dimension. In the preface, Mendele signals his use of allegory by referring to the analogue between the small world of humanity within the greater world. Subsequent lists include animal species, while beneath the surface they metaphorically describe diverse evils of humanity. For example, the word "lizard" (*yashtsherike*) also names a shrewish woman, "leech" (*piavke*) figuratively describes a human parasite, and "cockroach" (*prais*) may also refer to Prussians or to the poor. The compendium of evil spirits seems to suggest a full-blown, metaphysical demonology; however, these devils may equally well represent political enemies of the Jews. Since the book is, in short, a satire on life in Czarist Russia, this enumeration of evil spirits prepares for the allegorical dimension. Mendele has shed his early naiveté and has replaced it by deliberate irony and allegory.

Mendele's preface purportedly explains the origins of *The Nag*. Pretending to believe in divine providence, Mendele recounts "the great favor which God bestowed upon me, poor sinful creature, after first punishing me a little" (3). He explains that his horse has died of hunger in the time since its last appearance in *Fishke the Lame*. An acquaintance subsequently offers him a substitute: the manuscript of *The Nag*, supposedly written by Isrolik the madman. Mendele's newfound sophistication finds expression in his description of the book:

> *The Nag* is written in a high style, as the ancients used to write; everyone will understand it in accordance with his level. For commonfolk of lesser schooling it will merely be a wonderfully fine story, and they will be pleased by the simple meaning. Those of a higher level will, however, find in it a hint at sinful humanity. I, according to my level, found in it almost all Jewish spirits, all of our souls, and the *secret* of what they are doing in the world. . . . Someone else will say: Ai, Ai, I have found the secret of our taxes, of our benefactors, of our conduct. (5–6)

This passage incorporates a potent strain of parodic appropriation. In the description of layers of meaning, Abramovitsh has Mendele refer to medieval rabbinic notions about the interpretation of Scripture. According to a traditional view, biblical verses evoke four levels of signification: simple literal meaning (*pshat*), allusion (*remez*), moralistic or sermonistic content (*drash*), and mystical secrets (*sod*). Mendele proposes that we read *The Nag* in accordance with this rabbinic approach to Scripture. The consequences of such a reading are, however, far from being neutral or traditional. Here the allegorical levels do not add to the glory of God, but instead detract from the glory of Czarist Russia and all her inhabitants. Mendele draws from a rabbinic convention to point the way toward reading *The Nag* as a most unconventional attack on social mores.

The satiric allegory in *The Nag* continues the socially critical thrust of *The Tax*. Showing mock piety and obedience to religious authority, then, Mendele has asked the leaders of Glupsk whether *The Nag* fulfills a promise he made to print a sequel to *The Tax*; they purportedly agonized over this legal decision before concluding that the book contains the essence of its predecessor, thus satisfying his obligation. This is Abramovitsh's indirect means of indicating that *The Nag* continues in the satiric vein of *The Tax*.

The 1873 preface ends with a parodic prayer in the style of the Passover "Dayenu" ("It Would Have Been Enough"). Instead of thanking God for his role in the exodus from Egypt, in this parody Mendele thanks Him for the opportunity to taunt his reactionary enemies:

> "How many benefits God has bestowed upon us!" (*kama ma'alot tovot la-makom 'aleinu*). How many thanks I owe the Most High. If I had gotten hold of *The Nag* alone, without an advance to buy a horse, it would have been enough (*iz dokh dayenu*). If I had gotten it with an advance, and it hadn't contained the essence of *The Tax*, it would have been enough. If it had contained the essence of *The Tax*, and the judges hadn't freed me of my vow, it would have been enough. If they had freed me of my vow without scratching and squirming, it would have been enough. If they had scratched and squirmed without my knowing why, it would have been enough. (6)

Mendele adopts the form of the "Dayenu" only to undo its traditionalism. The opening line in Hebrew is a direct quotation from the Passover Haggadah. Abramovitsh's Yiddish parody intimates that the corrupt leaders of the Jewish community are analogous to the Egyptians who enslaved the ancient Hebrews. An attitude of pious acceptance may be suitable for the night of the Passover Seder, when Jews recall their deliverance from bondage in Egypt. But Abramovitsh questions whether this kind of passive faith constitutes a viable response to corruption among the Czarist officials and the Jewish community leaders. Hence Mendele ironically sees a minor miracle in his ability to torment the religious authorities with another harsh critique of their practices. As if to reaffirm the continuity between this Mendele and that of the mid-1860s, Abramovitsh has Mendele conclude the preface: "On my wagon with books between Glupsk and Teterevke, the insignificant Mendele the Bookseller" (7). Mendele's use of such conventional formulae camouflages his attack on the outmoded forms of Jewish life.

The title page of *The Nag* suggests that it is based on a manuscript found "among the writings of Isrolik the madman (*dem meshugenem*)."[6] Isrolik describes his solitary life, following his decision to renounce established ideas—especially concerning marriage. Isrolik's solitude intensifies as a result of his plan to study at the university. After reading incessantly while preparing for university entrance examinations, Isrolik suffers a breakdown and experiences hallucinations about a nag or mare, the *klyatshe* of the title. Finally the imbalanced narrator succumbs to further visionary encounters with the chief demon, Ashmodai. In terms of the allegorical content, this leader of the demons represents the Czar. The first-person narrative vividly enacts a journey between the realms of waking and sleeping fantasy in order to advance the allegorical tale.

From the outset, Isrolik explains the reason for his isolation: like Noah, he has survived a flood. In his case, this flood is "the misfortune of matchmakers" which has transformed his friends into impoverished householders. Resolved to avoid an early match, Isrolik plans to take the necessary exams and enter the university. This takes place in the context of the Russian Era of Great Reform when Jews were, for a short time, able to gain admittance to the state educational system.[7] A cultural clash ensues when Isrolik discovers that he must study history and Russian literature and lore [*slovesnost*]. He becomes utterly confused, *fardult,* after his encounter with this unfamiliar literary tradition. In his youth Isrolik had enjoyed fantastic stories such as the *Thousand and One*

---

[6]Quoted from the original edition of *Di klyatshe* (1873), which contains sixteen chapters; the later, expanded edition (1889) swells to twenty-four.

[7]In 1873, the same year that Abramovitsh published *The Nag*, Sholem Aleichem entered a Russian high school.

Nights, which was popular in an early Yiddish translation. According to his mother's later perception, however, books are the source of his mental disturbances (34). Isrolik is expected to learn about Russian "stories with transmigrated souls, with sorcerers and sorceresses" (11). Instead of passing his examinations, then, Isrolik falls prey to fantasies. His imagination combines folklore and broader concerns to create an allegorical figure of the Jewish people. Stretched out on the ground amid a natural scene, Isrolik becomes absorbed in thought.[8] This moment marks a decisive point in the evolution of a new kind of Judaic literature at the intersection of disparate traditions. Because he is dissatisfied with both Jewish customs and Slavic narratives, Isrolik must forge a new path through a secular, national story. Although he fails in his quest as a reformer, he is an important anti-heroic character in modern Yiddish fiction.

When his reality and fantasy become blurred, Isrolik discovers the nag being tormented by youths and dogs, who ultimately drive the old mare into a pit. After they depart, he brings her a bundle of hay and condescends to speak with her in horse-talk *(ferdish)*. To his amazement she responds with a Yiddish greeting, *borukh ha-bo* (16). He immediately wonders whether a demon is speaking to him, but the mare reassures him that, since Bilam's ass, stories and histories have described many such talking horses. This biblical allusion to Numbers 22:28–30 is a further means by which Abramovitsh sets his novel in the traditional context, preparing the way to expose shortcomings of that tradition. The mare then hints at her allegorical meaning: "I am not a demon, I tell you, nor am I a nag. My face, my form, is like a nag, but in truth I am really something else. If you knew what has happened to me in the world, you would understand me and stop being amazed" (17). The allegorical level is in fact explicit from the outset of *Di klyatshe* in the earlier editions, which print an epigram from Song of Songs 1:9, "I compare you, my beloved, to my horse among Pharaoh's chariots." The Yiddish translation of this epigram makes the alle-

---

[8]Although in the previous chapter Isrolik complains of the requirement that a university candidate learn to comment on the merest ornament *(melitse)* in an author's style, here he too resorts to a flowery phrase which shifts gradually from *batrakht* to *getrakht* and, finally, *fartrakht* (12). One form of the verb *trakhten* gives rise to another, which ultimately describes the speaker's excessively self-absorbed fantasy.

gorical implications of the Hebrew explicit. It specifies the tenor and vehicle of the simile in bold, enlarged letters: "To my *NAG* (*klyatshe*) in Pharaoh's chariots I compare you, *CONGREGA-TION OF ISRAEL* (*knesses-yisroel*)!" Presumably Pharaoh has been replaced by a new king, the Czar, who oppresses the Jews as beasts of burden. What began as an elegiac, loving evocation in Song of Songs becomes a bitter reproof. Isrolik's first conversation with the mare adds to this allegorical image, as when he asks her for how long she has experienced this condition, and she responds (in the expanded edition), "For as long as the Jewish exile (*goles*)!"[9] The mare justifies her existence by referring to biblical, classical, and folk tales. Recalling European myths concerning "the Wandering (or Eternal) Jew," she is also known as the eternal mare, *di eybike klyatshe*. Yet the equine form conceals an unfortunate prince, who represents the Jews' former glory prior to the destruction of the second Temple and their exile into slavery. On the linguistic level, certain biblical prototypes undergo an analogous degradation in Abramovitsh's parody.

When he revives from his "mad" state, Isrolik finds himself at home in bed. His mother and the servant Sender add a rational perspective to his fantastic recollections of recent events. If we read this as a realistic account, Isrolik seems to have had a kind of psychotic episode. But his madness bears specific literary weight, allowing Abramovitsh to provide a naturalistic framework for his allegorical tale. In other words, psychopathology in *The Nag* serves a literary purpose. Not until I. L. Peretz's story "The Mad Talmudist" ("Der meshugener batlen," 1890) does madness become a psychological theme in Yiddish literature.

Isrolik recovers for long enough to take and fail his exams. His failure reflects both his examiners' severity and his difficulty in remembering secular Russian literature and lore (*slovesnost*). Perhaps this deficiency also alludes to the Jews' resistance to assimilation and the problems associated with learning Russian. Afterward, his imagination exceeds all rational bounds. Isrolik's delusions include fears of a figure from Russian folklore, the witch Baba Yaga (38). At this point, his dealings with the nag return to haunt him. Once again, the emotional breakdown is charged with

---

[9]See *Ale verk fun Mendele Moykher Sforim (S. Y. Abramovitsh)* (Cracow: Farlag Mendele, 1911), vol. 3, p. 26; this late edition is henceforth cited as "MMS."

collective meanings, for Isrolik confronts broader issues related to modern Jewish learning, precisely when his own efforts at education falter.

One exchange between Isrolik and the *klyatshe* is particularly meaningful. In his delusionary efforts to help the mare, he writes a letter to the committee of a society for the prevention of cruelty to animals. Unimpressed by the self-aggrandizing rhetoric of this would-be Enlightenment author, the nag protests: "Rhetoric, rhetoric, rhetoric!" (*melitse, melitse, melitse!* [63]). It is sheer ornament, lacking content. At this moment, Abramovitsh's novel provides an image of an Enlightenment author's education by his audience. The mare stands as a figure for degraded and impoverished Jews; Isrolik's first-person narrative is analogous to Abramovitsh's ongoing dialogue with his prospective audience.

Isrolik's impotence as an enlightened, aspiring author is especially evident at the final stage of his delusions. His struggles to improve the mare (and himself) only lead him to Ashmodai's demon-land. Have the Enlightenment authors (*maskilim*) sold themselves to the devil? Efforts to teach the mare to dance (chapter 11) and assimilate to European culture are debunked, in the later edition, when Ashmodai has Isrolik join in a devil's dance (MMS, chapter 22). Recalling both Dante and popular lore, Isrolik extensively describes the darker realm. With dawning awareness of his folly, Isrolik has a vision of Ashmodai taking credit for the work of secular writers: "Those are my writers!" (103).[10] In the final chapter, Isrolik awakens at home as he did following his first fantasy sequence. His mother again blames his books (117), seeing a connection between them and his own "wild stories" (119). Exposed to new forms of learning, Isrolik succumbs to the hazards of a forbidden literary imagination.

Isrolik's difficulties indicate the traumas of young Jews who have received a traditional Jewish education but strive for a new kind of learning. The tormentors of the nag represent anti-semites, and Ashmodai suggests the Czar. *The Nag* thus extends Abramo-

---

[10]One of I. B. Singer's demon monologists shares this perception in the story "Mayse Tishevitz," in *Der shpigl un andere dertseylungen*, ed. Chone Shmeruk (Jerusalem: Magnes Press, 1975), pp. 12–14. In English, see "The Last Demon," trans. Martha Glicklich and Cecil Hemley, in I. B. Singer, *The Collected Stories* (New York: Farrar, Straus, Giroux, 1982), pp. 179–81. Compare Ken Frieden, "I. B. Singer's Monologues of Demons," *Prooftexts* 5 (1985), 263–68.

vitsh's social criticism beyond the narrow Jewish milieu to encompass general political causes of the Jews' poverty and backwardness. A multivoiced narrative by Mendele and Isrolik, together with parodic appropriations of Hebrew, Yiddish, and Slavic conventions, all serve Abramovitsh's satiric goals.[11] Again there is a tension between the implied author and his posited narrators, which renders palpable many of the social discrepancies and ambivalences in Russian-Jewish life.[12] In any event, this allegory was sufficiently transparent that, when the the book was initially translated into Polish, it was banned by the censor.

THE TRAVELS OF BENJAMIN THE THIRD

Abramovitsh's most severe satiric phase reaches its end with the preface to *The Travels of Benjamin the Third* (*Kitser masoes Binyomin hashlishi*, 1878). This mock-heroic novel follows a convention established by Abramovitsh's earlier Yiddish novels. According to Mendele's preface, it is based on a prior manuscript, in this case a longer book by Benjamin describing his travels. The Hebrew title actually suggests that the work is an abbreviated version (*kitser*) of Benjamin's full text. This pretense maintains Abramovitsh's custom: *The Little Man* incorporates a letter written by the character Isaac-Abraham; *The Magic Ring* is taken from Hershl's account, seemingly edited by Mendele and translated by a German-Jew; *The Tax* supposedly derives from a manuscript that was sent to Mendele; and *The Nag* is purportedly drawn from Isrolik's disorganized papers. Throughout the putatively translated novel *Benjamin the Third*, Mendele intersperses pseudo-quotations from Benjamin's own narrative.

Once again the "Preface by Mendele the Bookseller" opens with a mock prayer in the form of a blessing:

---

[11]There are obvious similarities between Abramovitsh's satires and those of Western European authors. As Edward A. Bloom and Lillian D. Bloom write, the satirist "might take additional cover behind allegory and beast fable. And he might shield himself in metaphor or other linguistic armor. Often as cunning as his own *eiron*, the satirist either erased the visible authorial self or created himself anew through a sheltering persona." See *Satire's Pervasive Voice* (Ithaca: Cornell University Press, 1979), p. 209.

[12]On the phenomenon of the "posited author," see M. M. Bakhtin, "Discourse in the Novel," in *The Dialogic Imagination*, ed. Michael Holquist and trans. Caryl Emerson (Austin: University of Texas Press, 1981), pp. 312–14.

Omar Mendele Moykher Sforim—sayeth Mendele the Bookseller: Praised be the Creator, who fixes the course of the planets
in the sky above and the course of all His creatures in the earth
below. Not even a blade of grass crawls out of the ground unless
an angel touches it and says: Grow! Crawl forth! How much
more likely it is, then, that a man has an angel that touches him
and says: Go, crawl forth! And how certain it is that fine people,
wealthy Jews, have a hundred bands of angels that come to each
one of them individually and say something like this . . . Dear
soul, go borrow money, as much as you can! Go, get as much
merchandise as you can from the Germans! . . . Go and silently
steal all of your merchandise from your own shop, and then
declare yourself bankrupt.[13] (3)

The outer form remains traditional, while Mendele distorts the
prayer formula and uses it to frame an unsparing critique of prevailing ills. Mendele begins by confirming God's part in all worldly
events, through the mediation of guardian angels, but he soon
shifts his aim to launch an implicit attack on mundane deception
and theft.

Mendele continues in the vein of his opening paragraph when
he explains his sense that a higher force has guided him: "I felt as if
someone were driving me from above with the words: Rise up,
Mendele, and crawl out from behind the oven! Go take a pile of
spices from Benjamin's treasure and make a banquet for your
brethren, just as they like it" (5). Most striking of all is Mendele's
explicit final statement of his moral commitments:

And I, Mendele, whose intention is always to bring usefulness to
our Jews to the extent of my ability, couldn't restrain myself. . . .
And if, God forbid, someone makes a mistake, let him turn
straight around as if he were gliding on ice and always remain
good and pious and just, as your true servant wishes you to be,
the insignificant Mendele the Bookseller. (5)

This moralistic entreaty employs mock piety to further its ends;
the final lines even fall into quaint rhymes (*kern . . . bagern*;

---

[13]Translations are based on *Kitser masoes Binyomin ha-shlishi* (Vilna: Rom,
1878); cited by page alone. For an English rendition, see Mendele Mocher
Seforim, *The Travels and Adventures of Benjamin the Third*, trans. Moshe
Spiegel (New York: Schocken, 1968). Another translation, by Joachim Neugroschel, is contained in *The Shtetl* (New York: Overlook, 1989), pp. 179–264.
See also Dan Miron's discussion of this preface in TD 143–44. Hillel Halkin
has prepared the best existing English version for a forthcoming volume.

feler . . . teler; *gerekht . . . knekht*). Yet Mendele hints at a form of piety that transcends the superficially righteous practices of the corrupt. Although Mendele repeatedly employs the outward forms of traditional Hebrew and Yiddish speech, he attacks false religiosity. He does this by adopting a superficially pious image that conceals Abramovitsh's radical exertions on behalf of social change.

The book's title informs the reader that this Yiddish text is translated from a Hebrew original entitled *Kitser masoes Binyomin ha-shlishi* (literally, *The Abridged Travels of Benjamin the Third*). In addition, the title page spoofs popular nineteenth-century Hebrew editions of religious works, which often carried a subtitle followed by a long synopsis of the contents. The subtitle translates the Hebrew into Yiddish: "That is, the Voyage or Travel-Description by Benjamin the Third." The synopsis adds, "Who, in his travels, went far away beyond the mountains of darkness, saw and heard many new and beautiful things; this travel account was published in all seventy languages and now also in our language." Mendele pretends to uphold the customary rabbinic view that there are seventy world languages.

The novel does have predecessors, though not of the same ilk as its title page implies. First, there are two prior Benjamins—the twelfth-century Benjamin of Tudela and Israel ben Joseph Benjamin (1818–64), also known as Benjamin the Second—who wrote travel books. Abramovitsh refers to "the actual sensation caused in the European press" by the nineteenth-century traveler's exploits.[14] Even more important is the parodic relationship to the classic parody of chivalric literature, Cervantes' *Don Quixote*, which Abramovitsh certainly knew; it is mentioned earlier in Mendele's preface to the 1865 version of *The Magic Ring*. Because of this link to Cervantes, Abramovitsh's *Benjamin the Third* has often been called "the Jewish *Don Quixote*."

The strengths of *Benjamin the Third* draw from Abramovitsh's earlier achievements. It combines the former emphasis on a multi-

---

[14]Dan Miron and Anita Norich, "The Politics of Benjamin III: Intellectual Significance and Its Formal Correlatives in Sh. Y. Abramovitsh's *Masoes Benyomin Hashlishi*," in *The Field of Yiddish: Studies in Language, Folklore, and Literature*, Fourth Collection, ed. Marvin I. Herzog, Barbara Kirshenblatt-Gimblett, Dan Miron, and Ruth Wisse (Philadelphia: Institute for the Study of Human Issues, 1980), p. 26.

voiced interweaving of first-person narratives with his later use of satire and parody. Part of the satire lies precisely in the combination of these features. The very fact that Benjamin is "the Third" suggests that he is intended as a parodic recycling of earlier heroes and anti-heroes.

Abramovitsh pretends that his book is merely a translation and reworking of the original, and that Mendele has merely translated and edited a preexisting work. In *The Magic Ring,* Mendele's text supposedly echoes a German subtext, employing cumbersome Germanisms interspersed with the Yiddish. In *Benjamin the Third,* Mendele pretends to convey snippets of the original Hebrew.[15] Thus Abramovitsh exploits both the Germanic and the Hebraic components of the Yiddish language, bringing out the pre-texts through subtle pseudo-quotations. For instance, following Mendele's preface, the work begins:

> *Kol yomai,* thus says Benjamin the Third himself, *Kol yomai nitgadalti be-Tuneyadevke.* "My entire life," that is, "until my great voyage, I grew up in Tuneyadevke; there I was born, there I was raised, and there I had the good fortune to be wed with *ishti,* with my better half, the modest Mistress Zelda, long may she live (*techieh*)." (6)

Abramovitsh takes advantage of the Jews' unusual bilingual situation, sometimes referred to as "diglossia." Because most traditionally educated Jewish men in Eastern Europe knew Hebrew, as their language of prayer and study, and because the vocabulary of Hebrew was extensively transferred to Yiddish, Abramovitsh is able to bestow upon Benjamin's narrative the aura of a nobler, more exalted age. At the same time, Abramovitsh uses this superimposed Hebrew for comic effect. In Benjamin's mouth, the Holy tongue comes out sounding overblown rather than exalted, and its degradation when juxtaposed to the poverty of Jewish life spoils his efforts at glorious rhetoric. In the passage cited this is partly the result of an incongruity between his high-sounding Hebrew (quoted here in italics) and his mundane Yiddish pronouncement that, until departing on his travels, he spent all of his days in Tuneyadevke—which signifies "a town of idlers" or "Parasitesville."

---

[15]This is another linguistic form of what Mikhail Bakhtin called dialogism or heteroglossia in the novel. See especially M. M. Bakhtin's essay "Discourse in the Novel," in *The Dialogic Imagination.*

Benjamin is a caricature, an unfortunate dunce or *shlemiel* who never does anything right; only his assistant Sender makes his survival possible. This duo is obviously taken from Cervantes, with the Don Quixote–Sancho Panza couple represented by Benjamin and Sender.[16] The differences are, however, as acute as the similarities. Don Quixote lives on the basis of chivalric legends, imaginatively framing himself after heroic knights in coat and armor, engaged in sublime episodes of love and war. While Benjamin also draws his inspiration from a high tradition of travel, his fantastic exploits attain none of the picaresque heights that made Don Quixote a favorite among later Romantic poets. Instead, Benjamin's efforts merely show the petty follies of the uneducated Jewish masses. Don Quixote remains a feudal lord, even if he is considered to be out of his wits, but Benjamin has no titles or social privileges on which he may fall back. Fantasy, one might say, is a luxury that only the rich can afford to indulge, while parody works equally well in the hands of titled and untitled satiric authors.

As Don Quixote steeped himself in a bookish tradition of chivalry, so according to Mendele's account "Benjamin, with great diligence, used to immerse himself in the travels of Rabba bar bar Chana, on sea and in the desert. Later he also got hold of the book *The Travels of Benjamin*, who traveled to the end of the world 700 years ago. . . . These books opened his eyes and simply transformed him into a new person" (11). Mendele then quotes the first-person narrator: "I used to be most inspired by the marvelous stories there; thus Benjamin expresses himself in his book. Ai, Ai! I cried out more than once, God help me to see even a drop of these things with my own eyes!" (11). Abramovitsh creates his multivoiced fictional work by embedding Benjamin's narrative within a mock-translation, which is in turn framed by Mendele's preface.

Benjamin's dubious status is mentioned in the heading of chapter three: "How Benjamin Becomes a Holy Man (*koydesh*) and Zelda an Abandoned Wife (*agune*)" (11). The townspeople, who consider him mad, ironically call him "Benjamin the Holy Man (*der koydesh*)" (19). By virtue of irony, the word "holy" comes to signify something quite different, closer to the traditional "holy fool" of

---

[16]For discussions of the relationship to *Don Quixote*, see Meir Viner, *Tsu der geshikhte fun der yidisher literatur in 19-tn yorhundert* (New York: YKUF, 1946), vol. 2.

literature and legend. His only claims to holiness are, however, a longing for the Holy Land and a smattering of Hebrew. Thus, when he and Sender meet a Ukrainian peasant, Benjamin proposes that Sender address him "in his coarse tongue"; later, he says, he will speak with the children of Moses in their language (36). Benjamin is "holy" only in his deranged struggle to live up to Hebrew proto-types, or in his proximity to "holy fools" like Don Quixote and the one in Alexander Pushkin's *Boris Godunov* (1831).

Abramovitsh's *The Travels of Benjamin the Third* succeeds as a parody, throughout recalling literary tradition while satirically mocking the parochial ideas and practices of *shtetl* life. This hu-morous sketch of Benjamin enables Abramovitsh, with tongue in cheek, to exert his sharpest criticism of Jews and small-town Juda-ism. He tells many painful truths in jest, allowing us to laugh at misfortunes that would otherwise provoke tears. On another level, *The Travels of Benjamin the Third* continues the political allegory of *The Nag*.[17]

Abramovitsh's second Yiddish phase concludes with his ex-panded version of *The Little Man* in 1879. This edition begins with an enlarged preface that has been transformed into a separate first chapter. The preface acquired special prominence in Abramo-vitsh's canon after it was adopted as the general preface to the editions of Abramovitsh's collected works that were published in 1888, 1907, and 1911. Yet this preface, written in 1879, actually marks a step backward in Abramovitsh's literary development. It revives his earlier, rather ingenuous Mendele, adding details to his 1864 characterization without shattering the original tone. Abra-movitsh presumably felt that the sharply satiric voice of Mendele in *The Tax*, *The Nag*, and *The Travels of Benjamin the Third* was inappropriate for the new preface to the revised edition of *The Little Man*.

In spite of regaining his naiveté in the political realm, Mendele moves forward with respect to his literary taste: in the 1879 preface he describes his wares as including "all kinds of story books—and some books of the current variety" (7).[18] On the whole he remains traditional, and after describing human foibles, he comments:

---

[17]See Dan Miron and Anita Norich, "The Politics of Benjamin III," pp. 70–83.

[18]Translations are based on *Dos kleyne mentshele oder a lebensbeshraybung*, 2d ed. (Vilna: Rom, 1879); cited by page alone.

"Such things are entirely ordinary; that has been the way of the world since ancient times, and to speak out against it would come out looking completely crazy" (3). The Mendele of *The Little Man* is a more accepting, fifty-two-year-old itinerant bookseller, nine years older than Abramovitsh in 1879. A good-natured humorist rather than a bitter satirist, this Mendele is a comic personality.

A decade later, another new preface introduces the revised version of *The Magic Ring* that was printed in Sholem Aleichem's anthology, *The Jewish Popular Library* (*Di yudishe folks-bibliotek*, 1888). This preface furthers Mendele's development in closer conformity to the prefaces from 1869–78. Its mock blessing is, however, less biting than are those of the earlier period:

> *Omar Mendele Moykher Sforim*—sayeth Mendele the Bookseller: Thanks and praise be unto God for the two communities of Kabtsansk and Tuneyadevke, near Glupsk—three saintly communities with which He beautified His world and in which He settled His beloved children of Israel. There He tested them with all His temptations, out of great love, to see if they would be able to keep their Jewishness: to renounce this world, to break the desire to eat and other such filthy desires, without which other people, mere flesh and bones, normally cannot live; in order that thereby they should be rewarded in the world—that is, in the world to come.[19] (2)

Mendele is only superficially pious, since he mocks the notion that all is for the best in a world that requires people to "break the desire to eat and other such filthy desires." This passage typifies Abramovitsh's third stage, when Mendele steers a course between traditionalism and anti-traditional satire.

THE HEBREW STORIES

After a significant interruption in his creative activity, Abramovitsh revised his Yiddish novels, produced Hebrew editions of his Yiddish writings, and wrote original Hebrew fiction (1886–96). As Abramovitsh translated his early Yiddish novels into Hebrew, he revised and expanded them, changing the image of Mendele the

---

[19]Translations are based on *Dos vintshfingerl*, in *Di yudishe folks-bibliothek*, ed. Sholem Aleichem, vol. 1 (Kiev: Jacob Sheftil, 1888); cited by page alone. Milton Himmelfarb has prepared the first English rendition of this 1888 text for a forthcoming volume.

Bookseller. His Hebrew stories also altered the Mendele persona, retaining his irony but rendering the overall effect less subversive.

In connection with the Mendele persona, Dan Miron interprets this period as "a phase of retreat" (TD 199). Miron points to Mendele's shifting role: he seems to play a less active part—as editor or alleged author of the fictions—in framing the stories he retells. Drawing upon Miron's observation, one may correlate Mendele's development as editor to tonal characteristics. Abramovitsh's third phase synthesizes the first, more naive persona (1864–69) and the second, primarily satiric character of Mendele (1869–78).

Mendele's persona was tempered with the return to Hebrew, which Abramovitsh had formerly used during the first decade of his literary activity, in a series of short stories. The very turn to Hebrew implied a higher, more dignified tone, coupled with piquant irony that prevents Mendele from slipping into the didactic style of an Enlightenment author. For example, "Shem and Japheth on the Train" ("Shem ve-Yefet ba-ʿagala," 1890) places Mendele amidst a crowd of Jewish passengers scurrying to find seats aboard a train, "as one of them" (45).[20] The pious tone of Mendele the bookseller emerges in his reference to the summer month Tammuz, "when the Holy One, Blessed be He, makes the sun to shine" (46), and at the same time he lightly mocks his own pious language, for instance when he describes the Jews' enthusiastic bargaining and adds, "the spirit of trade also rested upon me" (47). The Mendele of the Hebrew stories has comic limitations, then, which differentiate him from the educated author Abramovitsh. His traveling companion, Reb Moyshe, alludes to their difficulties brought about by the German Empire, saying in an effort to appease his hungry child: "Bismarck has made rules against (gazar ʿal) eating" (48). Mendele innocently asks who this Bismarck is, suspecting that he must be some newfangled doctor. At the close of the story, Mendele addresses God in a prayer that contains a germ of familiar irony: "Master of the universe! Grant us a few more such experi-

---

[20]Translations are from "Shem ve-Yefet ba-ʿagala," in *Kaveret* (Odessa: Aba Duchna, 1890), pp. 45–59; cited by page alone. A more readily accessible edition of the Hebrew stories is *Kol kitvei Mendele Moykher Sforim* (Tel Aviv: Dvir, 1947), pp. 377–447. For an English translation by Walter Lever, see "Shem and Japheth on the Train," in *Modern Hebrew Literature*, ed. Robert Alter (New York: Behrman House, 1975), pp. 19–38.

enced students as this—and Shem and Japheth will be brothers, and peace will come to the people of Israel" (59). On the one hand, this expresses a genuine wish for greater understanding among Jews and non-Jews. On the other hand, its pseudo-religious form and particular content suggest that Mendele has retained his parodic expertise and is speaking tongue-in-cheek.

The most important Hebrew text pertaining to the Mendele persona is the preface entitled "In Those Days" ("Ba-yamim ha-hem," 1894), which introduces Abramovitsh's autobiographical novel. Only the opening section of this autobiography, a "Preface of Mendele the Bookseller," appeared in 1894.[21] Representing the third phase in Mendele's development, it contains the subtlest characterization and the fullest statement of Abramovitsh's literary views.

This preface features a unique fictional encounter between Mendele and his creator Abramovitsh, in the guise of Reb Shloyme. The dichotomy between Mendele and Abramovitsh is one of the crucial devices in this Hebrew work. By clearly separating an old-fashioned Mendele from the intellectual Abramovitsh living in cosmopolitan Odessa, the author dissociates his fictional persona from his own reformist stance. Abramovitsh sought to regain a more innocuous Mendele whose moderated tone would be less threatening to traditional readers. Abramovitsh's successful reinvention of Mendele as a quasi-pious narrator may have influenced both Sholem Aleichem's Tevye stories and I. L. Peretz's neo-chassidic tales.

Mendele describes his travels to the city N., where he plans to peddle his wares. After he leaves his hostel, he is caught in a storm and arrives dripping wet at the home of Reb Shloyme. Earlier, in "Shem and Japheth on the Train," Mendele confronts modern technology; here he comes into contact with the current literary scene. Abramovitsh introduces Mendele to those gathered at his home, saying, "these are Yiddish writers, my good, faithful friends."[22] Mendele's reaction typifies his humorous style and un-

---

[21] The Yiddish versions became available in 1899–1901, and again in 1908, as part of a collection of stories translated from Hebrew; a new translation was printed in the Jubilee edition of Abramovitsh's works in 1911.

[22] "Ba-yamim ha-hem," *Pardes* 2 (1894), p. 176; "In yener tsayt," trans. Sh., in Mendele Moykher Sforim (S. Y. Abramovitsh), *Dray ertseylungen* (Warsaw:

pretentious sophistication: "Yiddish writers and faithful friends!" he responds, perhaps casting doubt on whether such a combination is possible.

The centerpiece of this short text is a discussion of writing and its purpose, structured on the model of Plato's *Symposium* with its discussion of love. One writer in the group states that writing is "a divine spirit in man." Mendele makes light of their debate, joking that "writing is no more than a madness, a kind of sickness, similar to the desire of many Jews to lead prayers in the synagogue, in order to show off their ringing voices before the congregation."[23] As usual, Mendele combines traditional language with irony, and his statements suggest an honest, commonsensical approach to life. When the late Mendele returns to his more innocent incarnation, this enables him to express himself at a safe distance from Abramovitsh's polemics.

Abramovitsh deliberately tempered his rhetoric in revising his Yiddish works for the collected edition of 1911–13. David Eynhorn, Abramovitsh's secretary, recalls his method of revising:

> Sitting and translating *The Nag* [from Yiddish into Hebrew], I noticed a remarkable phenomenon. Every time that he encountered overly sharp passages against the rabbis, yeshivas, and students, in the earlier text, Mendele [Abramovitsh] would, with a light heart, take a red pencil and quietly, without saying a word, cross out the phrase or change the style.[24]

The first editions of Abramovitsh's Yiddish novels, from 1864–78, contain the essence of his contribution to Yiddish letters. A later dulling of satiric barbs blurs the contours of Abramovitsh's career, obscuring the developmental progression of the Mendele persona. According to Eynhorn's account, the older Abramovitsh was more concerned to capture the voice of the common Yiddish speaker, the

---

Hoyz-fraynd, 1908), p. 10; under the heading "Omar Mendele," in *Shloyme reb Khaim's*, in *Ale verk fun Mendele Moykher Sforim (S. Y. Abramovitsh)* (Cracow: Farlag Mendele, 1911), vol. 2, p. ix. Cited by page alone, following the 1894 and 1911 variants.

[23]Translated from the 1894 Hebrew version (p. 177); also in the Yiddish edition (p. x).

[24]David Eynhorn, "Mendele at Work" ("Mendele bay der arbet"), in *Zikhroynes vegn Mendelen*, in *Ale verk fun Mendele Moykher-Sforim* (Warsaw: Farlag Mendele, 1928), vol. 20, p. 62.

simple Jew, than to retain Mendele's satiric messages. Whenever he had difficulty finding the right expression, Eynhorn recalls, Abramovitsh would appeal to a kind of alter-ego within himself: "Little Jew, what do you say?" (ibid., p. 59). At times he encouraged the conflation of his identity with that of his fictional Mendele, though in 1894 he saw fit to mark their difference. Both of them became more traditional in later years.

CRITICAL VIEWS

Yiddish literary studies have generally focused on biography, history, and theme. Literary interpretations and specific analyses of texts are rare. In studies of Abramovitsh's work, for example, few critics have contributed to the perception of the Mendele persona. There are two primary explanations for this neglect. First, Mendele is sometimes misunderstood to be merely Abramovitsh's pseudonym. Second, simplistic readings of Mendele have suggested a synchronic view, according to which this character remains essentially the same throughout the writings of Abràmovitsh.

An outstanding critic who provided more precise interpretations of Abramovitsh was Meir Viner (1893–1941). He drew insights from both Russian formalism and Marxist criticism in his essays on Abramovitsh, and he analyzed issues surrounding the author's tone and ideology. From these standpoints, Viner recognized that Abramovitsh's most original phase ended in 1879,[25] and that Abramovitsh's supreme achievement of the 1860s and 1870s rests on his participation in a "literature of demasking" (101). Rather than propose a positive solution to social ills, Abramovitsh employs "tragic, bitter mocking of the false paths" (109). Ridicule is both a literary strategy and an instrument of social change.

In *Fishke the Lame*, according to Viner, Abramovitsh takes a threefold approach to the Jewish masses. First, he exerts a "self-criticism" of the masses by the masses. Second, he writes an "apologetic" defense of the humanity of the common people. Third, he shows their economic straits, to make other classes in society aware of their situation (139). In short, Abramovitsh combines a

---

[25]Meir Viner, *Tsu der geshikhte fun der yidisher literatur in 19-tn yorhundert*, vol. 2, p. 156. Cited by page alone.

satiric and an apologetic style (163). In the diverse forms of satire, ridicule remains a central feature of classic Yiddish fiction from Abramovitsh to Sholem Aleichem and Peretz.

Other critics have prepared the way for a more satisfactory examination of the Mendele phenomenon. Shmuel Niger establishes the basic distinction when he writes: "*Mendele Moykher Sforim* is not S. Y. Abramovitsh, the government school-teacher [after 1881], the heretic. Mendele the Bookseller is a thread that is closely interwoven with the readers, and with the great fabric that, since ancient times, has traveled through the world under the name of Jew."[26] In another work, Niger explains that Abramovitsh employed the Mendele persona in order to make him a familiar insider to Jewish reading circles.[27] Meir Viner similarly writes that "Mendele the traveling bookseller is the embodiment of popular sincerity and wisdom; he is . . . a man of the people through and through."[28] Yet these general characterizations neglect modifications of the Mendele persona over the course of Abramovitsh's career, and they encourage a perception of Mendele as a static Jewish stereotype. Nachman Mayzel draws attention to changes in the image of Mendele: "We see that in Abramovitsh's works the Mendele figure is incomplete, unfinished." Without engaging in a close analysis, he notes that "there is thus a further development of the Mendele figure."[29]

Dan Miron presses further when he dismisses what he calls "the Pseudonym Fallacy" and "the *Folkstip* Fallacy." In his efforts to avoid the latter mistake, Miron sees Mendele primarily as a literary device, without reference to his changing image. Miron writes that Mendele's character "changes very little, if at all. Almost from the start, his character is a given entity, of which the author keeps making more and more extensive use, but which he hardly changes" (TD 185). Like Mayzel, Miron is most inclined to see differences regarding Mendele's supposed role as literary edi-

---

[26]Shmuel Niger, *Vegn yidishe shrayber: kritishe artiklen* (Warsaw: S. Sreberk, 1927), vol. 1, p. 38.

[27]Shmuel Niger, *Mendele Moykher Sforim: zayn lebn, zayne gezelshaftlekhe un literararishe oyftuungen* (Chicago: L. M. Stein, 1936), pp. 15 and 101.

[28]M. Viner, *Tsu der geshikhte fun der yidisher literatur in 19-tn yorhundert*, vol. 2, p. 51.

[29]"Di grenetsn tsvishn S. Y. Abramovitsh un Mendele Moykher Sforim," in *Dos Mendele bukh*, ed. Nachman Mayzel (New York: YKUF, 1959), p. 311.

tor.[30] More recently, however, Miron has modified his early outlook and noted that in *Fishke the Lame* Mendele "changes in the course of the story."[31]

Miron observes that when Abramovitsh's third creative phase began in the 1880s, Mendele's introductory monologues "had become Abramovitsh's trademark, so to speak, and were considered his unique and inimitable literary characteristic" (95). He also provides the best description of the Mendele phenomenon: "Whatever and whoever else Mendele is, he is also a humanist and an apostate. He can by no means be regarded as a genuine member of the traditional Jewish community. His beard, sidelocks, and old-fashioned gabardine are a mask, his biblical and rabbinical phraseology, a clever parody" (148). This interpretation is entirely convincing. As we have seen, however, it is necessary to distinguish between diverse phases in Mendele's development. In the search for Mendele's "true identity," Miron emphasizes his shifting pretense to have authored or edited the works he prints (pp. 191–202 and 233). He is therefore inclined to view Mendele as "a static character devised to operate a certain narrative-structural apparatus."[32]

Even more telling is the gradual shift in narrative tone that shows a marked change in Mendele's masks, especially in the first and second phases. Once Abramovitsh had captured the attention of Yiddish readers by introducing them to the affable Mendele, he employed this device while scrutinizing many of their popular beliefs. In particular, Mendele's mock blessings emphasize the error of trusting blindly in divine providence, when the world so painfully confronts us with contradictory conditions. Thus Abramovitsh slowly leads his readership from traditionalism to enlightenment, charting their course alongside Mendele's own journey toward a critical outlook in an ironic mode.

In his strategic use of satire, Abramovitsh has much in common with other European authors. Arthur Pollard observes that satirists

---

[30]See Mayzel, "Di grenetsn tsvishn S. Y. Abramovitsh und Mendele Moykher Sforim," pp. 315–16, and Miron, TD 191–202.

[31]Dan Miron, "'The Sentimental Education' of Mendele Moykher Sforim" (Hebrew), afterword to Mendele Moykher Sforim, *Sefer ha-kabtsanim* (Tel Aviv: Dvir, 1988), p. 229.

[32]Dan Miron, "Sholem Aleykhem: Person, Persona, Presence," *The Uriel Weinreich Memorial Lecture* 1 (New York: YIVO Institute for Jewish Research, 1972), p. 27.

commonly aim at religious targets: "Faced with the serious demands that religion imposes on man, the satirist delights to make
much of the discrepancy between profession and practice. Affecta-
tion and hypocrisy are ready topics for him at any time; they take
on additional point when those who are guilty of such faults are
committed by profession to a very different standard of behav-
iour."[33] Even when Abramovitsh responds specifically to ills
within the Jewish community, he does so by borrowing preexisting
literary forms.

Abramovitsh clearly makes the use of multiple voices a salient
feature of his fiction. Like works of music, his novels bring together disparate voices and themes, and all of his major novels employ interacting voices on several levels. First and foremost is the
voice of Mendele the Bookseller, which masks the implied author
S. Y. Abramovitsh. Second, Abramovitsh appropriates diverse literary traditions ranging from the Bible, Midrash, and Talmud to
contemporary European fiction. Moreover, within each narrative
by Mendele, another character speaks: in *The Little Man,* Isaac-
Abraham tells his life-story; in *The Magic Ring,* Hershl's story is
supposedly edited by Mendele; in *Fishke the Lame,* parts of the
story are narrated by Fishke himself as well as by other characters;
in *The Nag,* Isrolik "the madman" narrates his own demise; and
The Travels of Benjamin the Third contains purportedly direct
quotations from Benjamin's travel account.

Abramovitsh's essential literary accomplishments lie in his use
of first-person narratives, satire, and parody in his fictional works.
Enlightenment Yiddish and Hebrew drama had employed satire
since the 1790s; Joseph Perl (1773–1839) anticipated later Yiddish satires in his Hebrew work *The Revealer of Secrets* (*Megale
temirin,* 1819); and Y. Y. Linetsky (1839–1915) produced *The
Polish Boy* (*Dos poylish yingl,* 1867). Nevertheless, Abramovitsh
brought Yiddish prose to new heights with his detailed, first-
person accounts, confessions, and portraits. In *The Nag* he also
developed an innovative use of allegory, which Rabbi Nachman
had used earlier in an entirely different, spiritualistic framework.

Yet Abramovitsh curtailed his satiric polemics after the first

---

[33]Arthur Pollard, *Satire* (London: Methuen, 1970), p. 12.

edition of *The Travels of Benjamin the Third* in 1878. He subsequently disappeared from the literary scene until the mid-1880s and, having experienced the pogroms and worsening Jewish conditions in 1881, Abramovitsh further limited his use of the satiric mode. The later Hebrew stories employ parodic reformulations to question and critique, but the author felt that biting self-satire was no longer appropriate. Sholem Aleichem made a remark to this effect in a letter he wrote to Abramovitsh on 14 January 1890.[34] Perhaps aware that only those who are secure can afford to question their means of support, Abramovitsh toned down the attacks that once so antagonized the Jewish community of Berditchev. From Odessa, in the last decades of his life, he conveyed more reassuring signals, wrote nostalgic recollections, enjoyed celebrations in his honor, and basked in the privilege of reissuing his complete works in Yiddish and Hebrew.

The two early stages in Mendele's self-presentation, from 1864 to 1878, are especially incisive. Abramovitsh began to employ this figure in his effort to establish contact with a broad readership. As Miron states, Abramovitsh wanted to "keep the literal trustworthiness of his Mendele intact. This, he felt, would ensure his rapport with the Jewish masses" (TD 151). Starting with *The Tax*, however, Mendele is no longer "trustworthy" as a fictional narrator; his bitter irony transforms him into an "unreliable narrator."[35] In the second phase, we can no longer conceive of Mendele as a straightforward fictional character, since he only feigns naiveté in order to bring to bear devastating criticism. At different stages, Mendele has characteristics of both a "folk type" and a bitter satirist. He moved from the former to the latter, only to synthesize the two personae in Abramovitsh's late Hebrew stories.

According to Simon Dubnov, Abramovitsh more than once told him that "I am also an historian, but after another fashion. When you come to the history of the nineteenth century, you will have to consult my works to depict the lifestyle of those generations" (FZ 115). This claim suggests that Abramovitsh's aesthetic

---

[34]See *Tsum ondenk fun Sholem Aleichem: zamlbukh*, ed. I. Zinberg and S. Niger (Petersburg: I. L. Peretz-Fond, 1917), p. 84.

[35]See Wayne Booth, *The Rhetoric of Fiction* (Chicago: University of Chicago Press, 1961), p. 158.

incorporates a naive realism. David Frishman espouses a similar view in an early essay on Abramovitsh:

> Suppose that, for example, some flood came over the world and effaced from the earth the entire universe of Jewish street life, wiping out every remembrance and every trace of vestiges or survivors, so that no sign remained of what was. If by chance we were left with just the four large narratives by Mendele—*Fishke the Lame, The Magic Ring, The Travels of Benjamin the Third,* and *Shloyme, Son of Chaim*—together with his short stories, there is no doubt that using these remains a future researcher could reconstruct the entire picture of Jewish street life in the small town in Russia during the first part of the nineteenth century.[36]

Following the author's own assertion, Frishman proposes that Abramovitsh's stories straightforwardly describe past reality.

Dan Miron takes a more nuanced approach to Abramovitsh's and Sholem Aleichem's descriptions in his book *The Image of the Shtetl (Der imazh fun shtetl)*. Miron differentiates between the literary image and historical reality, commenting that "the classic image of the *shtetl* strives to create an idealized Yiddish world, an island of pure Jewishness." Even in his autobiographical novel, Sholem Aleichem "in fact created an idealized Jewish *shtetl*. However much he drew from his memory and observation, he also drew from the abstract, intellectual conception—which more closely mirrored an attitude toward historical reality than the historical reality itself."[37]

Abramovitsh and Sholem Aleichem both idealized and caricatured the Jewish communities of Eastern Europe. We may be tempted to rely on classic Yiddish fiction as a source of information about the world that has been destroyed, but it resists this use. Literary conventions frame the narrated world, and hyperbole is a prominent technique. Exaggeration served the polemical and humoristic purposes of Abramovitsh and Sholem Aleichem in their portrayals of an outmoded world that showed signs of crumbling from within, long before it was annihilated by external forces.

---

[36]David Frishman, "Mendele Moykher-Sforim (Sholem Yankev Abramovitsh): toldotav, ʿarkho ve-sfarav." In *Kol kitvei Mendele Moykher-Sforim* (Odessa: Vaʿad ha-yovel, 1911), vol. 2, p. vii.

[37]Dan Miron, *Der imazh fun shtetl: dray literarishe shtudies* (Tel Aviv: Peretz farlag, 1981), p. 25.

PART TWO

Sholem Aleichem

FIGURE 3
Sholem Aleichem (Rabinovitsh)

FIGURE 4
Sholem Aleichem's Russia and Ukraine

TABLE 2.
Chronology of Sholem Aleichem's Life

1859	Born in Pereyaslav, Poltav Province (Ukraine), on 3 March; childhood years there and in Voronkov (fictionalized as Mazepevke and Kasrilevke).
1872	Sent to Bohslov (Boguslav), Kiev Province, to live with his grandparents, after the death of his mother; soon afterward he returned to Pereyaslav, where he lived with his father and stepmother.
1873–76	Studied in the Russian school of Pereyaslav and graduated with distinction; gave Russian lessons there and in Rzhishchev.
1877–79	Worked as private tutor to Olga, daughter of Elimelech and Rachel Loyev, in Sofiovka (Zofjowka), Kiev Province.
1879	Lived in Pereyaslav and published his first Hebrew writings in *Ha-tsefira*.
1880–83	Held the position of government rabbi in Luben (Lubny, Poltav Province).
1881–82	Printed early Hebrew essays in *Ha-melitz*.
1883	Married Olga (Hodel) Loyev; published first Yiddish stories in the *Yudishes folksblat*, including his first work under the name Sholem Aleichem; moved to Sofiovka and Belotserkov (Belaya Tserkov).
1884–	Raised four daughters and two sons with his wife Olga.
1884	Lived in Belotserkov and passed summer months (until 1905) in Boyarka (fictionalized as Boiberik), Kiev Province; briefly worked for the Kiev millionaire Brodsky; published Yiddish short stories, essays, letters, and poems in the *Yudishes folksblat*.
1885	Lived in Belotserkov; inherited a fortune from his father-in-law and became active in business ventures in Kiev (fictionalized as Yehupetz).
1886–87	Published short fiction including *Street Scenes from Berditchev* (*Bilder fun der Berditchever gas*) in the *Yudishes folksblat*.
1887	Moved from Belotserkov to Kiev; published several Yiddish stories including "The Pen-Knife" ("Dos messerl"), which was favorably reviewed by Simon Dubnov in *Voskhod*.

(*continued*)

TABLE 2. (*Continued*)

1888	Serialized the first version of *Sender Blank* in the *Yudishes folksblat*; printed *The Trial of Shomer* (*Shomer's mishpet*); edited the first volume of *The Jewish Popular Library* (*Di yudishe folks-bibliotek*), including his "Jewish novel" *Stempenyu* and the first part of Abramovitsh's revised version of *The Magic Ring* (*Dos vintshfingerl*); traveled to Odessa where he met Abramovitsh and Y. H. Ravnitzky; mourned the death of his father and memorialized him in a volume of poems in prose (influenced by Turgenev).
1889	Printed the second volume of *The Jewish Popular Library*, which included the second part of Abramovitsh's revised version of *The Magic Ring* and his own novel *Yosele the Nightingale* (*Yosele solovey*).
1890	Prepared to edit the third volume of *The Jewish Popular Library* but was forced to abandon this plan in October, when he lost his fortune in the Kiev stock market and traveled to Odessa.
1891	Left Russia and visited Paris, Vienna, Chernovitz; returned to live in Odessa after his mother-in-law paid his debts; lost the rest of his fortune in the Odessa stock market; published in Russian.
1892	Lived in Odessa and published the first Menachem-Mendl letters under the title "London," in his *Kol mevaser tsu der yudisher folks-bibliotek*; published in Russian.
1893	Lived in Odessa, Fastov, and Kiev (where he and his family resided until 1899); was involved in business transactions at the Kiev stock exchange.
1894	Wrote a satire of the Kiev stock exchange that was confiscated by the Russian censor; wrote his first Tevye story, published in Mordechai Spektor's *Hoyz-fraynd*; again planned a third volume of *The Jewish Popular Library*, but was unable to carry out the project.
1895–97	Lived in Kiev; wrote little during this period in which few Yiddish journals were published; remained in Kiev and spent summers in Boyarka until 1905.

(*continued*)

TABLE 2. (*Continued*)

1897–98	Wrote Zionist essays and fiction.
1899	Published the second and third Tevye stories in *The Jew* (*Der yud*).
1900–09	Published his major monologues and additional Tevye stories; experienced his most creative and successful years, contributing fiction to numerous periodicals and edited collections; continued the Menachem-Mendl letters.
1903	Printed a four-volume Yiddish edition of his collected works in Warsaw; translated three stories by Lev Tolstoy from Russian into Yiddish for a volume he was editing in support of victims of the Kishinev pogrom; corresponded with Tolstoy, Maxim Gorky, and other Russian writers.
1904	Met I. L. Peretz in Warsaw and several Russian authors in Petersburg, including Maxim Gorky (mentioned in the story "Chava," 1906).
1905	Toured Kovno (Kaunas), Riga, Lodz, and other cities, where he read from his works; was enthusiastically received in Warsaw; lived in Vilna with his daughter and met Y. D. Berkovitsh, his future son-in-law; witnessed the Kiev pogrom in October, after which he emigrated with his large family to the United States; never resettled permanently in Europe.
1906	Lived in Lemberg, Geneva, London, New York; gave lectures and readings throughout Galicia and Bukovina, as well as in Switzerland, France, Belgium, and England.
1907	Lived in New York and Geneva; published in the American Yiddish press; failed to make his mark on the New York Yiddish theater; began to publish *Motl, the Cantor's Son* (*Motl dem khazn's*).
1908	Lived in Geneva and Berlin; gave readings in Warsaw, Vilna, Odessa, and elsewhere; fell ill in Baranovitch (Baranovichi) with an attack of tuberculosis, after which he recuperated in Italy; celebrated the twenty-fifth anniversary of his activity as a Yiddish writer.

(*continued*)

TABLE 2. (*Continued*)

1909	Lived in Italy and Switzerland for medical cures and published widely; published three volumes of his collected Yiddish writings in Warsaw; a Russian-language edition of his work was begun in Moscow.
1909–13	Lived in Italy, Switzerland, and Germany recuperating from tuberculosis; published numerous stories and essays; the Jubilee edition of his collected works was printed in Warsaw.
1911	Published three volumes of his works in Hebrew, in large part translated by his son-in-law Y. D. Berkovitsh.
1913–14	Published two additional volumes of his works in Hebrew, translated by Y. D. Berkovitsh.
1914	Gave readings in Poland, the Baltics, and Russia; traveled to New York after the outbreak of World War I; a volume of his stories was published in German translation.
1915–16	Lived in New York and contributed regularly to the New York Yiddish press; toured Cleveland, Detroit, Cincinnati, Toronto, Montreal, and elsewhere; published his autobiography *From the Fair* (*Funem yarid*) in serial form; crushed by the death of his eldest son, Misha.
1916	Died in New York on 13 May.

Sources: *Dos Sholem-Aleichem bukh*, ed. Y. D. Berkovitsh, 1926; Zalman Reyzen, *Leksikon fun der yidisher literatur, presse un filologie*, vol. 4, 1929; Y. D. Berkovitsh, *Ha-rish'onim ki-vnei-adam*, 2d ed. (Tel Aviv: Dvir, 1953–54), vols. 1–5; Dan Miron, "Shalom Aleichem" entry, *Encyclopaedia Judaica* (Jerusalem: Macmillan, 1971), vol. 14; *Guide to Yiddish Classics on Microfiche*, ed. Chone Shmeruk (New York: Clearwater, 1980); Chone Shmeruk, *Sholem Aleichem: madrikh le-chayav u-li-yitzirato* (Tel Aviv: Ha-kibbutz ha-me'uchad, 1980); *Leksikon fun der nayer yidisher literatur*, vol. 8, 1981.

CHAPTER 4

The Grandson: Trials
of a Yiddish Humorist

Sholem Aleichem once commented, to justify the simplicity of his prose, "Why should I write in the style of Yehuda Ha-Levi, and not in the style of Sholem Aleichem? Or, if I really must sing like another poet, I want to sing like the poet of poets—the people."[1] Although he excelled in conveying the voices of everyday people, he could not draw directly from life because other writers had set the literary precedents. He wanted to describe a Jewish bookseller, for example, but "it is very difficult now to depict one's own bookseller—after Abramovitsh's bookseller" (MBSA 196). An awareness of this crowded literary terrain led David Frishman to tell Sholem Aleichem in 1889 that "you could have written *Stempenyu* better, a thousand times better, if you had not fallen upon the unfortunate plan to imitate Abramovitsh."[2]

Sholem Rabinovitsh, or Sholem Aleichem as he came to be known, existed between the worlds suggested by two portraits that hung in his Kiev study: S. Y. Abramovitsh and Nikolai Gogol.[3] He published stories, novels, essays, polemics, and plays, and he achieved renown as an editor who solicited the best Yiddish fiction

---

[1]Volf (Vevik) Rabinovitsh, *Mayn bruder Sholem Aleichem: zikhroynes* (Kiev: Melukhe-farlag far di natsionale minderhaytn in USSR, 1939), p. 112. Henceforth cited as "MBSA" by page alone. Sholem Aleichem expressed himself in Yiddish but used the French phrase "à la" to mean "in the style of."

[2]*Dos Sholem-Aleichem bukh*, ed. Y. D. Berkovitsh (New York: Sholem-Aleichem bukh komitet, 1926), p. 161. Henceforth cited as "SAB" by page alone.

[3]Compare David-Hirsh Roskies, "Sholem-Aleichems veg tsu zikh (tsu zayn finf un zibetsikstn yortsayt)," *Di goldene keyt* 132 (1991), p. 6; Roskies' discussion relies on the firsthand accounts by Y. D. Berkovitsh and Osher Beilin. Compare Y. D. Berkovitsh, *Ha-rish'onim ki-vnei-adam: sippurei zikharonot 'al Sholem-Aleichem u-vnei-doro*, 3rd ed. (Tel Aviv: Dvir, 1976), p. 242; henceforth cited as "R" by page alone. See also Osher Beilin, *Sholem Aleichem* (Merchavia: Ha-kibbutz ha-'artzi ha-shomer ha-tza'ir, 1945), p. 16.

of the late 1880s. Before his death he became the most popular Yiddish writer and performed his stories in all the Jewish cultural centers of Eastern Europe. He was the worldliest of the three classic Yiddish authors and the only one to cross the Atlantic.

Sholem Aleichem was at home in nineteenth-century Russian culture to the point that he conducted most of his family life and much correspondence in Russian; his children were more fluent in Russian than in Yiddish (as I. L. Peretz's son was more fluent in Polish). While he lived for many years in Kiev, distant from the centers of Yiddish and Hebrew publishing, he also traveled extensively in Europe and the United States. Sholem Aleichem read widely and exchanged letters with contemporary Russian literati such as Leo Tolstoy, Anton Chekhov, and Maxim Gorky. He wrote prolifically and epitomized classic Yiddish fiction, combining oral-style narrative with other sophisticated literary devices.

In spite of his familiarity with world literature, Sholem Aleichem followed in the footsteps of S. Y. Abramovitsh. Their works differ substantially, yet the literary persona of "Sholem Aleichem" and the character Tevye owe much to Abramovitsh's "Mendele the Bookseller." To a greater extent than Abramovitsh, however, Sholem Rabinovitsh merged with his literary persona Sholem Aleichem, making it more than a fictional character or pseudonym. Even his autobiography was clearly influenced by Abramovitsh's autobiography—as in its use of third-person narration.[4] Thus Sholem Aleichem, like Abramovitsh, employs a third-person voice to describe "the hero of this biographical novel" (FY 26: 19).[5] He also seems to have recapitulated certain passages in Abramovitsh's autobiography, such as the description of his father. Nevertheless, Sholem Aleichem tried to avoid falling into autobiographical clichés, and

---

[4]Compare Shmuel Niger, *Sholem Aleichem: zayne vikhtikste verk, zayn humor un zayn ort in der yidisher literatur* (New York: YKUF, 1928), p. 166.

[5]Translations from the autobiography are based on Sholem Aleichem, *Funem yarid: lebensbashraybung,* in *Ale verk fun Sholem Aleichem* (New York: Folksfond Edition, 1917–23), vols. 26–27; cited as "FY" by volume and page alone. The standard volume numbers in Sholem Aleichem's Folksfond Edition are indicated by Uriel Weinreich in *The Field of Yiddish: Studies in Yiddish Language, Folklore, and Literature,* ed. Uriel Weinreich (New York: Linguistic Circle of New York, 1954), pp. 288–91. In English, see *The Great Fair: Scenes from My Childhood,* trans. Tamara Kahana (New York: Collier Books, 1970) and the more complete version *From the Fair: The Autobiography of Sholem Aleichem,* trans. Curt Leviant (New York: Viking, 1985).

he made a point of drawing attention to and parodying certain biographical customs (FY 26: 22).

SHOLEM RABINOVITSH AND SHOLEM ALEICHEM

We may differentiate between the man Sholem Rabinovitsh (born in 1859) and his literary counterpart Sholem Aleichem (introduced in 1883). Ideally, "Rabinovitsh" would refer to the flesh-and-blood man, while "Sholem Aleichem" would designate only the author as author. Yet for a century this distinction has been neglected, and it seems impossible to reintroduce now. In his childhood he was called Sholem. At his most Russified in Kiev, he was a businessman known as Solomon Naumovitsh Rabinovitsh. But after he used the pen-name Sholem Aleichem in 1883, it gradually became an essential part of his identity, and this persona has been adored by most Yiddish readers. In his letters to Simon Dubnov, written between 1888 and 1890, the writer wavered between signing his name "Sholem Aleichem" and "Sholem Rabinovitsh" (FZ 64–96). The letterhead on his stationery bore both the Russian name "Solomon Naumovitsh Rabinovitsh" and the Yiddish "Sholem Aleichem."[6] In Russian letters to his niece Natasha Mazor, he signed his name "Solomon" and "S. Rabinovitsh" from 1886 to 1908, after which he shifted to "Sholem Aleichem"; then in 1909 he reverted to signing "Solomon Rabinovitsh" or "Solomon."[7] At a great remove from his commonplace Russian name and patronymic, "Sholem Aleichem" literally means "Peace unto you" and is a traditional Yiddish greeting, borrowed from Hebrew, that carries amiable associations. Two decades earlier, Abramovitsh named his character Mendele "the Bookseller" using a Hebrew phrase (*mocher sefarim*) in Yiddish (*moykher sforim*).

The author's real name, then, was Sholem (or Solomon) Rabinovitsh. He chose the familiar greeting "Sholem Aleichem" as a vehicle for most of his Yiddish writings. But we should not confuse the author, who received a strong Russian education, with the

---

[6]Compare Nachman Mayzel, "Sholem-Aleichems briv tsu Yankev Dinezon," *YIVO bleter* 1 (1931), 387.

[7]See "Almost a Family Chronicle: Several Packets of Unpublished Letters by Sholem Aleichem" ("Pochti semeynaya khronika: o neskol'kikh pachkakh neopublikovannykh pisem Sholem-Aleichema"), *Vestnik evreiskogo universiteta v Moskve* 3 (1993), 228–56.

folksy Yiddish persona of Sholem Aleichem. Although clarity might dictate otherwise, the present work follows the accepted practice and refers to both the flesh-and-blood author and the literary persona as "Sholem Aleichem."[8]

A recurrent motif in the biography of Sholem Aleichem is the blurring of life and literature.[9] The fictional character Tevye of Boiberik virtually became a member of his household (SAB 51), and he had a flesh-and-blood twin named Tevye in Boyarka—who complained when "people laughed at him because my father wrote about him in the papers."[10] In some instances, it appeared that life imitated art. The motto of Sholem Aleichem's autobiography reads: "Why do we need novels, when life itself is a novel?" After his eldest daughter married suddenly, he wrote that her husband's plan to travel alone to Vilna "brings to mind, against my will, Tevye's daughter"—alluding to the story "Hodel," in which a young couple is separated immediately following their wedding (R 220).

Sholem Aleichem's son-in-law Y. D. Berkovitsh, like many other readers, tried to unite the man and the writer: "He was not *Sholem Aleichem* in literature and *Rabinovitsh* at home. In general, he totally detached the Rabinovitsh from himself soon after he truly felt his artistic mission. He was everywhere *entirely Sholem Aleichem*" (SAB 48; emphasis in original). His other son-in-law, Michael Kaufman, observed that "in his whole personal life he was always exactly the same as in his writings" (SAB 141). Yet Berkovitsh admits that this was not true in all social circles: "The great popularity that *Rabinovitsh* attained under the name 'Sholem

---

[8]Compare Dan Miron, "Sholem Aleykhem: Person, Persona, Presence," *The Uriel Weinreich Memorial Lecture,* 1 (New York: YIVO Institute for Jewish Research, 1972).

[9]Compare Nachman Mayzel, *Undzer Sholem-Aleichem* (Warsaw: Yidish-bukh, 1959), pp. 10–16.

[10]Marie W. Goldberg, "As I Remember My Father," in *Sholem Aleichem Panorama,* ed. Melech Grafstein (London, Ontario: The Jewish Observer, 1948), p. 209. This volume is henceforth cited as "SAP" by page alone. Goldberg recalls that her father "was immensely amused by the little man's Hebrew quotations." Compare the accounts by S. Shnayfal (in the Tel Aviv *Nayvelt* of 14 June 1946), cited by A. A. Roback (SAP 21) and by Nachman Mayzel, in *Undzer Sholem-Aleichem,* p. 57.

Aleichem' was no secret to the wealthy people of Kiev; but they understood it according to their own ideas as no more than the idle pastime of a merchant and intellectual, who enjoyed writing 'feuilletons in Jargon'" (SAB 287). Thus Sholem Aleichem's wealthy business associates looked down upon his literary involvement in Yiddish, which—as was then the custom—they referred to as "Jargon." A century of efforts to connect the man and the author cannot entirely efface the line between Solomon Rabinovitsh, who struggled to support his large family, and Sholem Aleichem, who signed humorous stories published in Yiddish.[11]

At the start of his autobiography, the author indicates that in this work "Sholem Aleichem the *writer* narrates the story of Sholem Aleichem the *man*" (FY 26: 15). Because the living author sought to merge with his literary presence, the distinction between Sholem Aleichem (the writer's persona) and Sholem Rabinovitsh (the man) has been noticed but not rigorously upheld in studies of Yiddish literature. Y. Y. Trunk, in the final chapter of his book on Sholem Aleichem, states his unconventional plan to "lead out, from the wings of the wonderful Sholem Aleichem stage, Sholem Aleichem personally, the corporeal and private Sholem Rabinovitsh."[12] He insists on the distance that separates the creative author and the family man, notwithstanding the fact that "Sholem Rabinovitsh" developed a life style in tandem with the literary style of "Sholem Aleichem" (ibid., 376–77, 433). During the 1980s some critics also noted the dichotomy between Rabinovitsh and Sholem Aleichem, but it has not been consistently observed.[13]

Pseudonymns are a fact of life in Yiddish letters, and "Sholem Aleichem" has often been viewed as simply the most prominent. Dan Miron reexamines the figure of Sholem Aleichem and corrects

---

[11]In somewhat different terms, A. Almi suggested a distinction between Sholem Aleichem the fiction writer and Sholem Rabinovitsh the activist who, for example, wrote Zionist pamphlets (SAP 61).

[12]Y. Y. Trunk, *Sholem Aleichem (zayn vezn un zayne verk)* (Warsaw: Kultur-lige, 1937), p. 375.

[13]See David Neal Miller, "'Don't Force Me to Tell You the Ending': Closure in the Short Fiction of Sh. Rabinovitsh (Sholem-Aleykhem)," *Neophilologus* 66 (1982), 102–10, and David Roskies, "Sholem Aleichem: Mythologist of the Mundane," *AJS Review* 13 (Spring and Fall 1988), 27–46.

many of the received ideas by concluding that this is "neither the author, nor a full-fledged character."[14] Miron points out that wheareas Mendele the Bookseller is a dominant character in Abramovitsh's fiction, Sholem Aleichem is not a fully developed, visible character in his work (ibid., 27). According to Miron, it is appropriate to speak of "the Mendele persona" but preferable to conceive of "Sholem Aleichem" as a literary *presence*. Neither is a pseudonym in any simple sense. Strictly speaking, we should refer to the flesh-and-blood person as "Sholem Rabinovitsh," and reserve "Sholem Aleichem" for the implied author that is suggested by his works. Following Wayne Booth's usage, we infer the presence of Sholem Aleichem as the implied author of his texts when we form "an ideal, literary, created version of the real man."[15] Convention dictates, however, that we refer to both the person and the author as Sholem Aleichem.

Sholem Aleichem's personal style engages the biographer on many levels, and the available primary materials are inexhaustible. Unlike Abramovitsh and Peretz, Sholem Aleichem left an immense paper trail in the form of letters that capture his ongoing experiences as a man and author. As Simon Dubnov comments, "large pieces of autobiography lie buried in Sholem Aleichem's thousands of letters."[16] But these documents also tend to obliterate the distinction between reality and art, since his personal letters in many ways resemble the letters he embedded in his fiction. For example, they parody biblical phrases and, instead of using a conventional postscript, they employ the droll Hebrew phrase ʿikar shakhachti—"I forgot the main thing." Simon Dubnov recalls that during the summer of 1891 "we carried on a humoristic correspondence . . . in the language of the *Revealer of Secrets* (*Megale temirin*)—the comic Jargon-Hebrew of two chassidim, which one cannot read without laughing. Sholem Aleichem was especially drawn to that comic style" (FZ 40). Shmuel Niger comments that Sholem Aleichem was essentially the first writer

---

[14]Dan Miron, "Sholem Aleykhem: Person, Persona, Presence," p. 42.

[15]See Wayne C. Booth, *The Rhetoric of Fiction* (Chicago: University of Chicago Press, 1961), p. 75.

[16]Shimon Dubnov, *Fun "zhargon" tsu yidish un andere artiklen: literarishe zikhroynes* (Vilna: Kletzkin, 1929), p. 63. Henceforth cited as "FZ" by page alone.

"to introduce the *epistolary* form into Yiddish literature,"[17] but his life was equally permeated by a witty, literary correspondence.

CHILDHOOD REVERSALS

Sholem Rabinovitsh was born in Pereyaslav in 1859, the third son of Nachum and Chaya-Esther's eight children who survived childhood. Soon afterward they moved to the even smaller village Voronkov, which served as a model for the fictional Kasrilevke. Later in life Sholem idealized his early years in Voronkov, although his satiric depictions show his awareness of the townspeople's foibles. The boy received a typical education in *cheder*. After the family returned to Pereyaslav he continued his studies of Bible and Talmud there. Soon after he became *bar mitzvah*, Sholem's mother died of cholera and his father remarried. This turn of events led to a permanent crisis in his family relations, since he felt life-long antagonism toward his stepmother.

The death of Sholem's mother marked the end of his childhood and the beginning of his literary calling. After the family had mourned her loss, the situation at home was further complicated by his father's remarriage. Death played a continual role in the Yiddish humorist's life: several siblings died of childhood illnesses, and especially painful was the untimely death of Sholem's closest brother Abe (ca. 1861–82), who was becoming a talented artist. A few years later his father-in-law Elimelekh (Mikhail) Loyev died. Then his own father died, and Sholem was moved to write a volume of Yiddish poems called *A Bouquet of Flowers* (*A bintl blumen*, 1888) in his father's memory. Soon afterward a niece whom he knew well died. For good reason, the author later became famous for his uncanny ability to evoke "laughter through tears."

Writing was the author's primary means of dealing with difficult circumstances. He often tried to work through his sadness by writing, as when near the end of his life Sholem Aleichem's eldest son Misha died unexpectedly. "He tried to write the misfortune away from his heart (as he always did in difficult moments): the same evening, after he received the difficult news, he locked himself in his study for several hours and stood at his writing stand like a mourner at the synagogue lectern" (SAB 53). This description as-

---

[17]Shmuel Niger, *Sholem Aleichem*, p. 221.

tutely suggests, moreover, that secular writing may have taken the place of religious activity. In one of his autobiographical sketches, Sholem Aleichem remarks that "the harder the struggle was, the more bitter his life, all the more frequently and stubbornly did his creative inspiration appear" (SAB 4–5). In some sense he compensated for loss by inventing fictional tragedies over which his humor prevailed. Mikhail Bakhtin refers to "irony (and laughter) as means for transcending a situation, rising above it."[18]

Like Sholem Abramovitsh, Sholem Aleichem had an early penchant and talent for imitating people.[19] In his autobiographical novel *From the Fair* (*Funem yarid*), where he speaks of himself in the third-person form, he confesses that "our Sholem was a devil when it came to copying, imitating, mimicking" (FY 26: 27). His brother recalls that Sholem, repaying their maid Frume for her punishments, imitated "how she would blink with her one eye as she carefully examined the knife while spreading honey on the bread, and how she caught drops of honey with her finger and licked them so that, God forbid, nothing should go to waste" (MBSA 16). At school he copied, laughed at, and mocked everyone (ibid., 19). When a grain merchant became a frequent guest at his father's inn, Sholem mimicked his Lithuanian-Yiddish accent (MBSA 23; FY 27: 80). Or he would imitate the way his teacher read from the Torah (FY 26: 159). In a related vein, his brother Abe was skilled at drawing sketches and caricatures (MBSA 62). Mimicry played a prominent role in the genesis of Sholem Aleichem's mimetic fiction: "If Sholem told a story in great detail, described the characters, imitated their gestures and language, one could be sure that he would also write it down" (MBSA 119). This underscores the oral roots of Sholem Aleichem's fiction, although mimicry was joined with caricature.

The author remembered hearing his father read aloud from a humorous Yiddish book. This "primal scene" of literary performance made a deep impression:

> Saturday evening all of the householders in town gathered at the home of Reb Nachum Rabinovitsh to usher out the Sabbath. . . . Reb Nachum reads a story book. Father reads while the

[18]M. M. Bakhtin, "From Notes Made in 1970–71," in *Speech Genres and Other Late Essays*, trans. Vern W. McGee, ed. Caryl Emerson and Michael Holquist (Austin: University of Texas Press, 1986), p. 134.

[19]Compare Shmuel Niger, *Sholem Aleichem*, p. 167.

audience sits around the table smoking cigarettes, rolling with laughter and holding their sides, and they constantly interrupt the reader to express their enthusiasm loudly. . . . Even the reader can't restrain himself and nearly chokes from laughter! The children don't want to go to sleep, and especially not Sholem. He doesn't understand what his father is reading, but he just enjoyed seeing how bearded Jews acted raucous, held their sides, and burst into laughter. (FY 27: 66)

Sholem Aleichem recalled that he was jealous of the writer's ability to make people laugh and wished he could grow up to produce such a book. The book has never been satisfactorily identified.[20] But most important was the boy's wish that he might learn to make humoristic writing his calling.

Sholem's earliest literary project was a list of his stepmother's curses and insults. Until her marriage to Nachum Rabinovitsh, she had lived in Berditchev and imbibed a wealth of local folk idioms. Sholem Aleichem ironically acknowledged a debt to her in his mature Yiddish writings, particularly in his use of invectives (FY 27: 10). Sholem expected to be punished when the pages were discovered, but on reading them even his stepmother broke into laughter (FY 27: 11–13). Ironic, humorous distance proved to be the most effective means to counter unpleasant realities.

Sholem's early parodic bent found expression after he read Mapu's *Love of Zion* (*Ahavat tsion*) and produced his own version entitled *Daughter of Zion* (*Bat tsion*). He also wrote *The Jewish Robinson Crusoe* in Russian at an early age (SAB 278). Later Sholem Aleichem followed the example of Abramovitsh's Yiddish *Travels of Benjamin the Third* by writing a Hebrew parody of this parody entitled "Don Quixote from Mazepevke."

Another source of material for his future fiction was the world of klezmer musicians.[21] The violinist Israel Benditsky attended Sholem's *bar mitzvah* celebration (FY 26: 183) and played all night at his older brother's wedding (MBSA 191). Traveling choirs fre-

---

[20]See Shmuel Niger, *Sholem Aleichem*, chapter 6; Noah Prilutsky, "Mekoyekh di kvaln fun Sholem-Aleichems humor," *Di yidishe velt* 4 (July 1928), 138–47; Shmuel Niger, "Polemik un visnshaft," *Di yidishe velt* 7 (October 1928), 137–43.

[21]A story that attests to Sholem Aleichem's early and enduring interest in klezmer music is "On the Fiddle: Narrative from Childhood Years" ("Oyf'n fidl: ertseylung fun di kinder yorn," 1902), in *Sholem Aleichem's ale verk* (Warsaw: Folksbildung, 1911), vol. 1, pp. 169–95, and in SA 8: 33–61.

quently visited the Rabinovitsh inn, thus familiarizing Sholem with the klezmer slang he used in his 1888 novel *Stempenyu* (see FY 27: 68–70). While writing this novel for publication in *The Jewish Popular Library*, he traveled to Berditchev to collect oral history about the musician Stempenyu:

> For my anthology I am writing a "*Jewish* novel" with the title *Stempenyu*. This name belongs to a personality who is, to a certain degree, historical. . . . Stempenyu was none other than a remarkable maestro, a fiddler in Berditchev. Today I returned from Berditchev, where I collected some information about that hero on location—and just imagine that all of the details that I described, his external appearance and so on, correspond precisely to the information provided by the elderly people of Berditchev. (Letter of 2 September 1888, in FZ 72; cf. FZ 77–78)

According to his brother, Sholem Aleichem would wander the streets of Berditchev talking to women and children, and "when he heard a new word or a characteristic expression, he immediately wrote it down in his notebook" (MBSA 120). He self-consciously followed in the footsteps of Abramovitsh, who had already made Berditchev the model for his fictional Glupsk (MBSA 123). The boundary between ethnographic research and fantasy faded when the author collected data for his fiction, yet Sholem Aleichem claimed that his imagination anticipated what he would find in Berditchev. Both his prior awareness and subsequent perception derived, in part, from Abramovitsh's novels. In any event, he insisted on the cultural bases of his novel and complained that his business obligations "do not allow me to remain longer in this Jewish Paris" (FZ 73). He published explicit descriptions of Berditchev in 1886–87, and he wrote fictionalized accounts under various names.[22]

EDUCATION

Sholem Aleichem received a traditional Jewish education until the age of fourteen. Sholem's father Nachum, a follower of the Talnoya Rebbe, was an unusual combination of "chassid and *maskil,*

---

[22]See "Bilder fun der Berditchever gas" [1886–87], in Sholem Aleichem's *Ale verk* (Moscow: Der emes, 1948), vol. 1, pp. 409–69; compare Sholem Aleichem, *Berditchever teater un andere ertseylungen* (New York: Reznick and Kaplan, 1908).

philosopher and prayer leader, a learned and inquisitive man, and by nature quiet, reserved, and melancholy" (FY 26: 23, 83). Nachum's religious bent did not deter him from reading secular Hebrew literature and encouraging his son's early literary efforts (MBSA 104). This blend of tolerant piety and open-minded secularism exerted an influence on Sholem Aleichem's writings.

Like Abramovitsh, the young Sholem Aleichem was an excellent Bible student who wrote Hebrew well (FY 26: 151–55). A friend of his father, Arnold of Pidvorke, engaged him in literary and philosophic discussions that led beyond traditional talmudic subjects. Moreover, this friend influenced Nachum to send his son to the Russian district school (FY 26: 165; 27: 37–40), an unusual step for a Jewish family of that time and place. As a result, Sholem Aleichem's education in Hebrew and Aramaic was somewhat weaker than that of Abramovitsh.

Sholem's years in the Russian school made a decisive change in his life. Until then he had studied Hebrew while speaking Yiddish with his family and friends. His subsequent secular education enabled him to become fluent in speaking, reading, and writing Russian. In turn, this training immersed him in nineteenth-century Russian literature and exposed him to most of the prominent European writers in Russian translation. His father's friend Arnold urged him to read Turgenev, Gogol, Pushkin, and Lermontov (FY 27: 65), all of whom he mentions in his letters. In conversation Sholem Aleichem "spoke very often about world literature, and even more often about contemporary Russian literature" (MBSA 128).[23] He was interested in the French writers Stendhal, Balzac, Zola, Flaubert, and de Maupassant; he hoped that Yiddish fiction would produce an equivalent to Balzac's "Human Comedy" (MBSA 143). According to many accounts, Chekhov was a particular favorite, and Sholem Aleichem reread his works frequently (SAB 188–89; MBSA 132). Berkovitsh recalls that "he read all of the humorists and satirists of world literature, from Cervantes, Swift, Dickens, Gogol, and Schedrin to Mark Twain, Jerome K. Jerome, and Chekhov. He felt closely related to Gogol" (SAB 188). In his youth he even wore his hair "à la Gogol" (FY 27: 149), and he compiled an album containing portraits of thirty-four

---

[23]Compare Nachman Mayzel, *Undzer Sholem-Aleichem*, pp. 89–104.

favorite philosophers and writers.[24] His personal library in Kiev included a wide selection of Russian literature as well as other European authors in Russian translations (MBSA 152–53).

Sholem graduated from his Russian high school with distinction in 1876, but government policies prevented him from studying at a university.[25] In order to receive higher education, he applied for admission to the Rabbinical Institute in Zhitomir, a center for the Jewish Enlightenment and Russian-Jewish intellectual life of the time. Abramovitsh attended this Rabbinical Institute in 1869, and Peretz hoped to study there at about the same time but did not carry out his plan. Sholem Aleichem was rejected by the Institute, however, on the grounds that he was one year too old and would be unable to complete the four-year course of study prior to entering obligatory military service (FY 27: 131). As it turned out, he was eventually exempted from serving in the Czar's army through the intercession of his future father-in-law Elimelekh Loyev.

Unable to pursue advanced education, Sholem Aleichem became a private tutor. His Russian studies served him well, and he gave lessons to Jewish children in Pereyaslav and Rzhishchev. In 1877 he was fortunate to be hired by Elimelekh Loyev to teach his daughter Olga. During the nearly three years in Sofiovka, he was influenced by Elimelekh, a wealthy Jewish landowner. Sholem benefited greatly from the new surroundings, in which

> he had enough time and freedom to do as he wished. Two or three hours daily sufficed for teaching his student. The rest of the time he could use as he wished—reading books or writing. And he read everything that came into his hands. The old man [Loyev] himself liked to read and spared no expense in constantly buying new books. And since he read only Hebrew, the library consisted mainly of Hebrew books (Yiddish was not yet fashionable). Kalman Shulman, Mapu, Smolenskin, Mandelkern, Gottlober, Yehalel, Isaac-Ber Levinson, Mordechai Aharon Ginzburg, Isaac Erter, Doctor Kaminer, Chaim-Zelig Slonimski—these were the names of the writers who graced the library. (FY 27: 192)

---

[24]The album included portraits of Descartes, Goethe, Shakespeare, George Sand, Turgenev, Lermontov, Pushkin, Gogol, Nekrasov, Saltykov-Schedrin, Mendelssohn, Heine, Spinoza, and Börne. See *Filologishe shriftn [fun YIVO]* 3 (1929), 153–56.

[25]Uri Finkl, *Sholem-Aleichem (monografie)* (Warsaw: Yidish bukh, 1959), p. 67.

In some ways, Elimelekh Loyev became a significant surrogate father figure.[26] With his financial support the young writer was able to read widely during 1877–79, while he lived on the Loyev estate and had access to Elimelekh Loyev's extensive library. At the time he still wrote in Hebrew, and he began to publish short prose in 1879–82.

During his three years on the Loyev estate, then, Sholem advanced his literary education. He took long walks with his student and discussed what they were reading. A romance developed between teacher and student, and when it became apparent, the Loyev family promptly dismissed Sholem Aleichem. Initially, the social discrepancy between the wealthy Loyevs and the poor tutor appeared insurmountable. Sholem Aleichem expresses this situation in his early fiction and in the Tevye stories "Hodel" and "Shprintse." Hodel falls in love with her tutor, while Shprintse has a romance with a boy whose wealthy family runs away suddenly on learning of the affair. Describing the repercussions of this debacle in his autobiography, Sholem Aleichem parodies a standard device of the autobiographical genre. He employs two lines of ellipses and then self-reflexively comments on them: "What do these dots signify? They signify a long, dark night. Everything is wrapped in a thick fog. The lonely wanderer goes his way" (FY 27: 226).

Exiled from the house of his beloved, Sholem next received the position of Government Rabbi in Luben, where he remained from 1880–83. This elected position had little to do with religious matters, but instead gave him administrative responsibility, mediating between the Czarist authorities and the Jewish population. In 1883 the Loyev family (like the fictional Tevye and Golda) acceded to the wishes of their strong-willed daughter Olga (whose Yiddish name was Hodel) and allowed her to marry Sholem. His new father-in-law insisted that Sholem give up his position in Luben as well as a subsequent job working for the millionaire Brodsky. The young couple then moved to Belotserkov, where they were supported by Elimelekh Loyev. Sholem devoted himself to literature and, as he wrote to his brother, "I frequently take up a pen and write one story after another in our mother tongue" (MBSA 76). Then, in 1885, Elimelekh died and Sholem became heir to the estate.

---

[26]Y. Y. Trunk, *Sholem Aleichem*, pp. 414–15.

WEALTH

"Money is filth," he wrote in 1888 (MBSA 79). But from 1885–90
Sholem Aleichem and Yiddish literature profited greatly from his
wealth: he spent large sums of money publishing *The Jewish Popular Library* (*Di yudishe folks-bibliotek*, 1888–89). He began to do
business in Kiev and lived there with his family from 1887 until
1905 (except for 1891–93, when they lived in Odessa). This was
an atypical milieu for an active Yiddish writer.[27] Kiev was a holy
city in Russian Orthodoxy, and the number of Jews residing there
was strictly controlled. In fact, Sholem Aleichem did not possess
the necessary permission to live permanently in the city.[28] He nevertheless invested actively in the stock market, which provided raw
material for the fictional letters of Menachem-Mendl (1892–
1913).[29]

Sholem Aleichem's literary efforts were advanced by his wealth
but in conflict with his responsibilities as an investor. As a result,
he commented, the novel *Yosele the Nightingale* (*Yosele solovey,*
1889) cost him 30,000 rubles—and the stock market lost him
what was left of his fortune in 1890. Pursued by creditors, he fled
the country and traveled to Paris, Vienna, and Chernovitz. Only
after his mother-in-law Rachel Loyev used her remaining funds to
help pay his debts could he return to Russia. He then moved to
Odessa with his family and lost the rest of his money there in 1891,
after which he was plagued by feelings of guilt. He nevertheless
continued to play the market and wrote a satire of the Kiev stock
exchange, *Yaknehoz* (1894), in the style of Pushkin.[30] Only after
1903 did Sholem Aleichem achieve sufficient fame to support his
family as a writer. In the late 1890s his wife Olga partly supported
them by means of her private practice as a dentist. This profession
brought little income but did provide legal residence permits in
Kiev for Olga and their children, though not for Sholem Aleichem
(MF 95–97).

[27]For a dissenting account of Kiev's literary world, see Nachman Mayzel, *Undzer Sholem-Aleichem*, pp. 23–42.

[28]He discusses the problem of Kiev residence permits in FY 27: 228.

[29]Compare Marie Waife-Goldberg, *My Father, Sholom Aleichem* (New York:
Schocken, 1971), pp. 102–10. Henceforth cited as "MF" by page alone.

[30]See Nachman Mayzel, *Undzer Sholem-Aleichem*, p. 90.

Money, or rather the lack of it, played a painful role in Sholem Aleichem's life. His father had been swindled by a business partner in Voronkov, which led to their ill-fated move to Pereyaslav. Thereafter his father eked out a living as an innkeeper and wine merchant (MBSA 29–34). As Sholem sat outdoors for hours trying to attract guests to the inn, he dreamed of wealth and longingly recalled his friend Shmulik's fantastic tales of buried treasure (FY 26: 32–35). Gambling had already entered his life with card-playing in the *cheder*, because it was "an epidemic in all of the Jewish schools, starting with Chanuka and lasting for the entire winter" (FY 26: 69–70). A cardsharp hustler appears in Sholem Aleichem's story "A Game of Sixty-Six," and the dream of winning a lottery motivates his play *The Jackpot*. For a decade he was obsessed by the Kiev stock market, with its potential for providing sudden wealth, and he expressed this mania in the Menachem-Mendl letters. Y. Y. Trunk comments that "in their essence, Sholem Aleichem's business transactions had more to do with the love of gambling (*shpil-lust*), in his naive but restless fantasy, than with his desire for wealth and material profit."[31]

Sholem Aleichem stood in an uneasy relationship to the Jewish "plutocracy" of Kiev. "Because of circumstances," he wrote, "it is my lot to move in circles that can least of all sympathize with my literary inclinations." He added ironically that "these circles are our exalted aristocracy, the merchant class, people with capital, who value my finances far more than my literary talent" (SAB 287). His true audience lived in poor Jewish neighborhoods and towns.

YIDDISH AND HEBREW

All three classic Yiddish writers began their literary careers in Hebrew: Abramovitsh in 1857, Peretz in 1876, and Sholem Aleichem in 1879. Like Abramovitsh in the early 1860s, Sholem Aleichem was confronted by the choice of language in the early 1880s. Abramovitsh published his first Hebrew essay about education in 1857, and Sholem Aleichem followed suit when he published an early essay on the same subject in a Hebrew periodical in 1879. In 1883 he began to print Yiddish stories and essays in a newspaper,

---

[31] Y. Y. Trunk, *Sholem-Aleichem*, p. 429.

the *Yudishes folksblat*. Simon Dubnov recalls that "the young writer was still searching for his path, and he himself was uncertain whether he had chosen the correct path when he began to write Yiddish" (FZ 33). As Dubnov notes, Sholem Aleichem possessed the talent and skill to make a name in either of the more established literary languages, Russian and Hebrew. But he felt that "one must describe Jewish life in the language of that life," and he chose to enter the less developed Yiddish literary scene (ibid.).[32]

In his autobiographical sketch dating from 1908, Sholem Aleichem echoes Abramovitsh's 1889 autobiographical essay when he refers (in the third-person) to his early decision to write in Yiddish:

> At that time (1883) the editor of *Ha-melitz* began to publish a newspaper in Jargon, *The Jewish Folkspaper* (*Yudishes folksblat*). The first number that fell into his hands astounded the writer with the simplicity of the idea. "So," he thought, "a newspaper is being printed in such a simple language that is accessible *for all Jews, even for women!*" From then on the thought stole into his head: Doesn't the Hebrew language, with its fine "rhetoric," nourish only a small number of selected readers who possess knowledge of it? That is one thing. And the second is that, in any case, if you write Hebrew you still think in Jargon—so isn't it better to write Yiddish in the first place, that is, to write as you think? (SAB 4; emphasis in original)

The problem was that Yiddish, or "Jargon" as it was then called, was commonly scorned as merely the language of women's prayer books (*tekhines*). According to Sholem Aleichem, this situation gave rise to his initial decision to write under a pen-name: "Then the pseudonym 'Sholem Aleichem' was thought up, behind which the author hid from relatives and acquaintances." This was especially important after he left his rabbinic post and lived among the Jewish plutocracy in Kiev: "In that environment (on the Kiev stock exchange) it was considered a disgrace to have dealings with writers, and particularly with those who wrote Jargon" (ibid.). Even the author's father would have preferred that he continue writing in Hebrew instead of lowering himself to the language of "cooks and servants" (SAB 4; MBSA 104).

---

[32]Compare Sholem Aleichem's essay, "A briv tsu a gutn fraynt," *Di yudishe folksbibliotek* 2 (1889), 304–10.

Sholem Aleichem was aware of the socio-political significance of Yiddish from the start. He wrote to the Russian-speaking woman Bertha Flekser: "I wonder if you read Yiddish. I understand that you are an educated, intelligent woman; it's a shame, if I may say so, for you not to know your native language. I am not speaking about Hebrew, of course, which is completely unattainable for our contemporary women. I mean, at least, the Jargon. The point is that a woman with your education would be very useful to our people in the pursuits of our newest folk literature."[33] Since women were not provided with an education in Hebrew, Sholem Aleichem hoped that they would become active in Yiddish literary circles.

Sholem Aleichem never found an original voice in Hebrew, but only "played the role of an Enlightenment writer" (SAB 24). Nevertheless, he made extensive use of Hebrew allusions in his Yiddish writing, and he explained to Leo Tolstoy in a letter of 1903 that "the richer the Yiddish dialect is in Hebrew nouns and verbs, the more beautiful it is."[34]

S. Y. ABRAMOVITSH AND SHOLEM ALEICHEM

The most important element in Sholem Aleichem's literary biography is his extended friendship with S. Y. Abramovitsh—the so-called grandfather of Yiddish literature. Abramovitsh had written the first versions of his major Yiddish works in 1864–78, and he returned to literary activity with Hebrew stories in 1886. Sholem Aleichem exerted a substantial influence in 1888, when he prompted Abramovitsh to write Yiddish fiction for *The Jewish Popular Library (Di yudishe folks-bibliotek)*. In a very real sense Sholem Aleichem carved out a place for himself by rediscovering and promoting his literary precursors, with Abramovitsh at their head.

Berkovitsh recalls that Sholem Aleichem learned a great deal from Abramovitsh (whom Berkovitsh calls "Mendele") during the years they both lived in Odessa (1891–93). Paradoxically, "under Mendele's personal influence he freed himself from Mendele's liter-

---

[33]Letter of 14–15 October 1889, in *Tsaytshrift far yidisher geshikhte, demografie un ekonomik, literatur-forshung, shprakh-visnshaft un etnografie* 1 (1926), 250; translated from the Russian by Mikhail Epstein.

[34]*Sovetish* 12 (1941), 239.

ary influence" (SAB 170). One of Abramovitsh's daughters describes her father's first meeting with Sholem Aleichem. When Sholem Aleichem arrives at the Abramovitsh household, the self-proclaimed grandson plays on the use of his name as a Yiddish greeting:

> We, the children, used to see him [Abramovitsh] very little during the day, primarily at dinnertime. And even at dinner he would sit and read a newspaper. . . . I remember one autumn day. . . . At the threshold there appears a man of middle stature and remains standing. . . .
>   —*Sholem-Aleichem,* he says.
>   Father, who was still immersed in the newspaper and preoccupied by eating, answers unwillingly, without removing his eyes from the newspaper:
>   —*Aleichem-Sholem.* In general he did not like it at all when one disturbed him or when unfamiliar people would come at dinnertime.
>   For a few seconds the unknown man stood without moving, and suddenly he turned to Father and embraced him.
>   —Grandfather, good evening! I am Sholem Aleichem!
>   A frightful tumult came over the room. Father lept up from his chair, caught on the tablecloth, and all the dishes crashed onto the floor.[35]

Later Abramovitsh and Sholem Aleichem met frequently and engaged in lively discussions together with other writers. Following the convention of referring to her father as "Mendele," Abramovitsh's daughter recalls that

> Sholem Aleichem was always in the center of everyone's attention. They used to debate, writers would read their works, and one would deal with questions concerning literary and social life.
>   During these discussions Mendele would become worked up, virtually frothing at the mouth as he defended his positions. He would often jump up from his place, gesticulating wildly, catching his opponent by the hand, so that once during such a discussion Sholem Aleichem's little daughter who was there broke into tears and cried out, "Grandfather wants to hit my Papa!" (Ibid., 266)

---

[35]Nadiezhda Abramovitsh, "Sholem-Aleichem un Mendele Moykher Sforim (zikhroynes fun Mendeles tokhter)," *Sovetish* 12 (1941), 265–66.

It is difficult to know whether to rely on such belated accounts by authors' family and friends, especially given the arduous conditions imposed upon Yiddish writing in the Soviet Union—where it was at best tolerated as a proletarian vehicle of expression.

According to tradition, Abramovitsh and Sholem Aleichem differed greatly in their practices of writing. "I rest while I am working," Sholem Aleichem stated in a letter to Dubnov (FZ 94). Sholem Aleichem also commented that he could write "at any time and place and under any circumstance; in the salon, in the kitchen, in a train, in a restaurant, even riding in a coach or lying in bed" (SAB 5). Dubnov attests to the difference in work habits:

> Mendele's way of writing was the opposite of Sholem Aleichem's. The latter could write wherever he was—on the streetcar, in the midst of noise and tumult, and he used to work without preparations, quickly writing page after page. Mendele used to lock himself up in his room, bent over the sheet of paper with quill in hand and think for a long time until he wrote down a single line. Then he would sit for a while, lift the manuscript up to his nearsighted eyes, and look over what was written—holding the quill nearby in order to throw out mercilessly every unsuitable expression. (FZ 47)

Such disparities are evident from their early correspondence, when Abramovitsh complained of the difficulty of writing and emphasized the need for further revisions of a book like Sholem Aleichem's *Stempenyu* (MB 148, 150, 163). Sholem Aleichem's dedicatory letter addressed to "grandfather Mendele" in *Stempenyu* quotes Abramovitsh as having written that "over a work, dear grandson, one must sweat, one must work to polish every word." In response, Sholem Aleichem admits that the younger generation "never has time" for such polishing.[36]

Dubnov recalls a simile Abramovitsh used to describe their differences in writing. Abramovitsh compared himself to a woman undergoing a difficult, protracted childbirth. Sholem Aleichem was more like a hen who sits for a moment and lays an egg (FZ 47). These similes suggested the contrast between Abramovitsh's slow method of composition and Sholem Aleichem's more impulsive approach, but Y. D. Berkovitsh presents a different picture and

---

[36]See *Stempenyu: a yudisher roman*, in *Di yudishe folks-bibliotek* 1 (1888), vii; reprinted in SA 11: 125.

explicitly rejects Abramovitsh's account (R 366). In any event, Sholem Aleichem was a remarkably prolific writer both in his fiction and in his letter-writing.

Michael Kaufman confirmed that Sholem Aleichem wrote "miraculously fast and easily. Nothing disturbed him. He could write standing, lying down, walking, even in the streetcar or on a train—anywhere" (SAB 140). He would laugh while writing, pointing to his manuscript and speaking as if his characters had lives of their own: "Just listen to what *he* says!" (SAB 141). As is clear from his letters, however, Sholem Aleichem carefully revised many of his works.[37]

Among many literary resemblances, a first similarity between the works of Abramovitsh and Sholem Aleichem lies in their basic ideology and goals. From 1857 to 1879, Abramovitsh was unmistakably a *maskil,* a proponent of the Jewish Enlightenment. His self-avowed intention was to educate the Yiddish-speaking masses. In Nachum Sokolov's *Sefer zikharon* of 1889, Abramovitsh explained his shift from Hebrew to Yiddish in 1864: "The desire to be useful outweighed the apparent honor, and I said, 'Come what may, I will have pity on Yiddish, the daughter without pity; it is time to do something for my people'" (SZ 123). Sholem Aleichem explicitly began in a kindred manner when he conceived his literary efforts as part of a social program. In this respect, both authors conformed to prevailing attitudes in Russian intellectual circles.

A second similarity is the means by which Abramovitsh and Sholem Aleichem launched their reformist ventures. In the 1870s and 1880s, both employed satire and caricature, exposing what they viewed as the errors of their day. They placed great emphasis on portraying anti-heroes, whom they used to combat typical foibles in the Jewish communities of Eastern Europe. Examples are Abramovitsh's Benjamin the Third, preceding Sholem Aleichem's Freydl in *Stempenyu* and Perle in *Yosele solovey.*

A third point of contact pertains to the structure of their novels. Both authors de-emphasized plot, placing greater weight on

---

[37]See, for example, his late 1894 correspondence to Mordechai Spektor concerning the first Tevye story, printed in *Der tog* on 23 and 30 September 1923. For Berkovitsh's description of Sholem Aleichem writing the story "Chava," see R 309–11.

character development and the process of narration itself. Hence a pivotal feature of Abramovitsh's novels is the narrative and editorial persona of Mendele the Bookseller; starting in the 1890s, Sholem Aleichem makes such personae even more central in his Tevye stories and other monologues.

Regardless of these and other significant similarities, Sholem Aleichem swerves away from Abramovitsh in his early novels. The points of divergence help to account for Sholem Aleichem's particular contribution to Yiddish fiction, but glimmers of originality appear even in the penumbra of his forerunner. First, despite Sholem Aleichem's efforts to become an enlightened author like Abramovitsh, he actually failed in this attempt; instead, as Shmuel Niger wrote, "he was destined to become the one who broke the utilitarian, moralistic, Enlightenment tradition of Yiddish literature."[38] What Sholem Aleichem did best was humoristic rather than satiric, and the early novels show his tentative steps in this direction. He gave legitimacy to comic narratives that did not serve a moralistic end.

Second, their narrative techniques differ. Abramovitsh's five novels from the 1860s and 1870s employ the first-person voice. In contrast, Sholem Aleichem's major novels of the 1880's—*Sender Blank, Stempenyu,* and *Yosele the Nightingale*—are all based on third-person, omniscient narration. In some respects, this places Sholem Aleichem uncomfortably close to rival Yiddish authors of the time, whose pulp novels announce on their title pages that they are "most interesting romances." Often Sholem Aleichem's presence is clearest in the chapter headings and in editorial asides, which make light of stereotypical novelistic strategies.

Third and most decisively, when Abramovitsh and Sholem Aleichem wax satiric, the objects of their satire differ. Abramovitsh satirizes antiquated Jewish beliefs and customs; Sholem Aleichem goes beyond this practice to satirize popular Jewish novels. Sholem Aleichem's satire turns inward, from external forms of life to the literature that (he believed) ought to reflect it. Both authors employ social satire, but Sholem Aleichem combines social criticism with literary satire. This clashes with Sholem Aleichem's commitment to realism and to the mimetic illusion. From a literary standpoint,

---

[38] Shmuel Niger, *Sholem Aleichem*, pp. 31–32.

Sholem Aleichem's self-reflexive fiction counterbalanced the realistic conventions he advocated.

SHOLEM ALEICHEM AND I. L. PERETZ

Whereas Sholem Aleichem was on friendly terms with Yiddish and Hebrew writers in the Ukraine, his relations with some Polish writers, and especially I. L. Peretz, were strained. The popularity of Sholem Aleichem's writings throughout Eastern Europe was unmistakable, but the Warsaw intelligentsia was skeptical.[39] Although Sholem Aleichem comfortably referred to Abramovitsh as his literary "grandfather," he would never have accepted the designation that later represented Peretz as a metaphorical "father of the literary family." It is significant that the grandfather–grandson family tree invented by Sholem Aleichem casts no one in the intervening role of father.

By 1901 I. L. Peretz stood at the center of Warsaw Yiddish culture. He had corresponded extensively with Sholem Aleichem when the latter was editing *The Jewish Popular Library,* and he submitted his Yiddish ballad "Monish" for the first volume. Sholem Aleichem was not particularly impressed and was far more concerned to receive a contribution by the poet David Frishman.[40] When he revised Peretz's poem, as editor of the volume, Peretz believed that Sholem Aleichem had spoiled his work. He had given Sholem Aleichem permission to change expressions that would be unclear to Yiddish speakers in Lithuania and Russia, but he asked to be informed of any such alterations.[41] The young editor ignored this request, and when *The Jewish Popular Library* appeared, Peretz sent a terse acknowledgment and requested that Sholem Aleichem return his manuscript. In 1892 he republished the original version of "Monish" with a note indicating that it had suffered from many changes at the hands of the editor of *The Jewish Popu-*

---

[39]Compare Shmuel Niger, *Sholem Aleichem,* pp. 10–13.

[40]See Nachman Mayzel, "Peretz un Sholem-Aleichem in zeyere perzenlekhe batsiungen," *Filologishe shriftn [fun YIVO]* 1 (1926), 268; *YIVO bleter* 2 (1931), 15–18.

[41]Letter of 4 July 1888; see *Kol kitvei I. L. Peretz* (Tel Aviv: Dvir, 1962), vol. 10, book 2, p. 215.

lar Library. Sholem Aleichem retaliated with a critical review of another poem Peretz printed at the same time.[42]

Peretz alienated Sholem Aleichem by publishing a Yiddish anthology under the title *The Jewish Library* (*Di yudishe bibliotek*), which appeared twice in 1891. Sholem Aleichem felt that this was a deliberate effort to take over the anthology that his financial setbacks had forced him to delay. The clearest and most reliable indication of their hostilities is preserved in letters written to Yankev Dinezon during 1888–89. After that time, evidently because of his friend Peretz's anger at Sholem Aleichem, Dinezon interrupted the correspondence with Sholem Aleichem for a decade.

When he and Dinezon resumed their correspondence in 1900, Sholem Aleichem tried to understand "why you have distanced yourself from me."[43] Dinezon mentioned Sholem Aleichem's mockery of Peretz's work, and Sholem Aleichem countered that Peretz was far more guilty of wronging him. After Sholem Aleichem lost everything he had in 1890, "Peretz thought it over, took Sholem Aleichem's sign from his door, and hung it on his own door—and from *The Jewish Popular Library* suddenly there became a *Jewish Library*. That is worse, dear Dinezon, than ten thousand reviews" (ibid., 348). Sholem Aleichem concluded his letter with a remark that he had seen Peretz "dancing on my grave" (ibid., 349).

The Sholem Aleichem–Peretz saga revolved around accusations by each that the other was "crazy" (*meshuge*). In an early letter to Dinezon of 1887, Sholem Aleichem commented that he was "crazy about Yiddish," and that "I am a great pedant and a little crazy."[44] Later he refered to the editor of the *Yudishes folksblat* as "the crazy Litvak."[45] In about 1893, Peretz wrote to Sholem Aleichem: "I have heard from a reliable source (Dinezon) that you are really a good man, but crazy."[46] Then in a letter to Mor-

---

[42]See *Kol mevasser tsu der yudisher folks-bibliotek* (1892). Compare Nachman Mayzel, "Peretz un Sholem-Aleichem," 271.

[43]Letter of 15/27 February 1900, *YIVO bleter* 3 (1932), p. 347.

[44]Letter of 28 December 1887, *YIVO bleter* 1 (1931), 390–91; see also *YIVO bleter* 2 (1931), 24.

[45]Letter of 11 January 1889, *YIVO bleter* 3 (1932), 342.

[46]Nachman Mayzel, "Peretz un Sholem-Aleichem," 272. Compare Berkovitsh, R 50.

dechai Spektor (5 January 1894), Sholem Aleichem wrote: "Apparently our poor Jargon is destined to have a madman"—first Levi and now Peretz.[47] On 20 July 1895 he expressed his annoyance that Spektor was collaborating with Peretz on his *Holiday Papers* (*Yontev bletlekh*). He sent Spektor a parodic poem, "To the Moon," in the style of "our great, mad poet L. Peretz" (ibid., 273).[48] These gibes on the theme of madness are pertinent to Peretz's contemporary fiction, which included "The Mad Talmudist" (1890) and "Stories from the Madhouse" (1895–96). In 1896 Peretz criticized Sholem Aleichem in an essay called "Sick Nerves" ("Di kranke nervn").[49]

Berkovitsh states that "in Sholem Aleichem's great popularity with the people, Peretz felt almost an insult against his own greatness, and for almost his entire life Sholem Aleichem remained cold to Peretz's work—*because he drew no enjoyment from it*" (SAB 158; emphasis in original). Moreover, Berkovitsh recalls debates over Sholem Aleichem's works in about 1904. At a literary gathering, Peretz spoke coldly of Sholem Aleichem while Bialik warmly defended him. Peretz stated that Sholem Aleichem "writes light prose, knows the people's language well—and this appeals to the audience. This fact alone, that Sholem Aleichem is so accepted by the masses, arouses suspicion" (R 60). Warsaw Jewish intellectuals frequently scorned Sholem Aleichem's work because of its apparent simplicity (R 67–69). On one occasion Peretz vociferously refused to participate in a literary evening if the organizers included a reading of one of Sholem Aleichem's stories (SAB 259).

For his part, Sholem Aleichem was skeptical of Peretz's way of garnering disciples. He compared Peretz's literary evenings to the inspirational gatherings of chassidic rebbes: "Peretz holds forth because he is basically more a chassidic rebbe than a writer" (SAB 158). Later Berkovitsh rephrased Sholem Aleichem's assertion: "Peretz organizes meetings of his chassidim because his greatness lies not so much in literature as in being a kind of modern rebbe" (R 97). What was worse, in Sholem Aleichem's eyes, was that

---

[47]See Nachman Mayzel, "Peretz un Sholem Aleichem," 272.

[48]See Sholem Aleichem's letter of 28 October 1895, printed in *Der tog* on 28 October 1923.

[49]Compare Nachman Mayzel, "Peretz un Sholem-Aleichem," 276–77.

Peretz held an elitist, arrogant attitude toward the people. Disputing Peretz's claims to authority, he stated that "only writers like Tolstoy and Chekhov have the right to be leaders of the young literary generation" (ibid.). Sholem Aleichem also complained that Peretz diminished the character of Yiddish by employing provincial Polish dialect (R 98).

Sholem Aleichem's skepticism toward Peretz's work was linked to his doubts about new trends in Yiddish writing. He apparently thought that the late *Folktales* were Peretz's best work. In 1906 he referred scornfully to young authors "with an entirely new style of decadence—or, as one calls it, 'mood.'" Sholem Aleichem blamed Peretz and his disciples for the turn away from plot, psychology, description, and characterization (SAB 76, 188).[50] In response to his son Misha, who had expressed pessimistic thoughts in a letter, Sholem Aleichem attacked "the philosophy of disappointment" and advised him: "don't read the contemporary idiots. Better, read the classics. The entire stream of contemporary decadence in literature (particularly in Russia) will pass very quickly!"[51] Closely tied to nineteenth-century realism, he was critical of the experiments by Peretz and his circle. Sholem Aleichem told Peretz that he would trade a thousand of his symbolist plays like *The Golden Chain* (*Di goldene keyt*) for one of his folktales.

On several occasions, nevertheless, Sholem Aleichem set aside their differences and expressed his readiness to make peace. When Peretz's twenty-fifth anniversary as a writer was celebrated in Warsaw, Sholem Aleichem sent congratulations from Kiev including the lines: "Two workers toil over one task with different tools. Two travelers move toward one goal from two paths. Two literati write for one people with two distinct pens."[52] Peretz was less forgiving.

The final drama unfolded when Sholem Aleichem visited Warsaw in spring 1914. Sponsored by the journal *Ha-zamir*, he was to perform his works in a large theater. The committee learned, however, that Sholem Aleichem planned a prior reading for another group, and as a result *Ha-zamir* threatened to cancel its engage-

---

[50]Compare H. Reminik, "Sholem Aleichems literarish-kritishe tetikayt," *Sovetish* 12 (1941), 172.

[51]Letter of 10 January 1909, in *Sovetishe literatur* 3–4 (March–April 1939), 274.

[52]Cited by Nachman Mayzel in "Peretz un Sholem-Aleichem," 277.

ment. Sholem Aleichem wanted to smooth matters over and made a special visit to Peretz's apartment, but "in protest Peretz went out. Sholem Aleichem waited a few hours, lay down on the sofa. Meanwhile Peretz was at Y. Dinezon's place and from there he sent word that he could not receive Sholem Aleichem at home. Sholem Aleichem rode to Y. Dinezon, caught Peretz there and was finally reconciled with him."[53] Sholem Aleichem's actions reflected his impetuous, gregarious style as aptly as Peretz's actions typified his more sullen and withdrawn disposition.

POGROMS

Sholem Aleichem was particularly shaken by the 1903 Kishinev pogrom, in which forty-seven Jews were murdered. Subsequently, he was enthusiastic about H. N. Bialik's energetic poetic responses, which bitterly describe the events and call for active self-defense. In 1906 Peretz translated Bialik's poem, "In the City of Slaughter," for a Warsaw newspaper. Berkovitsh records that Sholem Aleichem was appalled by the translation and concluded that Peretz must have intentionally spoiled the poem (R 314–21; SAB 175).

Following the Kishinev pogrom, Sholem Aleichem decided to edit a collection of writings in support of its victims. In this connection he corresponded with well-known Russian authors including Tolstoy, Chekhov, and Gorky.[54] He was eager to receive contributions from Tolstoy and Gorky, who "do not idly spill ink, but write with their blood" (MBSA 131). Sholem Aleichem was attracted to Gorky's social involvement, and in the revolutionary years 1903–05 he often wore the black, proletarian "Gorky shirt" (MBSA 132, R 86, 94). This black shirt is criticized by the bourgeois narrator of "Joseph" (1905), and Gorky is mentioned in the Tevye story "Chava" (1906). During 1905 Sholem Aleichem lived with his eldest daughter in Vilna, where he observed the socialist Bundists' activity and was inspired to write the story "Joseph" about them (R 150). As a result of Sholem Aleichem's social activism, including his correspondence with Russian authors, the Czarist authorites in Kiev placed him under surveillance and blocked his planned book in support of the Kishinev victims (MBSA 135).

---

[53]Nachman Mayzel, "Peretz un Sholem-Aleichem," 283.

[54]See the translations of Sholem Aleichem's letters in *Sovetish* 12 (1941), 234–48.

According to his brother, he often discussed revolutionary themes and wanted to write a book about a revolutionary hero (MBSA 185).

Sholem Aleichem and his family directly experienced a pogrom in Kiev. Following the October Revolution in 1905, Sholem Aleichem was initially exuberant over the prospect that Russia would receive a constitution (SAB 65). Then riots broke out in many cities of the Ukraine, and his family took shelter in the Imperial Hotel of Kiev. Immediately afterward they decided to leave Russia. For the same reason, Abramovitsh left Odessa and moved to Switzerland, where he occasionally met Sholem Aleichem and other Jewish writers.

In the final decade of his life, Sholem Aleichem traveled incessantly and never returned to settle in Eastern Europe. He lived in Lemberg, Geneva, London, and New York, giving public readings to support his family. He was attracted by the (unfulfilled) prospect of success in the Yiddish theaters of the Lower East Side in Manhattan. He was, however, disappointed by the United States: "In America there is everything except people [*mentshn*]," he wrote in 1907, "and people there have everything except a heart" (MBSA 170).

In 1908 he returned to live in Geneva but continued to travel and give literary performances. Then he fell ill in Baranovitsh and spent several years recuperating from tuberculosis in Italy, Switzerland, and Germany. After World War I began, he moved to New York City and lived there until his death in 1916.

PUBLIC READINGS, LITERARY PHASES, AND RECEPTION

Sholem Aleichem was the first major Yiddish writer to support himself by writing and by giving public performances of his works. The reading tours were necessitated by his financial difficulties, but they also reflected the effectiveness of his works when read aloud. There are numerous accounts of audience enthusiasm, and one writer comments that "like his great predecessor, the world-famous humorist and realist Charles Dickens, Sholem Aleichem was also a masterful reader of his own works."[55]

---

[55]Z. Venrop, "Etlekhe teg mit Sholem-Aleichemen (fragmentarishe zikhroynes)," *Sovetish* 12 (1941), 300.

His manner of reading was simple and direct, without histri-
onics. Sholem Aleichem's youngest daughter recalls his public
readings of 1905, when

> it was universally acknowledged that my father was his own best
> reader. His voice was soft, not very deep, but his diction was
> excellent and his voice carried, even in the halls that held a
> thousand, all the way to the highest balcony. He did not act,
> except for reading the funniest parts with a serious face; he did
> not raise his voice or overemphasize. He read simply, naturally, as
> the character himself might have spoken. But he had a brilliant
> sense of timing. A momentary pause at the dramatic turn, a
> slightest motion of the hand or even of a finger at the psychologi-
> cal moment, could bring the house down. (MF 157)

Gershon Levin also recalls his reading in Warsaw: "Sholem Aleichem read excellently, in a beautiful, pleasing, tenor voice, and
while the entire audience gasped with laughter, no trace of a smile
appeared on his face" (SAB 260).[56]

Sholem Aleichem's performances suited his literary style, with
its emphasis on the oral intonations of Yiddish speech. He swept
aside overblown literary pretensions and imitated common expression: "Sholem-Aleichem's ear perceived the slightest nuances in a
person's speech. . . . That is one reason why the monologue is so
peculiar to Sholem Aleichem's artistic form."[57] Moreover, he employs "hidden irony" to mock the exalted language of prayer.[58]
His public readings enabled him to exploit the contrast between
everyday Yiddish speech and parodied Hebrew style.

Sholem Aleichem wrote an immense quantity of prose, far
more than either of the other two classic Yiddish writers. Dan
Miron refers to three "cadences" of Sholem Aleichem's work: in
1883–90, when he actively contributed to the *Yudishes folksblat*,
wrote novels, and edited *The Jewish Popular Library*; in 1890–98,
when he produced at a far slower pace; and in 1899–1916, when

---

[56]Compare S. Dobin, "Sholem-Aleichem, vi ikh hob im gekent," *Sovetish* 12
(1941), 284.

[57]S. Dobin, "Sholem-Aleichem vi ikh hob im gekent," 285.

[58]Y. Reminik, "Sholem-Aleichem der novelist," *Sovetishe literatur* 3–4 (March–
April 1939), 231.

he contributed prolifically to numerous journals at a steady rate.[59] Miron provides both economic and literary explanations for these phases. During the first period he was supported by Elimelekh Loyev and, following Loyev's death, by the estate Sholem Aleichem and his wife inherited from him. After he lost his fortune in 1890, Sholem Aleichem also lost a large part of the literary momentum he had possessed as the editor of *The Jewish Popular Library.* Finally he was able to support himself from his Yiddish writing after 1899, when new newspapers and journals such as *The Jew* (*Der yud*) began to appear and commission his works.

Simon Dubnov encouraged Sholem Aleichem's literary career. Under the pseudonym "Kritikus," Dubnov printed a favorable review of Sholem Aleichem's early Yiddish story "The Pen-Knife" ("Dos messerl"); this reception in an important Russian-Jewish journal, *Voskhod,* made a deep impression on the aspiring author. Sholem Aleichem wrote that he hoped Dubnov would "return to our Jargon, which considers you as its *highborn relative* after ten or more years during which our emancipated sister, Russian-Jewish literature, has completely ignored her gifted younger sis-ter—Yiddish" (Letter of 9 February 1889, FZ 79). Six months later, Sholem Aleichem commented that "you are the only writer who relates sympathetically and humanitarily to the poor Jargon" (FZ 83).

Few serious critical essays on Sholem Aleichem's fiction appeared until the twenty-fifth anniversary of his Yiddish writing in 1908, when Bal Makhshoves wrote an essay about him.[60] Even after that time, Sholem Aleichem's fame was more established among common readers than among intellectuals. Shmuel Niger recalls the resistance many critics felt toward the most popular Yiddish writer: Sholem Aleichem's "closeness to the reader was for me—and not only for me—a defect. The closer he was to the reader, the higher grew the wall between him and us—the 'intelligentsia.' "[61] A collection of essays about him, *Tsum ondenk fun*

---

[59]Dan Miron, *Sholem Aleichem: pirkei masa* (Ramat-Gan: Massada, 1970), pp. 11–14.

[60]See Bal Makhshoves, *Geklibene shriftn* (Warsaw: Kletzkin, 1929), vol. 1, pp. 91–109. In English, see *Prooftexts* 6 (1986), 7–15.

[61]Shmuel Niger, *Sholem Aleichem*, p. 10.

Sholem Aleichem, appeared one year after his death, but few detailed studies followed.

The greatest contribution to serious analysis of Sholem Aleichem's fiction came from the Soviet Union in the 1930s and 1940s. Aware of inadequacies in the New York Folksfund edition of Sholem Aleichem's writings that was printed in 1917–23, for example, several Russian-Jewish scholars began work on a critical edition, three volumes of which appeared in 1948. Celebrated as a proletarian writer, Sholem Aleichem was widely read in Russian and other Slavic languages. According to one account, three million copies of his books were printed in the Soviet Union in 1935–45.[62]

Another aspect of Sholem Aleichem's reception in literary history is the story of his career on the Yiddish stage.[63] Three years after his death, for instance, the stories narrated by Tevye the Dairyman became the basis for an important play directed by Maurice Schwartz, who played the role of Tevye. In various forms, this drama became the vehicle for significant cinematic adaptations in 1939, 1971, and 1991.[64]

The distinctive life styles of the classic Yiddish authors are reflected in the nature of biographies about them. S. Y. Abramovitsh lived a rather secluded life, and only Lev Binshtok wrote a memoir of him prior to his Odessa period. Even at the height of his fame, he concealed his private existence behind the literary persona of Mendele the Bookseller. I. L. Peretz was also secretive about his family life, and biographers concentrated on his literary and intellectual life. Only Peretz's cousin Rosa Laks-Peretz told more intimate tales. The figurative "grandfather of Yiddish literature" and "father of modern Yiddish literature" were not in reality family men.

In contrast, Sholem Aleichem literally filled the roles of father and grandfather. As a child he was close to his brothers, one of whom wrote a memoir of their youth. After he married Olga Loyev in 1883, they raised a large family of six children, augmented by

[62]See *Yidishe kultur* 5 (May 1946), 17.

[63]See Kobi Weitzner, *Sholem Aleichem in the Theater* (forthcoming).

[64]See Ken Frieden, "A Century in the Life of Sholem Aleichem's *Tevye*," *B. G. Rudolph Lectures in Judaic Studies* (Syracuse: Syracuse University Press, forthcoming).

his mother-in-law Rachel Loyev and his sons-in-law Y. D. Berkovitsh and Michael Kaufman. His children as well as his sons-in-law wrote their memories of him. Sholem Aleichem's gregariousness meant that his memory could be preserved by many people who knew him personally, and not only by those who knew Sholem Aleichem the literary figure.

A more congenial impression of Sholem Aleichem emerges than of either Abramovitsh or Peretz, in part because his writings invented the likeable Sholem Aleichem presence. This warmth emanates from his writings, which include hundreds of letters, and in his attitude toward his readers. Early in his career he stated that "I write my novels mainly for the masses; that is, for a world of people who are still foreign to high thoughts or, as one calls them, 'ideas.' "[65] He was not deterred by skepticism on the part of some elitist authors, and his commitment to writing for all readers has made Sholem Aleichem's writings extraordinarily popular in Yiddish and in more than a dozen other languages.

---

[65] "A briv tsu a gutn fraynt," in *Di yidishe folks-bibliotek* 2 (1889), 307.

CHAPTER 5

Sholem Aleichem's "Jewish Novels"

After S. Y. Abramovitsh set a course for modern Yiddish fiction in the 1860s and 1870s, Sholem Aleichem wrote several novels in the 1880s that followed Abramovitsh's direction. He called Abramovitsh "the grandfather" of Yiddish literature in 1888 and fashioned himself as an obedient and devoted grandson. In this way, Sholem Aleichem simultaneously lent an appearance of stability to the shaky foundations of Yiddish literature and created a ready-made pedigree for himself.[1]

On the surface, Sholem Aleichem appears to have been unfamiliar with the writer's syndrome now called "the anxiety of influence."[2] But only on the surface. He played out the drama of his apprenticeship in relation to the best and the worst of his contemporaries—Abramovitsh and Shaykevitsh, who were familiar to general readers as Mendele and Shomer.[3] Sholem Aleichem did not, however, merely build upon prior literary history; he helped to shape it, especially in his role as editor of *The Jewish Popular Library* (*Di yudishe folks-bibliotek,* 1888–89). One of his stated goals was to reeducate Yiddish readers by shifting their attention from popular novels to superior works of fiction.

GRANDFATHER AND GRANDSON

Sholem Aleichem began writing to Abramovitsh in 1884—in Russian. At that time the inexperienced author introduced himself as "a young, but passionate, admirer of your talent; an admirer who is working the soil that you plowed, obstinately and diligently

---

[1]Compare Dan Miron, "Sholem Aleykhem: Person, Persona, Presence," *The Uriel Weinreich Memorial Lecture* 1 (New York: YIVO Institute for Jewish Research, 1972), p. 10.

[2]See Harold Bloom, *The Anxiety of Influence: A Theory of Poetry* (New York: Oxford University Press, 1973).

[3]Compare Shmuel Niger, *Sholem Aleichem: zayne vikhtikste verk, zayn humor un zayn ort in der yidisher literatur* (New York: YKUF, 1928), pp. 20–29.

following the footsteps you have left so clearly in the fields of our Yiddish literature."[4] When Sholem Aleichem presented himself as a humble laborer in this metaphorical field, he evidently hoped to be taken on as a trusted farmhand. He then called one of his own stories a "pale reflection of your splendid *Travels of Benjamin the Third*." Four years later, as editor of *The Jewish Popular Library*, Sholem Aleichem repeated his commitment to Abramovitsh by stating that "I am following [or obeying] you in *everything*" ("Ikh folg aykh in *ales*"), and he closed his letter with the phrase, "Your devoted grandson."[5]

An essay by Sholem Aleichem's close friend, Y. H. Ravnitzky, initially presents a comparable picture. Ravnitsky recalls that "like a fiery, passionate chassid of his rebbe, thus did Sholem Aleichem speak of the grandfather, Reb Mendele, even before he saw him with his own eyes." After Sholem Aleichem met Abramovitsh in 1888 and received a portrait of him, he placed it on his desk and "while writing he used to look at it often and ask himself, would the thing [he was writing] please him, Reb Mendele, or not?"[6]

Sholem Aleichem exchanged numerous letters with Abramovitsh in 1888. One letter from Abramovitsh is particularly relevant to the intertextual relationship between their works. Abramovitsh initially tells his self-proclaimed literary grandson:

> I would advise you not to write romances [*romanen*]. Your genre is something else entirely. You are indeed (as you yourself say) *my grandson*. You understand what that means? Understand it well, follow grandfather and, God willing, you will become a talented writer. In general, all Yiddish romances are worthless. They nauseate me. If there are romances among our people, they are entirely different than among other peoples. One must understand this and write entirely differently.[7]

---

[4]*Dos Sholem Aleichem bukh*, ed. Y. D. Berkovitsh (New York: Sholem-Aleichem bukh komitet, 1926), p. 191. Henceforth cited as "SAB" by page alone.

[5]Letter of 26 July 1888; in *Tsum ondenk fun Sholem Aleichem: zamlbukh*, ed. I. Zinberg and S. Niger (Petersburg: I. L. Peretz-fond, 1917), p. 84. Y. D. Berkovitsh discusses this correspondence in SAB 168.

[6]*Tsum ondenk fun Sholem Aleichem*, p. 51.

[7]Letter of 28 June 1888, reprinted in *Dos Mendele bukh*, ed. Nachman Mayzel (New York: Yiddisher kultur farband, 1959), p. 157; this volume is henceforth cited as "MB" by page alone. Abramovitsh's early letters to Sholem Aleichem were first printed in *Shriftn* 1 (1928), 247–72.

After counseling Sholem Aleichem not to write novels, Abramovitsh attacks the entire genre of Yiddish romances.[8] In this statement, the word *roman* means both "novel" in general and "a novel of romance" in its more original sense. Nineteenth-century European "romances" were literary works that often contained fantastic events and a "romance" between characters.

But Sholem Aleichem chooses to interpret Abramovitsh's statement sociologically as referring to actual romances, to love affairs among the Jews. He even misquotes Abramovitsh's letter to make this reading more plausible. In his dedication playfully addressed to Reb Mendele the Bookseller, which opens the novel *Stempenyu*, Sholem Aleichem modifies the phrase "If there are romances among our people," instead quoting Abramovitsh as saying that "If there are *romances* in the *life* of our people. . . ."[9] He emphasizes the reference to actual Jewish life rather than to a literary form, and to counter Abramovitsh's condemnation, Sholem Aleichem rephrases Abramovitsh's words in a way that suits his ambitions. Instead of accepting that all romances written in Yiddish are worthless, Sholem Aleichem concedes only that love and romance are expressed differently among Jews; corresponding to the particularity of Jewish customs, he affirms, Yiddish romances must be unlike those produced by other cultures.

This was a willful misreading. Sholem Aleichem did not wish to give up the genre of the novel; thus he twisted his mentor's words to mean that *if* he wrote a romance, it should accurately reflect Jewish mores. In one sense Abramovitsh's advice was probably right: Sholem Aleichem is best remembered for his short stories rather than for his novels. Yet Sholem Aleichem spent several years early in his career atttempting to show that he was capable of writing "Jewish novels." One of these works, *Sender Blank and His Household,* he later subtitled "a novel without a 'novel'" (*a roman on a 'roman'*). This seemingly paradoxical phrase employs the double meaning of the Yiddish word *roman* and might be translated more comprehensibly as "a novel without a romance."

---

[8]For a discussion of this correspondence in relation to Sholem Aleichem's novels, see Anita Norich, "Portraits of the Artist in Three Novels by Sholem Aleichem," *Prooftexts* 4 (1984), 237–51. Norich does not point out that Sholem Aleichem misquotes Abramovitsh's letter of 28 June 1888, which enabled him to respond in accordance with his predilections.

[9]In *Di yudishe folks-bibliotek* 1 (1888), v; emphasis in original. See also SA 11: 123.

Under the sway of his predecessor, he was not yet prepared to renounce this narrative form.

When Abramovitsh advises Sholem Aleichem "not to write romances," then, he is primarily telling him not to write fanciful love stories. In Yiddish, this was the domain of popular novels (*Shundromanen*) associated with the name Shomer, the pseudonym of Nachum Meir Shaykevitsh. Abramovitsh suggests that literary "romances" should take unique forms among Jews, rather than imitate a prevalent literary genre in other European languages. The literary figure Sholem Aleichem responds, in his dedication to *Stempenyu*, that this negative advice had an unforeseen effect: it actually provoked him to write the novel. The aspiring author felt impelled to attempt exactly what the master discouraged. Hence *Stempenyu* bore the subtitle *a yudisher roman*, meaning "a Jewish novel (or romance)."[10] Sholem Aleichem's burden was to show what this could mean, correctly framed and expressed.

In his dedicatory letter, Sholem Aleichem comments: "Your words penetrated deep into my thoughts and I began to understand the extent to which a Jewish novel (*a yudisher roman*) must be different from all other novels, because Jewish life in general, and the conditions under which a Jew can love, are not the same as with all the other peoples" (SA 11: 123). Sholem Aleichem accepts Abramovitsh's view that the Jewish (or Yiddish) novel should not be a "romance" in the usual sense, because it must reflect the particular pathways of love and romance among Jews. Sholem Aleichem then states that in the novel *Stempenyu* he sought to embody Abramovitsh's insight in shaping the character of the Jewish girl, Rachel. He implies that a Jewish novel can achieve success only by thwarting the expectations of readers who desire a typical romance. Instead of allowing the reader to become engrossed in the infatuations of unreal men and women, the genuine Yiddish author must disappoint such expectations by pointing to the failure of romance in a Jewish context.

Abramovitsh repeats his grandfatherly advice in another letter written to Sholem Aleichem six months later: "You have talent, great talent. I tell you once again, expressly, writing romances is

[10]As in the title *Di yudishe folks-bibliotek*, here the adjective *yudish* signifies "Jewish" rather than "Yiddish," since it had not yet become a widely accepted term designating the language.

not for you. Your genre is something else entirely. Where you describe life, it is a pleasure to read. There is wit and humor. But where you play out a love story, nothing comes of it" (letter of 17 January 1889, reprinted in MB 163). Abramovitsh admires Sholem Aleichem's wit and humor so long as he describes realistic situations of life, but Abramovitsh contends that Sholem Aleichem spoils his more legitimate effects when he employs fantasy and emulates the popular romances of his day. In Abramovitsh's own first five novels, only *Fishke the Lame* contains hints of a love story, and even this is framed within a sympathetic description of the life of the poor.

Abramovitsh's directives to his literary grandson transcend mere private advice; at issue is the proper quality of the emerging Yiddish tradition. Abramovitsh employs irony, parody, and first-person narratives to wield satiric social criticism. In a related vein, he respects Sholem Aleichem's effective "wit and humor." The problem is that *romance* casts an unreal haze over the actual conditions of Jews in Eastern Europe, whereas one of Abramovitsh's stated goals was to show their grim situation as clearly as possible.[11] Hence Abramovitsh discourages Sholem Aleichem from slipping into an unsuitable genre.

Sholem Aleichem essentially accepted Abramovitsh's aesthetic views and incorporated them into an unusual prose piece. In his devastating mock trial and literary polemic entitled *Shomer's Trial* (*Shomer's mishpet,* 1888), Sholem Aleichem passed judgment on the bestselling works of Nachum Meir Shaykevitsh, who published under the name Shomer. Although he continued to write novels after 1888, Sholem Aleichem publicly renounced the genre of the popular novel, the *shundroman,* and affirmed his commitment to the higher goals championed by Abramovitsh. The venom of this attack may have derived, in part, from Sholem Aleichem's self-critical awareness that he had been guilty of similar offenses.[12]

Another dimension of the relationship to Abramovitsh emerged in 1889, after Sholem Aleichem sent the manuscript of his second so-called "Jewish novel," *Yosele the Nightingale* (*Yosele*

---

[11]See Abramovitsh's letter of 1885, translated from Russian, in MB 131–34.

[12]See Sholem Aleichem's earliest love stories, discussed by Dorothy Bilik in "Love in Sholem Aleykhem's Early Novels," *Working Papers in Yiddish and East European Jewish Studies* 10 (1975), pp. 1–20. Sholem Aleichem's juvenilia were reprinted in *Ale verk* (Moscow: Der emes, 1948), vol. 1.

solovey), to Y. H. Ravnitzky in Odessa. Ravnitzky recalls that "in *Yosele the Nightingale* there were a few passages which, as I read them, seemed as if they had been copied from Reb Mendele, and I soon pointed this out to the author." Sholem Aleichem's response showed a new striving for independence: "*As far as I can tell,* there is no imitation of the grandfather, I swear it righteously. But should you still find that it repeats itself, I beg very emphatically that you either throw them out [that is, the imitative passages] or revise them; just indicate to me first what and where" (*Tsum ondenk fun Sholem Aleichem,* p. 54). Sholem Aleichem insists that there is a significant difference between following (*nokhfolgn*) and imitating (*nokhmakhn*) Abramovitsh. Another problem arises with respect to one of Abramovitsh's widely acknowledged strengths, the description of natural scenes. Ravnitzky complained about the weakness of Sholem Aleichem's descriptions, and he received this answer: "To tell you the truth, I wanted to describe nature *well;* I was simply afraid it would come out imitative of [literally "danced-after," *nokhgetantst*] the grandfather" (ibid.). At one and the same time, Sholem Aleichem followed in Abramovitsh's footsteps and feared that his writing would appear imitative, like an unoriginal and outmoded dance.

A further skirmish between grandfather and grandson occurred in 1890, when Sholem Aleichem acted as Abramovitsh's literary editor.[13] *The Jewish Popular Library* was to print a preface in the voice of Mendele the Bookseller, and the text proved unsatisfactory. Sholem Aleichem wrote to Abramovitsh that the use of obscure Hebrew expressions would make this preface incomprehensible to the general public; moreover, it was too critical of those who had suffered misfortunes. This reaction suggested his drift away from the type of satire employed by Abramovitsh. Still claiming to be an obedient grandson, Sholem Aleichem offered to rewrite the work.[14] The problem was resolved only by Sholem Alei-

---

[13]This editorial quibble was preceded by a similar incident in 1888, regarding Abramovitsh's new version of *The Magic Ring.* See Abramovitsh's letter to Sholem Aleichem of 20 June 1888 (MB 154–55), discussed by Dan Miron in *Der imazh fun shtetl: dray literarishe shtudies* (Tel Aviv: I. L. Peretz farlag, 1981), pp. 54–55.

[14]This may have been an adaptation from the Hebrew story "Be-seter ra'am" of 1887 (see the letter of 14 January 1890, in *Tsum ondenk fun Sholem Aleichem,* p. 84).

chem's bankruptcy, which laid to rest his plans for publishing a third volume of *The Jewish Popular Library.*

SENDER BLANK AND HIS HOUSEHOLD

Most pertinent to Abramovitsh's specific influence on his "grandson" are Sholem Aleichem's three major novels from the late 1880s: *Sender Blank, Stempenyu,* and *Yosele the Nightingale.* These works illustrate some direct lines of influence that run from Abramovitsh "the grandfather" to Sholem Aleichem "the grandson," including examples of parody. All three titles are the names of central male characters in the stories (like Abramovitsh's *Fishke the Lame* of 1869 and 1888)—yet all three novels break with the conventions of European "romance," even when they verge on becoming love stories, for their predominant goal is satire rather than seduction.

Sender Blank and His Household, the title of the canonical 1903 second edition, was first published in 1888 as *Reb Sender Blank and His Highly Esteemed Family (Reb Sender Blank un zayn fulgeshetste familie).* The original subtitle called this book "a novel without a love story" (*a roman on a libe*), while in his revised second edition Sholem Aleichem subtitled it "a novel without a 'romance'" (*a roman on a 'roman'*).[15] Irony is implicit in the original title, which refers to the "highly esteemed" (*fulgeshetst*) family although the novel pointedly uncovers its lowly motives and manners. At regular intervals, the narrator inserts humorous chapter headings and draws attention to the process of narration through self-conscious remarks. Such practices follow a literary tradition of eighteenth- and nineteenth-century authors such as Henry Fielding and Nikolai Gogol. On the issue of romance, Sholem Aleichem's narrator comments: "I see that my readers will guess that there is probably a beautiful girl involved, and Marcus is deeply in love . . . No! You must remember that my novel is 'a novel without a romance'" (*a roman on a ro-*

---

[15] The first edition was *Reb Sender Blank un zayn fulgeshetste familie: a roman on a libe* (St. Petersburg: Israel Levi, 1888). See Sholem Aleichem's *Ale verk,* ed. N. Oyslender and A. Frumkin (Moscow: Der emes, 1948), vol. 2, p. 306, and *Sholem Aleichem's ale verk* (Warsaw: Folksbildung, 1903), vol. 2, p. 157.

man).[16] The narrator pretends to have no control over his characters when he asks, tongue-in-cheek:

> But what can I do with my young hero, if chance has not yet favored him? Can I tell him forcefully: "Go, Marcus, fall in love, write passionate letters, melt away like a candle, hang yourself, drown yourself, so that I will have material for a 'most interesting novel'"? (Ibid.)[17]

Sholem Aleichem parodies the prevailing novelistic conventions that call for stereotypical events and mocks the popular authors who advertise "most interesting" wares on their title pages. At the same time that he asserts his awareness of such conventions, he affirms his commitment to other principles; Sholem Aleichem implies that Jewish life does not possess such melodrama as is contained in books like Goethe's *Sorrows of Young Werther.*

Ironic distance from popular novels is apparent from the start of *Sender Blank,* when Sholem Aleichem entitles his first chapter, "The Curtain Rises—and the Comedy Begins." Mocking the very conventions he assumes, the narrator writes: "All morning long, on the finest street of the city N. (thus begin all novelists, and thus I too begin), near a great two-storied wall, there arrive and depart carriages and cabs with diverse people; the passengers spring out and pay the coachman liberally, without haggling" (9). Except for the parenthetical remark, this sounds like the opening of any late-nineteenth century realist novel. Sholem Aleichem is not, however, willing to let the conventions stand uncontested. To write a novel he must follow European standards, but his antipathy to the novels by Shomer precludes any full-fledged acceptance of novelistic norms. Hence he takes away with one hand what he gives with the other: "thus begin all novelists, and thus I too begin." Rather than

---

[16]Translated from *Sender Blank un zayn gezindl,* in *Ale verk fun Sholem Aleichem* (New York: Folksfond Edition, 1917–23), vol. 11, p. 46; henceforth cited by page alone. This posthumous edition was based on Sholem Aleichem's 1903 version, which he revised extensively from the 1888 text. It was first issued in *Sholem Aleichem's ale verk* (Warsaw: Folksbilding, 1903), pp. 157–267. The original work has never been reprinted, but the editors of Sholem Aleichem's *Ale verk* (Moscow: Der emes, 1948), vol. 2, quote at length from passages that were omitted in the later text.

[17]These metafictional passages derive from the second edition of *Sender Blank* that was printed in *Sholem Aleichem's ale verk* (Warsaw: Folksbildung, 1903), vol. 2, p. 195. For a related discussion, see Shmuel Niger, *Sholem Aleichem,* p. 27.

merely use a standard opening scene, Sholem Aleichem draws attention to the fact that he is just pretending to do so. This dishonorable mention pokes fun at the seriousness with which other novelists employ mimetic conventions. Sholem Aleichem thus follows novelistic conventions at the same time that he calls attention to them and so places them in question.

As the chapter proceeds, we understand that the titular character Sender Blank is lying on his deathbed and that his critical condition is the occasion for these visits. From the outset, this situation raises issues of wealth, power, and social class. Sholem Aleichem's narrator shows his sympathies and preferences when he quickly turns from the wealthy family to the perspective of the house servants. The second chapter continues the dramatic metaphor with its heading, "The Actors Perform Markedly Well." At first this might suggest a self-congratulatory tone on the part of the author. Once again, however, irony surfaces: the "good" acting is only the hypocrisy of Sender Blank's family. Throughout the book, the narrator maintains this jocular tone and employs irony at the expense of a bourgeois household, simultaneously keeping his distance from novelists by mixing the novelistic conventions with hints of other genres.

By the end of the work, *Sender Blank* assumes a dramatic form and reaches its climax on the eve of Sender's death—when the "highly esteemed" family shows its true colors by playing cards and gambling late into the night. But since social satire is only one dimension of the book, Sholem Aleichem's narrator also takes this opportunity to parody the novelistic genre. He divides the ninth chapter into five theatrical acts, as if withdrawing his hand from the scenes they enact (98–105). Nevertheless, several introductory paragraphs in this chapter accentuate his irony: "It is a pleasure for me to have the opportunity to begin this chapter as would a genuine novelist, and to present my dear reader with heart-rending scenes and moving images, like all my friends, the novelists" (94). In a seemingly endless run-on sentence, the narrator subsequently shifts from mock-praise of his fellow writers to a fantasy in which all of their books are carted off and sold for paper.

The narrator next turns to the situation of the reading public, which will eventually realize that it has been duped by melodramatic writing. In the ninth chapter, he complains of popular Yiddish novels that "have about as much in common with Jewish life as you have with the Shah of Persia."[18] Because literary tastes remain corrupt, however, the narrator concedes that "we will also try just for a minute to follow the fashion and give the reader a romantic scene" (95). Sholem Aleichem then describes a stereotypical summer night with its pale moon, stars like diamonds, and silent earth. The narrator recalls his walk on such a moonlit night, in search of inspiration for his novel. Even here Sholem Aleichem's "Jewish novel" resists becoming like the scorned romances, instead only referring to the clichés it seeks to avoid. Adapting an idiom from current Anglo-American philosophy of language, we may say that Sholem Aleichem's work *mentions* the conventions of romance but declines to *use* these conventions in earnest. The satire attacks both bourgeois Jewish society and the fictions it has helped to spawn.

STEMPENYU

In *Stempenyu: A Jewish Novel* (*Stempenyu: a yudisher roman*, 1888), Sholem Aleichem tries to satisfy Abramovitsh's demands while continuing to question the novelistic genre. He dispenses with the usual elements of romance in order to produce Jewish fiction that supposedly reflects Jewish life. As Meir Viner writes, Sholem Aleichem was deeply impressed by Abramovitsh's "demand that literature must not represent imagined heroes and situations according to a traditional novelistic scheme, but the true, genuine reality of popular life."[19] In his dedicatory letter addressed to Mendele the Bookseller, Sholem Aleichem emphasizes that his Jewish novel is "truly taken from life," yet facilitated by fantasy concerning the character of Stempenyu (124).[20] Indeed, the author's younger brother recalled that many of his fictional charac-

---

[18]Sholem Aleichem omitted this passage from the second edition of *Sender Blank*. See *Ale verk* (Moscow: Der emes, 1948), vol. 2, note on p. 332.

[19]M. Viner, "Vegn Sholem-Aleichem's humor," in *Tsu der geshikhte fun der yidisher literatur in 19-tn yorhundert (etyudn un materialn)* (New York: YKUF, 1946), vol. 2, p. 340.

[20]Translations are based on *Stempenyu: a yidisher roman*, in *Ale verk fun Sholem Aleichem* (New York: Folksfond Edition, 1917–23), vol. 11; cited by page alone. For a partial English translation entitled *Stempeniu: A Jewish Romance*, see Joachim Neugroschel, *The Shtetl* (New York: Overlook, 1989), pp. 287–394.

ters were based on actual people who lived in their home-town.[21] Sholem Aleichem further establishes continuity with Abramovitsh's fictional world when he writes that Stempenyu is well-known "in your villages of Gnilopiatsk, Tsviatshitsh, and Tuneyadevke" (124). These intertextual references to Abramovitsh's fictional towns place *Stempenyu* on the proper literary map.

Sholem Aleichem continues his explanatory justification of the novel by describing its three main characters as "*the Jewish artist Stempenyu* with his fiddle, *the Jewish girl Rachel* with her beauty and Jewish honesty, and *the Jewish woman Freydl* with her commercial spirit and her trembling over every cent—each one with a separate world" (125). In the construction of the book, Sholem Aleichem admits, he has not entirely followed Abramovitsh, who would have included "a 'Story About a Story,' a 'Story in a Story,' and 'The Story Itself'" (126). The first and third of these headings are directly taken from Abramovitsh's *The Magic Ring* (concurrently printed in an expanded version in *The Jewish Popular Library* of 1888). Sholem Aleichem does not attempt to vie with the popular prefaces by Mendele the Bookseller; he does, however, introduce narrative commentary at several points in the story.

One of Sholem Aleichem's innovations in *Stempenyu* is his effort to convey the life and lingo of klezmer musicians. The dialogue between Stempenyu and another musician is so packed with non-Yiddish words that Sholem Aleichem appends footnotes to gloss them.[22] This device adds to the particularity of the Jewish artist-hero. Equally striking is Stempenyu's role as a wedding musician. His fiddle sounds mournful tones that seem to address all the women present: "Stempenyu stood in front of the bride and held a sermon on the fiddle, a fine, long, moving sermon, about the free and happy life of the bride until now . . . and about the dark, bitter life that awaits her" (137). This seductive tune places him squarely in a romantic tradition, but Sholem Aleichem does not permit him to carry through a romantic intrigue.

---

[21]See Volf (Vevik) Rabinovitsh, *Mayn bruder Sholem-Aleichem: zikhroynes* (Kiev: Melukhe-farlag far di natsionale minderhaytn in USSR, 1939), pp. 189–202. We must, of course, view such identifications with a measure of skepticism.

[22]This is the case in both the original edition of 1888 and in the canonical Folksfond Edition (SA 11: 135–36).

As a notorious womanizer, Stempenyu is a paradoxical enter-
tainer at weddings because he enlivens the festive occasion while
hinting at its folly. He is immediately attracted to one of the wedding guests, Rachel, and he attempts to reach her through his
melody. She, in turn, "stands and listens to the enchanting songs,
to the rare tones, and doesn't understand. Something pulls at her
heart and strokes her soul" (138–39 and, modified slightly, 143).
The novel represents Rachel's innocent efforts to maintain her
virtue and her marriage, in the face of Stempenyu's efforts to se-
duce her.

Stempenyu the klezmer musician has a charm that likens him
to Sholem Aleichem the writer, and in this sense the book is self-
reflexive. Yet Sholem Aleichem makes his book a "Jewish novel"
rather than a pulp romance by showing his readers how to resist
the appeal of sentimental romances in life or literature. The novel
about a Jewish musician thus contains a message for Jewish writers about their legitimate and illegitimate strategies. On the surface, then, Sholem Aleichem writes a love story about Stempenyu
and Rachel; he simultaneously undermines this plot and provokes
a reexamination of the entire literary genre.

Stempenyu begins to transform the romance genre by generalizing its characters, pointing to them as representative Jewish
types. For instance, Rachel follows the usual habits of Jewish dress
(151), and her friend Chaya-Etel has a typical life story, "the biography of many Jewish girls" (158). The latter has experienced a
roman, a love affair with a sad ending; Chaya-Etel's story adds to
Rachel's maturity: "True, Rachel knew nothing of heroes, of romances. . . . Rachel grew older by a few years thanks to Chaya-
Etel with her Jewish romance" (164).

The novel satirizes the way of life among Rachel's in-laws,
ranging from matters of food (168) to failures of communication
(169–71). A dialogue between the young woman and her husband
evinces their estrangement from one another. Rachel asks:

—What is it, Moyshe-Mendl?
—What, "what is it"?
—What are you looking at?
—Who's looking?
—You're looking.
—I'm looking?
—Who else? (170–71)

As their setbacks lead Rachel to search for more exalted exchanges, she resembles Jewish readers who escape from their un-
satisfying daily lives into the "most interesting" novels Sholem
Aleichem ridicules.

The satire strikes against both the bourgeois Jewish family and
the bohemian Jewish musician. Attempting to inspire a "romance," Stempenyu writes a love-letter to Rachel. While its hilari-
ous misspellings make it untranslatable, a rough English equivalent might read:

> My deerest Angle from heven when i saw yur brite form i became
> brite an mine ayes an my hart burn in a brite fire from redy lov
> for you my sole yur heven ayes dru me to yur brite form from
> first site you are my life the life of mine hart an don sleep an
> dreem of you but the brite sonne is dark an mine ayes lov you like
> mine own life. (181)

In this parody of the romance genre, nothing could be more germane than a spoof on the illiteracy of a would-be romantic hero.
Stempenyu poses as a kind of Jewish Casanova who breaks hearts
in every town. Yet in Sholem Aleichem's unconventional Jewish
novel, the conventional hero must fail in his quest; lacking education, the musician is insufficiently versed in Yiddish literacy, and
his failure as a writer justifies his failure to win Rachel's heart.
Stempenyu's dismal attempt to produce a high-sounding epistle
parallels the failure of many Yiddish writers in their overblown
imitations of European fiction. Moreover, because the European
novel has origins in the epistolary form, Sholem Aleichem parodies this genre at the same time that he satirizes the illiterate
musician.

Sholem Aleichem hovers between melodrama, psychology, and
satire in his undoing of the traditional romance. He expresses
mock-horror as he represents Rachel's conscience-stricken thoughts
in the third-person indirect style: "The pious Rachel, who in all
her life never neglected a single thread of Jewishness, never transgressed the most insignificant of all laws for Jewish women,
Rachel, a Jewish woman who reads the Bible in Yiddish, has a
strange man in her thoughts, receives a letter from him, meets
him" (215). Sholem Aleichem's narrator leads the reader along the
more familiar pathways of romance, but only up to a certain point.
Then he shatters the illusion with a self-conscious remark:

Readers who are accustomed to "most interesting novels" have suffered enough until now from this novel, which contains not a single moving scene or event. No one shoots himself, no one poisons herself. One meets not a single duke or marquis. One sees only simple folk, lowly musicians and ordinary Jewish women. These readers no doubt expect the familiar, dark Saturday night; they are waiting for the curious, piquant scene on Monastery Street. (225–26)

The narrator rudely disillusions such eager readers, telling them that "there will be no curious, piquant scene" (226). Although the reader may have been corrupted by other novelists, Rachel has no idea of such things: she has "never read any novels and has never known anything of love stories, except for the story of her friend Chaya-Etel" (ibid.). Hence she slips out of Stempenyu's seductive clutches and returns to her settled life.

Sholem Aleichem's fiction disrupts novelistic expectations. As a customary romance, *Stempenyu* might be simply a story of disappointed love, but instead this novel contains a derailed love story. In other words, the reader is both romanced and cured of the desire for romances. Encoded in the text, our progress toward a more enlightened literary taste is part of the plot.

As the novel leaves sentimental temptations behind and nears its conclusion, the narrator anticipates some readers' dissatisfaction: "A quiet repast! the reader says, obviously far from satisfied, since he has been raised on those 'most interesting' romances where one hangs oneself, drowns oneself, poisons oneself, shoots oneself, or where a teacher becomes a duke and a servant becomes a queen" (241). This narrator, like the narrator of *Sender Blank* who apologizes for Marcus' failure to fall in love, draws his justification from social realities: "What should I do if there are no dukes or princesses among us? Among us there are simple Jews, simple women, Jewish girls, and Jewish musicians" (ibid). Again, the implicit claim is that this Jewish novel is closer to reality and truer to life than are common romances. Cheap novels may have captured the imagination of many readers, but Sholem Aleichem attempts to reeducate the public.

YOSELE THE NIGHTINGALE

Sholem Aleichem's next "Jewish novel," *Yosele the Nightingale*, was published with the second volume of *The Jewish Popular Li-*

brary (1889). Twice the length of *Sender Blank* and *Stempenyu*, it is more ambitious in other respects as well. Rather than draw from the contemporary love story, this book takes the shape of a *Bildungsroman*, a novel of growth and education. We follow the maturation of Yosele, an aspiring cantorial singer from an impoverished family. In contrast to Sender, who is wealthy but struggling to overcome the emptiness suggested by the name "Blank," Yosele strives to merit his nickname "the nightingale" (*solovey*).

The plot of *Yosele the Nightingale* resembles that of the best Yiddish and Hebrew novels from the 1860s: Abramovitsh's *The Little Man* (*Dos kleyne mentshele*, 1864–65) and Peretz Smolenskin's *A Wanderer on the Paths of Life* (*Ha-to'eh be-darkhei ha-chaim*, 1868–71). Both of these Enlightenment novels employ the first-person form to retell a life story, and the latter includes a pertinent section dealing with a traveling boys' chorus. Yosele somewhat resembles Abramovitsh's heroes of the 1870s. Like Isrolik in *The Nag*, Yosele aspires to a better life than the one available to him in his small town. Like Benjamin the Third, Yosele "was never down to earth; his thoughts and imagination always carried him to the skies" (59).[23] The novel illustrates the perils associated with romantic fantasy. Formally, Sholem Aleichem's *Yosele the Nightingale* takes the European *Bildungsroman* as its point of departure, and the narrator is less immediately compelled to question his prototype than in the case of popular romances. Compared to his other parodies, this appropriation involves a greater measure of repetition and imitation with a lesser degree of critical distance.

Sholem Aleichem had not fully liberated himself from the romance genre Abramovitsh found inappropriate to a Jewish novel. Yosele spends three years as an apprentice to Mitzi, a famous cantor and choral leader, before returning home to Mazepevke and preparing for further travels. Then, at the age of sixteen, he meets his childhood friend Esther. Yosele and Esther are inspired by the thought of marriage, and the narrator hastens to distinguish their simple ideas of romance from fantastic, made-up romances (86). The narrator, skeptical of literary models, insists that his characters need no clues from novels because nature guides them

---

[23]Translations are based on *Yosele solovey: a yidisher roman* in *Ale verk fun Sholem Aleichem* (New York: Folksfond Edition, 1917–23), vol. 14; cited by page alone. An English translation is *The Nightingale: Or, The Saga of Yosele Solovey the Cantor*, trans. Aliza Shevrin (New York: New American Library, 1985).

(102). Yosele travels through fictionalized Jewish towns like those in Abramovitsh's novels, some of which are mentioned by name. We then lose sight of him, as do Esther and the townspeople of Mazepevke, and we learn of his exploits from his letters. The letters gradually taper off and Yosele disappears entirely. The trajectory of this book follows a familiar romantic course from love to separation, disappointment, and tragedy.

Arranged marriages play a central and tragic role in *Yosele the Nightingale,* as they do in Abramovitsh's *Fishke the Lame.* In a "Jewish novel," this time-honored practice is the predictable antithesis to romantic love. The battle between self-determination and parental guidance, in the form of arranged marriages, becomes one of Sholem Aleichem's primary themes in the later Tevye stories.

Literary influences dominate more than the style and structure of this novel: even the characters are subject to the influence of novelistic prototypes. During his travels, Yosele receives many offers of promising matches, but he initially remains faithful to Esther. In a stereotypical fashion, the plot thickens when a wealthy widow, Perele, encounters Yosele. Her chambermaid, Leah, indirectly brings about Yosele's fall by infecting her mistress with fantasies drawn from romances. When Perele elicits her perceptions of Yosele, Leah responds: "What should I say? . . . He is certainly handsome as the morning star, like that Solomon who is described in the novel: tall in stature, well-built, and with blonde hair" (123). The narrator explains that Leah "liked to read story-books that are inscribed on their title pages: 'a most interesting romance; reproduction forbidden'" (124). The irony is that such readers reproduce similar romances in their lives. Leah, for instance, sees her own fiancé as "an angel, tall in stature, well-built, and so she 'loved' him, just as it is described in those 'romances' (*romansen*) she reads" (ibid.). As in *Don Quixote,* the plot we are reading is guided by the antiquated literature its characters enjoy.

From a slightly higher social perspective, Perele disdains her servant's romances, yet she too falls prey to their charm after Yosele visits her town. A *shidekh* is hastily arranged and Yosele forgets Esther long enough to be married to Perele. The episode resembles a passage in Henry Fielding's *Tom Jones* (Book 9, chapter 5), and Sholem Aleichem even makes use of an ironic chapter heading similar to those employed by Fielding: "He Falls Into the Trap and Looks Around a Little Too Late" (139). Perele's own happiness derives from the pages of romance: she is enchanted by

"the single thought that such a 'hero,' an 'angel' whom one encounters only in a novel, is *hers*" (143). When the fog clears, Yosele
finds himself in a muddy hut rather than in a palace, and Perele
turns out to be an ordinary market woman (146–48). The song-
bird *solovey,* Yosele the Nightigale, turns into "a bird locked in a
cage" (147).

The remainder of the novel centers around Yosele's efforts to
extricate himself from the trap that was so cleverly sprung in the
romance tradition. He returns home to Mazepevke only to find
Esther betrothed to another man. Yosele finally rises to the occasion and makes an impassioned speech befitting the hero of a
romance, but the Jewish woman remains faithful to tradition and
to her new husband (244–47). Like a true romantic hero, Yosele
then becomes dangerously ill and loses his senses (255). A short
epilogue reviews the characters and concludes by portraying
Yosele as a beggar and madman. Children shout after him, taunt-
ing him with his youthful aspirations to become a singer. The
anti-hero of the book confronts and succumbs to the hazards of
romance, an art-form that appears unsuited to and destructive of
Jewish life.

SHOLEM ALEICHEM'S AESTHETICS

Sholem Aleichem published "A Letter to a Close Friend" in the
second volume of *The Jewish Popular Library* (1889). This letter
addresses several objections that were raised in response to *Stempenyu.* Specifically, Sholem Aleichem discusses the character of a
"Jewish novel" as it should reflect the character of the Jews. In
addition, he justifies his portrayals of the klezmer musician Stempenyu and of the cantor Yosele, who fall short of expectations for a
novelistic "hero." His final thesis is that lofty moralism is unsuited
to today's novels, which must instead provide a true picture of the
world.

First, Sholem Aleichem conveys his friend's skeptical query
using language that parodies the question in the Passover Seder,
"How is this night different from all other nights?" The unnamed
friend has asked Sholem Aleichem: "How is a *Jewish* novel different from all the other novels in the world?"[24] Based on the univer-

---

[24]"A briv tsu a gutn fraynt," *Di yudishe folks-bibliotek* 2 (1889), 304. Henceforth cited by page alone; emphasis in Sholem Aleichem's original text.

salistic ideology of the Enlightenment, his scholarly friend argues: "As long as physiology has not yet explained that the Jew has been created with a different heart, with a different kind of blood, with a different brain and nerves, I will not understand what is and what is not a *Jewish* novel" (304). Sholem Aleichem dismisses this physiological retort by explaining the *cultural* distinctiveness of Jewish life. At the same time, he locates the basis of his aesthetics in social practice. Since Jewish life is distinct, he asks, "Why won't one understand that the novel in which this life is depicted must also have a different appearance?" Thus Sholem Aleichem claims that his characters are drawn from "genuine Jewish life" and reflect this particularity. His heroine Rachel, for example, shows that a "romance" among Jews can be distinctly Jewish.

Sholem Aleichem states that "Rachel is first and foremost a *Jewish* girl . . . who must love *in accordance with Jewish law*" (ibid.). This differentiates her from a romantic heroine among other peoples who, "for the sake of her desire, her whim, her infatuation with someone, can do without everything that is beloved and holy and dear to her" (305). The Jewish heroine, in contrast, subordinates her desire to higher beliefs and obligations; as a result the Jewish heroine, like the Jewish novel, must frustrate expectations of wild surrender and social disruption. This is also what enables Sholem Aleichem to write a novel without a love story, as indicated by the subtitle of *Sender Blank*. Nineteenth-century Jewish romance, it appears, is always a frustrated affair, which justifies Sholem Aleichem's penchant for novels that frustrate the reader's expectations. Nevertheless, the successive rebellions of Tevye's daughters—not to mention the free-spirited behavior of Sholem Aleichem's pupil and future wife, Olga Loyev—show that the younger generation was indeed susceptible to romance.

Second, Sholem Aleichem refers to criticisms of his anti-heroes Stempenyu and Yosele. His initial response is that they are not so lowly as they might appear, since "such a talent as *Stempenyu*, among other people, might have become a great artist" (306). Moreover, Sholem Aleichem explains his ambition to reach the Jewish masses with his novels; in order to guide them to a higher world, he believes, he must begin at their level: "Writing for the people and speaking to them in their tongue, one must give them such scenes, and represent such characters, as are quite familiar to them; that is, the heroes must be taken from their sphere, from their level, from the *people themselves*" (307). Sholem Aleichem combines didactic goals with admiration for the Jewish masses, saying that there are more heroes among them than among the "intelligentsia" (308).

Third, Sholem Aleichem answers objections concerning the lack of moral teaching in his novels: "A hero—they say—must be able to serve as a model by virtue of his character, with his honesty, nobility, goodness" (308). Sholem Aleichem responds that a novel is not a sermon, and that contemporary novels are not what novels once were. Whereas novelists formerly wrote about imaginary heroes, "nearly angels, or instead . . . nearly demons" (309), literary fashions now favor realism: "today the public demands that all be in the *path of nature*. . . . A *contemporary* novel must give us only what life gives us" (ibid.). In place of moral teaching, today's novels must be a "mirror, in which everyone can find the reflection of genuine life" (309). In short, Sholem Aleichem claims that his "Jewish novels" hold a mirror to Jewish life. He asserts that he has shown Jewish heroes and heroines as they in reality exist, rather than as fantasy would have them be. As Jewish life in Eastern Europe underwent rapid transformations in the late nineteenth century, the changes affecting this community became a central theme in Sholem Aleichem's Tevye stories.

Shomer's Trial, or the Jury Trial of All Shomer's Novels (*Shomer's mishpet, oder der sud prisyazhnykh oyf ale romanen fun Shomer*, 1888) is Sholem Aleichem's most extensive statement of aesthetic views. Written concurrently with the "Jewish novel" *Stempenyu*, this satire helped to shape Sholem Aleichem's literary identity by means of its polemic. In part, Sholem Aleichem establishes his own reputation as the debunker of Shomer (Nachum Meir Shaykevitsh), then among the most popular Yiddish novelists. The mock trial has a precedent in Sholem Aleichem's *Sender Blank*, when the narrator conceives a dream of trashy novels being carted away and made into pulp (94). Sholem Aleichem may have later regretted the severity of his attack on Shomer, for he never reprinted this work.

Shomer's Trial follows a convention that had been established by Abramovitsh's novels of the 1860s and 1870s. Like the fictional Mendele, who is supposed to have edited preexisting works by Isaac-Abraham, Hirsh Rothmann, Isrolik, and Benjamin the Third, Sholem Aleichem pretends merely to have transcribed a recent trial of the author Shomer. Thus the title page announces that the trial was "taken down in shorthand (*stenografirt*) word for word."[25] The difference is indicative: while Abramovitsh's Mendele almost always purports to edit a written document, Sholem Aleichem reproduces an oral performance. In subsequent monologues by Tevye and other fictional characters, this representation of common speech in an oral mode becomes Sholem Aleichem's distinguishing forte.

The scene in court is set with a description of the judge, attorneys, clerk, jury, and defendant with his "half a hundred books"—ironically labeled as they themselves claim to be on their title pages, "most interesting novels" (3). Also present is an audience that "consists of simple Jews from the masses, who do not understand any language except Yiddish"; there are also "women, girls, half-educated mademoiselles, and schoolboys" (4). This audience reflects Shomer's gullible readership and shows that Sholem Aleichem did not blindly idealize the Yiddish speakers of his time. The secretary breaks the silence by reading the accusation, which provides historical perspective:

> It has been nearly twenty years since Yiddish (*der yudisher zhargon*) began to show signs of becoming a language, to stir and come to life. Three giants in Poland—Abramovitsh, Linetsky, Goldfaden—and Isaac Meir Dik in Lithuania were bold enough to stand Yiddish on its feet, and to carry it over from Bible translations (*Tsene rene mit'n Taytsh khumesh*) to vital literature, from the folktale (*Bove-mayse*) to the novel, from *In Praise of the Bal Shem Tov* to poetry, and from prayers for women (*tekhines*) to satire. (4)

This brief literary history emphasizes both the originality of modern Yiddish literature and its continuity with prior Yiddish traditions. Abramovitsh was not the only important model, and it may be that Sholem Aleichem's "early career was directly influenced by Linetsky's persona, much more than by the better-known Mendele Moykher-Sforim."[26] In any event, Sholem Aleichem notes that Abramovitsh and others were able to transfer or carry over (*ariber*

---

[25] *Shomer's mishpet, oder der sud prisyazhnykh oyf ale romanen fun Shomer* (Berditchev: Jacob Sheftil, 1888); cited by page alone.

[26] See Dan Miron, "Sholem Aleykhem: Person, Persona, Presence," *The Uriel Weinreich Memorial Lecture* 1 (New York: YIVO Institute for Jewish Research, 1972), p. 39. Miron refers to H. Reminik's extensive account of the relationship between Linetsky and Sholem Aleichem: "Linetsky un Sholem-Aleichem," *Shtern* 15 (1939), number 9, 80–90.

trogn) earlier genres to new forms of expression. Satire, the last mentioned literary mode in the quoted passage, is the most pertinent to this attack on Shomer, which also makes satire one of its overt themes. Much as *The Tax* marks a turning point in Abramovitsh's career, when his Mendele persona becomes sharply satiric, *Shomer's mishpet* is a watershed in Sholem Aleichem's development as an author. The statement of accusation pertinently mentions, as a counterexample to Shomer's work, Abramovitsh's play *The Tax* (5).[27]

Alluding to Abramovitsh's period of silence between 1879 and 1886, the accusation explains that the great new writers "have lain down their weapons and the people have slowly begun to forget about them" (ibid.). During the interim, a noxious breed of authors has sprung up. They have "so spoiled the taste of the public that no one wants to touch anything other than a romance!" (6). The worst offender, the accusation continues, is Shomer; he "corrupts the finest sentiment with such frightful fantasies, with such wild ideas, with such heart-rending scenes" (7). The prosecuting attorney concludes by listing ten accusations, the most essential of which are: "1. that all the novels [by Shomer] are, pardon me, stolen from foreign literatures," "3. that the romance-maker gives no real, no genuine images of Jewish life," and "5. that the romances excite only fantasy and not morality" (7). The bad influence has damaged both public literary tastes and the literature itself (9–10).

The subsequent mock trial focuses on Shomer's romances, casting Sholem Aleichem—in the guise of the prosecuting attorney—as a literary critic. By renouncing certain features of popular romances, Sholem Aleichem shows his own colors and establishes norms for the emerging Yiddish tradition. As in Sholem Aleichem's "Letter to a Close Friend," three prominent issues relate to the oppositions between foreign and Judaic elements, fantasy and reality, immorality and morality.

The prosecution demonstrates that Shomer's romances are merely stolen from French sources, without regard to their inappropriateness when applied to Jewish life (13). They have none of the originality that characterizes the source works by Eugène Sue

---

[27]Nevertheless, Abramovitsh was not pleased by being grouped together with Linetsky, whose virulent satire bore a different stamp than his own.

and Alexandre Dumas, and they sink into unreal fantasies (27); their satiric thrusts lack moral content (21–22), and they spoil the highest sentiment, love, by showing it in the most fantastic and sordid ways (13–14). Worst of all is the influence of Shomer's novels on the public, corrupting its morals as well as its literary taste and making it unreceptive to higher art forms.

This self-vindicating polemic against Shomer was crucial to Sholem Aleichem's evolution as an author. His underlying message was that Shomer's romances were worthless because they fail to convey a genuine picture of Jewish life. Sholem Aleichem believed that a Yiddish novel must, by its nature, reflect the lives of Yiddish speakers. Showing his commitment to this aesthetic view, Sholem Aleichem penned his early "Jewish novels" in which familiar Jewish types find their place.

The phrase "Jewish novel" (*yudisher roman*) might have initially appeared to be an oxymoron. But Sholem Aleichem's phrase secondarily connoted "Yiddish novel," which tautologically described any novel written in Yiddish. In appropriating the novelistic genre, at a distance from Abramovitsh's early novellas, Sholem Aleichem grappled with the question of how he could make it work for the emerging Yiddish tradition. He argued that the Yiddish novel should aptly reflect Jewish life and that, consequently, it should avoid the patterns that had been set by stereotypical European romances. Sholem Aleichem's early phase was his most parodic, perhaps because this intertextual mode enabled him to come to terms with his precursors.[28]

Sholem Aleichem's literary practice differs, however, from his stated theories. He claims to be guided primarily by real-life models, but he employs caricature to confront and counter literary norms. Perhaps what most distinguishes Sholem Aleichem's books as "Jewish novels" is their reliance on the intonations and articulations of everday Yiddish speech. Unlike Shomer's works that merely translated and adapted preexisting European novels, Sholem Aleichem's fiction drew inspiration from the oral, folk traditions of speech at home, in the market, or among klezmer musicians.

---

[28]Compare two related arguments about Henry Fielding, Jane Austin, and others who launched their novelistic careers with parodies: G. D. Kiremidjian, "The Aesthetics of Parody," *The Journal of Aesthetics and Art Criticism* 28 (1969), 231; Linda Hutcheon, "Ironie et parodie: stratégie et structure," *Poétique* 36 (November 1978), 471.

Sholem Aleichem has often been considered as an effortless writer. But the evolution of his work shows that he deliberately avoided the popular path of least resistance. Whereas Abramovitsh had formerly parodied Jewish communities in the 1860s and 1870s, Sholem Aleichem both satirized contemporary life and parodied popular Yiddish novels. In order to remedy the deleterious effects of writers like Shomer, Sholem Aleichem mimicked his conventions in order to upset them. Sholem Aleichem's "Jewish novels" initially appear to contain love stories of the usual sort, but their unwonted turns—and outbursts against the "most interesting novels" of the time—make them harsh critiques of prevalent literary norms. Entirely unlike customary romances, *Stempenyu* and *Yosele the Nightingale* are disappointed love stories, not stories of disappointed love.

CHAPTER 6

Tevye the Dairyman and His Daughters' Rebellion

The saga of Tevye and his daughters expresses broad social conflicts that threatened traditional Jewish life in the late nineteenth century. Love is the principal driving force while economic, political, and religious differences compete to obstruct fervent unions between men and women. In his tragi-comic mode, Tevye the Dairyman bows before changes that transform the stable world defined by his knowledge of Scripture, Talmud, Midrash, and Jewish prayer.

The Tevye stories effectively merge satiric and parodic elements. They satirize myriad social forms including the matchmaking institution, class hierarchies, political conditions, and relations between Jews and Gentiles. Sholem Aleichem's familial drama—taking the place of fantastic European romances—brings home many of the problems that confronted Jews as they entered the modern world. Ever since the Berlin Enlightenment, Jewish women showed their receptivity to secular culture, and Tevye's daughters epitomize the younger generation in late nineteenth-century Eastern Europe.

Tevye's daughters participate in broad social processes that shake the foundations of the Jewish community. At home they rebel against their father, who seems to preserve customs and beliefs as ends in themselves. Hence Tevye's daughters are essentially social reformers who take part in political upheaval by placing their own lives on the line. When Tevye discovers their innovations, he expresses dismay over the decline of the old world but accepts the disappearance of former ways with "ironic resignation."[1]

Tevye's own manner of speaking anticipates his daughters' re-

---

[1] Y. Y. Trunk coins this phase in his *Tevye un Menahm-Mendl in yidishn velt goyrl* (New York: CYCO, 1944).

bellions. His predominant mode is parody—in the extended sense of appropriation and repetition with a critical distance. In some ways like Mendele the Bookseller, Tevye the Dairyman incessantly quotes scriptural and rabbinic sources, often revising and remaking them for his own ends. Parody can operate in the service of both conservative and subversive impulses,[2] and Sholem Aleichem's Tevye illustrates these antithetical tendencies of parody in his quotations. On the one hand, Tevye's quotations reflect his obsessive reliance on the Hebrew and Aramaic locutions of traditional study and prayer. On the other hand, Tevye recycles these phrases by embedding them in his speech and freely reinterpreting them. Tevye mediates between the "high" rabbinic, masculine Hebrew culture and the "low" familial, female Yiddish culture of his wife and daughters. Y. Y. Trunk perceived feminine qualities in Tevye, but it might be more apt to observe his delicate balancing act. Whenever Tevye is on the brink of tears, responding to his daughters' misadventures, he catches himself and asserts: "But Tevye is no woman. Tevye restrains himself."[3] Tevye is an archetypal character in Yiddish fiction because his stories place traditional (male-dominated) Jewish values in direct confrontation with the forces of (female-driven) social change.

The Tevye stories draw inspiration from everyday Yiddish speech. Narrated by Tevye himself and purportedly transcribed by Sholem Aleichem, they create the illusion of spoken discourse. These stories employ oral-style monologue, which was called *skaz*

---

[2]See Linda Hutcheon, *A Theory of Parody: The Teachings of Twentieth-Century Art Forms* (New York: Methuen, 1985), especially chapter four, "The paradox of parody."

[3]SA 5: 114. Except where otherwise noted, translations from the Tevye stories are based on *Gants Tevye der milkhiker*, in *Ale verk fun Sholem Aleichem* (New York: Folksfond Edition, 1917–23), vol. 5; cited by page alone. The three seminal Tevye stories were originally published as follows: "Today's Children" ("Hayntike kinder"), *Der yud* 1 (1899), numbers 10–12; "Hodel," *Der fraynd* 2 (1904), numbers 193–96 (2–6 September); and "Chava," *Dos yudishe folk* 1 (1906), numbers 2–3 (24–31 May). See Chone Shmeruk, " 'Tevye der milkhiker'—l'toldoteha shel yetzira," *Ha-sifrut* 26 (April 1978), 26–38. See also Chone Shmeruk's forward to the Hebrew version of *Tuvya ha-chalban u-v'notav*, trans. Genia Benshalom (Tel Aviv: Ha-'asor, 1983). English versions include: *Tevye's Daughters*, trans. Frances Butwin (New York: Crown, 1949); *Tevye the Dairyman and the Railroad Stories*, trans. Hillel Halkin (New York: Schocken, 1987); and *Tevye the Dairyman and Other Stories*, trans. Miriam Katz (Moscow: Raduga, 1988).

and effectively analyzed by the Russian formalist critics, in particular Boris Eichenbaum, Dmitry Chizhevsky, and Viktor Vinogradov.[4] The formalists concentrated on *skaz* techniques of Nikolai Gogol, who wrote a generation before Abramovitsh, but they also recognized the accomplishments of Nikolai Leskov, a contemporary of Abramovitsh and Sholem Aleichem. *Skaz* was subsequently defined by Hugh McLean as "*stylistically individualized inner narrative placed in the mouth of a fictional character and designed to produce the illusion of oral speech.*"[5] This kind of prominent oral narration in Yiddish led Y. Y. Trunk to define the essence of Sholem Aleichem's monologists as "loquacity" (*baredevdikeyt*).[6] It also inspired Victor Erlich to write about the *skaz* quality of Sholem Aleichem's monologues.[7] In the Tevye stories, this oral pretense is counterbalanced by Tevye's obsessive literary allusions to the Bible, Talmud, Midrash, and prayer book.

Tevye, the most important of Sholem Aleichem's monologists, has a striking literary history. Sholem Aleichem began the Tevye stories in 1894 and continued to write them throughout the remainder of his life; the final story dates from 1914 or 1916.[8] They were not originally planned as a book, and they evolved as an episodic collection of stories rather than according to a novelistic

---

[4]See Boris Eichenbaum, "How Gogol's 'Overcoat' Is Made," and Dmitry Chizhevsky, "About Gogol's 'Overcoat,'" both contained in *Gogol from the Twentieth Century: Eleven Essays,* ed. Robert A. Maguire (Princeton: Princeton University Press, 1974), pp. 269–91 and 295–322. See also Boris Eichenbaum's "Die Illusion des *skaz*" and "Leskov und die moderne Prosa" as well as Viktor Vinogradov's "Das Problem des *skaz* in der Stylistik," in *Russischer Formalismus: Texte zur allgemeinen Literaturtheorie und zur Theorie der Prosa,* ed. Jurij Striedter (Munich: W. Fink, 1971), pp. 161–67, 209–43, and 169–207. A pertinent discussion by Mikhail Bakhtin is contained in *Problems of Dostoevsky's Poetics,* ed. and trans. Caryl Emerson (Minneapolis: University of Minnesota Press, 1984), chapter 5.

[5]Hugh McLean, "On the Style of a Leskovian *Skaz,*" *Harvard Slavic Studies* 2 (1954), 299.

[6]See Y. Y. Trunk, *Sholem-Aleichem (zayn vezn un zayne verk)* (Warsaw: Kulturlige, 1937), pp. 161–224.

[7]See Victor Erlich, "A Note on the Monologue as a Literary Form: Sholem Aleichem's 'Monologn'—A Test Case," in *For Max Weinreich on his Seventieth Birthday* (The Hague: Mouton, 1964), pp. 44–50.

[8]On the disputed date of the last Tevye story, see Chone Shmeruk, "'Tevye der milkhiker'—l'toldoteha shel yetzira," p. 26, and in particular p. 27 n.12.

scheme. Sholem Aleichem had an inkling of his accomplishment when he wrote to his friend and editor Mordechai Spektor in 1894: "Regarding your criticism [of the first Tevye story]—please don't be offended—the world will undoubtedly like it. I don't know whether this is because the world understands more than you, or because it understands nothing."[9]

Although Sholem Aleichem's Tevye is primarily an oral story-teller while Abramovitsh's Mendele is a more literary persona, in some respects the Tevye monologues derive from Mendele's prefaces. Both characters travel on horse-drawn wagons to sell their wares, and they are gregarious narrators who combine simplicity with traditionalism and book-learning. Mendele and Tevye frequently employ Hebrew and Aramaic quotations, and both are characterized by their repetition of key phrases. Mendele often repeats the self-corrective phrase, "But that's not what I'm getting at," while Tevye routinely begins each new torrent of words with, *bekitser,* "in short." Tevye always reverts to this locution just as he is about to narrate a long episode.

Sholem Aleichem's dependence on the Mendele the Bookseller model is apparent from his initial version of the first Tevye story. This short text was originally called "Tevye the Dairyman," as published in Mordechai Spektor's journal *The Home Companion* (*Der hoyz-fraynd,* 1895).[10] Even before Tevye's monologues begin, Sholem Aleichem echoes the title page of Abramovitsh's *The Travels of Benjamin the Third,* which boasts of its contents in a style that parodies popular Hebrew books of the nineteenth century. The title page affixed to the original "Tevye the Dairyman" announces that the story was "narrated by Tevye himself and transcribed word for word by Sholem Aleichem."[11] Then the text

---

[9]Letter of 24 November 1894, printed in the column entitled "Sholem-Aleichem's arkhiv" of *Der tog,* 7 October 1923, p. 8.

[10]A copy of *Der hoyz-fraynd* in the library of the Jewish Theological Seminary, containing "Tevye the Dairyman," is clearly dated 1895; compare *Guide to Yiddish Classics on Microfiche* [*Di yidishe klasikers oyf mikrofish*], ed. Chone Shmeruk (New York: Clearwater, 1980). In his "'Tevye der milkhiker'— l'toldoteha shel yetzira," p. 27 n.9, however, Chone Shmeruk gives the original date of publication as 1894. According to information provided on the verso of the title page, the volume passed the censor on 14 June 1894, but this was months before Sholem Aleichem had written his Tevye story. See his letters to Mordechai Spektor from September to November 1894.

[11]"Tevye der milkhiker," *Der hoyz-fraynd* 4 (1895), 63.

includes a letter from Tevye to the author, which recalls the epistolary traditions of eighteenth-century novels. Next Sholem Aleichem
frames Tevye's monologue by describing the speaker: "Tevye is
always ready to talk. He likes an honest saying, a parable, a bit of
Torah; he's neither a great scholar nor an ignoramus when it
comes to the fine print. In a word, Tevye is one of those village Jews
who eat good dumplings with cheese, live to ninety and have no
need for eyeglasses or false teeth, and know nothing of hemor-
rhoids or other Jewish troubles and misfortunes" (ibid., 67). Tevye
is a healthy representative of provincial Jewish life. Uncorrupted by
cities like Kiev or Odessa, he is in some ways "richer than the
richest man in Yehupetz." Sholem Aleichem's frame description
employs familiar strategies of pseudo-spontaneous narration; as he
sets the scene for Tevye's monologue, Sholem Aleichem digresses
and changes course before commenting, "but we return to Tevye
and to his story" (ibid.).

Tevye shares a number of characteristics with Sholem Aleichem's later monologists. They are generally passive, weak, beset
by difficulties, yet prepared to accept whatever befalls them. Other
characters who narrate their woes to Sholem Aleichem relate hardships involving their poverty, marriage, and the laws of *kashrut*.
Typical Sholem Aleichem characters have little to call their own
except their stories, and as they endlessly digress they indicate that
the telling is more important than the tale. In hopeless situations,
their only relief seems to come from sharing the suffering with
someone else. Despite his misfortunes, Tevye is a great affirmer of
all that occurs, combining confidence and nagging doubts in his
"ironic resignation."[12]

The three seminal Tevye tales—"Today's Children," "Hodel,"
and "Chava" (1899–1906)—revolve around the conflict between
generations.[13] This generation gap is most apparent in Tevye's
constant reliance on Scripture and Midrash, in contrast to his
children's rebellious actions. As Seth Wolitz writes, "Tevye lived in

---

[12] Y. Y. Trunk, *Tevye un Menahm-Mendl in yidishn velt goyrl*, p. 29.

[13] Y. Y. Trunk also asserts that these three stories illustrate "the central operative
motifs of the entire Tevye epic." See Y. Y. Trunk, *Tevye un Menahm-Mendl in
yidishn velt goyrl*, p. 52. In some places Sholem Aleichem gives Tevye seven
daughters, although elsewhere he has only five, as in "Lekh-lekha" where he
calls Beylke, his fifth daughter, his youngest (SA 5: 202). Compare Hillel Halkin's introduction to his translation of Sholem Aleichem's *Tevye the Dairyman
and the Railroad Stories* (New York: Schocken, 1987), pp. xvii–xviii.

a world of hierarchy, patriarchy, communal institutions, clear generational roles and arranged marriages. But this world was under two direct threats: external by market forces and anti-semitism, and internal by Western Enlightenment ideas of individualism and freedom of choice."[14] Wolitz comments that Sholem Aleichem "chose the theme of romantic love as the narrative ploy most likely to reveal the disruptive force of the new at the very heart of the traditional Jewish collective: the family" (ibid.). Whenever possible, Tevye shows his learning and escapes from troubling situations by referring to a Hebrew phrase. This peculiarity and linguistic trademark intensifies the battle between tradition and his daughters' untraditional ideas.

"TODAY'S CHILDREN"

"Today's Children" ("Hayntike kinder," 1899) begins *in medias res,* in the midst of a conversation between Tevye and Sholem Aleichem. They are discussing children, and Tevye immediately sets the tone by complaining: "Go have children, be humiliated, sacrifice yourself for them, work day and night—what's it all for?" (SA 5: 67). Tevye expresses his thoughts about children by drawing upon an ancient Hebrew context: he quotes God's words from Isaiah 1:2, "I have reared children and brought them up." This verse continues, "and they have rebelled against me." Sholem Aleichem injects humor into this passage by having Tevye use and identify with a biblical phrase spoken by God.

Tevye is an established dairyman in Boiberik, outside Yehupetz, and he expects to find suitable mates for his beautiful daughters. But this is not the way of the world—or rather, not God's way with the world: "There is a God, a God of mercy and compassion, who shows his great miracles and makes summer and winter, ascents and descents, and tells me: 'Tevye, don't get caught up in any nonsense and let the world take its own course!'" (ibid.). Tevye mixes colloquial phrases with snippets of traditional Hebrew prayer (for example, 'El rachum ve-chanun). He readily converses with God and conveys God's responses. Although he learns to expect only hard times, Tevye wishes to trust wholeheartedly in

[14]Seth L. Wolitz, "The Americanization of Tevye or Boarding the Jewish *Mayflower," American Quarterly* 40 (1988), 517.

divine providence (*hashgokhe*), and with the help of well-chosen words of wisdom he almost convinces himself to do so.

Recent critics have added to our understanding of Tevye's scriptural, talmudic, and midrashic quotations. Michael Stern disputes Frances Butwin's earlier view that most of Tevye's references are misquotations.[15] He reexamines many instances and concludes that "Tevye knows his source material, and his quotations are usually quite accurate."[16] Following Stern, Hillel Halkin states that Tevye's quotations are, in general, "accurate, apropos, and show an understanding of the meaning of the Hebrew words."[17] Yet the real issue is neither "Tevye's art of quotation" nor what Tevye purportedly knows, but instead Sholem Aleichem's art of ascribing quotations to Tevye. As an invented character Tevye has no real rhetorical strategies, and only Sholem Aleichem's devices are genuine. Although one might argue that Sholem Aleichem shows Tevye being ironic, and while it is sometimes meaningful to discuss the represented motives of a fictional character, the significance of Tevye's quotations is more closely linked to literary history than to individual psychology.

It is ultimately impossible to determine the measure of irony contained in Tevye's quotations. Sholem Aleichem incessantly places quotations in Tevye's mouth, without using them unequivocally to suggest Tevye's ignorance and without subordinating them to any single ideological slant. It would be inaccurate to say that Sholem Aleichem's Tevye always inadvertently misquotes—or, at the opposite extreme, that he always speaks ironically, with a de-

---

[15]See Frances Butwin's introductions to Sholem Aleichem's *Tevye's Daughters,* trans. Frances Butwin (New York: Crown, 1949), and *The Tevye Stories and Others,* trans. Julius and Frances Butwin (New York: Pocket Books, 1965). She writes in the former, for example: "In the fact that he misquotes more often than he quotes, and that usually his interpretation of what he is quoting is completely cockeyed, lies his all-pervading charm to the Yiddish reader . . . . The juxtaposition of a lofty phrase in Hebrew or Aramaic with a homely Yiddish phrase which is supposed to explain it but has no bearing on it whatever—that is the gist of Tevye's humor. Tevye, of course, has no idea that he is funny" (*Tevye's Daughters,* p. xv). There is at least some truth to this argument, since the incongruity of Tevye's Hebrew phrases is a key to the humor of these stories.

[16]Michael Stern, "Tevye's Art of Quotation," *Prooftexts* 6 (1986), 95.

[17]See Halkin's introduction to *Tevye the Dairyman and the Railroad Stories,* p. xxix.

liberate intention to distort. In some cases this enigma cannot be resolved, and that is part of the power of the Tevye stories. We may read Tevye as a realistically portrayed small-town character who likes to put on learned airs, but we may also see his quotations as a sophisticated literary device by which Sholem Aleichem chips away at the simple mimetic illusion. Most of all, these quotations enable Sholem Aleichem to situate his fictive world in a literary history that extends from the Bible to the nineteenth century.

Arranged marriages (*shidukhim*) are one object of social criticism in Tevye's tales, as they are in Abramovitsh's *Fishke the Lame* and in Sholem Aleichem's earlier "Jewish novels." But here Sholem Aleichem does not merely attack the matchmaking industry. Beyond his social commentary, he juxtaposes traditional expectations with contemporary events, illustrating the conflicts that arise from differences between parents' convictions and their children's actions. The inadequacy of arranged marriages is implicit in Tevye's reaction upon hearing that Leyzer-Wolf, the butcher, wants to see him. We have an inkling that his daughter Tsaytl is involved, but Tevye misunderstands: "What does he need me for so urgently? If he has in mind our fine cow, he can take a stick and knock this idea right out of his head" (SA 5: 68). The confusion continues when Tevye meets Leyzer-Wolf, who tells him that he has cast his eye on—and Tevye interrupts: "I know, I say, that you have been casting your eye on her, but it's useless for you to trouble yourself because it won't work, Leyzer-Wolf" (70). This comic mix-up intimates that the institution of matchmaking is barely distinguishable from the cattle trade.

Insofar as Tevye thinks in conventional terms, the suitability of a match depends primarily on questions of wealth and social status. Leyzer-Wolf possesses the necessary wealth, or petty bourgeois respectability (*balebatishkeyt*); he is, however, a bit short on learning and long on years. After Leyzer-Wolf clears up the confusion, explaining his interest in marrying Tsaytl, he expounds on the financial advantages. Tevye rebukes him, saying, "Excuse me, but you're speaking as if you were in the meat-market!" (73). Rejecting the mercenary dimension of marriage when it is explicitly presented, Tevye falls back on the traditional notion that suitable matches are destined to occur. Moreover, Tevye shows that he does not favor despotic parental authority when he tells the butcher, against the latter's protestations, that he must first "ask Tsaytl."

Yet the clash between meetings fated by Providence (*hashgokhe*) and those brought about by individual will (*kheyshek, rotsn*) is also the confrontation between parental guidance and children's self-determination, or between traditional practices and rebellion against them. The collision of values gives this story its title, "Today's Children," which craftily implies—in Sholem Aleichem's empathetic portrayal of Tevye's perceptions—that they are at odds with what children formerly were and ought to be.

One scene in "Today's Children" specifically recalls an analogous passage in Abramovitsh's *The Magic Ring* (1865). In his opening preface, Mendele recalls having said his prayers one morning, as he rode on his wagon, when suddenly he was jolted onto the ground by a collision. This scene recurs in Sholem Aleichem's tale, as Tevye is riding on his wagon praising God for bringing such a favorable match to his daughter: "Suddenly my horse lets himself go full speed down a slope, and before I raise my head to see where I am, already I'm lying on the ground with all of the empty pots and jugs, and the wagon on top of me!" (79). Mendele, in his scrape with disaster, takes it out on Sender; Tevye berates his horse. Sholem Aleichem again shows himself to be Abramovitsh's "grandson" by incorporating this allusive scene into Tevye's monologue.

Tevye interprets the accident as a bad omen, and he tells us that indeed it was (*kakh hava*). On the road home he meets his daughter Tsaytl who, overflowing with tears, asks him to "have pity on my youth!" (80). He has not troubled to ask her opinion of the match, and her opposition takes him by surprise. Suddenly aware of her independence, he tells her: "What need is there to cry? Say the word, no is no; no one is going to use force, God forbid, to hang an indifferent person around your neck. . . . If it's not to your liking, what can be done? Probably, I say, it's not meant to be" (80). The graphic detail of the Yiddish idiom is lost in translation. When Tevye says that "no one is going to use force, God forbid, to hang an indifferent person around your neck" he is actually using the language of butchers: "no one is going to use force, God forbid, to hang a lung and liver on your nose" (*onhengen a lung un leber af der noz*). By referring to this distasteful image, Tevye implicitly admits that the *shidekh* with a butcher was a nasty one. He literalizes the expression "lung and liver"—ordinarily used to refer to an indifferent, cold person—by suggesting that it might naturally suit a butcher with his trade in reeking inner organs.

In order to justify his daughter's uncustomary resistance to her father's plan, Tevye revises his ideas and affirms that it was apparently not meant to be or destined (*bashert*). According to tradition, "marriages are made in heaven," sanctioned by God. Since Tevye has no intention of forcing the match on his unwilling daughter, he declares that it must not have been God's will. Thus he determines destiny retrospectively. With stoical *amor fati,* he accepts that whatever has happened had to happen, while claiming that whatever he does not want to occur in the future is not meant to occur. Tevye's traditionalism is bounded by the limits of the practical that are imposed by his wife, his daughters, and the community around him.

Another genre of speech also typifies Tevye: pleading with God (*taynen mit Got*). He frames his metaphysical reflections as addresses to God and asks, for example, why God wants Tevye to suffer. Why does He run the world as He does? (81). These questions lead to broader doubts about the mundane social order. Concerning the wealthy people of Yehupetz, he asks: "Where is it written that Tevye has to work for their sake, and get up at the crack of dawn, when God Himself is still asleep? Why? So that they will have fresh cheese and butter with their coffee?" (83). As Sholem Aleichem makes Tevye his mouthpiece when he reexamines the justice of social hierarchies, he relies mainly on questions—somewhat like those posed by Abraham and Job. Tevye is sensitive enough to recognize injustice, but he is too traditional to draw pragmatic conclusions. His daughters have no such inhibitions.

Doubts about differences of class and status have captured the minds of Tevye's daughters, and the next thing he knows, a local yokel asks for Tsaytl's hand in marriage. This is a double blow to Tevye: first, because Motl is a poor tailor, while Leyzer-Wolf the butcher is the richest man in town; second, because it turns out that the young man and woman have already exchanged promises (85). The latter point is especially disconcerting: "What does that mean, *they have given each other their word?* What kind of world has this become?" (86). Although he recognizes their legitimate rights, he cannot accept this affront to parental authority. As the story ends, Tevye devises a scheme to convince the superstitious Golda, his wife, that the match to Motl is preferable. Pleading with

God takes a new form in complaints about "today's children." They are "too smart" and overturn venerable customs (91). Then again, Tevye's daughters give free expression to his own pertinent doubts about social classes and to his uncertainties about Providence.

"HODEL"

"Hodel" ("Hodl," 1904), one of Sholem Aleichem's stories that revolve around social activism, was written in the context of the events leading to the October Revolution of 1905. In this case, Hodel takes Tevye's own questions about the social order to their logical conclusion. Once again an unwanted match (*shidekh*) is in the making when the independence of "today's children" intervenes. In response to this misfortune, Tevye shows his unswerving faith: "I am, as you know, a great man of faith (*bal bitokhn*) and never have any complaints against the Eternal. Whatever He does is for the best. And, on the other hand, what good would it do to complain?" (SA 5: 95). His unresolved reflections juxtapose belief in God's justice with illustrations of possible evidence to the contrary. In one more instance of Sholem Aleichem's Tevye as a reworking of biblical motifs, this inner conflict associates him with the biblical Job.

As in his other monologues, Tevye frequently resorts to Hebrew sayings. Hebrew is his idealized reference-point, the domain of masculine rabbinic thought, while Yiddish vernacular is the matriarchal realm of the home. Golda cuts Tevye off as he spouts learned quotations, reminding him of more pertinent matters: "What do I want with Midrash? she says. We have a daughter to marry off. And after that, may the evil eye spare them, we have two more; and after those two—three more" (96). The couple enacts a comic rendition of the encounter between learning and life, or between sacred texts and everyday reality. In his unassuming way, Tevye represents the world of talmudic study, while Golda demands immediate solutions to mundane problems. Sholem Aleichem does not take sides in this confrontation, instead giving voice to both tradition and its contemporary challenges. He portrays Tevye as a sympathetic character, but he also depicts an astute Golda who is aware of his foibles.

Tevye's talk of his daughter Hodel wavers between irony, pride, and pity. He jocularly calls his daughters "fine merchandise," and in the next breath he uses a biblical phrase to describe Hodel as being "of goodly appearance" (*toyves ma're*). Drawing from the Book of Esther, Tevye shows his traditional learning and, at the same time, makes an unexpected connection to the non-Jewish world. Esther is indeed described as being *toyves ma're* (Esther 2:7), but the full Hebrew phrase quoted by Tevye actually comes from the description of Queen Vashti (Esther 1:11). This association to the foreign queen may elicit both laughter and a pertinent recognition that the match planned for Hodel conceals potential violence—like the Book of Esther.

The literary horizon of Tevye's household expands as his daughter reads widely in Yiddish and Russian. Tevye nearly always quotes ancient or medieval sources, while his daughters refer to contemporary secular writing. Tevye's second daughter, for example, is an avid reader of Yiddish and Russian books. This raises the question: "What kind of match is that, Tevye's daughter and books, since her father deals in cheese and butter?" (96). He does not understand the younger generation's affinity for education. This likens him to Isrolik's mother, in Abramovitsh's *The Nag,* who opposes her son's studious goals. A generation later, however, nothing can hinder the general drive toward enlightenment. Still, he asks his daughter's socialist friend Feferel, an impoverished student: "What's this studying? Who is studying?" (96). The class differences fade as children of tailors, cobblers, and of other craftsmen move to Yehupetz to study there. Feferel, the son of a cigarette-maker, is a specimen of this new breed.

One day Tevye meets Feferel returning from his university exams. Their discussion touches on study and social classes:

> "What," I ask, "is a boy like you studying for?"
> "A boy like me," he says, "doesn't know yet what he's studying for."
> "In that case," I say, "why does a boy like you rack his brains for nothing?"
> "Don't worry, Reb Tevye," he says, "a boy like me knows what he has to do." (98)

Later Tevye tries to persuade Feferel that university study is not befitting for children of his ilk. Feferel responds with a universalistic appeal to his rights as a human being. When Tevye suggests that Feferel shouldn't compare himself to the wealthy people of Yehupetz, Feferel agrees, placing them on a much lower plane. Tevye shares some of the new generation's socialistic ideas, and although their radicalism shocks him, Tevye is nonetheless attracted to Feferel. Somewhat like Sholem Aleichem in Sofiovke in the late 1870s, Feferel acts as tutor to Tevye's children in return for meals. As Tevye jokes, referring to the consequences of this arrangement, "An eye for an eye—a slap for a slap" (100). Here Tevye's ironic reformulation of the biblical phrase is evident. It does not challenge the scriptural source, but instead frames the present misfortune in a humorous "trans-contextualization." To replace this biblical echo, Feferel brings a new teaching: "What's mine is yours, and what's yours is mine" (101). When the subject of money arises, "he becomes full of anger and tries to convince me that money is the ruination of the world; from money, he says, all of the falsehoods in the world come into being" (ibid.). But concerning Tevye's eldest unmarried daughter Feferel voices only praise.

The plot takes a familiar turn when Tevye meets Ephraim the matchmaker. Tevye is interested to learn more about the wealthy client who wants to marry Hodel, but again he casts the matchmaking institution in an unfavorable light. Ephraim asks Tevye to bring his daughter to Boiberik for a looking-over, and Tevye mocks: "'What's that supposed to mean,' I say, 'that I should bring her along? One brings along a horse,' I say, 'to the fair, or a cow to be sold'" (104). While Tevye wishes to uphold the practice of arranged marriages, his fatherly concerns unsettle his traditionalism. Moreover, his penchant for rumination has developed in double measure among his children.

Returning home, Tevye again experiences the independence of "today's children." He spies a couple walking together and makes out that one of them is Feferel. In narrating he savors the moment of surprise: "Who is he, the shlimazl, going around with so late? I block the sun out of my eyes with one hand and take a closer look: who's the girl? Oy! Looks like—Hodel? Yes, it's her, as I'm a Jew, it's her! . . . So that's the way they've been studying grammar and reading books!" (105). This romantic consequence of private tutoring recalls Sholem Aleichem's own courtship with his student and future wife Olga—whose Hebrew name was in fact Hodel. In a private joke, Sholem Aleichem memorializes his late father-in-law's dismayed reaction to his daughter's romance with her young tutor. When Tevye greets them they are at first silent, but then Hodel tells her father to congratulate them:

> "Congratulations," I say, "and all the best. What's up? Have you found buried treasure in the forest? Or have you just been saved from some great danger?"
>
> "Congratulations are in order," he says, "because we're engaged."
>
> "What does that mean," I say, "That you're engaged?"
>
> "Engaged," he says, "don't you know what that means? It means that I'm the groom and she's the bride." That's what he says, Feferel that is, and looks me straight in the eye. (106)

The scene combines humor and pathos as a new order shatters Tevye's world; irony is his defense against expressing pain. He shows his disappointment by referring to the omitted custom of an engagement ceremony: "When was your betrothal party? Why didn't you invite me?" Tevye admits that, hidden behind his laughter, "worms gnaw at my insides" (108). He asks how there can be a match without a matchmaker or a wedding contract. When he uneasily agrees to the match, he wants to discuss practical matters of dowry, wedding attire, costs, food. Renouncing all of these traditional accoutrements, they tell him that they don't need anything, "just the wedding canopy and the ceremony" (108). This revolt in customs goes one step beyond the earlier breach in decorum when Tevye's first daughter, Tsaytl, chooses a poor tailor as her groom.

In the continuation of the monologue Feferel disappears, and weeks later Hodel learns that he has been imprisoned for subversive political activities. She resolves to join him in his distant exile. Thus Tevye loses his second daughter, subsequently heard of only in occasional letters. To close the tragi-comic story of changing morals, Tevye tells his listener Sholem Aleichem, "Let's speak about something more cheerful: what's the news of cholera in Odessa?" (118). Enlightenment ideas have indeed brought about an epidemic of changing customs.

While Tevye tries to permeate his household with the ancient lessons of the rabbis, his daughters teach him lessons of Jewish life in modern Russia. The "polyphonic" quality of Tevye's monologues arises from this embedding of disparate voices. Tevye has the first and the last word as he narrates his story to us by way of Sholem Aleichem, but Sholem Aleichem has him piece together quotations from his traditional learning with his daughters' contrary teachings from contemporary Russia.

"CHAVA"

Tevye's third and most extreme story of loss at the hands of social transformation is "Chava" (1906).[18] The potency of this tale has led successive adaptors to place it at the center of their stage and film versions of *Tevye*.[19] Tevye continues to cling to traditional Hebrew sayings as his world collapses. When the boundaries erode between the rich and the poor, the scholarly and the ignorant, or the daughters of a dairy merchant and the sons of lowly manual workers, Tevye has no choice but to let Tsaytl and Hodel take their chosen paths. In the case of Chava, however, her free choice threatens fundamental principles of Jewish life. In the continuum of assimilatory paths, perceived by Tevye from a distance, the treacherous extreme limit is intermarriage. For the first time, Tevye cannot accept the fate his daughter chooses.

From the start of his monologue, Tevye brings together the rhetoric of piety, resignation, and pathos. Following the dictates of pious acceptance, he resembles the overly passive characters in Abramovitsh's Hebrew stories of the 1880s and 1890s. He begins with the Hebrew phrase from Psalm 136, "Give thanks to God, for He is good," which he translates loosely: "Whatever God does is good." Then he adds ironically, "that is, it had better be good, because if you think you're so smart go and try to do better!" (SA 5: 121). He reviews his disappointments with Tsaytl and Hodel before he humorously portrays an exchange with the "God of mercy and compassion" who said to him: "'Wait a bit, Tevye, I'll do something to make you forget all of your sorrows.' And so it was, listen to this. I wouldn't tell this to anyone else, because the pain is great and the shame is even greater!" (122). Addressing himself to the educated author Sholem Aleichem, Tevye stands at the threshold between the religious and secular worlds. His daughters are in the process of crossing this threshold or leaving the fold.

---

[18] Y. D. Berkovitsh describes Sholem Aleichem at work on this text in *Harish'onim ki-vnei-adam: sippurei zikharonot 'al Sholem-Aleichem u-vnei-doro*, 3d ed. (Tel Aviv: Dvir, 1976), 309–11.

[19] See Ken Frieden, "A Century in the Life of Sholem Aleichem's *Tevye*," *B. G. Rudolph Lectures in Judaic Studies* (Syracuse: Syracuse University Press, forthcoming).

What good do his beautiful daughters bring, Tevye wonders, if they live in the provinces among non-Jews? He anticipates the upshot of the story when he abruptly mentions "the writer Khvedke Galagan, a tall gentile with an abundance of hair and high boots, and the priest, may his name and memory be blotted out" (123). With the clergyman he debates theological matters; this Christian leader tries to show his learning by reciting the first three words of the Hebrew Bible, while Tevye refers to Midrash. After their battle of quotations, the priest calls "Tal-mud" mere deception.

One day Tevye returns home, only to see Chava speaking with Khvedke the writer. Tevye questions her about this, asking "What do you have in common with Khvedke?" ("Vos far a mekhutn bistu mit Khvedken?" [124]). The idiomatic expression literally means "What kind of in-law are you to Khvedke?" This allusion to incongruous familial relations ominously anticipates what is about to transpire. When Chava asks whether Tevye knows who Khvedke is, Tevye responds with bitter irony. He embeds their quoted dialogue in his oral narration:

> "Who he is, I don't know, I haven't seen his letter of pedigree. But I understand that he must be descended from great men; his father," I say, "must have been either a shepherd or a janitor—or just a drunk."
> She says to me, Chava does, "What his father was I don't know and don't want to know. In my eyes all people are equal. But that he himself is no ordinary man—that I'm sure of." (124)

Sholem Aleichem depicts the conflict between Tevye's old-fashioned ideas of social hierarchy and Chava's revolutionary, universalistic beliefs. With his ironic reference to Khvedke's "letter of pedigree" (*yikhes-briv*), Tevye shows that he still thinks in terms of the letters that were formerly brought to demonstrate the status of prospective Jewish brides or grooms. At the very moment that he attempts to mock Khvedke by referring to his lowly origins, he gives an inkling that he knows where things are heading. Of course, as the retrospective narrator of his story, he does know exactly how it will turn out. But it is more germane to note, as in the case of Tevye's quotations, that Sholem Aleichem guides his rhetoric, using the words *mekhutn* (in-law) and *yikhes-briv* (letter of pedigree) to structure the narrative and anticipate future events.

When Tevye asks what manner of man Khvedke is, Chava tells him that he is "the second Gorky." Unfamiliar with the first

Gorky, Tevye asks, "Where is this sage [*tane*] of yours, what's his trade, and what kind of learned discourses does he preach?" (124–25). The humor of this passage derives from Tevye's naiveté—or irony—and his reliance on terms that normally refer to rabbinic scholars. As with Abramovitsh and Mendele, it is impossible to distinguish definitively between Sholem Aleichem's irony at Tevye's expense and Tevye's own ironic statements. After Chava shows him a picture of Gorky, Tevye says, "So that's him, your *tsadek*, Reb Gorky." A *tsadek* is a righteous, saintly man; this term is also used to name a chassidic leader; the *chassidim* often shunned all images except for portraits of famous rabbis. Thus when Chava takes a picture of Gorky out of her pocket, Tevye views him as her *tsadek*. Isolated from secular Russian culture, Tevye conceives of Gorky in more familiar terms, at the same time subjecting Chava to pointed sarcasm. Added ironies of this passage derive from the biographical facts that Sholem Aleichem was actually acquainted with the Russian author Maxim Gorky, and that during the prior year his eldest daughter married a writer (albeit from a less distant tradition), the Hebraist Y. D. Berkovitsh.

Chava attacks the separatism inherent in Tevye's worldview. She turns the tables by quoting poetical thoughts in a scriptural mode: "God created all human beings equal," she reminds Tevye, and continues: "You have a scriptural verse for everything! Maybe . . . you have a verse about why people went and split themselves into Jews and non-Jews, masters and servants, landowners and beggars?" Chava questions the underlying doctrine beneath Jewish insularity. Tevye reasons with her but concludes with dismay that his daughters have become enlightened thinkers (126). The religious conflicts resulting from enlightenment and assimilation emerge soon thereafter. The priest stops Tevye in order to inform him: "It is true . . . that you are your child's father; but you are ignorant of her. Your child aspires to another world, and you neither understand her nor do you want to understand her." The priest then explains that Chava is under his jurisdiction (*reshus*) and supervision (*hashgokhe*) (128). The priest's choice of words in the Yiddish rendering is especially significant. The word *hashgokhe* refers both to "supervision" and to "Providence"; Tevye himself affirms repeatedly that "I believe in Providence (*hashgokhe*)" (134). But in the first instance *hashgokhe* means "supervision": the priest is supervising Chava's conversion to Christianity prior to her planned marriage with Khvedke. The Christian supervision is directly at odds with Tevye's views of Jewish Providence, and no doctrinaire resolution can smooth over the discrepancy.

This development extends the pattern of his daughters' independence beyond acceptable bounds. Chava takes one step further than her elder sisters in a direction that Tevye will never accept. Golda admits that she had an inkling of what was going on, but she felt unable to tell him: "You I should tell? When are you home? . . . And when I talk to you, do you listen? When someone tells you anything, you answer right away with a scriptural verse; you stuff your head with verses and then get what's coming to you" (131). In the most explicit way, Golda denounces Tevye's continued reliance on Scripture. At every turn he quotes from Bible or Talmud, even though these works cannot extricate them from their current predicaments. Golda blames Tevye for relying too exclusively on the textual tradition and for living in a rabbinic world of pious quotations. Nevertheless, after Chava's departure from Judaism, they follow a strict custom and go into mourning for her as if she had died. Tevye tells his wife, "Let us sit *shive* as God commanded,for *the Lord gives, and the Lord takes away*" (133); Tevye "announced at home that *there shall be no remembrance* of Chava. Blotted out, that's all!" (135).

Tevye upholds traditionalism in spite of his doubts when he accidentally meets Chava in the woods one day. He resists the impulse to embrace her, instead turning away and refusing to speak with her. In Tevye's scriptural imagination, the scene echoes the Book of Numbers, chapter 22, when Bilam is riding to curse the Jews; God places an angel in his way to oppose him, and the ass swerves aside. Similarly, Tevye's horse stops short at the sight of Chava, whom Tevye perceives as an adversary. Perhaps this intertextual link hints that Tevye's decision to turn his back on his renegade daughter is as misguided as Bilam's intention to curse the Jewish people.

Sholem Aleichem does not openly mitigate the severity and finality of Tevye's decision to renounce Chava until, in his penultimate Tevye story, he engineers a reunion. When Tevye and his family are forced to leave town because of a pogrom, Chava returns and tells the family that "our exile is her exile."[20] But just as this poignant meeting threatens to become overly sentimental,

---

[20]See the story "Lekh-lekha," in *Ale verk fun Sholem Aleichem*, vol. 5, p. 218; henceforth cited by page alone.

Tevye distances himself by saying to Sholem Aleichem: "And what should I tell you, dear friend? It was exactly as it is described in your books" (219). In addition to including this self-reflexive gesture, Sholem Aleichem has Tevye end the story without resolving the family drama. Instead, the character Tevye presents his creator Sholem Aleichem with the task of completing his story: "What do you say, Mr. Sholem Aleichem? You're a Jew, anyway, who makes books and gives the world advice—so you tell me what Tevye should have done."[21] The mimetic illusion of Tevye narrating to Sholem Aleichem is jarred when the character stops and calls upon the author to finish what he has started. The saga of Tevye and his prodigal daughter ends unresolved, thrown back to Sholem Aleichem and the reader for refinishing.

Sholem Aleichem adds complexity to Tevye by presenting his confused reflections on whether he should reconcile himself with Chava. In broader terms, he wonders why Jews and non-Jews must live separately. Tevye ultimately gives up on his efforts to solve these questions "and it irks me, because I'm not clear enough, as others are, with regard to religious and secular books, to be able to find a proper justification" (138). He ingenuously assumes that there must be unambiguous explanations that he has not grasped. Continually troubled by having lost his daughter, Tevye concludes by comically blurring the boundary between fiction and reality:

> Sometimes I put on my Sabbath coat, go to the train station, and am ready to climb aboard and travel to see her, since I know where she lives. . . . I go to the ticket counter and ask for a ticket. He asks, "Where to?" I say, "To Yehupetz. . . ." He says, "I don't know of any such place." I say, "That's not my fault . . ." and I turn around and go back home. (139)

For this crucial passage that combines pathos and humor, Sholem Aleichem is again indebted to Abramovitsh. Tevye recalls Mendele the Bookseller, who breaks realist conventions at the start of *The Little Man* by saying that he stocks some copies of the newspaper *Kol mevasser*—in which the novel itself was first serialized. Now Tevye refers to Yehupetz, the fictional name used by Sholem Aleichem to name Kiev. At this juncture, however, a character in Sholem Aleichem's fictional world claims that this fictional city does not exist; hence the ticket agent slips away from Tevye's world onto another plane of being. This gives Tevye an excuse not to visit

---

[21] "Lekh-lekha," in SA 5: 220.

Chava, at the same time that it signals the fictionality of Tevye's world. After all, Tevye and his world are only fabricated from quotations, parodies, and representations of the contemporary Ukrainian-Jewish milieu.

Tevye is a symbol of the anachronistic older generation, unable to come to terms with the changes wrought by a new generation. Resisting Sholem Aleichem's art, according to the pretense, Tevye concludes his monologue by enjoining Sholem Aleichem not to "make a book" out of his story. Sholem Aleichem's supposed betrayal suggests the pseudo-realism of the story. Tevye is an intensely ironic figure in his traditionalism and resignation, and yet the irony is not always attributable to him. This ambiguity itself derives from the complex and evolving figure of Mendele the Bookseller. Sholem Aleichem sometimes uses Tevye as his mouthpiece to express satire, while in other contexts Tevye himself is satirized.

TEVYE'S QUOTATIONS

As we have seen, Tevye's use of quotations is his most characteristic feature, and it establishes a delicate balance between his colloquial speech and the traditions he strives to uphold. He thereby becomes a representative of tradition, of the Jewish attachment to Torah, and of the hybrid diversity of Yiddish with its fusion of Germanic, Hebraic, and Slavic components.[22] Tevye virtually becomes a symbol of Yiddish culture itself, entering the modern world laden with Scriptural associations and at the same time beleaguered by the contrary expectations of modernity. His wife Golda counters his old-fashioned learning with practicality, while his daughters contradict him through their rebelliousness. Like all archaic customs, Tevye's are in decline and the reader savors his hopeless efforts to maintain earlier beliefs, customs, and patterns of speech.

In his work on Abramovitsh, Meir Viner writes that "this wandering bookseller stems from the same family as the traveling dairyman. Mendele is Tevye's older brother."[23] Dan Miron disputes this filial bond by pointing out that the two characters exist

---

[22]On "hybridization" in the novel, see M. M. Bakhtin, *The Dialogic Imagination: Four Essays,* ed. Michael Holquist, trans. Caryl Emerson and Michael Holquist (Austin: University of Texas Press, 1981), especially pp. 75–78 and 358.

[23]M. Viner, *Tsu der geshikhte fun der yidisher literatur in 19-tn yorhundert (etyudn un materialn)* (New York: YKUF, 1946), vol. 2, p. 52.

on different fictional planes, since they do not "share the same dramatic status."[24] First, the scene of narration differs in kind: Tevye addresses his monologues to Sholem Aleichem, who purportedly transcribes them for us, while "Mendele's sentence is offered to our understanding and judgment without any mediation" (TD 179). Second, "as we read Tevye's monologues, they are already a thing of the past" (TD 173); in contrast, "Mendele's monologues are offered to us as they evolve" (TD 174). Miron argues that Tevye's monologues are always mediated by Sholem Aleichem, whereas Mendele's prefaces appear to reach us "without any mediation." Nevertheless, in some of Mendele's manifestations, the implied author Abramovitsh does employ traces of ironic humor that may undermine Mendele's stance.

The texts by Abramovitsh and Sholem Aleichem leave similar ambiguities, because in some passages it is undecidable whether they use irony at the expense of Mendele and Tevye, or whether Mendele and Tevye themselves are intended to appear in control of the irony. To recapitulate, then, Tevye both uses and abuses Hebrew quotations, often following them with more or less apt translations into Yiddish. In simple terms, there are two opposing views of these Hebrew appropriations. Frances Butwin initially suggested that Tevye is simply a comic figure who misuses Hebrew sources as a result of his inadequate learning. Butwin writes that Tevye's "speech is practically a series of Hebrew quotations from the Holy Books, most of which are, of course, misquotations, hilariously funny to the reader who could understand them."[25] Other critics such as Dov Sadan have rejected this view.[26] In some cases Sholem Aleichem may employ irony at Tevye's expense, meaning for us to laugh at his naiveté. But this is not the primary tone or effect of Tevye's quotations. Ruth Wisse argues that "Tevye's misquotations, puns, and freewheeling interpretations" should *not* be

---

[24]Dan Miron, *A Traveler Disguised: A Study in the Rise of Modern Yiddish Fiction in the Nineteenth Century* (New York: Schocken, 1973), p. 172; henceforth cited as "TD" by page alone.

[25]See Frances Butwin's introduction to Sholem Aleichem, *The Tevye Stories and Others*, trans. Julius and Frances Butwin (New York: Pocket Books, 1965), p. ix.

[26]See Dov Sadan, "K'mo she-ketuv: araynfir-bamerkn tsu Tevye dem milkhiker's toyre," in *Tsvishn vayt un noent: eseyen, shtudies, briv* (Tel Aviv: Israel-bukh, 1982), pp. 18–19.

taken as "proof of his simplicity and ignorance."[27] Michael Stern carries this thesis a step further and argues that "Sholem Aleichem meant his hero to be a self-conscious master in his use of quotations."[28]

Dan Miron begins with the view that Tevye's quotations "are often comically distorted and even when they are correct, his translations and interpretations of them are hilariously wrong. In any case, they never truly suit the context to which they are applied" (TD 176). Yet he also asserts that Tevye garbles his Jewish sources, "not always as is thought from ignorance, but rather intentionally with cunning charm."[29] Miron subsequently distinguishes Tevye's "attitude toward the Scriptures" from "the cunning destructiveness of Mendele." Tevye "never tries to explode the old text by quoting it":

> whatever his distortions, they are never malicious. The question whether they are intentional or unintentional is a delicate one, and in many cases cannot be settled with any certainty. There seems to be little evidence for the current notion that the comic effect of his misquotations and mistranslations stems *solely* from his ignorance, or from his genuine misunderstanding of the Hebrew and Aramaic expressions he hears and constantly repeats but is hardly able to decipher. This notion is undoubtedly correct in several specific cases, but as an overall explanation of this aspect of Tevye's comicality it is a gross simplification. A strong case can be made for a contrary notion claiming that in most cases Tevye is aware of his "mistakes"; he well understands at least a part of his quotations but chooses not to acknowledge the fact out of sheer high spirits. (177–78)

In Miron's interpretation, then, while Tevye is guilty of some unwitting malaprops, he also employs conscious distortions. In this sense he synthesizes aspects of the earlier and later incarnations of Mendele the Bookseller. In the 1860s, Abramovitsh's Mendele hovers between naiveté and irony, holding firm opinions but never wielding sharp satire. Starting with *The Tax* in 1869 and until *The*

---

[27]*The Best of Sholem Aleichem*, ed. Irving Howe and Ruth R. Wisse (Washington, D.C.: New Republic Books, 1979), p. xv.

[28]Michael Stern, "Tevye's Art of Quotation," *Prooftexts* 6 (1986), 79.

[29]See Dan Miron's entry on Sholem Aleichem in *Encyclopaedia Judaica* (Jerusalem: Keter, 1972), vol. 14, p. 1280.

Travels of Benjamin the Third in 1878, however, Mendele fully controls his satiric thrust. Sholem Aleichem's Tevye simultaneously expresses traditional views and persistent doubts about them. Instead of fixing Tevye in a single role as either an ingenu or satirist, Sholem Aleichem allows him traces of both. This permits Sholem Aleichem to take advantage of comic effects both at Tevye's expense and at the expense of his surroundings. As a result, the reader alternates between laughing at Tevye and laughing with him.

Hillel Halkin provides numerous comments on Tevye's quotations in the notes to his translation of *Tevye the Dairyman*.[30] In one passage, with regard to *The Ethics of the Fathers,* he notes that "Tevye's rhyme stands this adage on its head" (287). In other places, "Tevye is jokingly misquoting," "Tevye is clowning," and "Tevye's misattribution of the verse to Abraham is again deliberate buffoonery" (288–89). Other instances, helpfully documented by Halkin, show Tevye's apt reliance on biblical, talmudic, and midrashic citations.

The absence of critical consensus about Tevye's quotations may indicate that the question has been wrongly posed. We cannot resolve the issue by determining that Tevye is either consistently an ignoramus or thoroughly a wit. And while Michael Stern makes genuine contributions to our understanding with his essay on "Tevye's Art of Quotation," we need to focus our attention more closely on Sholem Aleichem's art. One may speculate on the fictitious motives of a literary character, but this has little to do with a literary-historical approach to Sholem Aleichem as author. Hence we should be more concerned with Sholem Aleichem's literary purposes than with Tevye's supposed strategies.

One might say that Sholem Aleichem uses Tevye's quotations "under erasure,"[31] much as he appropriates the conventions of

---

[30] Sholem Aleichem, *Tevye the Dairyman and the Railroad Stories,* pp. 286–303; henceforth cited by page alone.

[31] Drawing from Martin Heidegger's work, Jacques Derrida uses the suggestive phrase "under erasure" (*sous rature*) in several essays. See, for example, "Comment ne pas parler: Dénégations," in *Psyché: Inventions de l'autre* (Paris: Galilée, 1987), pp. 588–90. In English, see "How to Avoid Speaking: Denials," trans. Ken Frieden, in *Languages of the Unsayable: The Play of Negativity in Literature and Literary Theory,* ed. Sanford Budick and Wolfgang Iser (New York: Columbia University Press, 1989), pp. 56–57.

European realism in his early novels. Tevye's quotations enable him both to render present and to cancel the ancient sources that predetermine Yiddish speech. Without such quotations, Tevye's monologues would lack their decisive parodic dimension. Moreover, in appropriating scriptural models, Tevye alludes to the practices of "grandfather" Abramovitsh.

As with the use of social and literary satire in the "Jewish novels," Sholem Aleichem's Tevye figure shows the full measure of his debt to Abramovitsh. He seldom emulated the prefaces of Mendele, but instead created the oral narrator Tevye and his concomitant monologue form. Over the course of Abramovitsh's career, Mendele underwent a number of metamorphoses; Sholem Aleichem brought together diverse facets within a more static Tevye. In Tevye's words, quoting Genesis 1:5, *va-yehi ʿerev va-yehi boker*. Literally this means, "and there was evening, and there was morning." But Tevye reinterprets it as referring to a murky dusk "between day and night" (SA 5: 120). In Mendele's development, there is a temporal sequence that separates between modes that are as different as night and day. In the case of Tevye, this diversity is packed into a single time, an ambiguous dusk, in which he cracks jokes while cracks appear in his learned façade and literary persona.

The effectiveness of Sholem Aleichem's Tevye stories owes much to their hybrid quality. They alternately shift registers between "high" and "low" speech, between the masculine and feminine realms of Jewish culture, and between the liturgical intonations of Hebrew and the Yiddish vernacular. As Tevye blithely moves from Scripture and Midrash to everyday concerns and back again, Sholem Aleichem weaves together a literary fabric that transcends the sheer orality of Tevye's first-person monologues and daily *shtetl* life. In short, through his Torah-quoting oral narrator Tevye, Sholem Aleichem carries on a dialogue with the Judaic literary tradition. Tevye's memory of *loci classici* renders the body of Hebrew textuality present and accessible to emerging Yiddish fiction. Parody once again enables a belated Yiddish writer to inscribe his works into the ongoing literary-historical process, grafting together ancient *topoi* and vernacular commonplaces.

CHAPTER 7

Social Criticism
in Sholem Aleichem's Monologues

Sholem Aleichem's monologists take cues from Abramovitsh's personae of Mendele the Bookseller and Isrolik "the Madman," and they reinforce Sholem Aleichem's claim to be Abramovitsh's literary grandson by emulating the feigned directness of Mendele's address to his readers. Like Abramovitsh, Sholem Aleichem writes monologues that engage the reader, convey ideological positions, and satisfy aesthetic demands. While oral speech was the genius of Yiddish culture in the eighteenth and nineteenth centuries, modern Yiddish writers had to borrow literary conventions from European precursors even in their presentation of everyday speech.

The short monologue form suits Sholem Aleichem's creative propensities. Novels were not his strongest suit, in part because he seldom followed a carefully structured plot or imposed another principle of coherence. Instead, he created serially, as in the Tevye stories, the letters of Menachem-Mendl, the narrative by Motl the cantor's son, and the far-flung episodes of *Wandering Stars* (*Blonzhende shtern*)—which were most often written to be printed in newspapers or journals. Through the seemingly unpremeditated narratives of his characters, Sholem Aleichem shrewdly invented a fictive embodiment of his improvisational literary style. In other words, his associative manner of composition and the erratic conditions of publication spawned characters who free-associate.

Sholem Aleichem's monologues, which often hint at social commentary beyond the individual situations they depict, move in two ideological directions. In the commonest scenario, unfortunate men and women tell their woes to Sholem Aleichem, who purportedly transcribes them for the reader. While these characters are portrayed satirically, their miserable lives also reflect critically upon their society. In several contrasting stories, wealthy men show their corruption by exerting unprincipled control over other characters, and the implicit criticism falls upon the monologists themselves. Sholem Aleichem's monologues question the social order as reflected in both disadvantaged and privileged members of society.

The monologues, like Sholem Aleichem's Tevye stories written between 1894 and 1916, were penned over a period of decades. As presented in a posthumously published volume of his collected works entitled *Monologn,* they range from 1901 to 1916.[1] Of these sixteen tales, thirteen are narrated monologues while the remaining three are reported dialogues. Five are narrated by women, collectively representing Sholem Aleichem's most rigorous attempt to convey diverse feminine voices and experiences. In comparison to these female characters, even the archetypal Jewish wife, Golda, has a minor supporting role on Tevye's stage.

Like the Tevye stories, Sholem Aleichem's monologues employ the Russian literary mode known as *skaz,* that is, *"stylistically individualized inner narrative placed in the mouth of a fictional character and designed to produce the illusion of oral speech."*[2] Nikolai Gogol's *Diary of a Madman* (1835), "The Overcoat" and *Dead Souls* (1842), as well as Fyodor Dostoevsky's *Notes from Underground* (1864) illustrate Russian *skaz* and resemble Yiddish monologues. The subsequent use of *skaz*—as in Nikolai Leskov's *Night Owls* (1891) and Anton Chekhov's stories of the 1890s— predates and influenced Sholem Aleichem's creations. Dmitry Chi-

---

[1]Y. D. Berkovitsh notes, in *Dos Sholem-Aleichem bukh,* that the major monologues were originally published as follows: "The Little Pot," in *Der yud* (1901); "Geese," in *Di folkstsaytung* (1902); "A Bit of Advice," in *Der tog* (1904); and "A Game of Sixty-Six," in both *Di naye velt* and *Dos togeblat* (1910). "A Game of Sixty-Six" is one of the texts that were assembled in *Writings of a Commercial Traveler: Railroad Stories (Ksovim fun a komi-voyazher: ayznban-geshikhtn,* 1911).

[2]Hugh McLean, "On the Style of a Leskovian *Skaz,*" *Harvard Slavic Studies* 2 (1954), 299. McLean adapts his definition from Boris Eichenbaum's essays. Jurij Striedter discusses *skaz* at greater length in his introduction to his edition, *Russischer Formalismus: Texte zur allgemeinen Literaturtheorie und zur Theorie der Prosa* (Munich: W. Fink, 1971). This German collection includes three major essays on *skaz:* Boris Eichenbaum's "How Gogol's 'Overcoat' Is Made" and "The Illusion of *skaz,*" as well as Viktor Vinogradov's "The Problem of *skaz* in Stylistics." See also Mikhail Bakhtin's "Discourse Typology in Prose," in *Readings in Russian Poetics: Formalist and Structuralist Views,* ed. Ladislav Matejka and Krystyna Pomorska (Ann Arbor: University of Michigan, 1978), pp. 176–96.

zhevsky observes that "frequent repetition of exactly the same word is characteristic—in Gogol and in other writers—of conversational speech or *skaz,* as the literary historians now call it."[3] Much as Sholem Aleichem's monologues appear to be natural, unmediated expressions of Yiddish speech, they employ literary techniques and depend on prior literary models. The illusion of oral speech is common to monologues and dialogues, as the Russian formalists demonstrated.[4]

The two basic characteristics of *skaz*—oral pretense and repetition—are essential to Sholem Aleichem's monologues. The monologues purport to transcribe the oral discourse of fictional speakers, often within a frame narrative. Each character is rendered unique by distinctive patterns of speech, comparable to the recurring phrase "that's not what I'm getting at" in Mendele's prefaces. These tales are never purely monological or single-voiced, because they are purportedly addressed to their creator Sholem Aleichem. The author's ironies, to be decoded by the reader, frame the oral mode of his folk narrations.

"THE LITTLE POT" AND "GEESE"

"The Little Pot" ("Dos tepl," 1901) and "Geese" ("Genz," 1902) are monologues by hapless women whose stories refer metonymically to the general situation of impoverished Jewish men, women, and children. In spite of the putative subjects of their talk, they themselves and their class become the basic theme. Sholem Aleichem's fictive monologists bring themselves into being through their speech, which led Y. Y. Trunk to consider "loquaciousness"

---

[3]Dmitry Chizhevsky, "About Gogol's 'Overcoat,'" in *Gogol from the Twentieth Century: Eleven Essays,* ed. Robert A. Maguire (Princeton: Princeton University Press, 1974), p. 299. Chizhevsky's essay originally appeared in 1938. See also Boris Eichenbaum's "How Gogol's 'Overcoat' Is Made" (1918), contained in the same volume, pp. 269–91.

[4]See Boris Eichenbaum, "Leskov und die moderne Prosa," in Jurij Striedter, *Russischer Formalismus: Texte zur allgemeinen Literaturtheorie und zur Theorie der Prosa* (Munich: W. Fink, 1971), pp. 209–43. We may thus understand Sholem Aleichem's propensity to both the monologue and the dialogue. In addition to the three dialogues contained in the collected volume of *Monologn,* see his dialogue "Sholem-Aleichem" in the volume *Yidishe shrayber.* Sholem Aleichem also prepared several dramatic works for the Yiddish theater, but his stage dialogues are seldom as compelling as his narrated monologues.

(*baredevdikeyt*) the main feature of these short stories.[5] Sholem Aleichem's monologists delight in language itself and savor the process of making their voices heard. By inventing loquacious speakers, the author both projects his own narrative impulses onto them and creates collective voices that speak for the downtrodden. In some cases, the telling of a story seems to afford a measure of relief from misfortune, allowing the characters to escape from their reality into a second-order fictional narrative. This is, of course, only Sholem Aleichem's effective illusion, since the monologists are entirely fictional and have no reality to escape. Sholem Aleichem masks the devices that produce their deceptively simple narratives by pretending to transcribe their stories.

"The Little Pot" opens with a direct address by the monologist Yente to her listener: "Rabbi! I want to ask you a question, I do. I don't know whether or not you know who I am. I am Yente, I am, Yente the *kurelapnitshke*. I deal in eggs, I do, with chickens, with geese, and with ducks" (9).[6] The story's premise is familiar in traditional Jewish circles: a woman comes to a rabbi with a question concerning Jewish law (*halakha*). This situation brings into play the forces of rabbinic authority, the guide for everyday Jewish practices. The story, generalized by the woman's stereotypical name—which is also Mendele's wife's name in his canonical 1879 preface—dramatizes the tension between impoverished Jewish life and strict talmudic rules imposed upon Jews regardless of their financial constraints. Thematically, it also recalls Abramovitsh's bitter attack on corruption associated with the tax on kosher meat.

---

[5] See Y. Y. Trunk, *Sholem Aleichem (zayn vezn un zayne verk)* (Warsaw: Kultur-lige, 1937), chapter 3 on the *monologn*, pp. 161–224.

[6] The word *kurelapnitshke* means "chicken dealer." But it may also refer to "someone who paws (steals) chickens" or to "a short-legged woman." Translations of Sholem Aleichem's monologues are based on *Monologn* in *Ale verk fun Sholem Aleichem* (New York: Folksfond Edition, 1917–23), vol. 21; cited by page alone. For some English renditions of Sholem Aleichem's monologues, see *Favorite Tales of Sholom Aleichem*, trans. Julius and Frances Butwin (New York: Avenel Books, 1983), *Stories and Satires*, trans. Curt Leviant (New York: Thomas Yoseloff, 1959), *Old Country Tales*, trans. Curt Leviant (New York: G. P. Putnam's Sons, 1966), *Some Laughter, Some Tears*, trans. Curt Leviant (New York: Paragon, 1979), *The Best of Sholom Aleichem*, ed. Irving Howe and Ruth R. Wisse (Washington: New Republic Books, 1979), and *Tevye the Dairy-man and Other Stories*, trans. Miriam Katz (Moscow: Raduga Publishers, 1988). Remarkably and lamentably, there has never been an English edition of Sholem Aleichem's collected monologues.

At first glance it might seem that the rabbi in the story "The Little Pot" is completely unlike the modern author Sholem Aleichem. Yet from 1880 to 1883 Sholem Aleichem, then known only as Sholem Rabinovitsh, actually did serve as Government Rabbi in Luben. As a secularist he would not have presided over the enforcement of Jewish law. This was an official post rather than a religious role, but the young author undoubtedly received visits from members of his constituency. An awareness of Sholem Aleichem's biography, including his service in a marginal rabbinic role, intensifies the story's comic effect.

As Yente proceeds with her monologue, we learn that she is a poor widow with an only child, aged 13. Her son David is a diligent yeshiva student, so diligent in fact that he has ruined his health. To help him recover, Yente dutifully follows a doctor's orders that she feed him chicken soup every day, until one morning when she asks her neighbor to watch the soup for her. The neighbor decides to cook dairy fritters in a pot beside the chicken soup. During a quarrel, the neighbor spills her meal onto the oven, leaving Yente's soup in a questionable state. If more than a certain proportion of milk has fallen into the chicken soup, then according to the rules of *kashrut* it may no longer be eaten and the pot is no longer kosher. Since the legalistic ramifications are complex, the woman asks the rabbi to resolve her predicament. She hopes that her soup and pot can be declared kosher, so that her ailing son will be able to eat; Yente has no other pot for meat dishes, and so "if you pronounce my pot not kosher (*treyf*), I will remain without a pot" (24), and David will starve.

This quandary proves insurmountable for the rabbi. As the story closes, he collapses and Yente shrieks: "Rabbi! God be with you! What's the matter? . . . Rebbetsin! Rebbetsin![7] Where are you? . . . Come here! Faster! The rabbi isn't well! Became sick. . . . To the point of fainting! . . . Water! Water! . . ." (25). The rabbi's swoon shatters her initial confidence that he can solve her problem. Such misfortune proves to be more than the rabbi can handle, and he passes out at the end of the story because he sees no solution that satisfies both the laws of *kashrut* and the demands of an impoverished mother. At the same time, his collapse seems to be a weapon of self-defense against the endless stream of Yente's

---

[7]"Rebbetsin" refers to a rabbi's wife.

monologue. Unable to halt the flow of words, he escapes by losing consciousness. The story hints at a critique of excessive rigidity in ritual observances, as contrasted with the fluidity of the woman's speech.

As is typical of stories written in the style of Russian *skaz,* Sholem Aleichem's "The Little Pot" employs "frequent repetition of exactly the same word" or phrase.[8] This monologue is organized around the repeated sentence, "Yes, how did I get talking about that?" ("Yo, akegn vos iz dos gekumen tsu red?"), which serves as a point of contact after each digression. Following the opening paragraph, the story consists of fourteen paragraphs all beginning in this way. This linguistic reflex characterizes the speaker and, at the same time, gives her monologue a semblance of coherence precisely while emphasizing its digressiveness.

In "The Little Pot," the monologist addresses a rabbi and we read only her words, but the rabbi's impatient reactions may be inferred from her refrain, "Yes, how did I get talking about that?" Yente runs circles around her listener by digressing endlessly. Each time her rambling tale takes a step forward, she begins to move imperceptibly away from the matter at hand. For Yente the process of storytelling is more important than any goal, even if her stated purpose is to receive a ruling on the status of her pot. Or perhaps we could interpret her narrative wanderings as a means of postponing the legalistic decision she fears.

"Geese" is a similar monologue by another impoverished woman, Batia, who explains how one scrapes by as a trader of geese. Batia has no apparent reason for telling the tale, and her only motivation seems to be that of lightening her grief by unburdening herself. Linguistic patterns characterize Batia's monologue. As she explains her difficulties in supporting her family, for example, she frequently reverts to the phrase: "I'm not speaking any evil, God forbid, and I am also not one to slander. . . . But I'm mixing everything up. Don't get mad, it's just my nature, as you say, 'A Jewish woman has got nine measures of speech in her'" (30, 32, 33, 35, 36, 37, 40, 41). Each paragraph of "The Little Pot," except the first, opens with Yente's refrain, "Yes, how did I get talking about that?" Similarly, each paragraph of "Geese," except the first and the last, ends with her apology about gossiping, mix-

[8]Dmitry Chizhevsky, "About Gogol's 'Overcoat,'" p. 299.

ing everything up, and overflowing with "nine measures of speech." Only in the final paragraph does she break away from this cycle by catching herself: "But hush! . . . It seems to me that I wanted to tell you a fine tale. I haven't the faintest idea; even I have forgotten what it was" (44). The act of telling takes priority over imparting information, and the manner of presentation is more essential than the matter at hand.

Sholem Aleichem suggests a social message even in this comic monologue. After describing the poverty that surrounds her, Batia says, "Poor folk perish from cold, poor folk die, swollen with hunger; children fall like straw, like flies." Then she adds ironically, "It is merciful, as you say, that only poor folk die" (40). The stream of language catches the listener in its current for long enough to assert the needs of the poor. We do not hear the "fine tale" that was promised, but are instead reminded of the darker side of Jewish life in Eastern Europe that is usually excluded from humoristic fiction.

"A BIT OF ADVICE"

One of Sholem Aleichem's classic monologues, "A Bit of Advice" ("An eytse," 1904), carries further his expertise in the technique of *skaz*.[9] It contains an extensive frame narrative, which sets the scene for the monologue by a young man who shows signs of being an "unreliable narrator."[10] The listener, who resembles the implied author Sholem Aleichem, has an important role as interlocutor. The story could be read as a spoof of a psychoanalytic session, except that it predates widespread acquaintance with Freudian practices. Like the earlier monologues by women, "A Bit of Advice" portrays its male monologist as a helpless individual who is entirely incapable of making a major decision for himself. There arises a comic situation in which the young man wavers between

---

[9]"The Little Pot" and "A Bit of Advice" were soon reissued in popular editions. See *Dos tepl* and *An eytse* (Warsaw: Bikher-far-ale, 1905).

[10]See Wayne Booth, *The Rhetoric of Fiction* (Chicago: University of Chicago Press, 1961). Booth defines the unreliable narrator as one who does not speak or act "in accordance with the norms of the work (which is to say, the implied author's norms)" (p. 158). Unreliability need not be confined to matters of mimetic detail, but can extend to moral views, judgments, and standards of character.

two diametrically opposed alternatives, while the listener concurs with every decision that seems most convincing to the young man at the moment. This ultimately leads to a breakdown in communication similar to the rabbi's collapse at the conclusion of "The Little Pot." While the listener does not lose consciousness, he becomes so frustrated by the speaker's indecisiveness that he nearly resorts to violence as he rushes to throw him out. This final scene humorously suggests the author's own dissatisfaction with his fictional character, whom he hastens to dismiss as the story ends.

For the first time in Sholem Aleichem's monologues, the butt of criticism is a bourgeois narrator, whose equivocal speech follows different patterns and creates distinct effects. By 1904 Sholem Aleichem had been influenced by the social turmoil in Russia, and these changes are reflected in a new kind of comic monologue. Because the reader is not led to sympathize with the empowered speakers, the critique shifts from society as a whole to privileged social climbers. Sholem Aleichem's political position reflected his life among the Kiev "plutocracy," in which his own financial situation was always insecure.

In "A Bit of Advice," the monologist is a young man who (like Sholem Aleichem) has married into a wealthy family. Attempting to decide whether he should divorce his wife, he is paralyzed by uncertainty and hopes that his listener will be able to assist him. The listener or frame narrator, presumably Sholem Aleichem, hears on his return from a journey that a young man urgently wants to speak with him. He has narrow expectations:

> Probably a writer with an "opus"! That's what I thought and I sat down at my desk and went to work. Aha, someone's ringing, so early! The door opens and someone fumbles around, takes off his galoshes, coughs, blows his nose—all signs of an author. I was all ready to see the person. God lent a hand, and he came in. (73)

The frame narrative, merging satiric and parodic elements, prepares us to be skeptical of the monologist. Sholem Aleichem self-reflexively mocks the telltale signs of a writer. At the same time, he nods in the direction of the Mendele persona with his pseudo-pious remark that "God lent a hand, and he came in."

Sholem Aleichem, as the listener, misleads us by comparing the monologist to a young writer: "Soon he'll take a bundle of writings out of his breast pocket, no doubt a novel in three parts, long as the Jewish exile, or a play in four acts in which the characters are named Murderson, Erlichman, Frumharts, Bittertsvayg" (74). In line with his satiric attack on Shomer of fifteen years earlier, Sholem Aleichem mocks contemporary authors. Their characters are mere abstractions, with names that convey their villainy, honesty, piety, or bitterness. Readers well-versed in Yiddish literary history will catch a backhanded allusion to "grandfather" Abramovitsh, whose by then outmoded play *The Tax* uses just such transparent names. In any event, the young man has come "to express to you my bitter heart and to get some advice" (75). Sholem Aleichem had not expected to be confronted by flesh-and-blood problems, and here the monologue begins in earnest.

The young man hopes that his listener will be able to advise him: "A person like you will understand me. You write so much that you must know everything, and only you can give me proper advice. And believe me, whatever you say, I'll do" (ibid.). The mimetic character's first error is to assume that authors have special insight into life; at the same time, Sholem Aleichem makes a joke out of the character's ready obedience to his author. According to Sholem Aleichem's comic scenario, the character consults with his maker. It goes without saying that fictional characters generally follow the lead of their creators, but here the consultation becomes explicit. The meeting between the monologist and a writer-listener is reminiscent of the meeting between Mendele the Bookseller and S. Y. Abramovitsh in the 1894 Hebrew preface to his autobiography, *In Those Days* (*Ba-yamim ha-hem*), which later appeared in Yiddish as *Solomon, Son of Chaim* (*Shloyme reb Khaim's*, 1899).

Problems surface as soon as the young man begins his tale. He explains that he is from a "small town." Then he adds: "That is, the town isn't really so small, and it is quite a handsome town, a city one may say, but in comparison to your city it's a town" (75). From the outset, the speaker tends to be indecisive and self-contradictory. The listener apparently tires of this double-talk and interrupts to ask the speaker's occupation. His response is evasive: "My occupation, you want to know? Hm . . . I am occupied. . . . That is, at present I'm not doing anything, I'm still living at the expense of my in-laws; that is, not at their expense but together with them, ready for everything because she is, you should know, an only daughter" (76). As in the 1880s, under the impression of political unrest, Sholem Aleichem critically portrays bourgeois life. The young man reveals himself as an unreliable narrator whose story reflects more negatively upon him than he realizes. While the early "Jewish novels" use the technique of third-person narration to uncover foibles of the Jewish bourgeoisie, "A Bit of Advice" exposes social flaws from within.

The listener interrupts at regular intervals to ask the purpose of the visit. Like Sholem Aleichem's other monologists, the young man seems unable to get to the point or to tell his tale without digressions. His dissatisfaction revolves around a new doctor in town. The listener presses for details: "What, then, are you suspicious of her?" (83). But the speaker denies this, instead blaming the new doctor. Although nothing definite has happened, the young man recognizes his wife's attraction to the doctor, who has become a frequent visitor in their house. What's worse, the doctor's father is a gossipy tailor. The young monologist finally asks the listener: "What do you say? There's no other plan than to get divorced?" (85). The listener agrees, which provokes a new round of explanations on the part of the young man. One problem, he admits, is his lack of financial means. And how can he be so sure that another marriage would be better? To this line of reasoning the listener also assents, saying "of course, making peace is better than getting divorced" (87), as if trying to encourage the speaker to draw his own conclusions.

The listener's words again propel the speaker in the opposite direction. Their dialogue might seem to parody a talmudic debate, except that the young man himself represents both sides of the argument, continually wavering between the options of divorce and reconciliation. Paralyzed by two equally unpleasant alternatives, the speaker hopes that his interlocutor will make his decision for him. But this is precisely what the writer-listener avoids, instead merely agreeing with every self-contradictory conclusion the monologist reaches.

"A Bit of Advice" provokes two complementary lines of interpretation. The unhappy, nouveau-riche husband displays feelings of inadequacy that typify his social class. His thoughts are entirely engrossed by futile anxieties and jealousies, which take up the slack that is left by his sterile life. This charade continues until the listener becomes so impatient that he attacks him, if only to silence this endless chatter: "I don't know what happened to me. Blood rushed to my head, and my vision went dark. I grabbed my visitor by the throat, pressed him up against the wall, and in a voice that wasn't my own I shouted: You should divorce her, you bastard! Divorce her! Divorce her! Divorce her!!!" (90). The other members of the household burst in to see what is going on and to calm down the overwrought *pater familias*. The young man leaves quietly, apologizing for taking his listener's time and thanking him for the advice.

Beyond the level of social criticism, another interpretation of the story concentrates on the hostile relationship between the young bourgeois narrator and the intellectual listener, whom we identify with Sholem Aleichem. Several clues suggest that "A Bit of Advice" has elements of a self-reflexive narrative on the problems of writing, in which Sholem Aleichem, the implied author, enacts a drama that recapitulates the tense relationship between him and the literary world. First, in the writer-listener's irony concerning his visitor whom he takes to be an aspiring author, Sholem Aleichem seems to convey his dislike of young competitors. Second, the story dramatizes the author's antagonistic relationship to his own character, ironically designated as "my hero" (*mayn parshoyn*). This is the language of literature and, indeed, the monologist becomes Sholem Aleichem's hero or anti-hero in his story. Third, the encounter between author and character parodically reworks the discrepancy between the author and his Mendele persona in Abramovitsh's novels.

Thus the meeting in "A Bit of Advice" may be reconceived as the drama of an author encountering his fictional personage. On the one hand, Sholem Aleichem needs this wishy-washy character in order to make possible one of his most effective monologues. On the other hand, Sholem Aleichem's stand-in, the writer-listener, shows utmost impatience with this indecisive character who cannot rise to the occasion with a "most interesting" story or deed. This scene parallels a dilemma that beset the writer Sholem Aleichem himself. He excelled in the representation of oral speech but was less successful in framing novelistic plots. Finally, the uneasy relationship between speaker and listener resembles the relationship between author and reader: as readers, we may become impatient with Sholem Aleichem's amorphous fiction, short on plot and long on verbiage. Hence Sholem Aleichem solicits our sympathy in coming to terms with intractable fictional types; we join the author within the tale and share his impatience. Like the listener in the consultation, the reader may want to silence the monologist and end his flow of words. At the same time, we recognize this loquacity as Sholem Aleichem's trademark and strongest suit, incorporating the pretense of colloquial orality within evolving literary conventions.

Contemporary with the other monologues, Sholem Aleichem's *Railroad Stories: Tales of a Commercial Traveler* (*Ksovim fun a komi-voyazher: ayznban-geshikhtn*, 1911) explore related forms of mock-oral narration. The tales are united by a prefatory frame that transports the convention of Mendele's prefaces into a modernized context. In his standard preface, Mendele describes traveling on his wagon to ply his bookselling trade. The later Hebrew story, "Shem and Japheth on the Train," however, shifts Mendele into a more technologically advanced world. Sholem Aleichem takes the "traveler disguised" one step further with a businessman narrator who purports to have collected his book from stories he has heard while traveling on trains. We do not know what the commercial traveler is selling, but his literary pretensions associate him with Sholem Aleichem.

The opening paragraph of his preface, "To the Reader," clearly parodies the self-introductions by Mendele the Bookseller. In the 1864–65 version of *The Little Man,* Mendele begins:

> I myself was born in Tsviatshitsh, and my name is Mendele the Bookseller. I'm underway most of the year, here and there. People know me everywhere, because I travel throughout Poland with all kinds of books printed in Zhitomir—not to mention prayer shawls, *tales-kotns,* tassels, shofars, tefillin, amulets, *mezuzes,* wolves' teeth, and sometimes one can buy brass or copper utensils from me. In fact, since *Kol mevasser* appeared, I sometimes carry a few numbers of it. But that's not at all, not at all what I'm getting at; I want to tell about something else entirely.[11]

Echoing this self-presentation in an altered voice, Sholem Aleichem's commercial traveler begins: "I am a traveler. Nearly eleven months a year I am underway—generally by train, and for the most part third class. As is customary, I travel from one Jewish

---

[11]*Dos kleyne mentshele oder a lebensbashraybung fun Yitskhok Avrom takif* (serialized in 1864–65; repr. Odessa: Nitzshe and Tsederboym, 1865), p. 3.

town or village to the next, because I have no business wherever Jews are forbidden to live."[12] As in the case of Mendele the Bookseller, the economics of trade guide the narrator's travels, and he also wonders whether he "will earn anything" from his writings. Like the early Mendele, this business-minded traveler pretends to edit other people's narratives. A difference, in keeping with Sholem Aleichem's passion for the colloquial monologue, is that his traveler supposedly transcribes *oral* accounts. He tells us that "I went out and bought myself a fresh notebook and pencil, and everything I saw and heard along the way I entered straight into my book" (8).

This stenographic pretense is so congenial to Sholem Aleichem that he repeats it in the opening frame of "On Account of a Hat" ("Iber a hitl," 1913), another kind of railroad story written after the volume of railroad stories had been published. In this instance, the narrator pretends to have written down a merchant's story word for word, thus facilitating once again "the illusion of *skaz*" (in Boris Eichenbaum's phrase). Moreover, he claims tongue-in-cheek that the merchant is no writer, and he cannot have simply dreamed up the story. By means of this device, the frame narrator claims literal accuracy for his wholly improbable tale.[13]

In *The Railroad Stories*, Sholem Aleichem intensifies the ironic discrepancies between himself and his persona who comments, "Too bad I'm not a writer." Then the persona reverses himself and makes light of Sholem Aleichem's literary enterprise: "What sort of thing is that, really, a writer? Anyone can be a writer. Particularly in Yiddish. 'Jargon'—that's my business, too! One picks up a pen and writes" (7). Sholem Aleichem alludes to the popular image of Yiddish as a humble language that is more the province of simple folk than of any educated elite. The narrator's lighthearted disparagement of Yiddish writing establishes an obvious distance between him and the implied author. There are many similarities

---

[12]From "Tsu di lezer," in *Ayznban-geshikhtes: ksovim fun a komi-voyazher,* in *Ale verk fun Sholem Aleichem* (New York: Folksfond Edition, 1917–23), vol. 28, p. 7; translations are based on this edition and cited by page alone. When originally published, this collection bore a slightly different title: *Ksovim fun a komi-voyazher (ayznban-geshikhtn),* Jubilee Edition of Sholem Aleichem's *Ale verk,* vol. 8 (Warsaw: Progress, 1911). For an English rendition of the work, see *Tevye the Dairyman and the Railroad Stories,* trans. Hillel Halkin (New York: Schocken, 1987), pp. 133–284.

[13]See "Iber a hitl," in *Fun peysekh tsu peysekh,* in SA 2: 241–54.

between Sholem Aleichem's *Railroad Stories* and his other monologues.

"A GAME OF SIXTY-SIX"

One of the railroad stories, "A Game of Sixty-Six" ("A zekhs-un-
zekhtsik," 1910), exploits the dynamics of an unreliable internal
narrator. The commercial traveler frames the story descriptively
before he turns it over to a card player who relates a long-winded
tale of gambling on a train. The traveling writer is nearly ensnared
by this narrator, and up to a point the reader also falls into the trap
that has been set by both the card player and the commercial
traveler.

The card-playing internal narrator at first appears to be "a
completely respectable man, a commercial traveler like me."[14] After the listening traveler sets the scene, he purportedly "transmits
the story word for word" (155). In his monologue, then, the card
player tells of his experiences on trains, culminating with a grand
swindle in which he pretends to have lost a fortune to con-men. All
of this seems tame enough until the card player ends his story,
removes a deck of cards from his pocket, and invites the listener to
a game: "How did it all end up? —Don't ask. Better, let's forget
our worries and play a game of sixty-six in honor of Chanuka"
(170). The internal narrator takes cover behind the Jewish custom
of playing cards during Chanuka. Earlier in his story, in fact, he has
placed an alluring invitation in the mouth of the man who will
later swindle him: "During Chanuka it's a *mitsve* to play cards! A
game of sixty-six" (164).

The entire monologue takes on a new aspect as part of the card
player's scheme to win the listener's confidence and lure him into a
game. If the card-playing narrator himself has been cheated, the
listener is expected to believe, then he himself cannot be a swindler.
The frame narrator risks entering the internal story of deception
with roles reversed. But instead of falling into this gambler's trap

---

[14]"A zekhs-un-zekhtsik," in *Ayzenban-geshikhtes: ksovim fun a komi-voyazher,*
in SA 28: 155, henceforth cited by page alone. Sholem Aleichem mentions
having completed this story in a letter dated 6 December 1910, and he requests
that it be printed before Chanuka. See "Literarisher pinkes," *Bikher velt* 1
(1922), numbers 4–5, 465. For a related story, see "Knortn" (1912), in SA 22:
199–222.

and narrative hall of mirrors, the listener draws away: "I look at the man, as he shuffles the cards a little too skillfully, a little too smoothly and fast. His hands are a little too pale. Too pale and too soft. And a nasty thought flits through my mind . . ." (170; ellipsis in original). The frame narrator extricates himself by claiming total ignorance of the game's rules, much as he has claimed ignorance of literary devices, and at the next station the card player vanishes.

This otherwise quaint tale contains a pervasive element of deception that extends from card-playing to storytelling. Even the title, "A Game of Sixty-Six," turns out to be ambiguous. It refers to either the game that the card player has described or to the game that the card player hopes to play against his current listener and potential dupe. The title, which presumably has been affixed by the listening commercial traveler, marks the moment of deceit at which storytelling is intended to become a trap. The text exposes the very strategic principles of its own narration by thematizing an unreliable narrator. Whom can we believe? Have we been swindled by the commercial traveler or by Sholem Aleichem, the implied author? It is not so simple as merely accepting that the card player is fraudulent while the commercial traveler is trustworthy. Like the narrator of "A Bit of Advice," this narrator refers to the card player as "my hero" (*mayn parshoyn*), marking him as a fictional character. Sholem Aleichem's pretense of having characters relate others' stories "word for word" sometimes elicits an effect quite unlike what we initially expect: it arouses our awareness of the fictional status of the tale. His comic masks vary from the grotesque and ridiculous to the insidious and sly, and in spite of the realist aesthetic views Sholem Aleichem espoused, many of his stories employ perspectives that unsettle our initial impression of a stable fictional world.[15]

"MISTER GREEN HAS A JOB"

In the American context, monologue becomes the medium for some of Sholem Aleichem's most virulent social criticism. Once again, this form allows him to present Jewish life from within, from the standpoint of conniving narrators. Sholem Aleichem ex-

[15]For an extensive discussion of Sholem Aleichem's *Railroad Stories*, see Dan Miron's afterword to his Hebrew translation, *Sippurei rakevet* (Tel Aviv: Dvir, 1989), pp. 225–99.

pressed his interest in literary "pictures of the New York [Jewish] ghetto" in a contemporary letter to the American Yiddish writer Joseph Opatoshu.[16] Based on his own experiences in New York in 1906–07 and in 1914–16, Sholem Aleichem satirizes glaring corruption.

"Mister Green Has a Job" ("Mister Green hot a dshab," 1915) exaggerates a comic situation in order to poke fun at American-Jewish life. The critique addresses the Americanized Yiddish language and American Jewish religiosity, showing their joint demise. The monologist is a self-satisfied entrepreneur who boasts of his ingenuity in finding work for himself on the Lower East Side. His name, "Mister Green," makes him into a stereotypical new immigrant, a naive *griner* who must struggle to fit in and become "all right."

From his first words, Mr. Green shows his propensity for Yinglish: "How do you do, Mister Sholem Aleichem!" (245), he says, using this English phrase. Granted that it might be awkward to say, "Sholem Aleichem, Mister Sholem Aleichem," the speaker is downright proud of his English and draws from his newfound American resources whenever possible. He then adds a remark that places him in relation to Sholem Aleichem's fictional characters: "I don't know whether you know me. . . . We're distant relatives, second or third cousins. . . . That is, not you and me, but I'm related to your Tevye the milkman and his friend Menachem-Mendl from Yehupetz" (ibid.). The fictional character virtually acknowledges his own fictive status by placing himself on the same plane as other imaginary heroes. Alternatively, one might say that the present character elevates Sholem Aleichem's past fiction to a higher level of reality by jokingly associating himself with them. In any event, Sholem Aleichem shows interest in this speaker, who tells him: "Stand here with me on the sidewalk (*saydvok*) for just a little while, and we'll *shmuesn* a bit about America, what a Golden Land it is" (245). Implicitly, Mister Green also indicates that Sholem Aleichem can learn from him about Americanisms used in everyday speech such as the word *saydvok*. The lesson continues with references to American *biznes,* which enables one to find a job (*dshab*) and become "all right" (*alrayt*).

---

[16]See "Literarisher pinkes," *Bikher velt* 1 (1922), number 3, 326.

Mister Green's story is framed as a typical immigrant tale. His name has been shortened from Greenberg, and (mixing the real and the imaginary) he says he comes from "Odessa . . . from Yehupetz . . . from Kasrilevke . . . in short, from *those* places" (246). Moreover, on arrival in "Columbus' land" he joins the common struggle for survival. Rosh Hashana provides his big opportunity, when "I saw in the *papers* how one advertises (*advertayzt*) cantors, synagogues, and congregations. In the *stores,* I saw, one displayed daily prayer books, Holiday prayer books, *shofars,* prayer shawls" (ibid.). The corruption of New York Yiddish is apparent from the loan-word *papers* and from the fusion verb *advertayzn.*

The business-like approach to religion gives Mister Green his chance to "become all right." A synagogue congregation hears him blow the shofar on one occasion and contracts with him to be their shofar-blower during the Days of Awe. Already familiar with American capitalism, he drives a hard bargain, saying that he'll blow the shofar in their synagogue if he can "make a living from it" (*makhn derfun a lebn,* 247). He tells them that it would be beneath the dignity of a shofar-blower to be "a *drayver* . . . a *gabetshmen,* or a *strit-kliner*" (ibid.). They can't offer him a full-time job, but they do recommend him to another synagogue. Meanwhile he goes downtown (*dauntaun*), demonstrates his art whenever possible, and "my blowing was heard by judges (*dshadshes*), *kongresmens, asemblimens,* and all of them said: *vonderful*" (248). His business has grown steadily over the past two years, and now he expects to make a dozen appearances all over town. He will do his best to be on time, so as not to lose his *dshab* and his *reputeyshon.*

Having concluded his success-story, the narrator addresses Sholem Aleichem on the subject of his Yiddish: "You are amazed, Mister Sholem Aleichem, that I *yuz* more *engelshe* words than Yiddish? —That's because of the children. They're already real Americans and don't want to speak a single word in Yiddish. You should take a look at my *boys,* you'd never in your life guess that they're Jewish kids" (ibid.). This proud declaration appears as an unconscious tragedy of unquestioning assimilation and acceptance of prejudices against Jews. For the writer Sholem Aleichem, of course, the denial of Yiddish and Jewishness has more negative connotations—by 1915, Americanization already signaled the inevitable decline of Yiddish culture in the "Golden Land."

Not only the language of the Jews suffers at the hands of assimilation and business mentality. The entire culture surrounding religious life seems to have lost all dignity and weight. Only the outward forms remain: "And as for me, if you meet me after the Days of Awe, you won't recognize me. When the month of Elul rolls around, I get rid of my suit, grow a beard, and take on a 'homey' appearance. And as soon as the Days of Awe are over, I give myself a shave, put on my hat, and become a *dshentlmen* again—what doesn't one do in America for the sake of business?" (248). This passage shows Sholem Aleichem at his most socially critical, revealing the misguided mores of New York Jews. Even worse than this corruption, Sholem Aleichem suggests, is the proud way in which a Mister Green can tell his story—spoiling his Yiddish with incessant borrowings from English. His closing words ask Sholem Aleichem to include his address in the story he writes about him, since "for me it'll be an *advertayzment*" (249). Mister Green further affronts Sholem Aleichem's art by proposing to use the story as part of an advertising campaign.

The experience of Mr. Green the shofar-blower is not so distant from Sholem Aleichem's own experience in the United States. As an immigrant in 1906–07 and again in 1914–16, he struggled to make a living. In spite of his failing health, he became involved in numerous public readings, performances, and efforts to adapt his fiction for the Yiddish stage. Sholem Aleichem may have felt that, in the land of business, he was compelled to reduce his art to a cheap commodity for popular audiences.

In his later monologues from the "Period of Reaction" in 1905–07 and thereafter, Sholem Aleichem makes full use of unreliable narrators. In the case of such narrators, there is an ironic discrepancy between the stated views of the narrator and the implicit beliefs of the author. Whereas Mister Green thinks that his is an admirable tale of making it in America, for example, the implied author expects us to share his revulsion. This dissonance creates jarring effects, undermining the speaker through his own misguided words and leading us to question the narratives by shady characters. At the same time, Sholem Aleichem's unreliable narrators draw attention to the fictional scenario, including the persona of Sholem Aleichem. The monologues activate multiple voices to show moral tensions, and without always establishing a firm ground of ethical certainty.

In a continuation of his early program for Yiddish realism, Sholem Aleichem pretends to let everyday Jews, *yidn fun a gants yor,* speak in their own voices. He adapts this narrative genre from the Yiddish tradition of Abramovitsh's Mendele as well as from nineteenth-century Russian *skaz,* which in turn drew from folk narrative in deliberate opposition to the "high" literary language. This is one of Sholem Aleichem's major contributions to a Yiddish literature that taps broader cultural resources. But it is deceptively simple and constitutes only a feigned immediacy. The apparent directness of Sholem Aleichem's monologues has been mediated by his precursors who made his seemingly natural mode possible. As Sholem Aleichem appropriated conventions of the European novel in his early novels, and Hebrew and Aramaic sources in his Tevye stories, in other monologues he borrowed a convention from his Russian contemporaries.

Yiddish writers in the nineteenth century, as relative latecomers to European fiction, share with Russian authors an acute sense of belatedness. Both exploited the strong oral intonations of their languages, ostensibly inspired by vernacular folktales, but in order to create "the illusion of *skaz*" they required a panoply of literary devices. Sholem Aleichem appears to have delighted in working on a double register, evoking the folksy aura expected from him while subtly undermining it on another level. If there is a single fallacy that has distorted popular perceptions of Yiddish literature, it is the myth of a primitive, naive tradition.

CHAPTER 8

Sholem Aleichem's Monologues of Mastery

Sholem Aleichem is best known for impersonating the speech of common people, but he gives voice to a diverse cast of characters in his monologues. From a literary standpoint, his digressive style is often most effective when attributed to an "uncultivated mind of coincidental, associative, obsessive memory."[1] Another model arises when, as in the railroad story "A Game of Sixty-Six," a manipulative character uses storytelling to entrap his audience. Here the narrative rhetoric shifts from disorganized recollection to deliberate deception. Manipulative monologues of this kind, in which the speaker wields power and control, may be termed "monologues of mastery." Such monologues generally mimic unreliable narrators who provoke suspicion and thereby raise questions concerning the moral content of Sholem Aleichem's satire.

Previous commentators have touched on the social and political significance of Sholem Aleichem's work. Y. D. Berkovitsh suggests that Sholem Aleichem was "almost the only Jewish writer who came into close contact with all echelons of his people."[2] Although Sholem Aleichem lived among "privileged circles," he remained deeply rooted in the world of "simple Jews" (SAB 286). Berkovitsh cites a letter to Y. H. Ravnitzky in which he expresses his antagonism toward the wealthy Jews of Kiev: "Because of circumstances, it is my lot to move in circles that can least of all

---

[1]Compare Dan Miron, *A Traveler Disguised*, p. 179. The monologists' personae should not be confused with the Sholem Aleichem persona and presence, which Dan Miron discusses in "Sholem Aleykhem: Person, Persona, Presence," *The Uriel Weinrich Memorial Lecture* 1 (New York: YIVO Institute for Jewish Research, 1972).

[2]See Y. D. Berkovitsh, "Mit fraynd und yidn fun a gants yor," in *Dos Sholem-Aleichem bukh* (New York: Sholem-Aleichem bukh komitet, 1926), p. 285. Subsequent translations from this volume are cited as "SAB" by page alone.

sympathize with my literary inclinations. These circles are our exalted aristocracy, the merchant class, people with capital, who value my finances far more than my literary talent" (SAB 287). In connection with this rift between Sholem Aleichem and his milieu, Berkovitsh asserts that

> in his works Sholem Aleichem deliberately avoided touching directly on the circle of the Jewish plutocracy in Kiev. . . . Perhaps that was because he felt that then he would have to apply entirely the "principle of judgment" (*mides-hadin*), whereas his way was the "principle of mercy" (*mides-harakhmim*). And perhaps what stopped him was his personal tact—not wanting to involve people who stood outside Jewish life and looked down upon the "Jargon," who would have seen this as nothing more than a "mob" affront to their "aristocratic" majesty. . . . Thus he preferred to describe their kitchens and their servants rather than their palaces and the people themselves. (SAB 288)

While discretion does characterize the bulk of Sholem Aleichem's fiction, there are notable exceptions. Like Abramovitsh's early Yiddish works, Sholem Aleichem's youthful novels (such as *Sender Blank,* 1888) direct sharp criticism against the Jewish plutocracy.

Soviet Yiddishists were sensitive to and proponents of Sholem Aleichem's radical leanings. In a seminal essay entitled "The Social Roots of Sholem Aleichem's Humor," Meir Viner contradicts Berkovitsh, showing that Sholem Aleichem deliberately criticizes the wealthy Jews of Kiev.[3] Viner demonstrates that during the first period of his creativity and until 1895, Sholem Aleichem veers from the sympathetic "principle of mercy" toward the disparaging "principle of judgment." Viner emphasizes Sholem Aleichem's early novels and does not analyze the role of social criticism in his late fiction.

Hana Wirth-Nesher, in an article on "Voices of Ambivalence in Sholem Aleichem's Monologues," continues this socio-political line of inquiry with reference to the monologues written between 1901 and 1904. She observes that these stories illustrate "the victimizing of traditional men and women by historical change and

---

[3] M. Viner, "Di sotsiale vortseln fun Sholem-Aleichems humor" (1940), reprinted in *Tsu der geshikhte fun der yidisher literatur in 19-tn yorhundert (etyudn un materialn)* (New York: YKUF, 1946), vol. 2, pp. 235–37.

forces of modernism."[4] Wirth-Nesher then concludes, more or less in accordance with Berkovitsh's position, that Sholem Aleichem strives to preserve neutrality: "the linguistic disguises which Sholem Aleichem has draped around his speakers . . . permit the writer to escape from making the moral choices that his mutually contradictory and eclectic petit bourgeois social views would have eventually necessitated" (170). This conclusion is problematic because it neglects several distinctive stories from Sholem Aleichem's later writing. While some of his monologues do express ambivalence, others convey Sholem Aleichem's sympathies and antipathies. In several notable instances, Sholem Aleichem employs monologues as remarkable dramas of social criticism.

Interpreters of Sholem Aleichem's monologues have tended to concentrate on the major texts discussed in previous chapters.[5] As a result, critical and popular awareness seldom extend beyond "The Little Pot," "Geese," "A Bit of Advice," and the early Tevye stories. Reader reception has suppressed or overlooked another, potentially threatening world of Sholem Aleichem's work, which is epitomized by the monologues of mastery. The elements that comprise this mock genre may be found elsewhere, but they are particularly evident in the relatively unknown and atypical tales "Joseph," "Three Widows," and "A Story of a Greenhorn." Here the parodies of prior literary tradition intersect with satires of contemporary practices.

Sholem Aleichem's shifting political message is also evident in his concurrent Tevye stories. In "Shprintse" (1907), Tevye's fourth daughter plays out a tragedy that is even more definitive than Chava's decision to convert to Christianity. Shprintse falls in love with a young man, Arontshik, while his wealthy family is vacationing in their country home. Tevye tries to make the boy see that the match is impossible, speaking much as he argued in efforts to dissuade Chava from her liaison. Earlier he said to Chava: "What do you have in common with Khvedke?" ("Vos far a mekhutn

---

[4]Hana Wirth-Nesher, "Voices of Ambivalence in Sholem Aleichem's Monologues," *Prooftexts* 1 (1981), p. 169; henceforth cited by page alone.

[5]See, for example, Y. Y. Trunk, *Sholem Aleichem: zayn vezn un zayne verk* (Warsaw: Kultur-lige, 1937), pp. 161–224, and Victor Erlich, "A Note on the Monologue as a Literary Form: Sholem Aleichem's 'Monologn'—A Test Case," in *For Max Weinrich on his Seventieth Birthday* (The Hague: Mouton, 1964), pp. 44–50.

bistu mit Khvedken?"), which literally means "What kind of in-law are you to Khvedke?" Now, as the roles are reversed, he explains that Arontshik's family will never agree. Alluding to their class differences, Tevye asks Arontshik rhetorically: "What kind of groom are you for my Shprintse? . . . And the main thing is, I say, what kind of in-law am I to your mother?"[6] The problem here is not arranged marriages, ideological divisions, or religious differences, but social hierarchies. Tevye has internalized a class system, and only toward the end of the story does he reexamine his ideas and wonder: "Why should people be so evil, when they could be good? Why should people embitter others' lives and their own, when it is within their grasp to live well and happily?" (162). Nevertheless, the fictional world confirms Tevye's traditional notions about class differences: Arontshik's family prevents the match and Shprintse drowns herself. At the end of his good-natured monologue, Tevye interpolates a tragic conclusion that implicitly attacks the divisions between Jewish social classes.

The subsequent story, "Tevye Travels to the Land of Israel" ("Tevye fort keyn erets-isroel," 1909),[7] explores what might have occurred had Shprintse fulfilled her wishes. Beylke, daughter number five, has less of the idealism that characterizes her older sisters. They are inspired by love and ideological commitments, but Beylke openly marries for wealth. To describe her charm, Tevye employs a metaphor that fittingly projects a mercenary God: "Ever since God has traded in Beylkes, he has never made another Beylke like her" (170). Although Tevye compares her to gold, he claims that he never imagined she would "go and sell herself for money" (171). Pragmatism ultimately prevails when Ephraim the matchmaker succeeds in pairing off Beylke with the millionaire Podhotsur. An unforeseen consequence of this match is that the groom cannot bear the thought of having a father-in-law who is a dairyman, and he plans to send Tevye away to Palestine. The upshot of all this is that Beylke lives unhappily in her gaudy estate until (in the subse-

---

[6]*Gants Tevye der milkhiker,* in *Ale verk fun Sholem Aleichem* (New York: Folksfond Edition, 1917–23), vol. 5, p. 153; this and the subsequent Tevye story are henceforth cited by page alone.

[7]Sholem Aleichem's railroad stories were gaining momentum at this time, and so the present tale was subtitled: "Narrated by Tevye the Dairyman, Traveling by Train."

quent story) Podhotsur loses his riches.[8] Whereas the earlier Tevye stories confront the collapse of the traditional world under pressure from modernization, the later stories convey Sholem Aleichem's growing disapproval of social hierarchies.

The monologues of mastery are narrated by men whose wealth and education enable them to carry out sinister schemes. They often claim to be impotent or indecisive; unlike Sholem Aleichem's impoverished speakers, however, these narrators occupy a dominant position—both in their fictional worlds and in their acts of narration. As they address their monologues to Sholem Aleichem, we search for clues of unreliability. While the listener within the story betrays no reactions other than ambiguous smiles, there are hints of the author's stance beneath the surface of the narrative situation.

"JOSEPH"

Sholem Aleichem's "Joseph" ("Yoysef," 1905) carries the subtitle: "Narrative of a 'Gentleman.'"[9] This epithet at first appears as Sholem Aleichem's ironic designation, yet it also comes from within the story: "'The gentleman'—I had no other name," the narrator explains, among the revolutionaries he knows. Throughout, the speaker describes himself and the other characters vaguely, in accordance with their broad differences in status. The ensuing

---

[8]See "Get Thee Out" ("Lekh-lekha," 1914) in SA 5: 202. Compare Sholem Aleichem's play *Dos groyse gevins: a folks-shpil in fir aktn* (1915), also starring a young heroine named Beylke, in SA 4: 151–256. In English, see *The Jackpot: A Folk-Play in Four Acts,* trans. Kobi Weitzner and Barnett Zumoff (New York: Workmen's Circle Education Department, 1989).

[9]Translations of Sholem Aleichem's monologues are based on the volume of *Monologn* in *Ale verk fun Sholem Aleichem* (New York: Folksfond Edition, 1917–23), vol. 21; cited by page alone. "Yoysef" was first serialized in *Der veg*, September 22, 24, 25, 1905, and in *Dos yidishe togeblat*, October 5, 6, 8, 10, 11, 1905. Without substantial changes, the story was reprinted in Sholem Aleichem's *Nayeste verk* (Warsaw: Progress, 1909), vol. 1, pp. 21–41. These earlier printings bear lengthier subtitles than does the version in the Folksfond edition and do not place "Gentleman" in quotation marks. In *Der veg* and the Progess edition, the subtitle reads: "Narrative of a Gentleman and Retold Word for Word by Sholem Aleichem." *Dos yidishe togeblat* presumably chose its own punning title: "Narrative of a Gentleman and Retold Incidentally in '*Veg*' [Underway] by Sholem Aleichem." In a letter to Sholem Aleichem of 25 August/7 September 1905, Bal Makhshoves mentions having received a copy of this story from him.

rivalry between two men nearly becomes an allegory as it resonates with political overtones.

Y. D. Berkovitsh, having met Sholem Aleichem in 1905, provides inside information about the revolutionary context in which "Joseph" was written. During this period in the summer of 1905, Sholem Aleichem visited his daughter in Vilna. Berkovitsh recalls in his memoirs that after leaving Vilna "he immediately showed his renewed force in *Der veg* with his story 'Joseph,' a vibrant story that seethes with the wrath of the age, devoted to the Jewish youth, to the wonderful 'Yankelekh,' secretly brewing up the confection of the Russian Revolution. This was a kind of repayment for the days he resided in Vilna, the city in which the 'Bund' was born."[10] Berkovitsh does not mention the formal novelty of "Joseph": it tells the story, not from the perspective of its lead characters, but from the standpoint of a bourgeois observer.

"Joseph" reworks the family drama of "Hodel," written just one year earlier. In both cases, a strong-willed woman successfully asserts her independence against the oral narrator, a male authority figure. But here Tevye's fatherly protectiveness is replaced by a more sinister style of attempted control. Hodel must sweep aside Tevye's traditionalism, while the unnamed girl in "Joseph" has to counter the ascendancy of wealth. The girl's namelessness is one indication of the unreliable narrator's way of reducing her to a mere object of desire. In turn, the revolutionary socialists ironically restrict his authority among them by labeling him "the gentleman."

According to his own account, the gentleman admires and desires a poor girl who is the waitress in her mother's restaurant. Unfortunately for him, she is attracted to Joseph, one of the social revolutionaries who frequent the restaurant. Hence the drama centers around the question: Who exerts greater power, and by what means? Whereas the gentleman is primarily concerned with powers that vie for a woman's love, Joseph occupies himself with revolutionary ideas and actions.

The narrator evasively describes the girl who motivates the story: "You yourself probably understand that I will *not* tell *who*

---

[10]See Y. D. Berkovitsh, *Ha-rish'onim ki-vnei-adam: sippurei zikharonot 'al Sholem-Aleichem u-vnei-doro*, 3d ed. (Tel Aviv: Dvir, 1976), pp. 149–50. Henceforth cited as "R" by page alone.

she is and *what* she is, and *where* she comes from. She is a woman, a girl, indeed a beautiful girl, and poor" (108).[11] Despite his evasiveness, the gentleman quickly reveals what he considers to be the essential facts: she is beautiful and poor. He wishes to possess her but discovers that she is not as helpless as her financial and social position lead him to expect. That the gentleman views his beloved girl in capital terms is clear from his glowing account of her laughter, "which alone is worth all the money" one pays to eat in her mother's restaurant. In short, he wants to purchase her on the strength of his financial holdings, and is thwarted when her affections are not moved by monetary concerns.

The gentleman initially defies the hearer of his tale: "You can laugh at me, you can make a *feuilleton* out of me, even a book, if you wish—I'm not afraid of you" (107). Aware of Sholem Aleichem's usual satiric practices, the monologist insists on his imperviousness. Nevertheless, the final lines of the story undermine this initial bravado: "Give me your hand that everything I have told you here will remain between the two of us" (133). Despite the narrator's brash claim to make all decisions for himself, moreover, he admits that he broke off his studies and married a girl after being threatened by her brother (107). The gentleman tells us that he suffered for three years with her before regaining his freedom.

From start to finish, the narrator is aware of power struggles and is especially sensitive to those associated with language. Even Joseph's powers appear to him rhetorical, in the classical sense referring to persuasive oration. While he tells a story of his efforts to dominate others, he manipulates the fictional hearer of his tale, simultaneously manipulating the reader of Sholem Aleichem's story. But by writing the account which his character has supposedly asked him to keep secret, Sholem Aleichem hints at a betrayal of his fictional speaker.

The narrator boasts that women constantly fall in love with him and that matchmakers always chase him. His self-description is, however, unconvincing: "I am a modern, handsome young man, healthy, with a bit of a name, and a fine breadwinner, so that a

---

[11]References to Sholem Aleichem's volume of *Monologn* are by page alone in SA 5. An English translation of "Yoysef," entitled "Yosif: A 'Gentleman's' Tale," is available in Sholom Aleichem, *Tevye the Dairyman and Other Stories*, trans. Mirian Katz (Moscow: Raduga, 1988), pp. 374–96. See also Golda Werman's edited translation of "Joseph" in *Fiction* 11 (1992), 137–48.

ruble is nothing to me" (108). The gentleman resorts to this self-portrait in order to authenticate his status and it becomes a kind of nervous reflex, but his oft-repeated refrain only unsettles the identity it is intended to secure.[12] Rather than respect his position, we come to see it as a joke: he turns himself into a caricature of the up-to-date gentleman. Whenever he encounters a difficulty, an awkward pause, or a threat to his presumed power, he comically sketches out his profile. Although he claims to have "a bit of a name," in his own story he remains simply "the gentleman," and despite all his efforts only his rival's name, Joseph, will be remembered.

For the narrator who is so conscious of his image, class relations are clearly delimited by styles of dress. The socialist "Yankelekh" (generic "Jacobs") frequent the narrator's favored restaurant wearing long hair and black shirts. In contrast, the narrator wears a smoking jacket with a white vest. Tensions between the speaker and listener intensify with the former's remark that "you yourself, it seems, wear long hair and a black shirt, and if you think it handsome, excuse me, but you're wrong" (111). In their represented milieu, clothing is an unmistakable marker of social hierarchies, and this assault places the fictional hearer, Sholem Aleichem (the implied author's persona, not the flesh-and-blood Sholem Rabinovitsh) at odds with the speaker and closer to the revolutionary intellectuals.[13] As language becomes a medium of aggression, the reader should feel uneasy about the narrator's attacks and feints.

The politics of language also becomes an issue in connection with the socialist-Bundist terminology that is popular among the "Yankelekh." The speaker says that he has nothing against honest talk, but "I simply dislike it, when someone tells me that I am a 'bourgeois.' For the word 'bourgeois' I can deliver a slap on the cheek!" (112).[14] The monologist, familiar with socialist terms, uses them to establish legitimacy and approach Joseph's circle. On

---

[12]Compare SA 5: 109, 112, 115, 118, 122, 123, 128, 130, 132.

[13]When he wrote this story, Sholem Rabinovitsh actually did wear long hair and the black, "proletarian" shirt of the young Bundist activists, as attested by Y. D. Berkovitsh in R 86, 118. This garb was also called a "Gorky shirt."

[14]Compare Hana Wirth-Nesher, "Voices of Ambivalence in Sholem Aleichem's Monologues," p. 169.

occasion he even resorts to their key words: "proletariat," "Marx," "Bebel," "react" (*reagirn*), and "conspiratorial" (114, 123, 124, 126, 130). For the gentleman, however, these words merely form the mask by means of which he hopes to attain his ends. Where Tevye's quotations appropriate Scripture, this monologist parodies socialist jargon.

Although the narrator boasts of his good name, he discovers that another name is far better, in the mouth of his beloved: "She speaks the name 'Joseph' with an odd sort of sing-song. Only a bride [or fiancée, *kale*] uses such a sing-song, when she speaks the name of her destined groom" (*khosn*, 110). Impoverished, the desired girl asserts her freedom from the narrator by means of a word, one of her only words which he records: "Joseph." This word presents such an obstacle that it structures the narrative and provides its title. Like a spell against Satan, the name of the beloved keeps the narrator at a distance. Since the mildly satanic gentleman cannot become Joseph in order to correspond to her longings, he wonders how he can eliminate the rival.

The relationship between power and language is explicit in one central scene, when the gentleman attends a revolutionary meeting. While Joseph speaks and the narrator observes his success as an orator, he is especially struck by Joseph's sway over *her*: "That minute I envied him, not so much for the force of his speaking, not for the honor and the applause which he received afterward, when he finished speaking—not for these things was I so envious of him, as for the way *she* looked at him! For such a look of hers, I would give away—I myself don't know what!" (117–18). The narrator decides to eliminate his adversary, whom he credits with rhetorical skill: "one must get rid of him" (*me darf zayner poter vern*, 120). Having determined that Joseph's power resides in his language, the narrator resolves to fight him on this ground: "I'll have a chat with him alone" (ibid.). When they meet, the gentleman begins by showing off all the socialist vocabulary he knows. Then he transforms *reagirn* from a political term into a description of bourgeois emotions, to explain that he is not accustomed to "reacting" to a girl in this way. It remains unclear whether the speaker says anything more threatening to Joseph. We merely see that, in contrast to the gentleman, Joseph has concerns other than amorous pursuit.

The next we hear, Joseph—like Hodel's beloved—is in trouble with the authorities. Given the political environment of early

1905, one must assume that his trial turns out badly; he is presumably hanged or exiled. The gentleman's obstacle appears to have been overcome. He then makes a ruthless attempt to ambush his beloved's heart in a moment of weakness, but without success. He tells her that she need not *reagirn* (again this word!) so strongly to what has happened to Joseph; she should forget it all. Although he is momentarily surprised by his power of speech, his efforts fail (130). Soon afterward the girl, her mother, and their restaurant disappear. All inquiries are in vain, and their memory is like a dream. The gentleman can only tell the tale of a girl who revealed to him the limits of his power.

The narrator strives to manipulate the hearer of the story, at the same time that he pretends to be weak and a failure (108). Yet he evidently plays an active role at some points in his account, and we may wonder whether there is any connection between the narrator's schemes and Joseph's demise. This question is unanswerable, since it lies beyond the limits of the story. Nevertheless, a passing comment may hint that the gentleman contributed to Joseph's arrest. He explains that he keeps a record of the conspiratorial activity he observes: "I wrote it out in a notebook" (*ikh hob es farshribn bay zikh in bikhel*) (115). Sholem Aleichem employs irony when he has the narrator add: "Whether it will be of use or not, I don't know, but certainly it doesn't hurt" (ibid.). Of course, certain kinds of notes can have deleterious effects when furnished to the authorities in a repressive society. Language is a medium in which the narrator exerts power against Joseph and the listener, for writing and narrating have become his instruments of aggression.

"THREE WIDOWS"

A more intricate "monologue of mastery" unfolds in Sholem Aleichem's "Three Widows" ("Dray almones," 1907). The narrator of this monologue is similarly wealthy and literate, but the subtitle emphasizes an ungentlemanly characteristic: this is "a story of an old bachelor, an irascible man [*bal kasn*]." Anger is central to the story, in part because the speaker continually provokes the listener, implicitly Sholem Aleichem.

In "Three Widows," the narrator's belligerent relationship to his audience organizes the three sections of the narrative. His opening words immediately create a dramatic situation, following something the interlocutor has supposedly said: "You are wrong, my lord. Not all old maids are unhappy, not all old bachelors are egoists. Sitting there in your study with a cigar in your mouth and a book in your hand, you imagine you already know everything" (165). The reader is drawn into an aggressive scene for the duration of the narrative. At the same time, Sholem Aleichem employs irony against himself when he has a fictional character criticize his author's paper-thin conception of the world. In effect, this critique may grant a greater illusion of reality to the antagonistic speaker, who pretends to understand the real world better than does his creator.

Similarly, the second part begins: "Why have I made you wait so long?—Because I wanted to. When I tell a story, I do it when I wish, not when *you* wish" (190). The speaker insists that the hearer sit silently in an uncomfortable chair, and he sets the time and place of their meeting. After he concludes the second section, he tells the listener that to hear the rest of "the story about my 'widow number three,' you should trouble yourself to come to my home. If not—as you wish! I won't drag you by the coattails." He taunts, "You'll come by yourself" (*ir vet aleyn kumen*) (199). Sholem Aleichem sets the three sections of his story (originally serialized in more than three segments) in three separate scenes. For the initial readership of his work, made to wait for coming installments, this created a parallel between the fictional speaker-hearer situation of Sholem Aleichem's monologue and the real author-reader communication.

The plot of "Three Widows" is similar to that of the earlier "Joseph," but here the irascible speaker's account verges on becoming absurd. Thematically, both works recall the generational dynamics of the Tevye stories, but they take on a more ominous tone. The monologist begins his story by recalling the death of an acquaintance. He helps the bereaved widow and her daughter Roza, who is born a few months later. Although infatuated by the widow, he explains that indecisiveness prevents him from satisfying his desire to marry her. He claims to be impotent, like some passive characters in Chekhov's works such as "The Wife" (1892) and "A Dreary Story" (1899). Meanwhile, as Roza matures, the narrator's infatuation shifts from mother to daughter. Again, however, he never goes so far as to propose marriage. Roza eventually marries a bookkeeper who promptly poisons himself after a business failure.

She subsequently gives birth to Feygele, and the earlier pattern recurs. The narrator delays his marriage proposal to the daughter for so long that he finally transfers his attentions to the grand-daughter. In structure, if not in tone, this repetition of events *ad absurdum* associates the story with some of Sholem Aleichem's more familiar, comic tales. Insensitive to his charms, Feygele marries a chemist who, like Joseph, is arrested for conspiratorial activities and hanged. The speaker continues his close associations with the three widows, and he twice interrupts his storytelling to dine with them. As the monologue ends, he anticipates spending the night at their home. This narrative combines dark humor, perversity, and the absurd, in multiple layers of satire.

At every turn, the present scene of narration is relevant to the events narrated. The speaker initially challenges his hearer to grasp the paradoxical tale he will relate, since psychology is incapable of explaining such hard realities: "Why are you telling me about psychology? If you want to know the true psychology, you should sit down and listen carefully to what I tell you" (165). Only after listening to the tale, the speaker claims, may the hearer express an opinion on the origins of sadness and egoism, or concerning the character of old maids and bachelors.

The scene of monologue resembles a psychoanalytic session. The narrator demands freedom to narrate without interruptions, almost as if he were outlining the rules for Freud's talking cure. The narrator repeatedly toys with the prospect that he is *meshuge* (166, 171, 178–79, 181, 185, 191, 208). He directs the hearer to trade places, so that while narrating he may recline in a rocking-chair, and he adds that "by the way, it's better for you right there, you won't fall asleep" (166; cp. 186). The narrator openly states: "I'm speaking out my heart to you, and with you I want to analyze, to find out: where is the worm?" (185). The listener's brief reactions are not recorded, but instead implied by the monologist's words. Thus the burden of interpretation rests with the reader, who must gauge the narrator's level of reliability.

One early digression on buttons, revolving around a failure to marry, prepares the reader for the events of the story: "What is a button? A button, dear friend, with one of us, with a bachelor, is an important thing! An entire world! Over a button a nasty story once occurred: a bachelor came to look at a girl, and someone pointed out to him with a laugh that he was missing a button; he went away and hanged himself" (168). According to his own account, the bachelor narrator is a master of buttons, of reserve, to the extent that he never seems to undress or to have a lewd thought. He indicates that lapses of decorum, for bachelors, are no laughing matter.

Gradually the speaker reveals all the twists and turns of an unreliable narrator. His claim to speak "from the heart, without tricks" only arouses suspicion. He is evasive, self-contradictory, and at odds with established ethical norms: he withholds details (e.g., 166, 177–78), contradicts himself (e.g., 167/180–81/201), and repeatedly mocks social conventions (e.g., 185). Like the narrator of "Joseph," he is an individualist and an outsider. He also makes slurs against the Jewish people (172, 187), unlike the gentleman narrator who admits in passing that he is, in spite of everything, a Jew (120). He even predicts that the hearer will label him "an old bachelor, an irascible man," anticipating the criticism he knows he provokes. Still, the success of this fiction derives from the ambiguous—rather than obviously reprehensible—position of its speaker.

One early point of contention in the narrator's tale is his relationship to the first widow's husband: "I was acquainted with her husband. Not only acquainted, but friendly (*bafraynt*). That is, I don't say that we were friends. I say that we were friendly" (167). Later in the story, the narrator refers back to this "friend" (169, 180–81, 201); his relationship to the widow makes this a potentially sensitive point. Without being able to see beyond what the narrator tells us, we nevertheless sense that he is withholding information. He seems to exert a will to power over the listener at every turn.

Similar to Sholem Aleichem's other monologists, the irascible man digresses frequently and employs a linguistic catchword to bring himself back to the main thread. This repetition places him squarely in the tradition of Russian *skaz*, although the narrator's discourse shares few comic or colloquial patterns with Sholem Aleichem's other monologists. His rather pretentious, Germanic reflex is the connective adverb, *alzo*.[15] By means of this word the speaker indicates that he is returning to the earlier narrative line,

---

[15]Instances of this *daytshmerish* usage occur on pages 166, 167, 169, 171, 172, 173, 176, 177, 182, 184, 185, 190, 201, 203.

but digressions remain apparent. Nevertheless, this speaker's digressions seldom appear to be neutral or unpremeditated. Unlike Sholem Aleichem's loquacious female monologists, the irascible man seems to control his associative leaps, subordinating them to ulterior motives.

As he speaks, the narrator taunts the hearer: "I don't ask your opinion!" (167); "I won't enter into discussion with you" (172); "What does it matter to me what you think?" (173). He has only harsh words to say about "your writers" (197). The first widow's daughter grew and blossomed "like a delicate rose," he says, alluding to her name and mimicking "the language of your novelists, who know as much about the blossoming of a rose as a Turk knows about the *rabonan kadesh* [the prayer for the masters and disciples of the law]" (171).[16] Later, he refuses to narrate sentimental details, which "the novelists employ in order to squeeze out a tear from the foolish reader" (189; cp. 195). In particular, he rejects the word "love," which "your writers" have spoiled by indiscriminate use (197; cp. 210). The narrator thus employs parodic devices, recalling Sholem Aleichem's early attacks on "most interesting novels," in order to insult his listener. These polemics cover up his cool reactions to the lives of his loves and to the deaths of his rivals.

The speaker carefully monitors the hearer's reactions to his tale. He seems aware of his own covert, malicious tone, which is closer to black humor than is usual in Sholem Aleichem's work. He offsets the grim mood of "Three Widows" only by referring to the laughter of his female friends. When beset by difficulties, "they laugh": "With them everything is laughter! All of life is laughter" (183; cp. 191).[17] The redeeming laughter of the three widows differs sharply from the potentially critical or ironic smiles of the hearer. Hence this silent reaction is a threat and therefore unacceptable: "I dislike it when one smiles. You can laugh as much as you wish, but not smile" (200; cp. 168, 187; 107). In this case, most of the laughter occurs within the story rather than on the part of the reader.

---

[16]Compare "Joseph," 110, 120.

[17]In these monologues, laughter also occurs at the expense of their narrators, within the stories they tell. See, for example, the mother's play on the word *farzorgt* in "Joseph" (110).

Proud of his education, the irascible man explains that as guardian of the three widows he has received the name "Cerberus": "They gave me the name 'Cerberus'—a dog, that is, that stands at the entrance to paradise" (176). Yet his attempted gloss on a literary allusion backfires and shows his ignorance, since the mythological Cerberus guards the entrance to the underworld. Inadvertently reversing the classical myth, possibly because for him the widows' home is a paradise, he betrays the fact that he has turned it into a hell for them and for all other suitors. Sholem Aleichem uses this misunderstanding of the nickname "Cerberus" to satirize the narrator.

"Three Widows" ends in a situation of charged ambiguity. In a Chekhovian mode, the irascible narrator refers to his inability to fulfill his desires, saying that despite his infatuation for the first widow, "I had no courage to tell her" (181). There is no way to test his honesty, because the fictional world exists only in the story he tells. Yet internal inconsistencies unsettle the surface effects. The monologist claims never to satisfy his longings for those he calls "my three widows," but he manages to completely dominate their lives, apparently spending most of his days and even some nights with them. This is the conclusion of the story:

> You're ready to go? Come, I'll go with you. I have to be with my three widows. Just a moment, I want to arrange to have the cat fed, because sometimes I can sit there until dawn [*ikh kon mikh dort farzitsen biz tog oykh amol*]. We play Yerulash, sometimes Preference. We play for money. And you should see how everyone wants to win! And when someone makes a bad play, one doesn't show any mercy, neither they toward me nor I toward them. With me, if someone makes a bad play in cards, I'm capable of trampling on them, tearing them to pieces! What does your smile mean, for example? I know what you think now. I know you through and through and laugh at your grandma! You're thinking about me now: "An old bachelor, an irascible man." (212)

Curt Leviant's translation of this passage is perhaps intended to spare innocent readers by mistranslating the sentence that contributes most to our recognition of the speaker's unreliability. Leviant translates *ikh kon mikh dort farzitsen biz tog oykh amol* (212) by "I'm liable to spend the whole day there."[18] It is true that, given

---

[18]See Curt Leviant, *Stories and Satires*, p. 213.

the narrator's equivocations, day is night and night is day. But "biz tog" literally means "until dawn." "Farzitsen" here means "to sit," although (especially when applied to women) it can also mean "to remain unmarried." This is exactly what the narrator does, summed up in a phrase: he stays with the widows night and day, and yet remains unmarried. In the context of his confessional love story, the hostile relationship between the narrator and his three widows has never before been so evident. It cannot be purely coincidental that they play cards, like the unreliable narrator of "A Game of Sixty-Six," or that one of their card games is called "Preference." The narrator claims that he has never been able to express or enjoy his preferences. Why, then, does he haunt the widows' house, deep into the night?

There is no basis for further speculation on what "actually" happens between the narrator and his widows. He tells us that he has wasted his life as a result of his timidity with regard to women. And yet in another sense he has victimized the three widows, constantly hovering nearby like a bourgeois Cerberus—always about to propose marriage yet always delaying. The questionable nature of the irascible man's attentions becomes clear, from the standpoint of the first widow, when she once asserts that she has wasted her life because of him (178). Although the narrator claims to be a master in the ethereal world of chess strategy, he admits to having suffered defeat in real life (177–78). Yet even this resignation seems to be a guise that conceals a deeper strategy. Instead of choosing one of the three widows, he possesses all three, both as a sinister benefactor and as their narrative inventor. No amount of scrutiny can fully penetrate the story's layers of deceit, but the speaker himself alludes to Bismarck, saying: "Words were given to us in order to mask our thoughts" (196). To the extent that the narrator is obviously manipulative, his efforts fail to achieve their desired effect. We end the story with a critical smile on our lips, and (as in "A Game of Sixty-Six") we arrive at an uneasy awareness that we have been had.

"A STORY OF A GREENHORN"

"A Story of a Greenhorn" ("A mayse mit a grinhorn," 1916), one of Sholem Aleichem's last works, intensifies the earlier voices of mastery and Mr. Green's story of his career as a shofar-blower. On one level, it epitomizes Sholem Aleichem's scathing critique of America, and more specifically of business practices on the Lower East Side. But this monologue also extends the manipulative narratives by a gentleman and by an old bachelor. The subtitle of this satire informs us that in it "Mr. Baraban, business broker, tells how he taught a lesson to a greenhorn, who married for the sake of business" (251).[19] This narrator, Mr. Baraban—whose name means "drum"—pounds out a self-righteous account of his wrongdoings. Whereas the gentleman and the irascible man have somewhat ambiguous moral standings, Mr. Baraban possesses no positive features. His one-sidedness resolves the earlier uncertainties, producing a more straightforward effect of social criticism.

Like "Joseph" and "Three Widows," "A Story of a Greenhorn" opens with a reaction to the interlocutor: "You say: America is a land of business—nevermind. It has to be like this" (*Ir zogt: amerike iz a land fun biznes—nevermaynd. Es darf azoi tsu zayn*, 253). But where the narrator of "Three Widows" initially attacks psychological theories, this monologist refers to the practices of newcomers and states a moral:

> After all, to go and marry and sell oneself for the sake of business—that is really, excuse me, swinishness. I don't preach morality, but I'm telling you, it's a fact that ninety-nine percent of greenhorns among us marry for the sake of business. That vexes me, and when I catch such a greenhorn, he doesn't get away from me in one piece. (Ibid.)

By beginning with the relatively uncontroversial moral judgment that one should not marry for money, the speaker forestalls our recognition of his own immorality. Mr. Baraban tells a tale of his unethical actions, hidden under the mask of self-righteous criticism. The dual presentation produces the strained irony of the story, which the narrator calls a "comedy" (255). As in the other monologues of mastery, the drama centers around a desired woman, and recounts the elimination of a competing man.

---

[19] "A mayse mit a grinhorn" was first published in *Di varhayt*, 16 January 1916, with a long subtitle that was probably not written by Sholem Aleichem. An English rendition is contained in Sholem Aleichem, *Some Laughter, Some Tears: Tales from the Old World and the New*, trans. Curt Leviant (New York: Paragon Books, 1979), pp. 243–48.

An unsuspecting newcomer and his wife visit Mr. Baraban, the business broker. They ask for assistance in opening a stationery store. Because Mr. Baraban happens to have a laundry up for sale, he convinces the greenhorn to go into the laundry business. What most impresses the monologist is the greenhorn's well-favored marriage to a beautiful girl with a fine dowry.

Although the unnamed girl is a passive observer of the ensuing spectacle, she is the source of its drama. Mr. Baraban describes her enthusiastically, as he first sees her: "with him a woman—what shall I tell you?—blood and milk. Beautiful as the day and fresh as an apple, just off the tree" (253). His outrage against the greenhorn flares up when he compares their assets: "The bastard has only a few hundred dollars in his pocket and a woman at his side—fine gold! Why does he deserve it? Mr. Baraban, the biggest business broker of the East Side, has to have a wife, excuse me, a monster and what's more a Xantippe; and God has to send such a jewel to the greenhorn" (257). In "Joseph," the gentleman monologist learns the limits of his wealth, since his beloved is attracted to a poor intellectual. Mr. Baraban refuses to acknowledge forces greater than money, and in Sholem Aleichem's fictional world, the American milieu supports this attitude.

By means of several swindles, the business broker succeeds in completely bankrupting the greenhorn who, like the other mono- logists' competitors, is imprisoned. As the story closes, "I picked a lawyer for his wife who demands from him, on her account, three things: (1) her money, the thousand-dollar dowry; (2) a divorce; and (3) until she receives a divorce from him, he shall support her in accordance with the laws of the country" (259). Radicalizing the leanings of wealthy speakers in other stories, this last monologist embodies the triumph of evil. Through the mediation of a lawyer, Mr. Baraban unabashedly eliminates his opposition and takes con- trol of the woman's affairs. Financial power yields personal power and a self-assurance that blinds the caricatured speaker to the possibility of seeing his actions in a negative light. The story ends unresolved, since we do not know what may ensue between the usurper and the woman whose life he has dominated.

After perpetrating a violent scheme, Mr. Baraban narrates his misdeeds complacently and even moralistically. This is another example of how Sholem Aleichem's monological narrators betray themselves in the language of their narrations. Mr. Baraban's language is as violent as are the scheming actions he relates, and this violence is directed against people as well as against language itself. Specifically, the business broker wrecks the Yiddish language by slipping in English words at every turn. This perversion of Yiddish reaches such extreme proportions that the volume of *Monologn* includes an extensive dictionary of Yinglish (*farenglishte*) words.

Despite the power of the master monologists, we finally resist their attempted domination. Like the implied hearer of these stories within the fictional world, the Sholem Aleichem persona, we leave their narrators with a grimace. This happens both because we question their actions, as they narrate them, and because they undermine themselves through inconsistencies and questionable language. The bourgeois speakers put on airs and presume to know more than they do; they boast of their knowledge but garble socialist jargon, place Cerberus at the gates of paradise, and (especially in "A Story of a Greenhorn") do obvious violence to the Yiddish language.

These satiric stories are neither humorous nor comic in any usual sense, since we cannot laugh heartily *with* or *at* their speakers.[20] They contradict our expectations from a Sholem Aleichem monologue. Wealthy rather than poor, the domineering narrators are never folk characters (*folkstipn*) with whom we laugh in order not to cry. Nor do they make the best of an imperfect world; instead, they add to the world's imperfections. These narrators have the means to overcome most obstacles to the fulfillment of their desires. In fact, Sholem Aleichem's texts depend on the power of these speakers to impose their narrative wills. The gentleman, the irascible man, and the business broker are fictional authors of devious plots within their narratives and of their monologues. Hence these monologists enable Sholem Aleichem to exercise his mastery of form by transferring the burden of mastery to them. We

---

[20]Shmuel Niger, in *Sholem Aleichem: zayne vikhtikste verk, zayn humor un zayn ort in der yidisher literatur* (New York: YKUF, 1928), differentiates between laughter *with* humorous characters and *at* comic characters (pp. 102–04). In a related way, in *The Story of Yiddish Literature* (New York: Yiddish Scientific Institute, 1940), A. A. Roback writes that "Mendele wrote *to* the masses, while Sholem Aleichem wrote *for* them and Peretz wrote *about* them" (p. 150).

may, in consequence, admire the compositions while retaining a critical distance from the imaginary narrators of these mono- logues.

Monologue is an appropriate form for these stories, whose speakers live monologically. Dialogue hardly enters into their ex- perience, for they never exchange words or thoughts. We rarely hear a dialogue, and the desired women appear almost entirely mute. The monologists impose their wills, and are not concerned to suit their actions to others' needs. They are openly hostile to whatever the captive audience may say, preferring to do all the talking themselves, without interruption. Their failures reflect the limitations of a monological rhetoric.

In the erotic realm, both suppressed and decisive in these sto- ries, the monologists present themselves as voyeurs. They desire beautiful women from afar, but never seem to get beyond appear- ances. Ultimately, they desire only their own desire, in a fantasy that cannot be disturbed by any opposing will. Thus these monolo- gists never procreate; their only offspring are words. They never escape the boundaries of the mastery they desire.

Although it is tempting to interpret Sholem Aleichem's mono- logues of mastery on the mimetic plane, with an eye to clues of unreliability, even the unreliable narrators are only fictional per- sonae. Sholem Aleichem directs a wide range of narrative strategies toward irony at the expense of his monologists. When they are "low" characters, this irony achieves the effect of light comedy or humor. But when the speakers are more imposing personalities, the irony cuts deeper, challenging the social contexts that empower them. In the monologues of mastery, monologue has become a luxury—and a delusion—of the rich. Their wealth is no extra- neous detail, for it buys greater freedom from constraints and power to manipulate events. But these monologues are invariably marked by discrepancies. Allied with perversions of desire, the monologists are overthrown by their forced dependence on others.

Social criticism in literature often depicts corruption in one form or another. Sholem Aleichem's "monologues of mastery" employ a subtler means: in these stories the depiction itself is corrupt. There is no distance between the narrative voice and the world that is described. The monologists inadvertently turn their words against themselves, uncovering bourgeois foibles from within. Monologue, when it is a luxury of the rich, acts as a double-edged sword.

There is a significant break between Abramovitsh's novels of 1863 to 1878 and Sholem Aleichem's monologues that were written between 1894 and 1916. As Dan Miron observes in *A Traveler Disguised*, Abramovitsh's persona, Mendele the Bookseller, purports to be a self-educated, more or less straightforward literary editor. Mendele explains the circumstances that have enabled him to publish prior texts supposedly written by Isaac-Abraham, Hirsh Rothmann, Isrolik, and Benjamin the Third. According to this pretense, he deals with *written* documents, which he makes available to his readers after having tampered with them to varying degrees.

Sholem Aleichem's Tevye and his other monologists, in contrast, are supposed to be oral sources. This new turn is an essential part of Sholem Aleichem's genius, drawing from the inherent genius of the Yiddish language and its culture.[21] Until the nineteenth century, Yiddish was essentially an oral culture; its written glory dates only as far back as Abramovitsh. In the twentieth century, Sholem Aleichem goes several steps beyond the somewhat spontaneous persona of Mendele the Bookseller by reproducing an entire gallery of monologists. They range from Tevye and his underprivileged cohorts to the gentleman narrator in "Joseph," the old bachelor in "Three Widows," and the ruthless businessman on the Lower East Side in "A Story of a Greenhorn."

Sholem Aleichem started as a disciple of Abramovitsh and emerged as an original author in his own right. Abramovitsh began with socially conscious irony and satire, conveying social criticism through his amiable persona of Mendele the Bookseller. Sholem Aleichem took over where Abramovitsh left off, satirizing various aspects of Jewish life and the novelistic genre itself. In some respects Sholem Aleichem later curtailed his satiric impulse and placed the emphasis on humoristic sketches. This humor was most effective when it resonated with the voice of *yidn fun a gants yor,* everyday Jews. From Abramovitsh's greatest invention, Mendele the Bookseller, Sholem Aleichem extrapolated countless speakers

---

[21]Benjamin Harshav emphasizes this point in *The Meaning of Yiddish* (Berkeley: University of California Press, 1990), pp. 98–107.

whose rambling stories, pathetic uncertainty, quiet resignation, self-indulgent confessions, and comic errors represent the vanishing essence of popular Yiddish culture. At the same time, Sholem Aleichem never lost contact with social criticism, as is most evident in his monologues of mastery.

PART THREE

Peretz

FIGURE 5
I. L. Peretz

FIGURE 6
Peretz's Poland

TABLE 3.
Chronology of Peretz's Life

1852	Born in Zamosc (Zamoshtch), Lublin Province, on 18 May.
1864–67	Studied in yeshivot in Zamosc and Shevershin (Szczebrzeszyn); influenced by reading Maimonides' *Mishneh Torah* and secular Polish, Russian, French, and German books.
ca. 1871	Married Sarah, daughter of Gabriel Yehuda Lichtenfeld, a well-known Hebrew writer; moved to Apt (Opatow) and thence to Sandomir.
ca. 1874	Birth of Peretz's son Lucian; wrote Polish and Yiddish poems.
ca. 1875	Divorced his wife Sarah Lichtenfeld.
1875–76	Lived in Warsaw, where he gave Hebrew lessons and met Hebrew writers; published a fable in Peretz Smolenskin's journal *Ha-shachar* (Vienna).
1877	Published his first book with his former father-in-law, a collection of their Hebrew poems; passed examinations to become a lawyer.
1878	Married his second wife, Helena Ringelbaum.
1877–88	Worked as a lawyer in Zamosc.
1879	His volume of Hebrew poems from 1877 was favorably reviewed in *Ha-shachar*.
1886–87	Lived for a few months in Warsaw and published Hebrew fiction and poetry in leading publications: *Ha-'asif, Ha-tzefira,* and *Ha-yom.*
1888	Lost his right to practice law because of an accusation concerning radical activities; corresponded with Sholem Aleichem about Yiddish literature; published his Yiddish poem "Monish" in Sholem Aleichem's *The Jewish Popular Library* (*Di yudishe folks-bibliotek*).
1889	Moved to Warsaw permanently; published several short stories in the second volume of Sholem Aleichem's *Di yudishe folks-bibliotek.*
1890	Participated in a statistical and ethnographic expedition to small towns including Tishevitz (Tyszowce), Yartchovka (Jarczow), Lashtchev (Laszczow), and Tomaszhev (Tomaszow-Lubelski); published three

(continued)

TABLE 3. (*Continued*)

	Yiddish stories in his independent volume *Familiar Scenes* (*Bakante Bilder*).
1891	Worked for the Jewish Community of Warsaw as a records-keeper, which remained his occupation until the end of his life; published *Scenes from a Journey Through the Provinces* (*Bilder fun a provints-rayze*) based on his expedition.
1891–95	Published the first three volumes of *The Jewish Library* (*Di yudishe bibliotek*), including a wide range of poetry and prose.
1893	Published several Yiddish works in American newspapers, including "The Fur Hat" ("Dos shtrayml").
1894	Edited the Yiddish anthology *Literature and Life* (*Literatur un lebn*), including his stories "The Fur Hat" and "Bontshe the Silent"; edited a Hebrew anthology, *The Arrow* (*Ha-chetz*), which contained "The Teachings of the Chassidim" ("Mishnat chassidim").
1894–96	Edited *Holiday Papers* (*Yontev bletlekh*), including several of his own works.
1899	Arrested at a lecture for striking workers; imprisoned for three months.
1899–1901	Published his seminal neo-chassidic tales in *Der yud*; the first collected editions of his Hebrew and Yiddish works were published in honor of Peretz's twenty-five years of literary activity.
1904–	Wrote *Folktales* (*Folkstimlekhe geshikhtn*) and symbolist dramas.
1907	Published the first version of the play *At Night on the Old Marketplace* (*Baynakht oyfn alten mark*).
1909–13	Published the complete Yiddish edition of his works.
1911–12	Lectured in Vilna and elsewhere.
1913–14	Published *My Memoirs* (*Mayne zikhroynes*).
1915	Died on 3 April.

Sources: Zalman Reyzen, *Leksikon fun der yidisher literatur, presse un filologie*, vol. 3, 1927; *Guide to Yiddish Classics on Microfiche*, ed. Chone Shmeruk (New York: Clearwater, 1980); Shmuel Niger, *I. L. Peretz*; Nachman Mayzel, *Briv un redes fun I. L. Peretz* and *I. L. Peretz: zayn lebn un shafn*.

CHAPTER 9

The Father of Another Literary Family

Isaac Leybush Peretz came to be known as "the father of the literary family" after his death in 1915.[1] He exerted immense influence on twentieth-century Yiddish culture, most notably in Warsaw, and his coterie provided an alternative to the patrilineal descent from "grandfather" Abramovitsh to "grandson" Sholem Aleichem. Born seven years before Sholem Aleichem, Peretz was nonetheless more attuned to avant-garde literary trends. He never remained faithful to any ideological movement, but instead drifted among socialists, Jewish nationalists, and Yiddishists. Peretz also experimented with various literary styles, which led to debates over the relative importance of realism and romanticism in his stories. While Peretz's satiric barbs were tinged with the venom of the Jewish Enlightenment, he initiated a neo-chassidic trend in Yiddish and Hebrew. He inspired successive generations of young writers whose diverse experiments guided a revitalized Yiddish literature into the twentieth century. Peretz's short fiction acted as the seed crystal around which modernistic Yiddish fiction crystallized.

Although it is difficult to classify Peretz's writings into discrete literary periods, certain clusters are evident. Early in his career as a Yiddish writer, from 1888 to 1895, Peretz wrote passionately about psychological states, especially madness. At odds with bourgeois life and customary beliefs, he attacked social and literary norms. At this stage, Peretz's fiction combined psychological portrayals and satiric caricatures with more traditional elements. In the mid-1890s he was involved in the socialist workers' movement and wrote some stories that became popular in radical circles. After 1899, however, he dedicated himself to recreating folktales and writing symbolist plays.

---

[1]H. D. Nomberg, "I. L. Peretz: der foter fun der literarisher mishpokhe," in *Tsum yortsayt* (Vilna: Kletzkin, 1916), pp. 35–40.

231

Peretz was influenced by other European authors long before he read Abramovitsh or Sholem Aleichem. Partly in response to this distinct literary background, his works are characterized by a condensation that contrasts with both the leisurely pace of Abramovitsh's novels and the digressive manner of Sholem Aleichem's monologues. One of his great contributions to Yiddish writing was his borrowing of conventions from contemporary European fiction.

A vibrant literary center formed around Peretz between 1889 and 1915. In contrast to Sholem Aleichem, who was relatively isolated in Kiev and during his final decade of travels,[2] Peretz was the prominent cultural personality in Yiddish-speaking Warsaw. His group was rivaled only by the Odessa circle over which Abramovitsh presided.[3] But while Odessa became best known for its Hebrew publications, many Jewish writers in Warsaw remained more committed to Yiddish. Moreover, Peretz wielded influence through his editorial activities in 1891–96, 1904, and 1909–13, and he worked closely with the editors of *Der yud* after its début in 1899.

CHILDHOOD

There is no dearth of memoirs about Peretz. According to one admirer, almost everyone who visited him a few times became "his most devoted friend."[4] And because most of his friends were aspiring authors, virtually all of them later wrote about him. Yet there are few intimate memoirs, and Peretz's autobiography provides the only significant account of his childhood.

---

[2]Nachman Mayzel discusses the Kiev literary world in *Undzer Sholem-Aleichem* (Warsaw: Yidish-bukh, 1959), pp. 23–42.

[3]On the rivalry between Yiddish writers of these two cities, see B. Gorin [Isaac Guido], "Warsaw and Odessa (Peretz un zayne ershte kritiker)," *Di tsukunft* (1915), number 6, 548–52. For a concise account of this period, including mention of Peretz's role in Warsaw cultural life, see Ezra Mendelsohn's *Class Struggle in the Pale: The Formative Years of the Jewish Workers' Movement in Tsarist Russia* (Cambridge: Cambridge University Press, 1970), especially chapter 6.

[4]B. Gorin [Isaac Guido], "Isaac Leybush Peretz," *Di tsukunft* (1911), number 7, p. 392.

Peretz published *My Memoirs* (*Mayne zikhroynes*, 1913–14) in serial form, which only partly explains the unevenness of this text. His disregard for chronology reflects a greater interest in determinative events as he later recalled them subjectively. Peretz does not attempt a comprehensive autobiography, but states his wish to convey "the *characteristic*; the genuine, not the coincidental." At the same time, Peretz expresses doubts about handing over "the key" to his literary storehouse, observing that an autobiography cannot unlock the mysteries of a life. Moreover, he "will not write *everything*. Because not *everything* went into my *writings*, and only they belong to the reader."[5] Peretz's emphasis on his published works follows other modernistic authors' tendency to suppress the details of their lives. In spite of this reticence about his personal life, Peretz does reveal the lineaments of his early psychological development.

Peretz sets the tone of his autobiography with a description of internal conflict, referring to a fundamental dichotomy:

> I was, as people said, a child prodigy. I had a logical and lively wit and also—strong emotions.
>
> How are these two things reconciled? They are not reconciled. They don't come together. . . . A trial takes place between two elements (a logical mind and a heart full of feeling) in an "Of necessity must you live." (MZ 7)

By his own account, discord lies at the origin of Peretz's creative personality. This passage reiterates Peretz's basic theme of the antithesis between reason and emotion, conveyed through the rivalry between mitnagdim and chassidim in his masterwork "Between Two Peaks" (1900). Peretz confirms his reputation as a writer marked by contradictions, at the same time quoting the mishnaic saying "Of necessity must you live" (Pirkei 'avot 4:22) and alluding to one of his first stories, "Yankl the Pessimist" (1889). More explicitly, he then mentions his Yiddish poem "Monish," and he acknowledges that this ballad was intended as a self-portrait.[6]

---

[5]Emphasis in original. See I. L. Peretz, *Mayne zikhroynes*, in *Ale verk fun I. L. Peretz* (New York: CYCO, 1948), vol. 11, p. 5; henceforth cited as "MZ" by page alone. For an English translation, see Isaac Leib Peretz, *My Memoirs*, trans. Fred Goldberg (New York: Citadel Press, 1964).

[6]Compare David Roskies' essay, "A shlisl tsu Peretz's zikhroynes," *Di goldene keyt* 99 (1979), 136.

Peretz was born in 1852 in Zamosc (Zamoshtch), a town known for its opposition to the chassidim, and was raised in a traditional middle-class household. His father's commercial travels added a measure of worldliness to the observant family. In addition, Peretz received an inkling of chassidic lore from one early teacher, apparently a secret chassid (MZ 14–15). While he received the usual *cheder* education in Yiddish and Hebrew, and remained conventionally pious until his teens, he later learned Polish, Russian, and German. At the age of about 13, after studying sporadically at several yeshivot, Peretz enthusiastically began to read Maimonides' *Mishneh Torah*. This monument of medieval Hebrew style clearly shaped his subsequent attraction to modern Hebrew writing. He was allowed to study independently in the House of Study during a period when he sought to emulate his closest friend's father, who was an autodidact and a notorious skeptic. Peretz's penchant for difference was already established. Although the Enlightenment had scarcely reached Zamosc, the example of a few wealthy townsmen encouraged Peretz to forsake traditional clothes and to dress in modern European fashion, wearing a short, German-style jacket instead of a full-length gabardine.

One week, in order to leave the restless young Peretz no alternative but to study, his father confiscated his boots. Peretz disregarded this inconvenience and, to carry a message, he once raced through the streets wearing his house slippers; people called after him, "Madman!" (MZ 31). His eccentricity again aroused notice in about 1866, when Peretz was sent to study in the neighboring town of Shevershin (Szczebrzeszyn). Peretz recalls that the rabbi's wife commented about him, "If they say he's crazy, believe it!" Decades later, this phrase became the title of one of his short stories. Peretz earned the name of "the crazy Leybush" before being sent home as "really crazy" (MZ 45–49). Assisted by an aesthetic commitment to originality, Peretz retrospectively turned his reputation for eccentricity into a virtue, or at least into a kind of battle scar in the portrait of an artist.

Peretz recalls that Zamosc, known as "little Paris," was a center of Polish-Jewish culture outside Warsaw. People of Zamosc kept their distance from both chassidic and Lithuanian Jews; nevertheless, Peretz's exposure was eclectic, including mitnagdic orthodoxy at home, hints of Chassidism in the *cheder,* and leanings toward mysticism and skepticism. Peretz embraced no definitive ideology but dabbled in every trend that commanded his interest. "Problems and contrasts," he wrote, "were the two spools on which all my literary scrolls would wind themselves" (MZ 95–96). This phrase epitomizes Peretz's approach to dichotomies in his imaginative world: it transposes a traditional image of the Torah scrolls into a figure for the psychology of his secular writing.

Long before Peretz immersed himself in Yiddish writing he read Polish translations of French novels. A local man in Zamosc, having heard of the young Peretz's intelligence, provided the decisive bridge to world literature. Peretz relates this episode vividly, in the present tense:

> Suddenly someone touches my shoulder.
> Mikhl Fiddler, I remember, by the fence of his solitary house. . . . He had come out to me silently, smiling quietly, with sad, watery eyes; in one hand a small book, and in the other a lantern.
> —"They say that you're a prodigy. But can you interpret this?"
> He shows me a passage in the small kabbalistic book (I've forgotten the name), concerning transmigrations. . . . I read it through, understand it, and interpret it. . . .
> —"You really are a prodigy. . . . Well, wait a moment," and he disappears into the little house. . . .
> He comes back out with the lantern, but in his other hand, in place of the book, is a large, heavy, rusted key—
> The key to his closed library in the city.
> —"You deserve it." (MZ 109)

Peretz proudly comments to the reader that "the key opened up for me a new world of books, and for you, a new chapter." He remembers having read Polish translations of works by authors such as Alexandre Dumas, Eugène Sue, and Victor Hugo. Concerning their influence, he comments that "most of all I was attracted to and taken by the dialogues," and as a mature author "the love of dialogue and of painting with language has remained with me" (MZ 112). While this attachment to the literary presentation of oral speech associates Peretz with Abramovitsh and Sholem Aleichem, Peretz's early exposure to nineteenth-century French and Polish fiction played a major role in his development of new Yiddish styles.[7]

---

[7]Compare David Roskies' "A shlisl tsu Peretz's zikhroynes," 151.

Peretz nostalgically recalls a childhood romance with three sisters. But throughout his life he became closest to men, who were most often writers, and in particular he was intimate with Yankev Dinezon. S. An-ski (Solomon Rapoport) writes that the close relationship between Peretz and Dinezon went beyond friendship: "such an intimate bond develops only between an old couple who, living through half a century together in love and faithfulness, reciprocally blur the boundaries of their selves."[8] Peretz relied heavily on Dinezon for emotional support, "and apart from Dinezon—no one! Peretz had not a single intimate person near him" (ibid.). In June 1890, Dinezon wrote to Simon Dubnov that "on the horizon of Jargon there has appeared a new star: that is my beloved friend *Peretz*" (FZ 30). Dubnov recalls in his memoirs that thereafter Dinezon completely denied himself in order to "serve the fame of his holy rebbe as would a fiery chassid" (FZ 31).

At one time prior to his first marriage, Peretz secretly planned to leave home and study at the rabbinical school in Zhitomir. His traditional parents would have opposed this plan because the school was a leading institution in the Jewish Enlightenment movement. Had he carried out his scheme, Peretz would have received a more formal education from teachers such as Avraham-Ber Gottlober, one of Abramovitsh's mentors when both lived in Komenitz during the 1850s. Abramovitsh himself studied at the Zhitomir Rabbinical Institute in 1869, and Peretz might have met him there. But at the last moment Peretz cancelled his planned departure and, when his father returned from a business trip, he brought news of Peretz's arranged marriage (MZ 115–16).[9]

When he was to wed his first wife (Sarah Lichtenfeld) in about 1871, Peretz recalls that he was more excited about meeting his educated father-in-law than he was attracted to the bride who had been chosen for him. He told himself, "I will meet Gabriel Yehudah Lichtenfeld, my fiancée's father—a mathematician, philosopher" (MZ 119). Peretz looked forward to conversations with his father-in-law that would resolve his intellectual doubts, and "I didn't

---

[8]S. An-ski, "Isaac Leybush Peretz (erinerungen)," *Di yidishe velt* 4 (1915), vol. 2, books 1–2 (April-May), 26.

[9]For Peretz's elegiac rendering of his decision to stay home, see Ruth R. Wisse, *I. L. Peretz and the Making of Modern Jewish Culture* (Seattle: University of Washington Press, 1991), p. 72–73. Wisse's book provides the best account of Peretz's social, cultural, and literary life that is available in English. The present analysis places greater emphasis on the darker elements of Peretz's biography.

think about the bride." Peretz's friendship with Lichtenfeld is reminiscent of Abramovitsh's early friendship with Gottlober. In the absence of an adequate system of modern education available to Jews, the classic Yiddish authors gleaned much of their learning from older autodidacts. Peretz's memoirs end with his first wedding, which he renders in a tragi-comic vein: "They place the wedding canopy outside, in town. In the middle of the ceremony it begins to rain, and I run away from under the canopy to be indoors. The canopy follows. Gabriel Yehuda Lichtenfeld laughs. . . . His daughter cries" (MZ 116). Peretz returned to his traumatic experience of the wedding, as if attempting to work it through once more, in a later account he added to the memoirs (MZ 124).

Following the wedding, Peretz remembers, he suddenly felt sorry for himself and his wife—as one pities "two fish that squirm in a net" (ibid.). The failure of matchmaking customs, a theme common to Abramovitsh and Sholem Aleichem, alienated Peretz further from traditional practices. His autobiography ends with this anticlimax, hinting at the collapse of Peretz's first marriage in the 1870s. The match produced two offspring: a son, Lucian (born ca. 1874), and Peretz's book of Hebrew poems published together with his father-in-law (1876 or 1877). The name Lucian bears relevant associations in literary history: Lucian, a Greek writer of the second century, is renowned for his satiric and parodic works.[10] Peretz seems to have expressed his nascent literary leanings in the choice of his son's name.

In 1877, soon after he was divorced, Peretz met his second wife. According to the memoir by his cousin Roza Laks-Peretz, he acted with characteristic impulsiveness: "At the fair in Lentchna . . . Peretz went into a wine shop to drink a glass of wine—and saw the wine merchant's daughter, Helena (Nehama) Ringelheim. . . . She pleased him greatly and he immediately asked for her hand. Helena Ringelheim, a wealthy, educated girl who played the piano, at first did not consent—she was afraid of his 'dark, thin lips,' but Peretz conquered her heart."[11] The courtship continued from a distance in September-October of 1877, as documented by Polish and Russian letters written to his fiancée. Although his second

---

[10]See R. Bracht Branham, *Unruly Eloquence: Lucian and the Comedy of Traditions* (Cambridge, Mass.: Harvard University Press, 1989).

[11]R. Peretz-Laks, *Arum Peretzn (zikhroynes un batrakhtungen)* (Warsaw: Literarishe bleter, 1935), pp. 44–45. Henceforth cited as "AP" by page alone.

wife's practical disposition served to counterbalance his erratic nature, Peretz once commented that if he could relive his life he would not marry (AP 39).

From 1877 to 1888, after he passed the necessary examinations, Peretz practiced law in Zamosc. Y. H. Zagorodski recalls Peretz the lawyer in about 1884, when he was impressed by the "sharpness and directness" of Peretz's argumentations.[12] But when S. L. Tsitron met him in 1886, Peretz "complained bitterly of his spiritual misery in Zamosc, of his separation from literature and writers."[13] He published two Hebrew stories in that year, fortified by an extended sojourn in Warsaw. In the second instance, however, the editors of *Ha-tzefira* "found that Peretz expressed himself too freely against the Jewish clergy and scholars, and they began to delete the offending passages quite extensively" (ibid., 97–98). It is emblematic of Peretz's innovative work that it was censored by his more circumspect contemporaries. Peretz responded with undisguised outrage on seeing his works edited.

Peretz lost his license to practice law in 1888, apparently because a competitor informed the authorities of his purportedly radical activities. This event was a turning-point that returned Peretz to literary activity "in complete despair."[14] Prior to this time he had resided only temporarily in Warsaw and had published little. His permanent move to Warsaw in 1889 marked the beginning of a new period in his creative work.

PERETZ AND SHOLEM ALEICHEM

In 1888, as Peretz left the legal profession, Sholem Aleichem was taking steps to revive Yiddish literature by founding his new publication, *The Jewish Popular Library* (*Di yudishe folks-bibliotek*). Sholem Aleichem was in the process of becoming a recognized Yiddish author when he traveled to Warsaw to solicit contributions. S. L.

---

[12]Y. H. Zagorodski, "Isaac Leybush Peretz," *Achiasaf* 9 (1901), 357.

[13]S. L. Tsitron, "I. L. Peretz (erinerungen)," *Di yidishe velt* 4 (1915), vol. 2, books 1–2 (April–May), 96.

[14]According to Nachman Mayzel's editorial remarks in *Briv un redes fun I. L Peretz* (New York: YKUF, 1944), p. 137.

Tsitron recalls that Sholem Aleichem, together with the local writer David Frishman, went to Yankev Dinezon's small apartment and outlined his plan to print a literary anthology that would "put an end to the trash (*shund*) that had inundated Yiddish literature, and elevate it to new pathways."[15] His list of suitable authors excluded Peretz, and when Tsitron mentioned his name, Sholem Aleichem "looked at me totally astonished," never having heard of him. Frishman, who brutally satirized Peretz's work six years later, did not support the idea of inviting him to contribute.[16] Nevertheless, Peretz learned of the planned publication and sent Sholem Aleichem his ballad "Monish" and several stories. This led to one of the most interesting exchanges in the history of Yiddish literature, driven in part by Sholem Aleichem's newfound wealth and Peretz's sudden poverty. In his second letter Peretz admitted that "recently my sustenance has been greatly diminished, and there is not enough to live on."[17]

In his successive letters to Sholem Aleichem—whom he had not met but knew as Sholem Rabinovitsh—Peretz asserted his new identity as a writer at the same time that he confused his correspondent with Sholem Abramovitsh. Distant from the emerging Ukrainian centers of Yiddish literature, Peretz naively wrote to Sholem Aleichem as if he were addressing Abramovitsh; he questioned whether the renowned author, meaning Abramovitsh, would appreciate his work. Having read Abramovitsh's *The Nag* and *Travels of Benjamin the Third* in Polish translations from 1885–86, he had ample reason to doubt whether the author of these novels would welcome his stories.[18]

Peretz's earliest letter to Sholem Aleichem, written in Hebrew

---

[15]S. L. Tsitron, *Dray literarishe doyres: literarishe zikhroynes, karakteristikes un perzenlikhe erinerungen* (Warsaw: Achisefer, 1928), vol. 4, p. 6.

[16]See the hostile parody of Peretz's *Yontev bletlekh* entitled *A floy fun Tish'a b'Av: a shvarts, shpringendik, lebedik, baysendik bletl* (*The Tish'a b'Av Flea: A Black, Springy, Lively, Biting Pamphlet*) (Warsaw: Shuldberg, 1894), which Frishman printed under the pseudonym "Avrom Goldberg." This parody was, in its indirect guise, one of the first critical reactions to Peretz's work.

[17]Letter of 4 July 1888, in *Kol kitvei I. L. Peretz* (Tel Aviv: Dvir, 1962), vol. 10, bk. 2, p. 217. Henceforth cited as "KK" by page alone.

[18]See *Briv un redes fun I. L. Peretz*, 2d ed, ed. Nachman Mayzel (New York: YKUF, 1944), p. 141n.

and dated 17 June 1888, mentions four differences in their work
and provides evidence of his aesthetic commitments:

> First, I am certain that my poems and articles will not pleas-
> eyou from the standpoint . . . of form: our everyday speech and
> yours are very different. . . . Our colloquial language borrows
> images from Polish and yours from Russian, and moreover in
> ours there are more expressions directly from the German lan-
> guage.
>
> Second, I know the work of my lord. His will and striving (as
> far as I have been able to understand) is to write for the Yiddish-
> speaking public for the sake of Yiddish (*zhargon*), and I write for
> myself, for my own pleasure; and if I sometimes remember the
> reader, he is from the higher class in society, a person who has
> read and studied in a living language.
>
> Third: there is a great difference between the subjects them-
> selves. You dress up foreign, naked thoughts from another world,
> more from the world of action, while I, who write for my own
> pleasure and in accordance with my mood, when I am holding
> the quill, I draw simultaneously from all of the different worlds.
>
> And fourth, because writing itself is different here than in
> your parts, and it will be difficult for you to read. . . . I write as
> one speaks among us, and swallow syllables that one swallows
> here while speaking.[19]

It is remarkable that even before he published in Yiddish, Peretz
had such a strong sense of his literary program. The first and last
differences he mentions are linked to dialect variations, reflecting
the geographical and cultural distances between Zamosc (Poland)
and Kiev (Ukraine). The second and third points are more significant. Peretz aptly describes Abramovitsh's *Benjamin the Third* and
The Nag when he comments that Abramovitsh writes "for the
public," and Peretz sets himself apart from this didactic approach.
Because, as he comments, "I write for myself . . . in accordance
with my mood," the early Peretz replaces social criticism and allegory with individual psychology. Furthermore, Peretz is less concerned to portray social ills than to deal with "different worlds"
suggested by his imagination.

Peretz's initial comments about writing for his own amusement
create a false impression. In his second letter to Sholem Aleichem

---

[19]Translated from KK 212. For a Yiddish translation of the Hebrew original, see
ILP 11: 228–30, as well as *Briv un redes fun I. L. Peretz*, pp. 138–39.

he remarks at length on the need to work for the good of the Jewish community, and he criticizes those who have only lofty words to offer the poor. This critique implies a light self-reproach for his own belletristic writing that falls short of practical demands. He emphasizes the importance of expanding the horizons of the Yiddish language and offers to write on subjects ranging from psychology and sociology to physics, drawing from Russian, Polish, and German sources (KK 217). (He was aware of works by authors such as Wilhelm Wundt but had difficulty obtaining them in Zamosc.) He wrote to Sholem Aleichem that "I do not view Yiddish (*ha-zhargon*) as a 'second instrument' or as a temporary mediator. I desire that it shall become a language, and so we must broaden its treasures and add new expressions to it at every moment" (KK 226). Concerned to attract new talents to Yiddish, Peretz fears that writers may consider this medium "too cramped." His goals show a debt to the Enlightenment, and his educational project recalls the scientific editions translated by Abramovitsh in 1862–72. But Sholem Aleichem was apparently not enthusiastic and Peretz never produced the proposed books. Instead he focused some of his early fiction on psychological problems.

In spite of his claim to write only for his own pleasure, then, Peretz frequently mentions social goals. He tells Sholem Aleichem his views on nationalism, assimilation, and the role of women (letter of 18 July 1888, in KK 218–21). Moreover, Peretz's letters anticipate his later, socially critical depictions of chassidic life, while at the same time they indicate his renunciation of Enlightenment writing and his wish to invent more individualized characters by creating the illusion of psychological depth.

Because of their disparate literary experiences, Peretz and Sholem Aleichem expressed different outlooks concerning foreign influences on Yiddish writing. Although Sholem Aleichem read widely in Russian literature, he was a purist when it came to Yiddish fiction, attacking Nachum Meir Shaykevitsh (Shomer) in *Shomer's Trial* (*Shomer's mishpet*, 1888) for his dependence on foreign models. But the young Peretz, who had little familiarity with Yiddish literature and admired Polish, Russian, French, and German authors, did not share this attitude. Sholem Aleichem sent Peretz a copy of *Shomer's mishpet*, which explains his aesthetic credo and his rejection of certain poems Peretz submitted. As we may guess from Peretz's response, the unpublished works touched on universal problems rather than specifically Jewish themes. Such universalism was contrary to Sholem Aleichem's goals in his contemporary "Jewish novels." In his second letter to Sholem Aleichem, Peretz concludes that he does not understand the exclusive interest in Jews, asking rhetorically: "Isn't it necessary for our nation to know about the life of the other nation in whose midst it dwells?" (KK 217). From Peretz's universalistic beginnings he gradually drifted toward a narrower Jewish cultural nationalism.

At the start of their correspondence, when Peretz confuses his addressee with Abramovitsh, he admits that he has read his work only in Polish translations. To account for this neglect, he adds hyperbolically that in Zamosc there is not a single Yiddish book (KK 214). Embarrassed by his ignorance of their faraway literary world, Peretz corrected his earlier gaffe—when he confused "Rabinovitsh" with "Abramovitsh"—in a letter to Sholem Aleichem of 22 July 1888. Peretz's distance from Jewish literary circles in 1888 is also evident from his unrestrained attack on Sholem Aleichem's co-worker Avraham-Ber Gottlober. Peretz writes bluntly that Gottlober has a big mouth, a small mind, and that "I have never found in him a single new idea" (KK 214). Peretz thus earned his reputation for honesty bordering on tactlessness and cruelty, unaware that this same Gottlober had a decisive influence on Sholem Aleichem's "grandfather" Abramovitsh in the 1850s. Meanwhile, an amicable correspondence between Abramovitsh and Sholem Aleichem had developed since March 1888.

Peretz's first Yiddish publications were printed by Sholem Aleichem, but tensions surfaced immediately because Sholem Aleichem heavily revised Peretz's ballad "Monish." He may have felt justified in this by Peretz's own admission of linguistic discrepancies between their usages; in fact, Peretz's letter of 4 July 1888 gave Sholem Aleichem permission to alter his poems as needed to make them more comprehensible to Lithuanian, Russian, and Ukrainian Jews. Yet Peretz added two requests that Sholem Aleichem did not honor: to heed the poetic meter and to inform him of the editorial changes (KK 214–15). Critics have disputed the merits of the editing by Sholem Aleichem, who never excelled as a poet.[20] Peretz

---

[20]See S. L. Tsitron's article, "I. L. Peretz (erinerungen)," 99–101, and Shmuel Niger's contrasting discussion in *I. L. Peretz*, pp. 170–79.

soon reprinted the work in its original form, yet he incorporated some of Sholem Aleichem's revisions in later versions. The fact remains that Peretz was deeply offended because he felt that he, the artist, knew best in such matters. He wrote brusquely: "It never occurred to me that a day would come when I would be forced to support myself from my pen. To my misfortune that day has come, and I am forced to permit you to revise [my works] because I am in dire need of the money" (KK 227). Peretz sent Sholem Aleichem additional Yiddish writings for the next volume of *The Jewish Popular Library,* but this ill-fated exchange ended their correspondence for the next twenty years.[21]

S. L. Tsitron recalls the manner in which Peretz's unpublished work was first discovered by the writers of Warsaw: "In the winter of 1889 Peretz sent me a small notebook with a dozen new stories of the same genre. These stories were then read aloud in a small circle of writers in the apartment of the late, well-known novelist Mordechai Spektor, and they caused a great furor."[22] One consequence of such readings was the publication of Peretz's first independent volume.

In 1890 Yankev Dinezon edited three of Peretz's stories and had them printed under the title *Familiar Scenes* (*Bakante bilder,* 1890). In his preface, Dinezon introduced the obscure author and astutely portrayed Peretz's work at this early stage in his Yiddish career: "Mr. Peretz doesn't write to flatter the coarse taste of the lower class of readers. On the contrary, he wants to refine and improve it."[23] This description echoes the author's concurrent statements, as when he wrote to Sholem Aleichem that "if I sometimes remember the reader, he is from the higher class in society, a person who has read and studied in a living language." By refer-

---

[21] Y. D. Berkovitsh sheds further light on the long history of tensions between Peretz and Sholem Aleichem in his—undoubtedly partial—memoirs. See *Harish'onim ki-vnei-adam: sippurei zikhoronot 'al Sholem-Aleichem u-vnei-doro,* 3d ed. (Tel Aviv: Dvir, 1976), pp. 45–61.

[22] S. L. Tsitron, "Fun mayne zikhroynes: Peretz's ershtn arayntrit in der yidisher literatur," *Literarishe bleter* 2 (10 April 1925), 7. See also Tsitron's *Dray literarishe doyres,* vol. 4, p. 8.

[23] Yankev Dinezon, "A Few Words from the Editor," in Leon Peretz, *Bakante bilder,* ed. Y. Dinezon (Warsaw: Boymriter, 1890), p. 3. The popularity of these stories is attested by the appearance of a second edition in 1894.

ring to "a living language" he excludes Hebrew, and by referring to study he intimates that his ideal reader would have received an education in Polish or Russian.

Familiar Scenes contains the best of Peretz's psychological fiction: "The Messenger" ("Der meshulekh") and "The Mad Talmudist" ("Der meshugener batlen"). Each of these stories probes into a character's individual psychology using the technique of internal monologue. B. Gorin emphasizes the novelty of Peretz's psychological approach: "Not only the style was new; not only the form was new; but also the soul was new, the psychology of the scenes. It was the soul of the individual and not of the community; it was the psychology of the human being and Jew, and not only of the Jew as a Jew."[24] In the perception of many readers, this differentiated the fiction of Peretz from that of Sholem Aleichem and especially from that of Abramovitsh, who tended to represent Jewish types and caricatures rather than unique individuals.

An important influence on Peretz's early Yiddish writing was his participation in a statistical expedition funded by the millionaire Jan Bloch and designed to uncover data about the Jewish population of small towns in Poland. Like Abramovitsh's journey with Avreml Khromoy, this expedition afforded Peretz an opportunity to travel extensively and observe the varied conditions of Jewish life. It resulted, most immediately, in his publication of *Scenes from a Journey Through the Provinces* (*Bilder fun a provints-rayze,* 1891). This book describes Peretz's visits to *shtetlekh* such as Tishevitz, Lashtchev (Laszczow), and Tomaszhev (Tomaszow). Yudel Mark observes that "this collection does not deal with the mundane, everyday aspects of life, but with the curious, strange and unusual aspects. Peretz as a writer was almost always intrigued by the difficult and peculiar types, the most vivid images, and the most astounding answers."[25] For instance, one chapter describes a memorable town "madman" who supports himself by begging. Dan Miron comments that Peretz combines an

---

[24]B. Gorin [Isaac Guido], "Isaac Leybush Peretz," 389–90.

[25]Yudel Mark, *I. L. Peretz (1852–1915): His Life and Works,* trans. J. Noskowitz (New York: Workmen's Circle, 1952), p. 13. On Peretz's interest in "rare phenomena," compare N. Oyslender, "Vegn tsvey shtromen in Peretz's kinstlerisher shprakh fun di 90-ker yorn," *Afn shprakhfront* 5: 1–2 (26–27) (January–April 1931), 59 and 70.

ostensibly documentary style with a psychological study of "the narrator's frame of mind."[26] As in his autobiography, Peretz superimposes a deliberately subjective framework over the descriptive context.

PERETZ'S ANTHOLOGIES AND HIS "RADICAL PERIOD"

From 1889 until his death, Peretz held a position as records-keeper for the Jewish community in Warsaw. This job ended his financial hardships and enabled Peretz to devote his remaining time to literature. After Peretz began to publish in Yiddish, he followed Sholem Aleichem's example and established himself as an editor. Sholem Aleichem had gone bankrupt before issuing the third volume of *The Jewish Popular Library* (*Di yudishe folks-bibliotek*), planned for 1890; Peretz boldly lept into the breach with three volumes of *The Jewish Library* (*Di yudishe bibliotek,* 1891–95). This step antagonized Sholem Aleichem as much as Sholem Aleichem's editorial changes had annoyed Peretz. But Peretz did not content himself with taking over the initiative that Sholem Aleichem had been forced to abandon. During the early 1890s he produced numerous other editions including *The Arrow* (*Ha-chetz,* 1894) in Hebrew and *Literature and Life* (*Literatur un lebn,* 1894) in Yiddish. One peculiarity of these volumes was that Peretz, disguised behind myriad pseudonymns, filled them almost single-handedly with his own work. Seldom satisfied by the submissions he received, he insisted on printing only what he judged to be of the highest quality—his poems, stories, and essays.[27]

Peretz's most ambitious and sustained publishing project was the series of pamphlets collectively called *Holiday Papers* (*Yontev bletlekh,* 1894–96). Because of the difficulties involved in securing authorization to print a regular journal, Peretz dispensed with this detail and produced pamphlets of 32 or 64 pages for special occasions in the Jewish year. This arrangement permitted a stimulating and sometimes comic interplay between the Jewish holiday and the secular literature written for the occasion. As if to give such dichotomies visual form, these editions employ a typographical conven-

---

[26]Dan Miron, *Der imazh fun shtetl: dray literarishe shtudies* (Tel Aviv: I. L. Peretz farlag, 1981), p. 105.

[27]B. Gorin [Isaac Guido], "Isaac Leybush Peretz," 391.

tion of interweaving belletristic essays and fiction, with one text juxtaposed above the other, running for many pages and divided by a dark line. According to Peretz's most active collaborator at this time, David Pinsky, Mordechai Spektor soon dropped out of the project because the pamphlets became too radical.[28] Peretz was respected by Jewish students in Warsaw and his editions were circulated among those in the workers' movement, but he could not afford to sustain his publishing efforts. M. Mikhelzon recalls Peretz's patient editorial work with twenty-year-old students: "he read his things to them and seriously conferred with them over every small detail, while in fact he had to do the entire job—both the literary and the financial side—himself."[29]

According to a tenacious critical view, from 1893 to 1899 Peretz underwent his "radical period."[30] During these years he showed his debt to the Enlightenment when he satirized the traditional Jewish establishment. Bal Makhshoves describes the social concomitant of Peretz's satire: "In his exploits there was more often a destructive force than a constructive one. . . . Peretz's destructive mania always conveyed a protest against idleness, comfortable bourgeoisie, against the lazy, slow steps of our people who like to take a rest after the first little triumph."[31] Bal Makhshoves situates Peretz squarely in Judaic literary tradition when he adds that all Jewish writers, "from Heinrich Heine to Peter Altenberg, tore down the accepted artistic forms" (ibid., 36). He observes that Peretz was particularly aware of the need to alter literary forms.

[28]See David Pinsky's introduction to *Di verk fun Isaac Leybush Peretz* (New York: Farlag "Yiddish," 1920), vol. 1, p. 20. Another reason for Spektor's withdrawal may have been his conflicting friendship with Sholem Aleichem.

[29]M. Mikhelzon [Mikhl Rubinshteyn], "Fun I. L. Peretz's radikal-sotsialistishe yorn," in *I. L. Peretz: a zamelbukh tsu zayn ondenken* (New York: Literarisher farlag, 1915), p. 39.

[30]The most thorough-going study of this phase is Isaac Rozentsvayg's *Der radikaler period fun Peretz's shafn (di "Yontev bletlekh")* (Kiev: Melukhe farlag far di natsionale minderhaytn, 1934). Prior to Rozentsvayg, A. Gurshteyn emphasized the problems inherent in any effort to classify Peretz's work into discrete periods. See "Der itstiker tsushtand fun Peretzes biografie," *Tsaytshrift* 1 (1926), especially 78–80. Ruth R. Wisse discusses the contradictions in Peretz's literary styles and commitments in *I. L. Peretz and the Making of Modern Jewish Culture*, pp. 93–94.

[31]Bal Makhshoves [Isidor Eliashev], "I. L. Peretz," *Di yidishe velt* 4 (1915), vol. 2, books 1–2 (April–May), 32.

Although Peretz later renounced his debt to Heine and rejected the satiric mode, he continued to employ parody in his reworked folktales.

Peretz sympathized with the workers' movement and sometimes used allegory and other devices to convey his political agenda. Peretz's diverse allegiances, however, presented obstacles for his contemporary readers. Kalman Marmor recalled that young Jewish socialists would argue over the meaning of Peretz's allegories, especially those included in *Small Stories for Big People* (*Kleyne mayses far groyse mentshn*, 1894): "in nine stories we all agreed on what Peretz meant. But concerning one story we could on no account reach agreement. Most read into it the struggle between labor and capital. I didn't agree. I said that I. L. Peretz was simply referring to the Hovevei Zion."[32] The Hovevei Zion were proto-Zionists in the Hibat Zion movement that was founded in 1882. Peretz initially supported them, but as they became popular in the 1890s he renounced their territorial goals.[33] His commitments were closer to the "spiritual Zionism" of Ahad Ha-Am and the "diaspora nationalism" of Simon Dubnov. Yet Peretz never became friendly with Dubnov—both because he resented an early review of the poem "Monish" which Dubnov printed in *Voskhod*, and because Dubnov was close to Abramovitsh and his Odessa circle.[34] In any event, during the 1890s Peretz was considered to be an important ally of the workers' movement.

Shortly after his abortive correspondence with Sholem Aleichem, Peretz diverged from his initial literary direction, and his psychological studies gave way to social satires. M. Mikhelzon attests to the popularity of Peretz's works among socialists in the 1890s: "Peretz's 'The Fur Hat' fully conformed to our entire world view and therefore made a great impression on us."[35] When Peretz actually attended a workers' meeting, however, no one was satis-

---

[32]Quoted by Shmuel Niger in *I. L. Peretz*, pp. 236–37. In response to an inquiry, Peretz concurred with Marmor's interpretation.

[33]See S. L. Tsitron, *Dray literarishe doyres*, vol. 4, pp. 19–20.

[34]See Sophie Dubnov-Erlich, *The Life and Work of S. M. Dubnov: Diaspora Nationalism and Jewish History*, trans. Judith Vowles and ed. Jeffrey Shandler (Bloomington: Indiana University Press, 1991), chapters 8 and 9.

[35]M. Mikhelzon [Mikhl Rubinshteyn], "Fun I. L. Peretz's radikal-sotsialistishe yorn," p. 38.

fied. David Pinsky recalls that "it did not please the workers that he behaved like a visitor, and it irked him that he could not be more than a visitor."[36]

In honor of Peretz's Jubilee celebration in 1901, the socialist Bund sent him a special gift, "a copy of his *Jewish Library* that was kept in the Warsaw prison, the 'Tenth Pavillion,' where it had been secretly passed from one political prisoner to the next. The pages were soiled, greasy, and torn from having been read over and over. Many letters in the book were underscored in pencil. The underscored letters formed messages that one prisoner sent to another."[37] Peretz's writings became a secret code in the hands of political activists, regardless of whether Peretz had encoded radical messages in them. Mikhelzon muses on "the hardships, which the censors suffered from Peretz's writings. The socialist movement was beginning to spread among the Jewish workers, and the need for Yiddish literature with a radical thrust grew. There was as yet no party literature in Yiddish. Since Peretz's collections expressed certain radical opinions, people read and studied his stories with the workers, and when arrests began to occur among the workers, the police found Peretz's pamphlets everywhere."[38] Peretz was forced to state before the government authorities that his works contained nothing subversive. In August 1899, Peretz was arrested because of a lecture he gave to striking workers.[39] Peretz's arrest and the subsequent three-month prison term "put an end to his period of socialist-radical activity, both literarily and personally."[40] Mordechai Spektor wrote to Y. H. Ravnitzky on 1 May 1900: "Since Peretz spent time in prison he's become quite mad. Before, as you know, he was already well on his way, but since his

---

[36]From Pinsky's introduction to *Di verk fun Isaac Leybush Peretz*, p. 17.

[37]See Sholem Ash, "Mayn ershte bakantshaft mit Peretz'n," *Di tsukunft* (1915), number 5, 463.

[38]M. Mikhelzon [Mikhl Rubinshteyn], "Fun I. L. Peretz's radikal-sotsialistishe yorn," p. 40.

[39]The fullest accounts of Peretz's imprisonment are contained in M. Spektor's *Mit I. L. Peretz in festung* (Odessa: Farlag "literatur," 1919), and "In tseyntn pavilyon (fun mayne zikhroynes)," in *Tsum ondenk fun I. L. Peretz* (Odessa: Yidishe sektsye bam "gubnarobraz," 1920), pp. 22–24.

[40]M. Mikhelzon [Mikhl Rubinshteyn], "Fun I. L. Peretz's radikal-sotsialistishe yorn," p. 42.

imprisonment he wants to play the martyr, though he was no more guilty than you or I."[41]

PERETZ AS FOLKLORIST AND NATIONAL AUTHOR

During his imprisonment Peretz prepared to write "If Not Higher," one of his seminal neo-chassidic tales; like Abramovitsh after his hardships in the early 1880s, Peretz returned to Judaic traditions. Peretz became increasingly interested in Jewish folklore and ethnography as expressions of linguistic and cultural nationalism. S. An-ski, who later authored *The Dybbuk,* attested that Peretz was fascinated by the folktales An-ski collected during an ethnographic expedition:

> Peretz and Dinezon were delighted by the undertaking. Every time I was in Warsaw, Peretz would 'sit me down' to tell him chassidic tales. Often I would sit for hours and tell him one story after the other. . . . As I was telling the story, Peretz would hear it, assimilate it, throw out the inartistic strands, add new ones, join it with details from another story. And I had scarcely finished when Peretz was already telling me the same story, revised into one of his *Folktales (Folkstimlekhe geshikhtn)*, which was as far from the original version as a polished diamond is from a raw stone that has just been unearthed. The next day one such story had been written down and in a few days it was printed with the dedication: "To An-ski, the Collector."[42]

This folk-inspired oral mode was the focus of Peretz's creative attention in the last decade of his life.

At a time when Sholem Aleichem showed the consequences of modernization in Tevye's monologues and in his railroad stories, Peretz looked backward to draw strength from an earlier period. Sholem Ash tells of Shabbat evenings with Peretz, during which "we sat in the darkness and sang folksongs." In more general terms, "from that apartment emanated the idea of Yiddish—the poetic rebirth of chassidism, the love of the folksong and the folktale."[43] A significant measure of nostalgic revivalism suffuses Per-

---

[41]Cited by Ruth R. Wisse in *I. L. Peretz and the Making of Modern Jewish Culture,* p. 118 n.18.

[42]S. An-ski, "Isaac Leybush Peretz (erinerungen)," 27.

[43]Sholem Ash, "Mayn ershte bakantshaft mit Peretz'n," 462.

etz's later writings and cultural involvements. In Peretz's reap-
propriations of folk motifs, however, he sometimes injected critical
distance.

After Peretz renounced his short-lived support for the Hovevei
Zion, he implicitly embraced spiritual or diaspora nationalism.[44]
His public role culminated in 1908 at the Chernovitz Language
Conference, where he was the leading spokesman for Yiddish as
the Jewish national language. This activity on behalf of Yiddish
culture gained him widespread popular support at the same time
that it alienated some of the Hebraists based in Odessa. In his
inspirational speech at the Chernovitz Language Conference, Peretz traced Yiddish literature back to its origins in chassidic tales,
especially those concerning the Bal Shem Tov (*Shivchei ha-Besht*)
and Rabbi Nachman's stories. He then linked Yiddish literature to
the increasing role of Jewish women and workers as social forces.
More broadly, he proclaimed that the modern State had lost its
attraction and had been replaced by "the people"—including
Jews—as separate nationalities: "Weak, repressed peoples are
awakening and fighting against the State for their language, for
their particularity, and we, the weakest, have joined their ranks!"
(ILP 11: 294). Reasserting the "particularity and individuality" of
cultures, Peretz insisted that Yiddish is the language of the Jewish
people: "And in this language we shall collect our treasures, create
our culture, awaken our soul, and unite culturally amid all coun-
tries and at all times" (ibid., 295).

Because of his commitment to the revitalization of Jewish culture, Peretz was disappointed by some young writers' work and
commented: "It's beautiful, of course! But what good is it if you
are all Gentiles (*goyim*)? There isn't a shred of Jewishness in all of
you."[45] His literary efforts began to assume a more partisan character, and he asserted in 1910 that "Yiddish literature is only one
link in the chain and must be viewed just as a moment in the

---

[44]See Moyshe Shalit, "Peretz in Vilna," *Literarishe bleter* (1925), numbers 49–
50, in which Shalit quotes Peretz as having stated in a lecture: "To you, Zion-
ists, I *do not* belong." Shalit adds that Peretz "does, perhaps, belong to the
youth . . . that has devoted itself, heart and soul, to the Jewish national life and
its *spiritual* content" (9).

[45]Menachem [Goldberg], "Mit Peretz'n (erinerungen)," in *I. L. Peretz: a zamlbukh tsu zayn ondenken* (New York: Literarisher farlag, 1915), p. 33.

eternal Jewish culture."[46] With this metaphor Peretz alludes to his play *The Golden Chain: A Drama of Chassidic Life* (*Di goldene keyt: a drame fun khasidishn lebn*).

In his final phase, then, Peretz renounced "foreign forms" much as Sholem Aleichem had rejected Shomer's European romances twenty years earlier. Viewing assimilation as the enemy, Peretz perceived two pathways: "One path to Europe, where the Jewish forms must be destroyed, and the second path back—to our former days, to our past" (ibid., 303). Hence Peretz greatly valued Yiddish translations of the Bible and modern rewritings of Jewish folk traditions.

LITERARY PERIODS AND CONTRADICTIONS

In spite of the difficulties involved in any periodization, Peretz's mature literary career has often been divided into phases. During 1886–94, in Hebrew and Yiddish, he distinguished himself with his attention to individual psychology. The years 1893–99 formed the core of his so-called "radical period," when he often used outright satire to confront social issues. Chassidic themes played a role as early as 1886, but Peretz wrote his seminal chassidic tales in 1899–1901. After 1901, following the Warsaw literary community's celebration of Peretz's twenty-five years as a writer and fiftieth birthday, Peretz most characteristically produced folktales (*Folkstimlekhe geshikhtn*, 1904–15), wrote avant-garde symbolist dramas (1906–08), and gave public speeches (1908–12).

As early as in 1901, Bal Makhshoves published an essay that illustrated Peretz's dual proclivities.[47] Years later he recalled that "even then it was clear to every critic that Peretz's relationship to Jewish life was double-edged, realistic and romantic. One noted that whenever he approached Jewish life with a realist's instrument he couldn't free himself from Enlightenment tendencies. But when he started to dream of Jewish life in the past or future, he assumed the bent of a modern European who is permeated by a certain

---

[46]I. L. Peretz, "Vegn der yidisher literatur," in *Ale verk I. L. Peretz*, vol. 11, p. 300.

[47]See J. Eliaschoff [Isidor Eliashev/Bal Makhshoves], "Leon Perez: Ein moderner jüdischer Volksdichter," *Ost und West* 1 (1901), 299–306.

PERETZ

aesthetic and mystical-religious culture."[48] Bal Makhshoves observes Peretz's diverse styles that coexisted in the 1890s, suggesting that they cannot be relegated to wholly independent periods.

Yet Peretz gradually distanced himself from satiric realism as he began to specialize in artistically remaking folktales. Some critics such as Bal Makhshoves viewed Peretz's development from realist to romantic as an improvement, whereas the Soviet critics were inclined to condemn it as a lapse into sentimentality and outmoded, atavistic nationalism. Bal Makhshoves pointed to the historical context of Peretz's evolution, noting that a broad social movement shaped and propelled him in the early twentieth century: "Only from the time when a strong nationalistic movement began among Jews—and thanks to it, an audience was created for the Jewish poet, artist, social activist, and so on—did a new chapter begin in Peretz's creative life, and precisely the most beautiful chapter" (ibid., 28). According to Bal Makhshoves, the "radical period" combined disparate elements, while the romantic phase was more univocal: "If, fifteen to twenty years ago, Peretz was more realist than romantic, in the final period of his life he became a pure romantic" (ibid., 29). Nevertheless, some critics have pointed to ironic elements even in Peretz's late folktales.

Peretz continually modified his views and altered his style, combining positions that others considered contradictory. Thus Isaac Rozentsvayg, in his study of "the radical period in Peretz's creativity," concludes that his work was characterized by contradictions. He comments on "the immense contradictoriness" of Peretz's work and argues that "Peretz's contradictions may be seen, not only in different periods of his creativity . . . but also within every period."[49] This, Rozentsvayg believes, reflected his erratic and pessimistic character, which precluded a thorough-going critique of social ills. Whereas Bal Makhshoves applauds the later phase in Peretz's work, Rozentsvayg sees it as a conservative relapse, a period of decline after his strongest, most socially critical work.

---

[48]Bal Makhshoves [Isidor Eliashev], "I. L. Peretz," in *Tsum yortsayt* (Vilna: Kletzkin, 1916), p. 27.

[49]Isaac Rozentsvayg, *Der radikaler period fun Peretz's shafn*, p. 3. Rozentsvayg's position reflects the prevailing Soviet views of the 1930s.

David Bergelson argued that Peretz "was too full of seething impetuousness to remain a consistent artist."[50] H. D. Nomberg perceived Peretz's inconsistencies in a more favorable light, as a sign of his originality: "Until the last day of his life he remained a *beginner!*"[51] Psychologically, "with his boiling, seething temperament," Peretz could never rest content with any single style. Nomberg describes Peretz's loose attachment to causes such as the socialist workers' movement: "this great and powerful talent had a dilettantish relationship to his work. A passing acquaintance with a few Jewish socialists" could suddenly inspire him (ibid., 38). Gradually, "without discussions or logical deliberations, there crept into Peretz's circle the belief in the Jewish masses" (ibid., 39). In 1898, having left behind their more subversive skepticism, Peretz and many other Jewish intellectuals enthusiastically received the proletarian message of Maxim Gorky's work as a sign of "healthy optimism."[52]

After Peretz's death, An-ski recalled the social changes at the turn of the century and Peretz's shifting position: "the mood in the outlying Jewish colonies became daily more nationalistic. And Peretz played an important role in this. No one could dismiss Peretz, not even the most stubborn social democrats. Peretz was an argument, a banner. In his works young people studied the Jewish people and Judaism, and because of him assimilated boys and girls learned Yiddish. There was seldom a Jewish soirée, whether Zionist or Bundist (both parties considered Peretz 'theirs'), that passed without a reading from Peretz's works."[53] The changes during Peretz's later period led him to a new manner of giving public readings. In about 1908, for example, when Peretz was reading from his work in St. Petersburg, members of the audience requested that he read "The Fur Hat" ("Dos shtrayml") or "Bontshe the Silent." He was not satisfied with these satiric scripts and instead improvised a folktale orally (ibid., 20).

---

[50]David Bergelson, "I. L. Peretz un di khasidishe ideologie," *Literarishe bleter* (1925), numbers 49–50 (April), 3.

[51]H. D. Nomberg, "I. L. Peretz: der foter fun der literarisher mishpokhe," in *Tsum yortsayt* (Vilna: Kletzkin, 1916), p. 36.

[52]H. D. Nomberg, *Dos bukh felyetonen* (Warsaw: S. Jaczkowski, 1924), p. 184.

[53]S. An-ski, "Isaac Leybush Peretz (erinerungen)," 18.

FATHER OF THE LITERARY FAMILY

After 1901 Peretz was somewhat spoiled by his success. He was "accustomed to being shown respect, and everything that seemed to him a slight would simply shatter him" (AP 23). One grotesque incident occurred circa 1910 at a theater performance by the well-known actress Esther Rachel Kaminska. Peretz had received complimentary front-row tickets for himself, his wife, his cousin, and Dinezon. Their seats, however, had been mistakenly sold:

> After the play had been going on for a few minutes, the real owners of the seats came up and asked us to leave. At first Peretz didn't understand what they wanted. But he soon sprang up and went out with all of us after him. The play was interrupted. Kaminska and other actors ran after Peretz, took him by the hand and by the cloak, and asked forgiveness from Peretz's wife and Dinezon. But Peretz looked frightful. It was the first time I saw him angry.
>
> We remained silent. Silently we took the streetcar and rode standing up to Dinezon's. Dinezon leaned over to me and said, "Don't tell anyone about this!". . . The incident was never mentioned again. (AP 35–36)

The mix-up became a minor tragedy that had to be concealed; Peretz's honor had been blemished, and Dinezon's patient devotion was required to smooth it over. Humor and self-irony were not among Peretz's strengths.

If Peretz was "the father of the literary family," it is not surprising that Oedipal rivalries surfaced. When one student wrote a sharp article against him, Peretz told Menachem Goldberg: "I am too great in all of your eyes. You all think that I am taking your place, that because of me no one notices you."[54] Peretz would repeatedly "discover" new talents and encourage their progress until they drifted away from him. Each young writer experienced an early period with Peretz that "had almost the character of an infatuation. He not only conveyed this impression to the young man himself; he spoke about him, told stories about him, went around with him. In all this there was a great deal of the disposition of a man who would jump from one literary form to another, from one idea to another—and the same thing was noticeable in

---

[54]Menachem [Goldberg], "Mit Peretz'n (erinerungen)," p. 29.

relation to people. The intense friendships always cooled off and led to a 'separation.' I really can call it separation because each interrupted relationship of that kind carried something in the nature of an extinguished love affair" (ibid., 30–31). Hence Peretz became close to successive generations of writers, inspiring and encouraging each one in turn before passing on to new talents. When Peretz once reproached him for distancing himself, Menachem Goldberg answered, "who is at fault if you drive everyone away?" (ibid., 35).

The relationship between Peretz and Sholem Aleichem was, as frequently noted, strained. Whereas Sholem Aleichem established his authenticity by declaring himself Abramovitsh's "grandson," Peretz set out on a unique path. Sholem Aleichem's editorial revisions of "Monish" were the first point of contention; soon thereafter, Peretz antagonized him with his anthologies that copied the ones Sholem Aleichem had been editing. Later there were reports of Sholem Aleichem's scorn for Peretz's literary circle in Warsaw, with young writers treating him almost as if he were their chassidic rebbe.

Peretz felt deep respect for Sholem Aleichem mingled with jealously. Y. Y. Trunk recalls that Peretz once told him, "I am jealous of only two writers, Shakespeare and Sholem Aleichem."[55] From the standpoint of readers, "in the hierarchy of popularity, Sholem Aleichem then stood as the most deeply beloved of the Jewish masses; but with respect to artistic fame, Peretz stood on the highest plane" (ibid., 122). When Peretz's *Folktales* appeared in book form in 1909, Sholem Aleichem wrote a letter to Peretz in which he said that he blamed himself "because he had never known how to recognize Peretz's value." For many days, Trunk remembers, Peretz carried this letter with him in his breast pocket and showed it to everyone (ibid.).

The movement toward a revival of Judaic tradition in Peretz's later writing is epitomized by a letter he wrote to Yehoash (Solomon Bloomgarden) in 1907. Repudiating the early influence of Heinrich Heine, Peretz comments that "the 'ingenious' mockery is really nothing more than—impotence . . . and in the best case: self-contempt. We must not make mockery . . . There is a need for

---

[55] Y. Y. Trunk, *Poylen: zikhroynes un bilder*, vol. 5: *Peretz* (New York: "Unzer tsayt," 1949), p. 121.

building and planting; if one sometimes needs to make a wry face, one should do it privately in front of a mirror, not in public. Let us become prophets and leaders, not field-marshalls."[56] Peretz no longer valued the undermining literary effects he had achieved a decade earlier, and he wished for a new generation of pride and confidence.

Shmuel Niger compares Peretz's written style to his everyday speech. This style carries on the element of oral narration but is distinct from that of Abramovitsh and Sholem Aleichem. Abramovitsh's novels, with their archaic, classical tone, seem to be written "not on paper but on parchment."[57] His persona Mendele speaks in the vernacular of a folk character while peppering his Yiddish with learned references. Sholem Aleichem achieves an oral quality in his monologues, but in so doing he imitates the speech of diverse characters unlike the flesh-and-blood author. In contrast, Niger states, Peretz's writing reveals his own personality: "Peretz writes as *he* used to speak, not just as one speaks, and he would always speak in a choppy manner, tersely and allusively."

Peretz's aphoristic, improvisatory style expresses his impulsiveness (ibid., 94). There are many testimonies to Peretz's impulsive character, and one critic argued that this trait prevented him from writing novels.[58] This notion disregards the modernistic influences on Peretz the writer: "In everything else he was capricious," but "concerning his literary activity Peretz was very patient. He revised his works dozens of times and persevered for long hours sitting at his writing desk" (AP 23). The condensation of Peretz's short fiction was essential to his modernistic literary tastes, and he incessantly revised the dramas that he wrote in his later years.

Many Yiddish writers perceived Peretz as the heroic champion of modern Yiddish fiction. One encomium referred to him as "the eagle from the high mountains" (AP 25). In one of many poems written on the occasion of Peretz's death, Moyshe Leyb Halpern raises the question, "What, then, were you to us?" Halpern responds with a sequence of images that liken Peretz to

---

[56]Translated from *Ale verk fun I. L Peretz* (New York: CYCO, 1948), vol. 11, p. 215; ellipses in original.

[57]Shmuel Niger, "Vegn Peretz's Yiddish," *Di yidishe velt* 4 (1915), book 2, vols. 1–2 (April–May), 73.

[58]Y. H. Zagorodski, "I. L. Peretz," *Achiasaf* 9 (1901), 357.

A last charred log at night
Smouldering on the steppe in a gypsy tribe's camp;
A ship's sail struggling with the wind and sea;
The last tree in an enchanted, mazy wood
Where lightning cut down at the roots
Oak giants, thousands of years old.[59]

Or, as one disciple transposed this forest imagery, "we had great respect for Mendele. He was the powerful oak, fully formed and shaped, without a spot or blemish. From him we learned, and we were charmed by Sholem Aleichem. But Peretz was our guide."[60]

In some respects Peretz represents the end of the classical period in Yiddish fiction. Though himself a classic author for later Yiddish writers, he did not create a harmonious image of Yiddish culture. Thus Shmuel Niger argued that "Peretz, in his life and creativity, was no classicist but instead a romantic—and his style was not classical, as was Mendele's, but romantic."[61] Peretz did not feel constrained by fixed conventions, because "the romantic style is *not bound*! It has no traditions, it knows no models." According to Niger, Peretz broke the limitations imposed by Abramovitsh's style by employing a spoken manner that contrasted with Abramovitsh's bookishness (ibid.).

Peretz led an intense and private inner life. He passed days of depression and self-doubt during which "he stood beside his bookshelf and every moment looked into another volume. He read long passages from his books, paced up and down the room and looked again into the book. His face expressed suffering, almost despair, and this condition lasted until Dinezon arrived. With a warm look and a few sincere words Dinezon was able to disperse and drive away Peretz's painful thoughts" (AP 15). When his cousin once fell into a gloomy mood, Peretz proposed an introvert's cure: "lock yourself up in your room for a month, don't let anyone in, and everything will heal itself" (AP 22). Peretz himself had ample expe-

---

[59]Translation by Kathryn Hellerstein in the bilingual edition of Moyshe-Leyb Halpern's *In New York: A Selection* (Philadelphia: The Jewish Publication Society of America, 1982), p. 103.

[60]B. Epelboym, "Unzerer (tsum finfyorikn yortsayt fun I. L. Peretz)," in *Tsum ondenk fun I. L. Peretz* (Odessa: Yidishe sektsye bam "gubnarobraz," 1920), p. 10.

[61]Shmuel Niger, "Vegn Peretz's yidish," 76.

rience with solitude and depression: "Standing at the center of the emerging Yiddish literature—almost of the entire Yiddish culture —Peretz was frightfully miserable."[62]

Peretz was an extraordinarily talented writer marked by his eccentricities. His major creations were short and condensed while his commitments to social causes were short-lived. Often depressed, he sought relief in literature, and as he wrote to Yankev Dinezon, "For me literature is a refuge, a help station, the drink that intoxicates me and allows me to forget."[63] Peretz hovered at a safe distance from his contemporaries while producing strikingly original Yiddish fiction in the form of psychological studies, social satires, and folktales.

---

[62]S. An-ski, "Isaac Leybush Peretz (erinerungen)," 26.

[63]Letter of 3 November 1893, translated from ILP 11: 270.

CHAPTER 10

I. L. Peretz: Monologue and Madness in the Early Stories

After Abramovitsh created the predominant style (or *nusach*) for modern Hebrew and Yiddish writing, I. L. Peretz became one of the leading practitioners of an opposing style (or anti-*nusach*). For Peretz had already been deeply influenced by Polish, Russian, and French literature when he encountered the works of his forerunner Abramovitsh in the late 1880s. Peretz learned from Abramovitsh's literary techniques; moreover, several of his stories from the 1890s depict imbalanced characters like Abramovitsh's Isrolik in *The Nag*. But Peretz modified Abramovitsh's conventions, combining literary borrowings with a new psychological realism that extended the boundaries of Yiddish fiction. Whereas Sholem Aleichem shifted from Abramovitsh's written monologues into the genre of orally narrated monologues, Peretz moved beyond Abramovitsh in a different direction by representing silent, internal speech.

Peretz was aware of obstacles that faced Yiddish writers, and soon after he began to publish in Yiddish he planned a long poem entitled "Where Shall I Find a Hero?"[1] Eastern European Jewish culture seemed to lack heroic figures, particularly after it turned away from the ideals of the Enlightenment. From a literary standpoint, Peretz needed to choose between heroic, mock-heroic, and outright satiric genres. In prose he began by representing the inner lives of everyday anti-heroes. He later replaced psychological fiction with complex presentations of chassidic leaders who are ambiguously suspended between heroic and non-heroic modes.

In Abramovitsh's *The Nag*, Isrolik's fantastic narrative shows how he and the Jewish people are victims of the social order. Peretz's characters are more limited to their personal experiences,

---

[1]David Pinsky's information about this early poem "Vu nem ikh a held?" is contained in his edition of *Di verk fun Isaac Leybush Peretz* (New York: Farlag yidish, 1920), vol. 1, p. viii.

reacting to their specific milieux and speaking only for themselves. Even more solitary than Abramovitsh's Isrolik, Peretz's early narrators are oblivious to broader political horizons. Although works such as "The Fur Hat" show Peretz's debt to Enlightenment satire, most of his initial Yiddish stories contrast sharply with the didactic bent of *The Nag*.

FAMILIAR SCENES

Peretz contributed immeasurably to Yiddish fiction with his first book, a collection of three stories entitled *Familiar Scenes* (*Bakante bilder*, 1890).[2] He had formerly published the poetic ballad "Monish" and some insubstantial fiction in *The Jewish Popular Library* of 1888 and 1889; the three new stories constituted a radical departure from prevailing Yiddish literary norms. Unlike popular authors who merely imitated the romantic plots of European novels, Peretz drew from current trends in psychological realism—and from his own experiences in childhood, when he was known as "the crazy Leybush" (MZ 49).

Edited by Peretz's friend Yankev Dinezon, *Familiar Scenes* contains "The Messenger" ("Der meshulekh"), "What is 'Soul'?" ("Vos heyst 'neshome'"), and "The Mad Talmudist" ("Der meshugener batlen"—more literally, "The Mad Idler"). The first conveys an old man's experience of traveling through a snowstorm, the second contains a narrator's youthful metaphysical reflections, and the third expresses the thoughts of an unbalanced yeshiva student. The first and last texts share thematic and stylistic characteristics: they depict desperate situations employing internal monologue to represent extreme human experiences. "The Messenger" and "The Mad Talmudist" are milestones in Peretz's development of psychological complexity in modern Yiddish fiction. While guided by European fiction in other languages, *Familiar Scenes* also responds to his major Yiddish precursor: Peretz had read Abramovitsh's novel *The Nag*, which was first published in 1873, in a Polish translation that appeared in 1886.[3]

---

[2]Leon Peretz, *Bakante bilder*, ed. Y. Dinezon (Warsaw: Boymriter, 1890).

[3]Letters of 4 and 22 July 1888, in *Kol kitvei I. L. Peretz* (Tel Aviv: Dvir, 1962), vol. 10, book 2, pp. 214 and 221–22. This volume of Peretz's Hebrew works is henceforth cited as "KK" by page alone. For Yiddish translations of these letters, see *Briv un redes fun I. L. Peretz*, ed. Nachman Mayzel (New York: YKUF, 1944), pp. 141 and 148–49.

Peretz's story "The Messenger" portrays a relatively balanced character in a state of crisis. The old man, carrying money and a contract through a blizzard, tries to ignore painful sensations in his chest. The narrative follows his thoughts, memories, and fantasies as he trudges through the snow. While resting he drifts into a dreamy state and ultimately freezes to death. Alluding to this story, the second edition of *Familiar Scenes* (1894) bore the sensationalistic subtitle: *Frozen! (Ferfroyren gevorn!).*[4]

In "The Messenger," Peretz experiments with techniques of internal monologue, combining them with occasional third-person descriptions. The story opens: "He walks, and the wind chases at his clothes and white beard."[5] Peretz employs limited omniscience to follow the thoughts of the old man, who worries from the outset whether he will be able to complete his mission. A sharp pain stabs him again and again in the chest, "but he does not want to admit it" (30). The narrator even informs the reader of what the character hides from himself.

As the messenger tries to distract himself from his chest pain, the story follows his fantasies. First the messenger imagines what he would buy if he possessed wealth. Then he recalls his twenty-five years as a recruited soldier under the harsh Cantonist system of Czar Nicholas I (32). There follows a long recollection of his marriage to the sharp-tongued Shprintze, who died many years earlier (33–36). Finally, after his weak heart compels him to sit and rest in the snow, he imagines entering a warm, friendly household. Dream takes the place of reality, offering the messenger an imaginative escape from the snowstorm just as he is on the verge of death. Peretz employs internal monologue technique to represent the psychology of an individual in extremity.

The narrator of "What Is 'Soul'?" recalls a sequence of contemplations on the soul and the afterlife, from the time of his

---

[4]I. L. Peretz, *Bakante bilder: ferfroyren gevorn*, 2d ed., ed. Y. Dinezon (Warsaw: Funk, 1894).

[5]Translations are based on I. L. Peretz, "Der meshulekh," in *Ale verk I. L. Peretz*, vol. 2 (New York: CYCO, 1947), p. 30; cited by page alone. English translations are contained in Isaac Loeb Perez, *Stories and Pictures*, trans. Helena Frank (Philadelphia: Jewish Publication Society, 1906), pp. 101–13, and in I. L. Peretz, *Bontche the Silent*, trans. A. S. Rappoport (Philadelphia: David McKay, 1927), pp. 37–48. See also *In This World and the Next: Selected Writings of I. L. Peretz*, trans. Moshe Spiegel (New York: Thomas Yoseloff, 1958), pp. 176–85.

childhood to maturity. This story bears some resemblance to Abramovitsh's *The Little Man,* in which Isaac-Abraham recalls his childish notions about the soul. Peretz's story antedates his mature chassidic tales and suffers from the absence of plot, narrative force, and dramatic effects. Peretz had not yet mastered the nuanced tone and suspense of his later works, in which first-person narrative enables him to subtly question customs and superstitious beliefs. "What Is 'Soul'?" is an instructive transitional piece, though not a successful work of fiction.[6]

"The Mad Talmudist," the third and final story in *Familiar Scenes,* innovatively explores the meanderings of an individual mind. Peretz's rigorous use of internal monologue precedes that of Western European authors such as Arthur Schnitzler in "Lieutenant Gustl" (1901).[7] Like Schnitzler, Peretz represents his character's thoughts in coherent, well-formed sentences. Peretz's method differs from that of Abramovitsh, who presents Mendele as having edited Isrolik's written draft of *The Nag.* Following Abramovitsh but placing new emphasis on oral speech, Sholem Aleichem pretends to have transcribed word for word the tales his monologists narrate to him. In contrast, Peretz represents his Talmud student Beryl thinking the words that constitute his monologue. The inwardly spoken monologue depends on an omniscient narrator who represents Beryl's inexpressed thoughts. With the exception of several short third-person descriptions, the narrative consists of the mad talmudist's represented thoughts. This internalized narrative technique allows for a detailed portrait of an abnormal, unbalanced mind. In place of first-person narrative, then, Peretz develops internal monologue in a way that diminishes the apparent distance between the narrator and his story.

Like Abramovitsh in *The Nag,* in "The Mad Talmudist" Peretz represents an eccentric character who suffers from the discrepancy

---

[6]In English, see "What Is the Soul? The Story of a Young Man," trans. Michael Stern, in *The I. L. Peretz Reader,* ed. Ruth R. Wisse (New York: Schocken, 1990), pp. 93–104. For an earlier translation by Helena Frank, see Isaac Loeb Perez, *Stories and Pictures,* pp. 117–32.

[7]For an English rendition of this important story, which has often been credited with popularizing the internal monologue technique, see "Lieutenant Gustl," trans. Richard L. Simon and revised by Caroline Wellbery, in Arthur Schnitzler, *Plays and Stories,* ed. Egon Schwarz (New York: Continuum, 1982). Compare my discussion of Edouard Dujardin and Arthur Schnitzler in *Genius and Monologue* (Ithaca: Cornell University Press, 1985), pp. 171–77.

between his readings and his life. Isrolik in *The Nag* strives to enter the university; Beryl in "The Mad Talmudist" remains in a traditional context of Jewish education, the yeshiva. Peretz explores the consciousness of his protagonist, whereas Abramovitsh uses irony, satire, and allegory to convey a social message. Unlike Abramovitsh, who raises issues of education and social reform, Peretz probes the repressed desires of his talmudist.

"The Mad Talmudist," like a dramatic soliloquy, could be performed onstage with a one- or two-man cast. At several points the narrative provides cues that resemble stage directions. The opening sentence sets the scene by means of a third-person description: "He ran back and forth by day, alone in the House of Study (*bes-hamedresh*), and suddenly stood still" (18).[8] The story then shifts to a sequence of contemplations, as Beryl the talmudist begins by questioning his identity. Since he is alone, he addresses himself to God: "Master of the Universe, who am I?" (ibid.). He answers his own question in accordance with what other people say about him: he is a Talmud student, a madman, an orphan, possibly a thinker, and a thirty-year-old yeshiva boy who eats only five days a week (18–19).

In light of his paralyzing internal conflict, psychologists today might diagnose a young man like Beryl as having a personality disorder. From his standpoint, however, as a student of the Bible and Talmud, he concludes that a *dybbuk*—an evil spirit—must have entered him. He notices the internal division when, tempted to steal a cake, part of him says "yes" and the other part warns "no" (21). In the language of the Talmud, he concludes that he is like a room in which the good spirit or impulse (*yetser-tov*) and the evil spirit or impulse (*yetser-hore*) dwell.

Beryl, as he suffers from hunger and other untoward drives, continues to reflect on his identity. His malaise also results from his excessive absorption in texts, to the exclusion of the world, as is the case with Abramovitsh's Isrolik. His search for an identity also reflects Peretz's search for a literary identity, influenced by and yet

---

[8]Translations are based on "Der meshugener batlen," in *Ale verk fun I. L. Peretz,* vol. 2 (New York: CYCO, 1947); cited by page alone. An English translation of "The Mad Talmudist," by Irving Howe and Eliezer Greenberg, is contained in *A Treasury of Yiddish Stories,* ed. Irving Howe and Eliezer Greenberg (New York: Penguin, 1990), pp. 234–42. No single English word can convey the multiple senses of talmudist, idler, and impractical person that are connoted by the Yiddish word *batlen.*

distinct from Abramovitsh. Like Abramovitsh's Isrolik, Peretz's Beryl is aware of his difference from his contemporaries, who have taken ordinary jobs (19). And like Peretz himself, who had recently lost his position as a lawyer in Zamosc, the talmudist is troubled by his lack of all standing, which hinders him from answering the question, "Who am I?"

"The Mad Talmudist" enacts a kind of displaced Oedipal drama. Since his real father has died, no actual process of working through his conflicts is possible. He is forced onto the imaginary plane by his transferred relationship to those who feed him: the couple Wolf and Taybele. The merchant Wolf stands between Beryl and Taybele, who is the only person who cares for the talmudist and "gives a sigh, because she knows that I'm a poor orphan" (18). She mends his clothes, without which he would be "naked as Adam" (19). In the second part of the monologue, with the arrival of Wolf at the House of Study, Beryl's solitary ruminations intensify. Projecting his own identity crisis onto Wolf, Beryl wonders "how may birds sing in his cage?" (24). He contemplates Wolf's many identities and discerns "a pious lamb that sits and studies tractate Nedarim . . . a thief . . . a murderer who beats his wife with murderous blows" (ibid.). This reflection awakens further thoughts of Wolf's wife.

After the first part of the story shows the talmudist's internal confusion, the subsequent two parts suggest its cause. The spirit that has entered him is in fact Taybele, the wife of the merchant Wolf. What he understands as his "evil impulse" is, in Freudian terms, repressed sexual desire. "I often dream of her," the talmudist thinks, and "sometimes she begs me, at night while sleeping, to help her" (24). Yet social norms preclude the longed-for interaction: "That is, she doesn't ask with her mouth, she doesn't speak, God forbid; a Jewish girl doesn't speak with a man . . . but she looks at me with such . . . with such a . . . a kind of gaze . . ." (ibid.; ellipses in original). Beryl fantasizes that Taybele will ask him to defend her against her brutal husband, yet—as a kind of Yiddish Hamlet—he is incapable of acting on this fantasy, and can only continue to suffer from his internal conflict (25).

Desiring the forbidden contact with a married woman, Beryl imagines murdering Wolf. He cannot do this without the urging of a voice (*bas-kol*), preferably that of Taybele, but moral guidelines prevent him from engaging in conversations with women. He allows himself only a fantasy of killing Wolf, or at least of doing away with the most violent of Wolf's three identities. After a terse dialogue with his rival, Beryl becomes so agitated that he unthinkingly slices through his bootleg with the knife he is clutching. "The Mad Talmudist" ends with Beryl's continued thoughts of Taybele. As he wavers between ideas of suicide and murder, he concludes: "I should be able to commit suicide, and see for myself what will be, what will remain, after the head, hands, feet . . . fall off . . . then perhaps I would know something? Wouldn't it be justice to try? . . . If only she were to command! Maybe I would try it on him" (29; ellipses in original).

The talmudist figures his condition metaphorically: a stranger thinks within him, like a bird inside a cage. On one level, this image represents the soul that is trapped inside the body. More specifically, however, the bird is a little dove, in Yiddish a *taybele* (23), which is also the name of the woman he loves. She, or his desire for her, is trapped inside his more rational self. In short, she is the repressed subtext of his thoughts, a dove (Yiddish *taybele* = Hebrew *yonah*) like the woman in the Song of Songs, always desired and frequently absent. The doubling of the self in this monologue simultaneously reveals a personal unconscious, the presence of the desired other, and a biblical source. This becomes clear at one moment of reflection, when Beryl seems to internalize the woman-dove. A stranger has penetrated his thoughts: "Am I a cage, and it—a bird? . . . King David, peace unto him, says: *yonati*, that is, my dove [*taybele*]" (ibid.). Both container and contained, Beryl is both himself and the one he desires, both the cage and the bird it holds. The hypothetical, figurative decision is between killing oneself or one's father. For Beryl, the displaced father is Wolf the merchant, who has possession of the "dove" Taybele.

These early tales contain little irony or satire and differ from the chassidic stories for which Peretz is best known. Peretz does not describe the messenger and talmudist in order to criticize them, but rather to recreate their particular states of mind. This distinguishes him sharply from Abramovitsh, who first and foremost directs his portrayals toward the pedantic goals of the Englightenment. Whereas Abramovitsh sought to satirize and render obsolete the superstitious *shtetl* world, Peretz did not yet aim at social ends. As he initially wrote to Sholem Aleichem, mistaking him for Sholem Abramovitsh, "I know the work of my lord. His will and striving (as far as I have been able to understand) is to write for the Yiddish-speaking public for the sake of Yiddish (*zhargon*), and I write for myself, for my own pleasure; and if I sometimes remember the reader, he is from a higher class in society" (letter of 17 June 1888, in KK 212). Peretz deliberately sets himself apart from Abramovitsh's didacticism.

Shmuel Niger confirms the significance of the emphasis Peretz placed on the individual consciousness. Whereas Abramovitsh and Sholem Aleichem deal with the "soul of the people," Peretz probes his own mind.[9] In contrast to Abramovitsh's Yiddish style, which "derives from the folk-tradition," Niger states that Peretz's style "comes from him alone" (ibid. 172). This is something of an exaggeration, since Peretz learned from precursors who wrote in Yiddish and in other European languages. Yet even when Peretz follows the Enlightenment authors by satirizing ignorance and superstition, he does so in a subtler, more individualized way.

When I. L. Peretz published his highly original collection of stories under the deceptive title, *Familiar Scenes,* only some of the scenes were familiar, and the style Peretz employed to depict them was previously unknown in Yiddish. Peretz did not subordinate his portrayal of a messenger or mad talmudist to any ideological position but sought to simulate the depths of particular minds. While Abramovitsh remained Sholem Aleichem's revered "grandfather," Peretz thus became the father of another Yiddish literary family.

"THE FUR HAT"

At one extreme in his fictional creativity, Peretz produced an outright satire spoken by another Beryl, an elderly cap-maker in "The Fur Hat" ("Dos shtrayml," 1893). The fur hat of the title becomes a symbol of religious authority and those who possess it. Under cover of a simple monologue by a cap-maker, Peretz unfolds a slashing critique of the *shtetl* world. As a narrated monologue, this text initiates the period represented by "Stories from the Madhouse"; at the same time, its satiric bent intensifies the irony that was beginning to emerge in Peretz's chassidic tales.

This story was written at the start of Peretz's so-called "radical

---

[9]Shmuel Niger, *Dertseylers un romanistn* (New York: CYCO, 1946), vol. 1, pp. 163–64.

period," which continued through his involvement with the *Holiday Papers* (*Yontev-bletlekh*) until about 1899. It was first published in an American newspaper (*Di arbeter tsaytung* or *Di tsukunft*) before being reprinted in *Literature and Life* (*Literatur un lebn*) in 1894.[10] Also contained in this volume, which Peretz edited, was his kindred story "Bontshe the Silent." In Peretz's collected writings of 1901, these two stories were printed side by side; in 1911, Peretz again emphasized their interconnections by printing them together under the heading "Humoresques and Satires" (*humoreskn un satirn*).[11]

"The Fur Hat" begins with Beryl's self-presentation, illustrating the primary colors of narrated monologue:

> I am a cap-maker, but the main thing is—a *shtrayml* maker. It's true that most of my sustenance comes from peasants' coarse clothes and porters' coats.
>
> And occasionally Leyb Milner comes in with a raccoon fur. . . .
>
> It's true that one seldom, very seldom, happens upon a *shtrayml*. For who wears a *shtrayml* these days? A rabbi! And a *shtrayml* always outlives him.[12]

Implicitly, this passage suggests a scene in which the speaker stands before his audience. The implied audience does not, however, consist of his immediate circle of acquaintances; in contrast, some of Peretz's chassidic narrators appear to speak to other chassidim who share fundamental beliefs and experiences. Nor does Peretz hint at his own presence in the way Sholem Aleichem purports to hear and transcribe monologues word for word. This introduction follows a literary convention far different from that of "The Mad Talmudist" (where the protagonist and internal monologist begins *in medias res* with his agonized reflections) or "Between Two Peaks" (in which the narrator gradually reveals his

---

[10] "Dos shtrayml," in *Literatur un lebn: A zaml-bukh far literatur un gezelshaft*, ed. I. L. Peretz (Warsaw: Isaac Funk, 1894), pp. 119–34. Reprinted separately as *Dos shtrayml* (Warsaw: Halter, 1896).

[11] See I. L. Peretz, *Shriftn* (Warsaw: Halter, 1901), part 4, and I. L. Peretz, *Ale verk* (Warsaw: Progress, 1911), vol. 6.

[12] "Dos shtrayml," in *Ale verk I. L. Peretz*, ed. Shmuel Niger (New York: CYCO, 1947), vol. 2, p. 249. Henceforth cited by page alone. For an English rendering, see "Shtraimel," in *In This World and the Next*, pp. 80–89.

identity). "The Fur Hat" places the speaker at the center of attention, as is the case with Abramovitsh's Mendele the Bookseller in 1864–79.

The narrative by this worker is less a psychological portrait than a critique of the world he cheerfully pretends to accept. Rhetorically, "The Fur Hat" is based on irony and metonymy. The irony devolves from the tension between Beryl's simple praise of the fur hat (*shtrayml*) and an undercurrent of social criticism. Metonymy is a figure of speech that names relationships by association, including the relationships of a crown to a king or a *shtrayml* to a religious Jew. A *shtrayml* was a fur hat worn on Shabbat and holidays by wealthy, orthodox Jews in Eastern Europe. When Beryl speaks of the *shtrayml* he has made, he also refers metonymically to the person who wears it and to the power vested in that person. In the *shtetl*, it held special significance insofar as it was predominantly worn by religious leaders.

On the surface, Beryl appears naive. He unreflectively admires his *shtrayml* and the inordinate power it commands. Taking the metonymy literally, he assumes that the *shtrayml* constitutes the role performed by the rabbi. Like Mendele the Bookseller in the early 1860s, on the surface he does not seem to question the world he describes. Yet as in the case of Abramovitsh's Mendele, Peretz's Beryl hints at his doubts:

> I've acquired a filthy habit: Whatever I see, I like to ask, "*Where* does it come from! *Why* is it as it is? Can't it be *otherwise*? And when I get hold of Leybl Milner's coat I start to think: Master of the Universe? Why have you created so many kinds of coat? Why does one have a raccoon fur, another a porter's coat, and a third person a peasant's clothes? (251)

To further sharpen the effect, Peretz later added, "and a fourth person has nothing at all" (ibid.). Again the use of metonymy is clear: each kind of garment is associated with a social class or role. While reflecting on clothing, Beryl simultaneously reconsiders class differences. The social criticism becomes most overt in the next line: "I know that Leyb Milner doesn't pay for his raccoon fur until he first extorts a *groshn* from the peasants for a sack of grain. Well, should *that* leave me satisfied?" He refers to the peasant metonymically as a "coarse cloth" (*siermienge*) while suggesting the injustice of this system of exchange. But for the most part Beryl presents his observations lightly, without drawing conclusions.

Beryl is a marginal member of his community, similar in his reflective nature to Beryl "the mad talmudist." He states that "in town, thank God, they never ask my opinion; I'm never called to meetings, and since I'm no tailor I don't go to such things anyway—I barely leave the house! I have no fixed place in the synagogue, or in the House of Study, or in any congregation! . . . So what am I? A nothing!" He adds, however, that "once in a while I unleash a *shtrayml* on the community, and they bow down before me!" (253). His day of glory comes when he makes a fur hat for a rabbi, since according to his interpretation the metonymic power of the *shtrayml* extends to its maker as well.

The following section dispenses with all suggestions that the power of the *shtrayml* resides in what is *beneath* it (254). This eliminates part of the metonymic association, replacing it with a kind of cynical animism: the *shtrayml* itself emerges as the source of a rabbi's power and authority. Beryl implicitly shifts the focus from the *shtrayml*-rabbi association to the relationship between a *shtrayml* and the community that authorizes rabbinic actions and judgments. A rabbi can officiate at marriages and deliver legal rulings only because the community empowers him to do so. The *shtrayml* comes to stand for such empowerment.

Beryl asserts that his *shtrayml* has even greater power than policemen and soldiers. He phrases this superiority in terms of a second metonymy. Across from his shop is a lace-maker who produces epaulets, associated with law enforcement and the military. Given the nature of Jewish society, such institutions cannot compete with the force of his *shtrayml*:

> Let one of his epaulets or shoulder-knots try to say "Treyf!" over one ox and "Kosher!" over another. But in the case of a *shtrayml*, let's see what happens! When my *shtrayml* pronounces that four oxen, one after the other, are "treyf," the butcher is beside himself, his apprentices fall silent, the whole town goes without meat for a week, a company of cossacks gets inexpensive meat, and that's it! No one complains! (253–54)

Peretz's text recalls Abramovitsh's satiric play of twenty-five years earlier, *The Tax*, which attacks and satirizes corruption surrounding the supervision of kosher meat. In contrast to the situation in which a rabbi holds total authority, Beryl gives the example of an epidemic during which sheep become sick and die: "The veterinarian came and said: *Treyf*! But do the people listen to him? He brought along a bunch of policemen and officers! They stole all of the meat, and within three days the whole town had cheap, kosher meat for supper!" (254). This episode emphasizes that the townspeople are less concerned with medically defined hygiene than they are with blindly obeying the *shtrayml* and the religious laws it represents. For the purposes of his social critique, Peretz invents an ironic persona, a narrator who naively embraces and ingenuously praises the backwardness of his community.

Beryl refuses to interpret the *shtrayml* as a conventional symbol, or as the arbitrary metonymy it is. He insists that the community's slavish obedience must derive literally from his *shtrayml,* a kind of idol before which everyone readily bows down (256). Its authority extends to a number of domestic customs practiced by the narrator's wife and by people throughout the Jewish community. Hence the *shtrayml* comes to embody rabbinic authority as a whole, and the narrator defies this authority. He tells us that on fast days he goes to a certain tavern: "in any case, I'm not obliged to fast; it is my own *shtrayml*" that rules the community.

Following this introduction, the narrator begins his main story, inspired by the tavern-keeper's identical twin daughters who were "born in the tavern, and they were princesses!" (258). Their beauty initially makes him question whether they may be even more powerful than the *shtrayml* of religious authority. The events he recounts reaffirm that the *shtrayml* is all-powerful: "Both got boyfriends, and soon both had to let out their skirts. Don't be ashamed; that's the way of the world. If it is God's will, what is the shame? Yet how different it was with them!" (259). The first sister bears her child openly, gives birth, and holds a celebration for the newborn boy. The second sister bears her child secretly, has birth pains, and misfortune takes her child away: "Her little boy has already lain for a long time outside the fence [of the cemetery], and she won't have any more children! Only God knows what has become of her! —She ran away!" (260). The narrator then explains the subtle distinction between them: "The only difference was that the first [match] took place in the schoolyard, in a rubbish heap, under a filthy woolen canopy with silver letters . . . but with the *shtrayml.* The second happened in some warbling woods on a meadow of grass and flowers, under *God*'s blue skies bestrewn with stars, but—without the *shtrayml*" (ibid.). The first daughter was married according to traditional Jewish customs, while the second was united with her lover in nature. Since society destroys the second sister, Beryl concludes that only his *shtrayml* has power—not the flowers, forest, skies, stars, or even God Himself.

The narrator of this tale pits religious authority—embodied in the rabbi's *shtrayml*—against all other powers that be, including God, and decides that the authority vested in a fur hat is greatest. This satiric monologue is somewhat unusual in Peretz's canon, taking an individual approach to the Enlightenment ideology that attacks the backwardness of unexamined beliefs or customs. In "The Fur Hat" the townspeople allow themselves to be ruled by an ignoramus, and a girl is ruined because she does not marry in accordance with convention. This story expresses Peretz's individualistic inclinations, combined with his anti-traditional criticism of social ills; his essays attest to dissatisfaction with the religious world epitomized by the *shtrayml*.[13]

From a distance, Peretz continues the line of Abramovitsh's Mendele the Bookseller. Peretz's *shtrayml*-maker says, "But that's not what I'm getting at" (258)—echoing the key phrase in Mendele's seemingly spontaneous and digressive narrations. In a surprising moment of convergence, Peretz developed this disciple of Abramovitsh's Mendele in 1893, just before Sholem Aleichem began to invent the character of Tevye.

From another standpoint, we may view the *shtrayml* as a figure for the art object, and more specifically as a symbol for Peretz's own chassidic stories. Externally it looks like any other religious artifact, similar to Mendele's pseudo-blessings, but it contains within itself the seeds of its undoing. The *shtrayml* begins with its metonymic association to a rabbi or to rabbinic power, shifts toward metaphorical resemblances to art objects, and further suggests a synecdochal relationship to Peretz's own fiction. Through the association of part for whole, Peretz's fictional fur hat represents the genre of chassidic narrative that later becomes a focal point of his literary production.

"STORIES FROM THE MADHOUSE"

In his *Complete Works* (*Ale verk*, 1909–13), Peretz published seven stories that further develop the themes of madness and social criticism, under the heading "From the Madhouse" ("Fun dul-hoyz").

---

[13]For some of Peretz's critical remarks (1891–94) about rabbis' fur hats, and the authority vested in them, see ILP 8: 7, 11, 53.

Probably influenced by Chekhov's *Ward Six* (1892), these are transitional works in Peretz's development from psychological realism to new trends. One of the most striking features of this group is its lack of coherence, for there is a significant stylistic discrepancy between the first three and the last four tales. The disparity between the former and the latter stories may be explained from bibliographic, literary, linguistic, and psychological standpoints. Although these stories are not central to Peretz's achievement, their checkered textual history reveals much about how Peretz composed and edited his work.

When Peretz published his initial three "Stories from the Madhouse" ("Mayse'lekh fun dul-hoyz") in 1895, he both continued his earlier leanings and responded to a long tradition. Major nineteenth-century Russian authors from Gogol to Dostoyevsky and Chekhov, among others, had experimented with stories by and about madmen. In Yiddish, Abramovitsh had produced the 1873 and 1889 editions of *The Nag,* purportedly based on writings of Isrolik "the Madman." As in Gogol's *Diary of a Madman* (1835) and Abramovitsh's *The Nag,* Peretz's speaker—presumed to be mad—views animals, plants, or inanimate things anthropomorphically. In Hebrew, there are elements of madness in Peretz Smolenskin's *A Wanderer on the Paths of Life* (*Ha-to'eh be-darkhei ha-chaim,* 1868–71). Formally, Sholem Aleichem's early work, "The Intercepted Postal Letters" ("Di ibergekhapte briv oyf der post," 1883–84), was another precursor to Peretz's monologues.[14] In turn, Sholem Aleichem's fictional letters drew from Hebrew parodies such as Joseph Perl's *Revealer of Secrets* (*Megale temirin,* 1819).

The first story *fun dul-hoyz,* "The World to Come" ("Oylem ha-be") consists of seven scattered reflections. The speaker opposes the verdict of madness which others have imposed upon him: merely because of his metaphysical ideas, he says, and because he doubts the reality of this world, "they say that *I* am mad!" (433).[15] In fact, he directs the diagnosis against everyone else, saying that "this is not a world!. . . . It is a madhouse" (434). As is typical of some paranoid schizophrenics, the speaker "from the madhouse" is troubled by the multitude of masks around him: "there is a masquerade, a Purim-play, with only the disguised, and not one is in its proper

---

[14]See Sholem Aleichem, *Ale verk* (Moscow: Der emes, 1948), vol. 1, pp. 54–194.

[15]Translations of the "Mayse'lekh fun dul-hoyz" are based on *Ale verk fun I. L. Peretz,* vol. 2 (New York: CYCO, 1947); cited by page alone.

skin!" (435). This reflection leads to a second tale about a jack-of-all-trades (*kol-bonik*) who, like Beryl the talmudist, has multiple identities.

In the third and last of the original "Stories from the Madhouse," entitled "A Dream" ("A kholem"), the narrator describes the experience that brought him to the asylum: he entered what he perceived as an enchanted garden. His madness is revealed by personification, the imaginary nature of which he remains unaware. The opening two stories from the madhouse mock superstitious ideas about the World to Come and Angel of Death; the third monologue recalls the well-known legend (*aggada*) of entering a garden, contained in the Palestinian and Babylonian Talmuds, Tractate Hagigah, and in the Tosefta to Hagiga.[16] Peretz undoubtedly alludes to the talmudic narrative in which four men enter a garden (*pardes*) and one dies, one is smitten, one "cuts down the sprouts" (becomes insane), and only the last, R. Akiba, remains whole.[17] This traditional tale serves as the basis for Peretz's text, which thus combines psychological description with a parodic recasting of the ancient source.

The narrator of "A Dream" has been smitten by his encounter with what lies beyond the familiar, material world. This speaker, who is not necessarily the same as that of the first two tales, begins by responding to a question: "You wish to know where I come from? I'll tell you; I have no secrets" (440). He then explains that he was mentally well until the advent of his dreaming visions. His fantasies have much in common with those of Abramovitsh's Isrolik, except that they are less obviously allegorical. The story describes the mad fantasy that has destroyed the speaker's life: in his dream, he enters a wealthy estate and longs to eat from its natural abundance. Yet as he reaches out to pluck a piece of fruit, talking trees and corn stalks reproach him for wanting to eat them. They chant:

> "*You* did not set us,
> *You* did not plant us!"
> (*Nisht du host undz gezetst,*
> *nisht du host undz geflantst!*). (441)

---

[16] On the three basic versions of this talmudic story, see David J. Halperin, *The Merkabah in Rabbinic Literature* (New Haven: American Oriental Society, 1980), pp. 86–92.

[17] See the Tosefta to Hagiga 2:3–4, the Palestinian Talmud, Hagiga 77b, and the Babylonian Talmud, Hagiga 14b, 15a,b. Scholars have not agreed as to whether this story should be interpreted literally, mystically, or both.

After this delusionary experience, the speaker finds himself in bed, attended by his wife. He concludes, "I fell asleep and woke up already here" (443), in the madhouse. There would be little reason to dwell on these three modest stories if not for their ambitious effort to enter the speech of madmen. Peretz was obviously intrigued by phenomena of madness, and was interested enough in madness to begin the "Stories from the Madhouse," but other forces intervened before he completed them.[18]

Peretz's seven stories "from the madhouse" were not initially published together, nor—despite appearances—were they originally intended to form a single unit. In fact, they were not even written in the same language. The language shift had serious implications, particularly for the attempted representation of vernacular, oral discourse. To recognize the character of Peretz's madhouse sequence, as well as to better understand Peretz's creative process, we first need to review its publishing history, which is outlined in Table 4.

In 1895, as this table illustrates, Peretz printed three "Stories from the Madhouse" ("Mayse'lekh fun dul-hoyz") in his *Yontev-bletlekh,* successively entitled "The World to Come" ("Oylem ha-be"), "Jack-of-All-Trades" ("Kol-bo"), and "A Dream" ("A kholem").[19] Although the letters *Feh-Feh* on the final page (an abbreviation for the expression *forsetsung folgt*) indicate that a continuation will follow, the closest approximation published in the subsequent *Yontev-bletlekh* of 1895 is an independent monologue, "If They Say He's Crazy, Believe It!" ("Az men zogt meshuge—gleyb!"). In place of the promised continuation, Peretz then switched to Hebrew and published four madhouse tales in the journal *Ha-tzefira* in 1896.[20]

In Yiddish, for his 1901 *Shriften,* Peretz appears to have trans-

---

[18]In the story "Madmen" ("Meshugoim"), dating from after 1900, a first-person narrator tells about the deranged from an analytical perspective; his own sanity is not in question. See ILP 3: 359–64.

[19]The "Mayse'lekh fun dul-hoyz" were first published in the issue "Bekhurim," in *Yontev-bletlekh,* Second Series (1895), number 3, pp. 7–23.

[20]*Ha-tzefira* 23 (1896), numbers 195, 196, and 198, on pages 948, 952, and 962–63. The first Hebrew edition of Peretz's *Ketavim* collects the same four stories, with one additional tale, in 1900. See "Be-'agaf ha-meshuga'im" in Peretz's *Ketavim,* part 2 (Warsaw: Toshia, 1900), vol. 4, pp. 213–25. This edition does not include the three earlier tales.

TABLE 4.
Peretz's "Stories from the Madhouse"

Yiddish	*Hebrew*
1895—Stories 1–3 published as "Stories from the Madhouse" ("Mayse'lekh fun dul-hoyz") in *Yontev-bletlekh*: "The World to Come" ("Oylem ha-be"), "Jack-of-All-Trades" ("Kol-bo"), and "A Dream" ("A kholem")	1896—Stories 4–7 published as "In the Insane Asylum" ("Be-'agaf ha-meshuga'im") in *Ha-tzefirah*: "Doctor or Patient?" ("Rofe' 'o chole?"), "A Talk with Vaporman" ("Siach ve-sig 'im ba'al ha-'edim"), "The Holy One" ("Ha-kadosh") and "The Fire and After the Fire" ("Ha-sreifah ve-achar ha-sreifah")
1901—Stories 1–3 and 4–7 published separately in *Writings (Shriftn)* as "Stories from the Madhouse" ("Mayse'lekh fun dul-hoyz"; same titles as in 1895) and "In the Insane Asylum" ("In fligel far meshugoim"): "A Doctor or a Patient" ("A rofe tsi a khule"), "A Talk with Vaporman" ("A shmues mit gazeman"), "The Holy One" ("Der koydesh"), and "The Fire and After the Fire" ("Di srayfe un nokh di srayfe")	1900—Stories 4–8 published as "In the Insane Asylum" ("Be-'agaf ha-meshuga'im") in *Ketavim*: same titles as in 1896, supplemented by "In the Wide World" ("Be-'olam ha-gadol")
1911–Stories 1–7 published together in *Ale verk* under the heading, "From the Madhouse" ("Fun dul-hoyz"; same titles as in 1901)	

lated the Hebrew text of stories 4–7.[21] He did not combine the later four tales with the earlier "Stories from the Madhouse," but instead gave them an independent title, taken directly from their Hebrew source: "In the Insane Asylum" ("In fligel far meshugoim").[22] In this edition of Peretz's works, moreover, the two series are separated by nearly one hundred pages of unrelated fiction. Not until the 1911 edition of Peretz's *Complete Works* did these tales appear together under the single title, "From the Madhouse" ("Fun dul-hoyz").[23] Peretz apparently authorized this decision to unite the two sequences, despite the fact that he published them separately in his *Shriftn* of 1901. The unity of the first three and the latter four or five tales has been imposed retrospectively.

While Peretz originally intended to continue his Yiddish "Stories from the Madhouse," the continuation came in Hebrew under the title "In the Insane Asylum." The change in title is concurrent with an unmistakable stylistic shift that reflects a turning point in his literary development. The explanation for Peretz's interruption and stylistic change may be approached in a variety of ways. In his madhouse monologues, Peretz attempts to enter the minds of madmen; or, more precisely, he impersonates their speech. His experiment fails for several reasons, in connection with the progression from Peretz's *Familiar Scenes* of 1890 to his separate sequences of madhouse stories.

Peretz innovates remarkably when he employs internal monologue in the stories "The Messenger" and "The Mad Talmudist." Using the language of common speech, Peretz's characters attain a

---

[21]There is internal textual evidence that the Yiddish version of stories 4–7 is later than the Hebrew text of 1896. During the narrator's conversation with "Gas man" concerning his divorce, for example, the narrator says in the original Hebrew, "And you did not give it?" (*ve-lo natata?*). In the Yiddish, he asks, "And you did not want to?" (*un ir hot nisht gevolt?*). This apparently later modification also figures into the subsequent Hebrew version: "And you did not wish to?" (*ve-lo khafatzta?*). Peretz must have modified the Hebrew text on the basis of changes he made while translating it into Yiddish. There are many other examples suggesting the priority of the Hebrew stories 4–7, including expansions in the Yiddish version. In contrast, there was no early version in Hebrew of the initial three Yiddish "Mayse'lekh fun dul-hoyz."

[22]I. L. Peretz, *Shriftn* (Warsaw: Halter, 1901), part 4. The "Mayse'lekh fun dul-hoyz" are printed on pages 30–38, while the "In fligel far meshuga'im" stories appear on pages 124–37.

[23]*Ale verk I. L. Peretz* (Warsaw: Progress, 1911), vol. 6, pp. 219–53.

psychological complexity that was generally absent from earlier, nineteenth-century Yiddish fiction. The talmudist's furious thoughts revolve around his unstable identity and the figure of Taybele, a woman he unconsciously loves. Thematically, Beryl's *meshugas* returns to haunt the characters in Peretz's original three "Stories from the Madhouse." Yet in the later tales 4–7 Peretz modifies his conventions, following the first-person form of "The Fur Hat." He no longer purports to transcribe the internal speech of his characters; instead, his monologists address an audience in a dramatic situation. In contrast to his early stories that center on the consciousness of a Talmud student or messenger, Peretz's later tales emerge "from the madhouse." Mysterious voices speak from indefinite situations in the asylum. In a more abstract Hebrew, however, the latter narratives lose much of this situational power. Peretz seems to waver between the psychological mode of his *Familiar Scenes* and the satiric mode of "The Fur Hat."

After *Yontev-bletlekh* folded in 1896, Peretz published the continuation of "Stories from the Madhouse" in a Hebrew newspaper rather than in a Yiddish serial. This shift necessitated a number of modifications. Because the newspaper *Ha-tzefira* was primarily concerned with political realities, its editor would have discouraged personal, monological narratives like those of the earlier madhouse stories. Accordingly, Peretz recast his original project in more philosophical terms, making the mental hospital appear as a microcosm for the mad world, ending with a kind of self-inflicted apocalypse. Under pressure from the demands of Hebrew publishing, Peretz developed the later madhouse stories into harsh indictments of traditionalism, specifically attacking false messianic ideas by showing their catastrophic consequences.

There is also a linguistic explanation for the radical swerve that differentiates the Yiddish and Hebrew madhouse stories. While represented direct speech was effective in Yiddish writing, such first-person, "spoken" narratives were foreign to contemporary Hebrew literature. When he switched from Yiddish to Hebrew, then, Peretz necessarily gave expression to the difference between the literary forms that had developed in both languages. The genius of Yiddish fiction was epitomized by its ability to emulate patterns of everyday speech; in contrast, Hebrew was still most effective in the written mode that drew from ancient and medieval literary and liturgical models. Thus the languages themselves asserted a decisive influence over the respective Yiddish and Hebrew tales "from the madhouse." In the Hebrew version, for example, the narrator indicates that he is writing his memoirs, while the corresponding Yiddish version of stories 4–7 continues to suggest an oral narration.

Before he wrote his two series of "Stories from the Madhouse," Peretz had already attempted to transfer his Yiddish accomplishment in "The Mad Talmudist" into a comparable Hebrew text. In 1893 he printed the ambitious Hebrew story entitled "A Night of Horror" ("Leil zeva'ah").[24] To assist the reader in comprehending the scattered thoughts of Mr. Finkelmann, and perhaps also to assert a safe critical distance, Peretz added the subtitle: "A Study in Mental Illness." Peretz's remarkable experiments with internal monologue in Hebrew were not appreciated by his contemporaries, presumably because the immediate effect of unspoken thoughts was so difficult to achieve in late-nineteenth-century Hebrew.

Peretz's writing in Yiddish and Hebrew gradually evolved away from the representation of individual psychology and toward ironic effects. After his Yiddish experiments in "The Mad Talmudist" and "The Messenger," and his efforts with introspective Hebrew writing that culminated in "A Night of Horror," Peretz turned away from the use of internal monologue. Primarily in Yiddish, he shifted to satires, allegories, and oral narrations in a pseudo-chassidic mode. This was an integral process in Peretz's literary evolution, at the same time suggesting motives beyond aesthetic criteria.

From a psychological standpoint, Peretz may have been uneasy with the personae he was attempting to create. Having been called "the crazy Leybush" in childhood, and more recently dubbed "our great, mad poet L. Peretz" by Sholem Aleichem, he was both drawn to and anxious about his imaginary madmen. Thus in the later stories "from the madhouse," he only dimly explored abnormal mental states. Peretz took a step toward and then quickly withdrew from madness, after which he chose to experiment with other narrative forms.

The subsequent issue of *Yontev-bletlekh* contains no continuation of the madhouse tales, but instead a story called, "If They Say

---

[24]Peretz's "Leil zeva'ah" was first published in the journal edited by Nachum Sokolov, *Ha-'asif* 3 (1893), 136–46.

He's Crazy—Believe It!" ("Az men zogt meshuge—gleyb!").[25]
This story does continue some thematic aspects of the third story
"from the madhouse," yet Peretz distances himself from the madness in his story by creating a third-person narrator who tells
about the eccentricities of a certain Moyshe. As with some of
Sholem Aleichem's later unreliable narrators, a direct tension
arises between the purportedly mad Moyshe and the narrator who,
perhaps motivated by malice and self-interest, exposes his foibles.
Peretz retains the theme of madness but distances the narrative
mode, possibly employing a defensive mechanism.

In producing the later madhouse tales, Peretz shifted to Hebrew
and made the identity of the speaker more complex. For example,
the second Hebrew text, entitled "Doctor or Patient?" ("Rofe' 'o
chole?"), asks whether the "I" of the narrative is inside or outside
the mental asylum, as one of the patients or one of the doctors.[26]
The fourth Hebrew story, the last of those subsequently translated
into Yiddish, ends on the same note of ambiguity: "If I have not yet
gone mad, I will go mad tomorrow."[27] The Yiddish version concludes by referring back to the ambiguity between being a doctor
or a patient: "I don't even wonder any more who I am, a doctor or
a patient, for I'm sure that, if I'm not yet mad, I will go mad
tomorrow" (ILP 2: 459). Thus in the final series of madhouse
stories, Peretz shies away from his former project. He begins to
allegorize the mental hospital, obliquely likening the diverse illnesses it houses to the varying customs of world nations. What
began as a psychological study ends as a political allegory.

In his mad monologues, Peretz presented psychological portraits of madness in the words of the madmen themselves. He fell
short of his goal, perhaps because of a reluctance to probe deeper
into the madness that intrigued him. He had reached the limits of
Yiddish realism, and shifted toward satire. Instead of reaching
further into the mad mind, Peretz withdrew and contented himself
with depicting eccentric speakers from a safe ironic distance.
Moreover, from the linguistic standpoint, he bowed to the respective strengths of the current Yiddish and Hebrew literary tradi-

---

[25]This story appeared in "Tammuz," in *Yontev-bletlekh*, second series (1895),
number 4, pp. 38–54.

[26]This confusion is very much in the spirit of Chekhov's *Ward Six*, published four
years earlier.

[27]See *Kol kitvei I. L. Peretz* (Tel Aviv: Dvir, 1950), vol. 5, p. 153.

tions. What was possible in Yiddish fiction was not yet possible, or at least not yet accessible to readers, in Hebrew.

Peretz succeeded in some of his early monologues by "mad" characters, but when he sought to give psychological complexity to a mad narrator "In the Madhouse," following Isrolik in *The Nag*, his experiment fell short. In retrospect, too, it appears unlikely that Peretz could have matched the contemporary successes of Sholem Aleichem in the monologue genre. Peretz did not master the improvisational oral form that Sholem Aleichem had already begun to employ with unprecedented success in Tevye's earliest spoken monologue of 1894. Rather than vie with Abramovitsh and Sholem Aleichem through the use of loquacious speakers, Peretz turned to a less personalized narrative voice and parodic effects, epitomized by the later chassidic tales. He never returned to the kind of personal, individualized monologues that launched his career in Yiddish fiction. In place of mad monologists who have lost control of their lives, Peretz created first-person narrators whose subtle narratives rework spiritualistic conventions in the chassidic world.

CHAPTER 11

Irony in I. L. Peretz's Chassidic Tales

Peretz's creativity reached its zenith in 1899 to 1901 with his innovative return to chassidic traditions. He had taken tentative steps in this direction with several Hebrew stories as early as 1886, but his Yiddish fiction initially carried him toward psychological realism ("The Messenger" and "The Mad Talmudist," 1890) and social criticism ("Bontshe the Silent" and "The Fur Hat," 1893–94). In his best fiction of 1899–1901, Peretz surpassed his former narratives with reworked chassidic tales that are neither wholly romantic and nostalgic nor entirely realistic and satiric; they suspend the reader between contradictory positions. Peretz repeats certain aspects of the classic chassidic tale while retaining a critical distance; he never imitates so much as he *refashions,* using irony as his mark of parodic difference.

In the 1890s, Peretz's major stories shift from internal monologue and first-person satire to the understated first-person narratives of his chassidic tales. While Peretz adapts many plots from folk traditions, he supplements them by accentuating the dramatic process of retelling. Peretz's texts, which have been widely circulated in the volume entitled *Chassidic (Khasidish),* convey subtle impressions through narratives about traditional characters. In a latter-day transformation of Abramovitsh's Mendele persona and concurrent with Sholem Aleichem's Tevye, Peretz invents a variety of seemingly pious narrators. Commenting upon a story by H. N. Bialik, Robert Alter discusses the use of what he calls an "as-if pious" narrator—"'pious' because throughout he uses the language of tradition to be found in the mouths of the devout; 'as-if' not only because he is the artful invention of a sophisticated modern writer, but because he clearly manneuvers his pious rhetoric for comic effect."[1] The difference is that Peretz balances his texts more shrewdly between traditional echoes and ironic effects, so that we cannot always be certain where the piety ends and the irony begins.

---

[1] See Robert Alter's introduction to Bialik's "The Short Friday" (1925) in his anthology *Modern Hebrew Literature* (New York: Behrman House, 1975), p. 106.

Peretz wrote his early Yiddish fiction under the influence of foreign models, but after 1899 Peretz increasingly grafted or superimposed his fiction onto Jewish folktales. As Peretz became disillusioned by his socialist involvements, his neo-chassidic genre was affected by two contemporaneous trends: the growing interest in ethnography throughout Europe, and the revival of Jewish nationalism in the wake of Theodor Herzl's First Zionist Congress in 1897. Having deliberately situated modern Yiddish fiction in a line beginning with chassidic narratives, Peretz produced "as-if" chassidic stories in a new key.

In Peretz's later first-person narratives, irony often plays the decisive role. Peretz's narrators are less developed as characters than are Abramovitsh's Mendele or Sholem Aleichem's monologists; nevertheless, they do constitute significant fictional personae. "Irony" is broadly defined as dissembling speech, "saying one thing and meaning another." Peretz's ironies unsettle his narrators' overt expressions, and several of the major chassidic tales revolve around narrators whose own implicit ambivalences are essential to their meaning.

The title *Chassidic* indicates the underlying genre of the stories in this volume. They describe chassidim and borrow stylistic features from chassidic folktales. Two obvious reference points are *In Praise of the Bal Shem Tov* (*Shivchei ha-besht*, 1815), comprising popular recollections of the revered originator of the chassidic movement, and the tales that were told orally by Rabbi Nachman of Bratslav—and printed in a bilingual Hebrew-Yiddish edition by his scribe Nathan Sternharz (1815). Peretz draws from the conventions established by these works, appropriating their spiritualistic genre for his literary purposes. The tone of many genuine chassidic tales is adulation, directed toward the leader (the Rebbe) or other righteous person (*tsadik*). Peretz takes on and modifies this genre by sketching scenes of greater complexity and conflict. In this vein, some of Peretz's most characteristic stories are "Kabbalists," "If Not Higher," "The Teachings of the Chassidim," and "Between Two Peaks."[2]

Like his "Stories from the Madhouse," Peretz's volume *Chassidic* does not represent a single conception, but is instead a pragmatic grouping that was imposed retrospectively. Most Yiddish scholars are

---

[2]H. D. Nomberg, who was close to Peretz's circle in Warsaw, also argues that "the highest expression of his particular style, of his originality, unfolds in two short stories": "The Teachings of the Chassidim" and "Kabbalists." See H. D. Nomberg, "I. L. Peretz (a literarisher dor)," in *Dos bukh felyetonen* (Warsaw: S. Jaczkowski, 1924), pp. 188–89.

familiar with the canon of chassidic tales that was established by the 1909–13 edition of Peretz's collected works. It includes twenty-two stories, divided into five unnamed parts; the grouping is broadly thematic rather than chronological.[3] When Shmuel Niger edited a new collection of Peretz's works in 1947, however, he altered the canon slightly and reorganized the stories chronologically. This helpfully breaks the illusion of an undifferentiated unity in the *Chassidic* volume; on the other hand, it disregards the interpretive act Peretz performed when he organized these tales into five distinct clusters.[4]

The textual history of Peretz's neo-chassidic writings elucidates their evolution as a meaningful group. The title *Chassidic* (*Khasidish*) dates from the earliest Yiddish edition of Peretz's collected works, printed in 1901. Yet this novel heading initially encompasses only six stories plus the first three of "Yochanan Melamed's Stories."[5] The Hebrew edition contains the same six tales under the somewhat different title *Chassidism* (*Chasidut*), most of them translated by Peretz from his 1900–01 Yiddish texts.[6] This reveals that the original inspiration for the collection called *Chassidic* came in about 1900, specifically in connection with the key Yiddish tales "If Not Higher" and "Between Two Peaks." These masterpieces have antecedents, however, in "Kabbalists" and "The Teachings of the Chassidim"; in fact, these linked stories are grouped together in sections three and four of the volume *Chassidic* in the 1909–13 edition of Peretz's Yiddish works. It is additionally significant that

---

[3]See I. L. Peretz's *Ale verk* (Warsaw: Progress, 1909–13), vol. 5.

[4]Shmuel Niger acknowledged objections to his method of editing Peretz's chassidic tales. See his *I. L. Peretz: zayn lebn, zayn firendike perzenlekhkeyt, zayne hebreishe un yidishe shriftn, zayn virkung* (Buenos Aires: Alveltlikher yidisher kultur kongres, 1952), pp. 281n–282n.

[5]The six tales are "Kabbalists" ("Mekubolim"), "If Not Higher" ("Oyb nisht nokh hekher"), "A Conversation" ("A shmues"), "Joy Dwells with Him" ("Shehasimkhe bemoano"), "Between Two Peaks" ("Tsvishn tsvey berg"), and "The Metamorphosis of a Song" ("Gilgul shel nign"). See I. L. Peretz, *Shriftn*, part 5 (Warsaw: Halter, 1901).

[6]The Hebrew sequence runs: "Joy Dwells with Him" ("She-ha-simcha bema'ono"), "Between Two Peaks" ("Bein shnei harim"), "The Metamorphosis of a Song" ("Gilgul shel nigun"), "A Chassidic Conversation" ("Sichat chasidim"), "If Not Higher" ("'Im lo le-ma'ala mi-zeh"), and "A New Song" ("Nigun chadash"). See I. L. Peretz, *Ketavim*, part 4, book 10 (Warsaw: Toshia, 1901). In this edition, as compared to the Yiddish edition, "A New Song" ("Nigun chadash") takes the place of "Kabbalists." On the distinction between *Khasidish* and *Chasidut*, see Shmuel Niger *I. L. Peretz*, chapter 12.

both of the forerunners, "Kabbalists" and "The Teachings of the Chassidim"—as well as "The Kaddish"—were first written in Hebrew. The Hebrew context provided the inspiration, while the transfer of this Hebrew form into Yiddish enabled Peretz to make a particular contribution to Yiddish prose.

"THE KADDISH"

Peretz published four Hebrew stories in 1886, which was also the year in which Abramovitsh emerged from his period of silence and published the first chapter of his story "Be-seter ra'am." Both contributed to the new Hebrew daily *Ha-yom*, but their stylistic differences are obvious: in contrast to Abramovitsh's *nusach*, Peretz's prose is spare, he employs extensive dialogue, and the overall structure of his fiction is highly condensed.[7]

Peretz's first work in a pseudo-chassidic mode, his Hebrew story "The Kaddish" ("Ha-kadish," 1886), predates his earliest Yiddish texts. It has never been printed as part of the *Chassidic* canon, but it clearly anticipates these later tales. It opens dynamically with the description of a traditional yet mysterious event: "After the evening prayer an old man approached the pulpit lectern and read the Mourner's Kaddish in a trembling voice. The entire congregation, which had not paid attention to the earlier Kaddish prayers, suddenly turned to face the Eastern Wall and a silent stillness overcame the House of Study."[8] Unlike Abramovitsh, who constructs his narratives around leisurely reflection and observation, Peretz turns immediately to a dramatic scene. He then draws the reader into the scene with a dialogue:

> I wondered at the sight, and I stood amazed and astounded even after the Kaddish had ended and the old man returned from the lectern.
> —Young man, he said as he was passing me, you are astonished at what you have seen . . . that is Rabbi Isaac's Kaddish!
> —Excuse me, sir, if I ask you who the man was whose memory was blessed before all of you.

---

[7]Shmuel Niger characterizes Peretz's mature literary style along these lines in his *I. L. Peretz,* pp. 177, 258–61.

[8]"Ha-kadish," *Ha-yom* 1 (1886), number 14, p. 2; henceforth cited by page alone.

—I shall tell you, young man. . . . Thirty years ago, the old man began in his trembling voice, there lived among us here a generous man, Rabbi Isaac, son of Rabbi Joseph, may God bestow favor upon his remains. (2)

As recalled by this internal narrator, Rabbi Isaac and his wife Esther led virtuous lives but remained childless. One apparent source of Esther's childlessness was her husband's excessive zeal as a scholar: "On Friday nights, when Rabbi Isaac sat all night in the House of Study, as was then the custom, Esther did not shut her eyes and all night prayed and read various supplications, until the neighbors heard her crying bitterly, but they did not tell Rabbi Isaac" (ibid.). Although the narrator conveys neither praise nor blame, the custom of late-night study appears cruel and at odds with the circumstances. Esther died an early death in consequence of the medications and regimens imposed upon her by doctors seeking to render her fertile. Subsequently Rabbi Isaac turned over his merchandise to the now aged narrator and transformed his house into a hostel for the poor. Until his death he lived among the sick and the poor in his house. Thereafter they and the narrator said the Kaddish prayer in his memory.

This story functions on two distinct levels. Most basically it reflects a nascent "cult of personality" in which the admirable Rabbi Isaac is praised for his goodness. This genre was popularized by the chassidim in their recollections of the Bal Shem Tov and other leaders. On the first level, then, the story simply recounts the unselfish deeds of an outstanding man. Equally significant, however, are hints of criticism. Peretz's innovation lies in his subtle combination of these antithetical modes of praise and censure. As the older narrator within the story explains the meaning of his Kaddish for Rabbi Isaac, he betrays doubts about outdated practices.

Rabbi Isaac was so pious, the narrator recalls, that he spent entire nights in the House of Study, leaving Esther to her sorrow. Esther tried zealous remedies including fasts in order to fulfill the commandment, "Be fruitful and multiply," but they only brought about her premature death. After recalling that Rabbi Isaac and Esther were childless, the internal narrator comments that "at that time there were no chassidim or miracle workers to cure barrenness." The young listener then adds parenthetically, "a mocking smile (*sechok la'ag*) appeared on the old man's lips." The man next explains that Esther sought remedies from gypsies and shepherds, and he cynically remarks that these so-called doctors "realized a good profit from their labors, although all of their efforts to cure Esther came to nothing." A further cause of Esther's death was "the wound buried in her heart" from being childless; "Esther feared lest Rabbi Isaac would divorce her and take another wife to bear children." This was not his intention, but perhaps the traditions that dominated their lives were faulty, and "once when the rabbinical judge remarked that he was not fulfilling the commandment to 'be fruitful and multiply,' Rabbi Isaac became bitterly angry and even cursed him vehemently" (2).

At the time of the story chassidim were scarce; now, the narrator concludes his tale, "the rich men of the city are great chassidim but not *men of deeds*." That is, he intimates, their piety is inert and does not necessarily influence their conduct. The narrator says Kaddish for thirty years in memory of the admirable man, yet he cannot dispel his impression that something went amiss. After all, he is saying the Kaddish that—according to tradition—a son should have said. Peretz's early story anticipates his best works, in which he exposes a tension between competing perspectives.

"KABBALISTS"

Five years elapsed between the publication of "The Kaddish" ("Ha-kadish") and "Kabbalists" ("Ha-mekubalim," 1891). During those years Sholem Aleichem edited *The Jewish Popular Library* (*Di yudishe folksbibliotek*). The high quality of his two anthologies—as well as the large honoraria paid by the editor—improved perceptions of Yiddish literature, and Peretz contributed to these editions. Even after Peretz had been outraged when Sholem Aleichem modified his ballad "Monish" for the 1888 collection, Peretz submitted several stories for the 1889 volume. When Sholem Aleichem had to shelve further volumes because of his bankruptcy, Peretz took over by producing the imitative journal entitled *The Jewish Library* (*Di yudishe bibliotek*) and several other literary collections. Suddenly he was even more committed to Yiddish than he was to Hebrew. His contemporaneous essay on education ("Bildung," 1891) asserts that "with Hebrew alone, for the time being, we cannot get by."[9] At least for didactic purposes (and financial rewards), Peretz favored writing in the language of the three million Yiddish speakers in Europe.

9ILP 8: 9.

Apart from this didacticism, Peretz's turn to Yiddish had significant consequences: his stories of 1889–94 brought about his development as a bilingual writer. In one early case, Peretz translated his 1889 Yiddish text "Venus and Shulamit" into Hebrew in 1890, which forced him to test the limits of Hebrew as a language of spoken dialogue. Two other stories, conversely, began in Hebrew and later appeared in Yiddish. Instead of focusing on the actual process of translation between languages, which was not always carried out by the author, it is revealing to analyze how Peretz's best fiction indirectly gained from his experience with writing in both Hebrew and Yiddish.

Two highly condensed stories frame section three of the canonical (circa 1911) volume *Chassidic.* The narrators of "Kabbalists" and "If Not Higher" do not play prominent roles, yet they hint at restrained irony. Both tales end with a single sentence that gives a sharp turn to their meaning; this rhetorical device is the Yiddish analogue of an "O. Henry ending." The last sentence, by showing an unexpected dimension, suddenly sheds new light on all that has come before.

The effect of Peretz's abrupt endings is epitomized by his "Bontshe the Silent" ("Bontshe shvayg," 1894). The first part of this story describes Bontshe's quiet life of poverty and suffering, while the second half shows his fate in the world to come. In accordance with popular beliefs, Bontshe should then receive his just compensation for bearing lifelong suffering in silence. When asked by the Heavenly Throne to name his reward, however, Bontshe merely pleads: "Every morning, I want to have a hot roll with fresh butter!" The story concludes abruptly: "Judges and angels lowered their heads in shame; the prosecutor broke into laughter."[10] Bontshe's spirit has been so crushed by his subservient life that he cannot rise above such material needs. In what previ-

---

[10]ILP 2: 420. For English translations attesting to the popularity of this tale, see "Bontzye Shweig," in Isaac Loeb Perez, *Stories and Pictures,* trans. Helena Frank (Philadelphia: Jewish Publication Society, 1906), pp. 171–81; "Buntcheh the Silent," in *In This World and the Next,* trans. Moshe Spiegel (New York: Thomas Yoseloff, 1958), pp. 58–65; "Bontsha the Silent," trans. Hilde Abel, in *A Treasury of Yiddish Stories,* 2d ed., ed. Irving Howe and Eliezer Greenberg (New York: Penguin, 1990), pp. 223–30; "Bontshe Shvayg," trans. Hillel Halkin, in *The I. L. Peretz Reader,* ed. Ruth R. Wisse (New York: Schocken, 1990), pp. 146–52; and "Bontshe Shvayg," trans. Eli Katz, in *Selected Stories: Bilingual Edition,* selected and ed. Itche Goldberg and Eli Katz (New York: Zhitlowsky Foundation for Jewish Culture, 1991), pp. 192–213.

ously seemed to be an edifying tale, the heavenly court is shamed, which gives force to skeptical doubts about the merits of pious self-sacrifice.

Written at the outset of Peretz's so-called "radical period," this tale became a favorite in the workers' movement. It draws from Jewish customs and beliefs in order to shock the reader with a dissonant impression. The ironic balance is such that some readers persist in finding only sentimental, noncritical meaning, while others perceive an outright attack on religious norms. A more suitable approach observes the hybrid character of Peretz's story, bringing together contrary strands from disparate narrative traditions. Ruth Wisse, for example, refers to the "tension between the radical and the conservative impulses."[11]

"Kabbalists" ("Ha-mekubalim" and "Mekubolim") employs a similar device. First published in Hebrew in 1891, Peretz's 1894 Yiddish version was the earliest of his tales that were included in the 1901 selection called *Chassidic*. "Kabbalists" antedates the core chassidic stories by a decade and in some ways it sets Peretz's pattern and agenda for the coming years. Peretz's original choice of the Hebrew language appropriately defines the parameters of his superficially traditional narrative. This linguistic distance sets off the neo-chassidic tales from the more secular psychological studies that characterize his prior Yiddish writing.

The Hebrew version of "Kabbalists" has a dignified, exalted tonality that derives in part from the current conventions of Hebrew writing. Peretz's transfer of the staid Hebrew diction into more fluid Yiddish prose produces remarkable effects, and this linguistic opposition later reemerges in the parallel contrast between the scholarly mitnagdim and the inspirational chassidim.

The opening sentence in the 1891 Hebrew text is long and slow-moving:

> In times of trouble and distress the value of all merchandise falls, including that of Torah, the best and dearest of all merchandise; out of the entire Tshakhnovka Yeshiva, a light to the People of Israel, there remained only two remnants, Rebbe Jacob, the head of the yeshiva himself, a tall man, thin as a reed, with a beard down to his knees and dark, wandering eyes; and the other,

---

[11]Ruth R. Wisse, *I. L. Peretz and the Making of Modern Jewish Culture* (Seattle: University of Washington Press, 1991), p. 47.

Lemekh, his beloved student, a boy of eighteen, thin, pale, with feverish lips and black, burning eyes; both of them were wrapped in worn-out rags, their chests exposed, without shirts. The other students (about ten boys) had been scattered to the four corners of the earth.[12]

In contrast, the first sentence (and paragraph) of the 1894 Yiddish version is shortened to the barest statement: "In bad times even the value of Torah—the best merchandise—falls."[13] For stronger effect, Peretz uses short phrases and single-sentence paragraphs, as in the second sentence: "Nothing more remained of the Lashtshiver Yeshiva than the Head of the Yeshiva—Reb Yekl—and a single student." Peretz's narrator explains that, for lack of food, all of the other students have dispersed.

The opening words solidly place the story in relation to popular sayings, assuming the genre of a chassidic narrative while retaining an aesthetic and ironic distance. This combination of tradition and a break from tradition is implicit in the opening line. First, Peretz alludes to the expression, "Torah is the best merchandise" (*tova torah mi-kol schora*), which derives from medieval Hebrew literature;[14] Yiddish has the literally translated equivalent *toyre iz di beste skhoyre*. Thus in this initial phrase, Peretz's story takes on a familiar theme. Its metaphor merits closer examination: the superlative construction likens Torah to merchandise in order to assert that traditional learning exceeds the value of material goods.

Yet the notion that the value of Torah falls in hard times contradicts this view. In turn, it alludes to the more pragmatic saying that "If there is no flour there is no Torah, and if there is no Torah

---

[12]"Ha-mekubalim (sippur)," *Gan perachim* 3 (1891), 83; henceforth cited as "H" by page alone.

[13]"Mekubolim," in *Ale verk fun I. L. Peretz*, ed. Shmuel Niger (New York: CYCO, 1947), vol. 4, p. 20. The following analysis refers to this Yiddish version as "Y," henceforth cited by page alone. The original Yiddish text of "Kabbalists" was appropriately printed in "Der tones" ("The Fast"), in *Yontev bletlekh*, first series (1894), number 4, 3–13. The earliest translation was by Helena Frank, in *Stories and Pictures*, pp. 213–19. English translations by Moshe Spiegel and Shlomo Katz are contained in *In This World and the Next*, pp. 171–75, and in *A Treasury of Yiddish Stories*, pp. 219–23 (reprinted in *The I. L. Peretz Reader*, pp. 152–56).

[14]See Avraham Even-Shoshan's dictionary, *Ha-milon he-chadash* (Jerusalem: Kiryat-Sefer, 1985), vol. 4, p. 1442.

there is no flour" (Pirkei 'avot 3:17). This ancient proverb notes that while men and women do not live by bread alone, we cannot live without it, either. Thus Peretz's opener conveys the weight of wide-ranging cultural attitudes toward learning. Taking on the language of popular conviction (*toyre iz di beste skhoyre*), Peretz ironically suggests the limitations of this view. When times are bad, the supposedly transcendent value of religious learning is affected. These words balance piety—referring to "the best and dearest" Torah—with literalizing humor, which observes that Torah stock may also fall. In a tension that characterizes the story "Kabbalists," bringing together esoteric mystical teachings and mundane concerns about satisfying hunger, Peretz's first sentence combines diametrically opposed views.[15]

The teacher and student are sharply contrasted. The Rebbe has "wandering," "extinguished" eyes—while his student Lemekh's eyes are "burning" and "black" (H 83, Y 20). They become kabbalists, immersing themselves in mystical texts and spiritual regimens, by virtue of necessity: "Both of them occasionally suffer from hunger. From eating little comes insomnia, and from entire nights without food or sleep comes—a longing for Kabbalah!" (Y 20). The narrator continues the irony of his opening sentence when he describes the men's path to the Kabbalah by way of starvation. Because the town can no longer support them, they consider what to do about their "impetuous and bitter hunger," and decide "to deal with theoretical and practical Kabbalah, and so their fasts would become a source of blessing" (H 83). Study of Kabbalah serves as a stopgap, a means to turn hunger into holy fasts.

The main body of the story consists of the Rebbe's teachings, which center around a musical metaphor. Like the chassidic leaders in "The Teachings of the Chassidim" and "Between Two Peaks," he emphasizes song; and he most values the melody that is furthest from articulated words. The Rebbe speaks of several levels of song, from those with words to *nigunim* without words and those that sing themselves inside us, purified of all materiality. This speech contains a mystical charm that is interrupted by the subsequent events of the story.

---

[15]Ruth Wisse presents a similar reading of this opening passage in her *I. L. Peretz and the Making of Modern Jewish Culture*, pp. 30–31.

After making the chassidic context believable and even showing its possible attractions, Peretz disrupts these impressions. A boy loudly enters the room and announces: "Reb Solomon sends food for the Rebbe." As soon as this bowl of soup appears before him, the Rebbe loses interest in his lecture. Naturally the student is distracted by the sight of his teacher eating, and he covets the food. When another bowl soon arrives for the student, he refuses it and states his decision to fast one more day. The Rebbe, rather than express concern over his student's failing health, reproaches him, "Why didn't you tell me?" Lemekh explains that his fourth consecutive fast is one of repentance: "When you began to eat I transgressed the commandment, *You shall not covet*" (H 84). The Rebbe accepts his student's excessively harsh self-criticism.

During the night, Lemekh awakens his teacher and tells him of a "mystical" experience of light and song. The Rebbe encourages him, saying excitedly, "I am not your teacher, fool . . . I am your student! . . . I have not reached as high as your ankle" (H 85). Lemekh then cries out, begins to say the prayer "Hear, O Israel," and collapses. Throughout this scene the rapid exchange of dialogue adds to the effect, intensifying until Lemekh's death. The final lines withdraw from this ecstatic climax to portray its aftermath:

> The entire town was in a fervor; all of the men, women, and children wished for themselves and their kin such a holy death, yet Rebbe Jacob said with a light reproach:
> —If he had reserved the strength for another four fasts, he would have died with the Divine kiss! (H 85)[16]

The words used to describe the Rebbe's "light reproach," *t'luna kala,* recalls his early complaint (also *t'luna*) when he objects that Lemekh plans to fast without him. There is a direct relationship between these two moments. In the first case, the Rebbe's pride leads him to resent Lemekh's independent fast; he shows no compassion and does not try to prevent his student from starving. At the close, he virtually censures Lemekh for dying too soon. Rather

---

[16]The Yiddish conclusion of this story is slightly different:

> All of the people in the town were of one mind in wishing such a death for themselves, but for the Head of the Yeshiva this was not enough.
> —Just a few more fasts, he wheezed, and he would have died with "the Divine Kiss" on his lips. (Y 25)

than recognize his own errors leading to the death of his last student, the Rebbe places the blame on Lemekh. Like the ending of "Bontshe the Silent," this conclusion turns against its protagonist, giving the story a new twist. Until this final point we may be unsure of how to interpret Bontshe's silence or Lemekh's hunger. But the prosecutor's laugh and the teacher's complaint shift our response to a different register. At once the description of two starving kabbalists becomes an indictment of their practices. As intense irony disrupts the sentimental, romantic effects of this scene, counterpoint begins to jolt the Rebbe's song out of key.[17]

Peretz's appropriation of chassidic motifs is parodic in the original sense of the word *para-odos*: it is a countersong to the Rebbe's mystical philosophy of music. This multilayered text merges Kabbalistic lore with modern narrative technique. On the surface, it is a chassidic tale about a great student of the Kabbalah. On another level, it might be read as a sentimental, neo-romantic tale about life in the Jewish *shtetl*. But these dimensions are subtly counterbalanced by implicit irony and a critical thrust. At first Peretz seems to address a pious audience with a wondrous tale of devotion, only to interpolate a contrary message.

"IF NOT HIGHER"

"If Not Higher" ("Oyb nisht nokh hekher: A khasidishe dertseylung," 1900) brings together several of Peretz's major themes and stylistic devices. It employs a first-person narrator who seems to address his audience orally, and as Shmuel Niger has shown, it draws from a folktale that Peretz modifies to enhance the literary effect.[18] At issue are the tensions between chassidim and mitnagdim, or between Polish Jews and Lithuanian Jews ("Litvaks"), as well as the opposition between spiritual conditions and material realities or between superstitious beliefs and pragmatic actions. Moreover, the tale places immense weight on its final sentence, which is anticipated by the title.

---

[17]For another reading of the Yiddish version of "Kabbalists," see Ruth R. Wisse, *I. L. Peretz and the Making of Modern Jewish Culture*, pp. 30–34.

[18]Shmuel Niger, *I. L. Peretz*, pp. 286–87. Compare David Cortell Jacobson's extensive analysis in "The Recovery of Myth: A Study of Rewritten Hasidic Stories in Hebrew and Yiddish 1890–1910," Ph.D. diss., University of California, Los Angeles, 1977.

The subtitle, "A Chassidic Narrative," openly links the story to the original collection called *Chassidic (Khasidish)* in Yiddish and *Chassidism (Chasidut)* in Hebrew. Both the contents and the narrative voice are ostensibly chassidic. "If Not Higher" immediately places the reader in a scene of chassidic storytelling, starting *in medias res*: "And the Rebbe of Nemirov, every morning at the time for penitential prayers, used to disappear completely!"[19] The narrator's exclamation echoes the enthusiasm of an inspirational context. Moreover, his first word, "and," suggests that the story is part of a larger narrative in which a circle of chassidim are telling adulatory tales about their leader. Although there is no single major historical figure known as the "Nemirover," it is relevant that Rabbi Nachman and his disciples lived for some time in Nemirov. Peretz draws from folklore that originated in Ukrainian Jewish towns distant from his native Poland. This tale is not directly based on an actual leader, nor does it describe magical or miraculous events. Instead it reveals a mundane action that lifts the Rebbe "even higher" than a wonder-rabbi could go.

The rhetoric of the story mimics the aura of a chassidic gathering. After recalling the Rebbe's mysterious disappearance, the narrator adds:

> Where could the Rebbe be?
> Where should he be? In Heaven, of course! Does a rebbe have little to take care of before the Days of Awe? Jews—no evil eye—need livelihood, peace, health, marriages, and want to be good and pious, yet the sins are great and Satan with his thousand eyes watches from one corner of the world to the other, and he sees, lodges complaints, turns people in . . . and who should help, if not the Rebbe? (98)

By employing questions and answers, the narrative approximates the character of a dialogue between disciples. "This is what the people thought," the narrative tells us, summing up popular chassidic views of their Rebbe.

---

[19] *Ale verk fun I. L. Peretz*, ed. Shmuel Niger (New York: CYCO, 1947), vol. 4, p. 98; henceforth cited by page alone. The Yiddish text was originally published in *Der yud* 2 (1900), no. 1, pp. 12–13. For English renditions, see *Stories and Pictures*, trans. Helena Frank, pp. 13–18; *In This World and the Next*, trans. Moshe Spiegel, pp. 76–79; *The I. L. Peretz Reader*, trans. Marie Syrkin, pp. 178–91; and *Selected Works: A Bilingual Edition*, trans. Eli Katz, pp. 270–81.

Subsequently the narrator introduces the element of tension that drives the story forward:

> But once a Litvak arrived, and he laughed! You know the Litvaks: they don't think much of moralistic (*muser*) books; instead they stuff themselves with Talmud and commentaries. So the Litvak points out a clear passage in the Gemara that hurts your eyes. Even Moses, he shows, couldn't rise to Heaven during his lifetime, but remained ten hands' breadths beneath Heaven! Well, go argue with a Litvak! (Ibid.)

Whereas the chassidim tended to exalt their rebbes with adulatory tales, the mitnagdim often viewed this practice as fostering an inappropriate personality cult. The former conceived the *tsadik* as an ideal and a model for humanity, while the mitnagdim concentrated on study of the Talmud. The remainder of the story presents the Litvak's mission to spy on the Rebbe and get to the bottom of his mysterious disappearance. Meanwhile, the narrator has underscored his standpoint and that of his listeners by pronouncing scornfully: "You know the Litvaks," and "Go argue with a Litvak." Like the narrators in "The Teachings of the Chassidim" and "Between Two Peaks," this narrator is part of the world he describes.

The body of the story relates the basic tale, which Peretz drew from folklore: the Rebbe disguises himself as a peasant, goes into the forest, cuts down a tree and chops it into firewood, then takes it to an old, bedridden woman and lights a fire for her. This solves the mystery of the Rebbe's disappearance. Instead of engaging in prayer and study alone, he turns his faith into action. This is a revelation for the Litvak:

> The Litvak who saw all that became a disciple to the Nemirover Rebbe.
>
> And thereafter, if a chassid told of how the Nemirover Rebbe, every morning at the time for penitential prayers, rises up and flies to Heaven, the Litvak never laughed, but added quietly:
>
> If not higher! (102)

Here the final irony is on the part of the Litvak, a character within the narrative. This masterful reworking turns the folktale on its head, making a supernatural journey into a tale of simple virtue, and creating the impression that the narrator slides between the two positions he represents. The chassidim emerge victorious in that the Litvak becomes one of them and accepts the greatness of the Rebbe. And yet the Litvak's discovery reveals the erroneous, superstitious beliefs of the chassidim. His closing exclamation "If not higher!" intimates that mundane acts of goodness are even more praiseworthy than magical intercessions, wonder healings, or mystical insights. Without exerting overt criticism, Peretz's story suggests that some chassidim misunderstand the essence of their Rebbe's spirituality.

"THE TEACHINGS OF THE CHASSIDIM"

"The Teachings of the Chassidim" is a turning-point in Peretz's development, at the intersection of his Hebrew and Yiddish fiction. Although first published in Hebrew (1894), the Yiddish version (1902) is integral to the fourth section of the canonical volume of stories entitled *Chassidic* (circa 1911). "The Teachings of the Chassidim" establishes several precedents for Peretz's later work, and it directly anticipates "Between Two Peaks."

"The Teachings of the Chassidim" alludes to the genre of traditional chassidic tales about righteous men (*tsadikim*). In a number of ways, however, Peretz modifies these conventions for his literary ends. The opening lines take on the adulatory tone of a chassidic disciple, pretending to restate common knowledge:

> It is known to all (*yadu'a le-kol*)—the whole world knows that our master and teacher from Nemirov served God out of joy. Happy is the eye that was privileged to see the fire, the enthusiasm, the joy itself that emanated from him, may his memory be blessed, like a sun, and which lit up and bathed the entire world in a golden, fiery light! What a delight that was![20]

This translation is from the 1902 Yiddish text, which Peretz expanded from his Hebrew version of 1894. The original Hebrew version employs a more explicit narrative persona who signs the story "The Orphan of Nemirov," but seldom reappears in Peretz's works.[21] In Yiddish, the added exclamations intensify the impression of this narrator as an admiring, almost fawning disciple.

---

[20]"Mishnas khasidim," in *Der yud* 4 (1902), number 19, p. 11. Peretz's Yiddish version is henceforth cited as "Y" by page alone.

[21]This intriguing persona does recur as narrator of the stories "Dem reben's tsibek," in *Yontev bletlekh*, second series (1895), number 2 ("Der omer"), 36–46, and "Der feter Shakhne un di mume Yakhne," *Di yudishe bibliotek* 3 (1895), 42–50.

Peretz makes the most of the Hebrew narrative persona by emphasizing his emotional involvement in the events he relates. The orphaned narrator from Nemirov frequently expresses his love of the Rebbe. In the opening paragraph of the Hebrew text he states, "Happy was the eye that had the fortune to see the enthusiasm and the joy that sprang forth from him like water from a fountain, and flowed to us, showered us with abundance, attached itself to us, so that we forgot all of our worldly sorrows, all of the misfortunes and evildoers."[22] As in the Yiddish version, this adulatory sentence suggests the narrator's excitement in speaking of the Rebbe. By using the first-person plural form, he underscores the collective response; the fiction intimates that his ideal audience would be a circle of Nemirov chassidim. For this inspirational context he punctuates his talk with elements of eulogy. The narrator closes the first section with the phrase, "Happy were the ears that had the fortune to hear Torah from his holy mouth," and he opens the second section, "And happy was the eye that had the fortune to see him serve God joyfully" (H 36). He comments that the spirituality of the Rebbe's wedding was so great that it could have brought back to the fold all of the non-believers in the world.

By 1894, Peretz had shifted from the internal monologues of *Familiar Scenes* (*Bakante bilder,* 1890) to first-person, narrated monologues. The earlier tales—in particular "The Mad Talmudist" and "The Messenger"—enter the fictional minds of two characters in borderline states, near madness and death, and the exploration of their psychology constitutes the story. Subsequently, after Peretz passes through a satiric phase, he employs first-person narrators in which some of his strongest effects derive from the tone of the narrative voice. Peretz sharpened the tonal effect when he translated the story "The Teachings of the Chassidim" into Yiddish, yet his breakthrough is already evident in the 1894 Hebrew version.

"The Teachings of the Chassidim" embeds significant dissonances within what at first appears to be merely a traditional chassidic tale of the Rebbe. The entire first section presents a glowing portrait of "our master and teacher, the Rebbe of Nemirov,"

---

[22]"Mishnat chasidim," in *Ha-chetz: yalkut sifruti,* ed. I. L. Peretz (Warsaw: Shvartsberg, 1894), p. 35. This Hebrew version is henceforth cited as "H" by page alone.

who "every day of the year until the day of his death was full of joy, song, and dance" (H 35). These are familiar elements of chassidic life; while the story does not refer directly to any historical personage, it is again pertinent that Rabbi Nachman lived part of his life in Nemirov. There follows a quotation from one of the Rebbe's speeches in which he describes the world as a song before God: "Every individual person sings only a syllable of the melody before he dies, and the rest of what he does in this world prior to death is just a groan and worldly matters" (H 35–36). In contrast, the righteous man "knows all or most of the melody, and thus he finds constant joy" (H 36).

The next passage, a continuation of the Rebbe's sermon, is the first point in Peretz's tales that sets chassidic teachings against the rationalistic learning of the mitnagdim. The Rebbe does not refer to them as mitnagdim, but rather as *ha-lamdanim be-nigleh*, scholars of the manifest, mundane world. He compares them to skilled workmen who "know how to repair musical instruments and how to make new instruments, but they do not know the song itself, nor can they play the harp that is their handiwork" (ibid.). In contrast, "the hidden *tsadik* knows the melody." Hence "the scholars, he said, are the garment, and we are the person. In his own words, *un mir zaynen mentshn* [and we are people]; the scholars are the body, and we are the soul! The scholars are the Torah and we are the secrets of the Torah" (H 36). The Rebbe makes his rivals appear extrinsic, yet at the same time his metaphors show that they, as workmen, bodies, or garments, are also necessary. They exist in a relationship of uneasy opposition and interdependence. In the Hebrew version, the inserted Yiddish phrase (*un mir zaynen mentshn*) reminds the reader that, like Rabbi Nachman, this Rebbe holds his discourses in Yiddish.

The remainder of the story describes the wedding of the Rebbe's daughter. This event is charged with significance for the disciples of the Rebbe, since his son-in-law will presumably carry on his teachings. The narrator enthusiastically recalls the Rebbe's song and dance of joy, but a darker coloring comes over this scene. The narrator interrupts his account of the wedding and tells us mysteriously:

It is known to all the world that, following the death of our master and teacher, the Rebbe of Nemirov, and after what happened to his son-in-law, I traveled to holy men throughout the land and did not find one whom my soul could cherish. I saw the great and wonderful, I saw reformers, healers, and miracle-workers, but *joy* I did not see. (H 38)

The Hebrew description of uninspiring leaders does not explain the failure of the Rebbe's son-in-law. We may speculate that he deviates from the chassidic way of life or fails to meet expectations in other respects. Peretz's later revision in the Yiddish text clarifies the outcome, informing us that "there happened, what should not have happened, with the son-in-law, Feygele's husband, may he rest in peace, and I was left like a sheep without a shepherd" (Y 13). This sympathetic mention of the son-in-law's death dispels much of the threatening mystery of the Hebrew version.

During the wedding of the Rebbe's daughter, the spiritual leader exalts his disciples with songs and dances. The narrator merges hearing and vision in a synesthetic image that recalls the giving of the Torah at Sinai. In Exodus 20:15, "All the people see the voices (*ro'im et ha-kolot*) [the thunder] and the torches [the lightning] and the voices (*kolot*) of the *shofar*." Peretz's narrator follows the biblical fusing of sight and sound when he describes the celebration: "the Rebbe stands in our midst and sings and dances; we stand around him in circles, and we see the voices (*koyles* or *kolot*) and hear the dance—and everyone around began to sing and dance" (Y 13).[23] On the one hand, this intertextual echo links the Rebbe to Moses and "the teachings of the chassidim" to the original giving of the Torah. But there is also a hint of critical, perhaps ironic, distance in an allusion to another biblical passage connected to the giving of the Torah. When Moses returns from Sinai with the two tablets, he finds the people singing and dancing around the golden calf (Ex. 32:18–19). This secondary allusion suggests something a chassidic disciple would never consciously intend: that the followers of a rebbe are like idol worshipers.

A further linguistic association connects the description of dancing chassidim to the biblical scene of idol worship. The narrator writes in both Hebrew and Yiddish that they stand around their Rebbe in circles (*'iggul betokh 'iggul*). The three root letters of the word "circle" (*'iggul*) are identical to the letters in the word "calf" (*'egel*)—as in the golden calf, *'egel ha-zahav*. Peretz increases the tension in this story by placing a hint of irony in the mouth of the

---

[23]The earlier, Hebrew version presents the scene more conventionally: "we hear and see the voices and the dances" (H 39).

unwitting narrator. A genuine chassidic narrator would not permit this shocking linkage of chassidim and idol-worshipers. This dramatic moment thus suggests an ironic doubling by means of which Peretz establishes a gap between his story and the chassidic tradition. Some opponents of the chassidim actually did argue that they went too far in the adulation of their leaders, almost to the point of idol worship; Peretz hints at this challenge in his language describing the chassidic celebration. The traditional references were beyond the ken of at least one editor (or typesetter?) of Peretz's collected works: Shmuel Niger's New York edition of this story eliminates the biblical allusion by amending "we see the voices and hear the dance" to the tame and literalistic "we hear the voices and see the dance" (ILP 4: 184).

The orphaned narrator does not deliberately exert such ironic distance from the scene he describes, but emphasizes his active participation: "I was favored to sing and dance face to face with our master, the Rebbe." A disruptive element enters the scene when "our groom stood aloof and did not join in the song" (H 38). His silence threatens the foundations of this adulatory tale, and the narrator asks his Rebbe for reassurance. This is a moment of recognition for the Rebbe's disciple:

> —Rebbe! I cried to him, even the musicians are singing along, but not the groom!
> —Don't worry, he answered me, I have faith in my daughter's good fortune! . . . Don't worry, during the meal he will speak Torah from my dance.
> And so it was. (H 39)

Tension and uncertainty differentiate Peretz's story from traditional tales in praise of a rebbe. As "Kabbalists" contains unsettling hints that disturb the familiar genre, here ample evidence suggests that all is not well with the chassidic circle of Nemirov. The narrator later confirms that, in its essence, the groom's speech contains the master's dance, and the chassidim are inspired by it. Only the Rebbe himself resists:

> —Do you see that thief? he said to me exultantly. He is repeating my dance and saying it in his own name.
> —But, the Rebbe (*tsadik*) added petulantly, just as he didn't enter into my song, I won't enter into his Torah!
> I suddenly felt as if a sharp knife had lodged itself in my belly. (H 40–41)

The Rebbe conveys his ambivalence toward the groom's Torah although he views it as a restatement of his own teachings in another medium. Earlier he asserted that "the scholars are the body, and we are the soul!" Now a kind of reversal occurs when the Rebbe places his teachings on the side of dance and associates the groom with a more abstract Torah.

For the first time the narrator senses that even the Rebbe has doubts, because a deeper conflict lies beneath the difference in personality. After the disciple raises a probing question, there is a poignant revelation:

—Rebbe, I asked in a whisper, where does he come from?
—He is the student of the Vilna Gaon, he answered me.
I felt thunderstruck. Then the *tsadik* said:
—Go order whiskey for the peasants and fodder for the horses.
—And to this day I do not know the secret meaning of these words. (H 41)

The revelation of the son-in-law's background swiftly alters the tone and meaning of the story, explicitly sharpening the context of rivalry between chassidic and mitnagdic groups. This dimension is more obvious in Peretz's Yiddish adaptation. Whereas the Hebrew text includes only the disciple's doubts about the groom, the Yiddish version indicates his Rebbe's dissatisfaction. After the narrator observes that the son-in-law does not sing together with the group, his Rebbe comments, "the Vilna Gaon's student. . . . Ah!" and the narrator adds that this exclamation "entered my heart like a knife" (Y 14). Moreover, in the Yiddish version the narrator specifically describes the groom as having spoken with a Lithuanian-Yiddish accent (Y 13), as opposed to the Polish- or Ukrainian-Yiddish dialects of most chassidim.

The Rebbe's disclosure that his new son-in-law is a student of the Vilna Gaon is charged with meaning. The Gaon of Vilna—or Elijah Ben Solomon Zalman (1720–97)—was a renowned Talmudic scholar who led opposition to the chassidim. By choosing one of the Vilna Gaon's students as his successor, he has either made an unaccountable blunder or has broken the line of continuity for unspecified reasons. Thus the story ends with a final twist that resembles the sudden conclusions of "Kabbalists," "Bontshe the Silent," and "If Not Higher." The narrator assumes there must be a secret (*sod*) concealed behind his Rebbe's words, as in kabbalistic teachings or in Rabbi Nachman's tales.

The closing lines leave room for interpretation, especially in connection wih the Rebbe's remark: "Go order whiskey for the peasants (*'arelim*) and fodder for the horses." Even the narrator admits that "to this day I do not know the secret meaning of these words" (H 41). The Rebbe employs a measure of irony, saying one thing and meaning something else, in an allusive gesture which his follower wishes to interpret as a sacred allegory. On one level, this could be the Rebbe's way of rejecting the groom's learned discourse. By thinking of the peasants and horses during the groom's speech he perhaps shows that his own teachings move in another direction, away from conceptual abstractions and toward concrete action. On another level, the reference to "peasants" (*'arelim*) may suggest a less positive meaning. The word *'arel* in Hebrew names a non-Jew as one who is "uncircumcised." But it may also refer to an obtuse, ignorant person (as in the expression *'arel-lev*). The Rebbe's phrase, "whisky for the *'arelim*," could thus refer metaphorically to his non-chassidic in-laws, using an insulting term to mark these wedding guests as outsiders.[24] They need whisky to help them overcome their resistance to chassidic fervor.

The effect of this story revolves around the narrator, who is a disciple of the Rebbe and unconvinced by his son-in-law. The reader is left with two unresolved questions. First, what occurs after the death of the Rebbe? In the Hebrew story, the narrator refers obscurely to "what happened" to the son-in-law. Second, what does the Rebbe mean by his final words at the wedding, ordering drinks for the peasants? The two mysteries are linked: the latter is an instance of the Rebbe's teaching through enigmatic statements, while the former shows the narrator himself having recourse to hints rather than making direct revelations. "The teachings of chassidim" are sometimes nonverbal, based on gestures and songs. Although the mitnagdim might view them as extrinsic to the Torah, the narrator views these chassidic expressions as the most essential teachings. Ignoring his son-in-law's speech and ordering drinks for the peasants, the Rebbe perhaps emphasizes the incompatibility of the two rival strands of Judaism, while exemplifying his this-worldly inclinations. Or he may hint that rationalistic Jews who are unable to share chassidic enthusiasm are as far from the spirit of Judaism as non-Jews. Ultimately, the story concludes on an ambiguous note: the Rebbe's acceptance of the Vilna Gaon's student as his son-in-law suggests either a tragic error, leading to a break in continuity, or shows his deliberate effort to

---

[24]Rachel Glazer suggested this surprising interpretation to me.

foster understanding between the chassidim and the mitnagdim. Peretz ends his Hebrew narrative on this unresolved note, and in Yiddish he intensifies the antagonistic situation that pits the two groups against one another.

Like "Kabbalists," "The Teachings of the Chassidim" is an exemplary instance of Yiddish parody, in the sense of a counter-song (*paraodos*). It alludes specifically to the song of the Israelites who worship the golden calf even after they "see the voices" of revelation. Peretz's counter-song is that of the chassidim who are at odds with the extreme legalists, the mitnagdim. This parody both appropriates the biblical narrative and, by means of the juxtaposition, implies an unspoken critique of chassidic practices.

"BETWEEN TWO PEAKS"

"Between Two Peaks" ("Tsvishn tsvey berg," 1900) is Peretz's masterpiece in this genre. Like "The Teachings of the Chassidim," it employs a first-person narrator who is a follower of a rebbe; again the narrator witnesses the encounter between chassidic and mitnagdic leaders. Peretz recognized the similarity between these stories and placed them together in section four of the canonical volume of chassidic tales.

Peretz's chassidic tales subtly deal with broader questions of identity. "Between Two Peaks," in particular, stages an encounter between two extremes of personality, embodied in diametrically opposed religious leaders. Chassidic motifs become the backdrop for a drama of modern identity in which both the narrator and the reader are hard-pressed to establish their own positions. "Between Two Peaks" opens with the narrator's address to his audience:

> You have no doubt heard of the Brisker Rov and the Bialer Rebbe, but not everyone knows that the *tsadek* of Biala, Reb Noah, was formerly a brilliant student of the Brisker Rov, that he studied with him for several years; afterwards he disappeared, went into "exile" for a few years, and was revealed in Biala.[25]

---

[25]Translated from *Ale verk fun I. L. Peretz*, ed. Shmuel Niger (New York: CYCO, 1947), p. 103; henceforth cited by page alone. For English renditions, see "Between Two Mountains (Between the Rabbi of Brisk and the Rebbe of Byàle): A Simchas Torah Tale Told by an Old Teacher," trans. Helena Frank, in *Stories and Pictures* (Philadelphia: Jewish Publication Society, 1906), pp. 429–46; "Between Two Peaks," trans. Nathan Halper in I. L. Peretz, *Selected Stories*, ed.

Peretz employs a number of narrative strategies. In addition to establishing a fictional rapport between the narrator and his audience, he assumes the shared knowledge of a culture. By asserting that "You have no doubt heard of" two religious leaders, he implies a familiar world of learning and lore. The line between fact and fiction is blurred, however, since the Brisker Rov was an historical personality, in contrast to this Bialer Rebbe, who is a fictional creation. Brisk is the Yiddish name for Brest-Litovsk; "the Brisker Rov" presumably refers to Aaron ben Meir, an eighteenth-century Lithuanian rabbi, known for his Talmudic learning.[26] While Biala is the name of an actual town to the west of Brisk, Peretz inserts an imaginary element—the Bialer Rebbe—into the eighteenth-century context. (In fact, Peretz claimed that the only rebbe he had ever seen was a latter-day Bialer Rebbe.)[27]

Peretz sharpens the effect of this first-person narrative by implicating the speaker in his story. The narrator does not pretend to be neutral but explains that he is a follower of the Bialer Rebbe (106). Nevertheless, he finds himself living as a tutor in Biala with a family of mitnagdim, in which one daughter-in-law is the Brisker Rov's child. Like the story itself, then, the narrator is delicately balanced "between two peaks": "And the two peaks met. . . . It is a miracle from heaven that I was not crushed between them" (114).

The simple plot extends the basic features of "The Teachings of the Chassidim." The Brisker Rov's daughter experiences a difficult childbirth, and the Rov travels to Biala. After her delivery, the Rov asks to see his former student, the Bialer Rebbe. They discuss their disagreements and celebrate the holiday of Simchat Torah together. Although they do not resolve their differences, after this meeting the Brisker Rov stops persecuting chassidim. The opposition between the Brisker Rov and the Bialer Rebbe corresponds to a universal tension between reason and emotion, or individualism and communality, and it also reflects a duality between realist and romantic styles in Peretz's creative expression. The essence of this seemingly neo-romantic story lies in the psychological and emotional dispositions it describes.

Irving Howe and Eliezer Greenberg (New York: Schocken, 1974), pp. 83–95, and "Between Two Mountains," trans. Goldie Morgentaler, in *The I. L. Peretz Reader*, pp. 184–95.

[26]*The Jewish Encylcopedia* (New York: Funk & Wagnalls, 1901), vol. 1, p. 18.

[27]See his letter to Israel Zinberg in ILP XI, 282.

The narrator recalls the reason for the original break between the Brisker Rov and the Bialer Rebbe. As a student the Bialer Rebbe felt that the Rov's Torah was dry and lifeless, and a dream strengthened his resolve to leave the Rov's Yeshiva. In his dream, the Rov led the future Rebbe into an earthly paradise, which was a palace made of ice. This vision turned nightmarish as they continued through endless rooms, isolated from the world. Finally he burst out: "Rabbi, take me away from here! I don't want to be alone with you! I want to be together with the People of Israel!" (105). This rejection of solitary learning initiated the Rebbe's calling. According to his account, he wished to address his teaching to common people, furthering community rather than isolated scholarship.

The climactic moment of the story comes with the reunion of the two leaders. The narrator plays a central role in bringing them together both within the story and in his narrative; at the same time, he shows his superstitions (108–09). Although the narrator is a follower of the Bialer Rebbe, his account does not favor him one-sidedly. The strength of this story lies in its success in balancing the "two peaks" of antithetical leaders. For instance, rather than merely boasting of his Rebbe, the narrator vividly describes the Brisker Rov as he arrives in Biala:

> That was a man, I tell you, a pillar of steel! A very tall man, of tremendous stature . . . and he cast fear wherever he went, like a king! As if it were today I remember his long, pointed, white beard. . . . His brows—white, thick and long—covered half of his face. When he raised his eyes—my God!—the women fell backward, as if struck by lightning, such eyes he had! (111)

Himself stricken with fear, the narrator observes that the Rov represents "another path, another world." After his daughter has given birth, the Rov delivers a speech. The description is more elaborate than the report of a comparable speech by the Rebbe's son-in-law in "The Teachings of Chassidim": "If the Torah is a sea, he is the Leviathan in the sea: with one motion he swims through ten tractates; with one gesture he brings together the Talmud and its commentators! It echoes and spurts, boils and seethes, like the sea itself" (112). Subsequently the Rov meets his former student, and their conversation heightens our sense of the opposition between them. The Rebbe explains that the Rov's yeshiva choked his soul:

Your Torah, Rabbi, is all judgment, without mercy! . . . And, what's more, it is without joy, without freedom. It is all steel and brass, iron laws, copper strictures . . . all high Torah, for scholars, for the select few. . . . And tell me, Rabbi, what do you have for the people of Israel? For woodcutters, butchers, workmen, for the simple person? (115)

The Rebbe complains of incompatibility between strict law and a joyous life, as between scholarship for the elite and the everyday existence of the poor. At this point the narrator evidently favors the position of his Rebbe, sharing his dissatisfaction with the dry teachings of the Rov.

The Rov asks about the Rebbe's Torah, and the former student tells his erstwhile teacher that he will show it to him. The occasion is the celebration of the Torah, Simchat Torah. The narrator comments that it was "as if a curtain dropped from before my eyes," and he describes the scene in one of Peretz's most lyrical passages:

Across the sky swam white, silvery clouds, and when one looked closer, one saw that they were trembling with joy, that they were dancing with joy of the Torah! A bit farther off a green belt, dark green, surrounded the town, but it was a living green as if a life force were floating among the grass; sporadically it seemed that one could see little flames that leapt and danced among the grasses, as if they were embracing and kissing. (116)

This is a kind of epiphany for the narrator, in which he sees that "the soul of the world is singing" (117). The scene of spiritual revelation suddenly fades, however, when the Rov calls out, "It is time for afternoon prayer!" The exalted followers of the Rebbe are once again "simple chassidim in torn coats." The imagery of light and flame disappears, and the Rebbe's face, like the natural scene, goes dark (ibid.). Throughout this story, the narrator's figuration animates Torah and nature. In the beginning he paraphrases the Rebbe's early dissatisfaction with the Rov's teaching: "Torah must live!" The life and soul of the Rebbe's Torah are revealed in the songs and dances of his chassidim; their celebration brings out the spirit of nature. But when the Rov brings them back to the mundane world, they are once again confronted by material poverty and a figurative death in the image of darkness.

The narrator is a follower of the Rebbe, standing "between two peaks" (literally "between two mountains," *tsvishn tsvey berg*), and his narrative itself balances the two extremes. Beneath the narrator's attraction to his chassidic leader lies a suppressed admiration for the mitnagdic Rov. The concluding lines, moreover, suggest a softening of the polemic between the two groups: "They reached no reconciliation; the Brisker Rov remained a mitnaged as before. . . . But it did have an effect! He no longer persecuted the chassidim" (117).

Peretz's views remain unspoken, since nothing the narrator says clearly establishes the position of the implied author. Although he seems to approve of the chassidic fervor, Peretz may also question several superstitious elements. For example, the narrator tells us that the daughters of the Rov all had difficulties in childbirth, adding, "everyone saw and knew that this was a punishment" meted out to the Rov because of his opposition to the chassidim. Later, in the midst of a storm, the narrator takes courage in the thought that, after the Rebbe's blowing of the shofar, "for an entire year, thunder and lightning have no power" (109). Similarly, the narrator believes that when the Rebbe speaks to his disciples, "one feels that angels hover over the room, and one actually hears the rustling of their great white wings" (112). In view of such superstitious beliefs, it is evident that the implied author Peretz does not agree with everything his narrator utters. As Ruth Wisse argues, "Rather than put down one combatant at the expense of the other, Peretz presents the conflict between the rationalist and the ecstatic through the eyes of a disciple who reveres the learned Rabbi and adores his holy Rebbe. Both sides of the Jewish inheritance—its civilizing legal demands and its liberal compassion—are characterized with appreciation for their grandeur of mind and spirit."[28]

Peretz's goal is not to subvert this narrator through ironies or satiric thrusts, but to balance the narrator's enthusiasm and superstition. Chassidism becomes a figure for a certain form of life, at odds with the sometimes sterile intellectualism of the mitnagdim. The meaning of the text is, in part, summed up by the reader's potential response—an existential self-questioning. The universal choice between emotion and reason, collectivity and individuality, or populism and elitism shines through this tale of chassidim and mitnagdim.

In a highly condensed and controlled manner, Peretz's chassidic stories present folk materials in a literary form, combining neo-

---

[28]Ruth R. Wisse, *I. L. Peretz and the Making of Modern Jewish Culture*, p. 58.

romantic and satiric elements in masterful parodies. Following his example, several other authors experimented with such voices, allowing full reign to the oral genius of the Yiddish language while drawing from the spiritual aura of Hebrew.[29] Peretz's literary contribution is thus linked to his translations from Hebrew to Yiddish and from Yiddish to Hebrew. His chassidic stories, even those first written in Hebrew, were influenced by his contemporary Yiddish fiction.

Peretz was a pathbreaker in Yiddish and Hebrew. Sholem Aleichem vowed to work the soil that had been prepared by Abramovitsh, and he presumably meant that his early stories and novels would follow Abramovitsh's path of social criticism. Later Sholem Aleichem moved toward narrative personae like those of Abramovitsh's Mendele, most notably in his Tevye stories. Peretz also appropriated aspects of Abramovitsh's Mendele persona, with its ambiguous combination of traditionalism and antitraditional satire. Whereas Sholem Aleichem's late "monologues of mastery" clearly subvert their narrators, Peretz's monologues of mystery suspend the reader uncertainly between antithetical worldviews. Peretz's strongest chassidic tales share the incongruity of Mendele the Bookseller's prefaces, when they subtly undermine the positions they overtly represent. Peretz's first-person narrators tell traditional tales with a difference in tone, pressing against tradition with their irony and threatening hints of transgression.

When Peretz organized his Yiddish fiction into his collected works in 1901 and again in 1909–13, he necessarily generated new patterns and principles of order. The volume entitled *Chassidic* was one consequence of this reorganization, but in spite of its popularity there is still debate over the exact nature of its contents. These chassidic tales have, too often, been misunderstood as sentimental retellings of folk traditions. Some of Peretz's later stories, collected in the volume *Folktales* (*Folkstimlekhe geshikhtn*, 1909), lapse toward this

---

[29]For example, M. J. Berdichevsky produced *Stories of a Distant Relative* (*Ksovim fun a vaytn korev*; written in 1902–06); Z. Y. Anokhi (Aronson) wrote monologues by a traditional character called *Reb Aba* (1911). In Hebrew, S. Y. Agnon created a range of narrators who assume tones of piety and traditionalism, and H. N. Bialik wrote tales such as "The Short Friday" ("Yom shishi ha-k'tzar," 1925) employing what Robert Alter calls an "as-if pious" narrator. Among many others, two important authors in this neo-chassidic mode were Hillel Zeitlin and Yehuda Steinberg.

stereotype and have contributed to misreadings of the more complex works.

The power of Peretz's best chassidic stories derives from their subtle juxtaposition of chassidic themes, first-person narrative, and ironies that suggest conflict. His use of first-person narrators enables him to pit distinctive personalities against the conflicts within their stories. Peretz exploits the traditional aura implicit in these Hebrew and Yiddish tales, allowing it to encounter opposition in various guises. The style is surprisingly colloquial, although it incorporates passages that simulate chassidic teachings. In spite of the pious personae of the narrators, contrary impressions emerge, for Peretz's work is permeated by contradictions.[30]

Peretz's importance as a Hebrew writer has been underestimated. His small but significant Hebrew output has been neglected in consequence of his reputation as a Yiddish author. Moreover, when early Israeli critics such as Aharon Ben-'Or and Fishel Lachower interpreted Peretz's stories in Hebrew, they did not differentiate clearly enough between his original Hebrew writings and those that were translated from Yiddish.[31] As a result, Peretz's specific Hebrew contribution has not been adequately understood.

Peretz made several major advances in modern Yiddish and Hebrew fiction. Specifically, he helped to create the genre of the retold chassidic story, fashioning it into a highly condensed literary form. Two of Peretz's pivotal chassidic tales first appeared in Hebrew before being translated into Yiddish versions. At the same time, Peretz placed an emphasis on spoken language, which is evident in his preference for first-person storytellers and in his use of dialogue. Finally, Peretz combined the neo-chassidic genre, tending toward romanticism, with hints of post-Enlightenment irony and satire. This synthesis brings together aspects of the ongoing Hebrew and Yiddish traditions.

Peretz wrote several tales in Hebrew before translating them into Yiddish, which had a determinative influence on his Yiddish style,

---

[30]Isaac Rozentsvayg, *Der radikaler period fun Peretz's shafn* (Kiev: Melukhe farlag far di natsionale minderhaytn, 1934), p. 3.

[31]See Aharon Ben-'Or (A. Orinovski), *Toldot ha-sifrut ha-'ivrit ha-chadashah* (Tel Aviv: Izreel, 1951), vol. 2, chapter 7, pp. 115–19, and Fishel Lachower, *Toldot ha-sifrut ha-'ivrit ha-chadashah* (Tel Aviv: Dvir, 1951), book 3, part 2, pp. 46–49.

resulting in a combination of dignified written Hebrew and Yiddish oral fluidity. Peretz's most effective texts operate "between two peaks": they coordinate the religiosity of Hebrew chassidic tales with the individuality of Yiddish presentation. These peaks are cultural forms as well as human personality types; they may suggest Peretz's wavering between the intellectualism of contemporary Hebrew writing and the greater populism of Yiddish literature.

It has been said that when S. Y. Abramovitsh shifted back from Yiddish to Hebrew fiction after 1886, he bestowed some of the colloquial aura of everyday speech on Hebrew.[32] Peretz traversed the opposite path, bringing the spiritual associations of Hebrew writing into his Yiddish fiction. Hence much of the power of late nineteenth-century Hebrew and Yiddish fiction derived from the effects of auto-translation and, more generally, cultural transfer. Interlinguistic transactions produced results that cannot be attributed to inspired individual creativity in a single language.

In his speech at the Chernovitz Conference of 1908, Peretz traced Yiddish fiction back to Rabbi Nachman's tales, which were told in Yiddish but recorded in both Yiddish and Hebrew. By reappropriating this and other sources in his pseudo-chassidic stories, Peretz combined cultural depth and social commentary. A delicate parodic balance holds in suspension nostalgia and criticism, archaic Hebrew diction and everyday Yiddish cadences.

---

[32]See, for example, Robert Alter, *The Invention of Hebrew Prose: Modern Fiction and the Language of Realism* (Seattle: University of Washington Press, 1988), p. 29: when Abramovitsh returned to Hebrew in 1886, he tried "to make Hebrew sound as though it were the living language of the Jews about whom he wrote. He worked to give it the suppleness, the colloquial vigor, and the nuanced referential precision of the Yiddish he had fashioned."

Conclusion

This survey of Yiddish fiction does not simply present each author's major works in chronological order, because Abramovitsh, Sholem Aleichem, and Peretz were close contemporaries. They were called the "grandfather," the "grandson," and the "father" of modern Yiddish writing, yet they died in 1917, 1916, and 1915, respectively. Classic Yiddish fiction is a trio rather than a sequence of solo performances. It would be as misguided to isolate their musical voices as it would be to analyze a melody without regard to its harmonic context.

Modern Yiddish literature developed to a large extent without heroes. Lacking an aristocracy or any other firmly established elite, Yiddish culture was often skeptical of individual claims to self-importance, power, or authority. Furthermore, classic Yiddish writers scorned the heroic romances that had become popular in nineteenth-century European fiction. Peretz ultimately sought his heroes in chassidic folk traditions, which exalted the Rebbe or another righteous person. But even when Peretz drew from folktales, he altered them by maintaining ironic distance. Yiddish fiction attacks corruption more often than it presents a positive model.

Abramovitsh, Sholem Aleichem, and Peretz specialized in irony and parody, as when they portrayed Mendele the Bookseller's mock-prayers, Tevye the Dairyman's mock-quotations, or chassidic disciples' mock-piety. Abramovitsh takes his ironic starting-point from liturgical contexts and veers sharply toward satire. Sholem Aleichem initially parodies the "most interesting novels" of his day but employs social satire when he condemns corruption among the Russian-Jewish bourgeoisie or the unprincipled businessmen of New York. Peretz maintains nuanced irony in his chassidic tales, opting for ambiguous situations that combine elements of psychological analysis, neo-romanticism, and satire. In distinctive ways, all three classic Yiddish authors appropriate aspects of Judaic literary history, including biblical and talmudic language as well as folk traditions. From Abramovitsh's early Mendele narratives to Peretz's chassidic tales, the three canonical authors reexamine literary and social norms.

In first-person narratives and simulated oral presentations, monologue is fundamental to modern Yiddish literature. The monological device in classic Yiddish fiction takes advantage of the oral bases of popular Jewish culture. The classic authors remain close to the spoken word, rhetorically conveying the intonations of speech by representing the act of storytelling itself. Nineteenth-century Yiddish literature reflects the oral genius of Yiddish language and culture. At the same time, the evolution of the written word in Yiddish quickly recapitulates stages in the progress of European writing.

Classic Yiddish fiction is also inseparable from social commentary. It begins with the ideology of the Enlightenment, represents the questioning voices of untrained speakers, and concludes in the early twentieth century with critical retellings of chassidic folktales. Abramovitsh, Sholem Aleichem, and Peretz advance Yiddish literature by responding both to literary trends and to the social milieu of its readers. There was virtually no "art for art's sake" in classic Yiddish writing, since this was a luxury that neither the authors nor the audience could afford. Even Peretz, the founder of Yiddish modernism, wrote tales about traditional Jewish life in Poland. As a result, Yiddish fiction from 1864–1916 is always engaged and committed to effecting social change, even when it entertains and elicits laughter.

A. A. Roback stated that Abramovitsh wrote *to* the Jewish people, Sholem Aleichem wrote *for* them, and Peretz wrote *about* them. There is some truth in these generalizations. Abramovitsh wrote *to* the Jews from an enlightened distance, seeking to educate and bearing a message for individual improvement and social reform. Sholem Aleichem produced fiction *for* the people, meeting them on their own ground and in their vernacular. Sholem Aleichem offered entertainment combined with social criticism and strove to educate his readers by improving their taste in literary matters. Peretz deliberately stood further above his audience than either Abramovitsh or Sholem Aleichem. He wrote *about* the people, employing techniques of psychological realism, and he conveyed the splendors as well as the misadventures of the chassidim. In each case, the implicit audience was essential. These authors wrote in Yiddish for a broad readership, which influenced the tone and tenor of their narratives. Irony, satire, and parody drew authors and readers together in an overtly or covertly conspiratorial group. While the characters in these fictions are seldom heroic, the authors heroically confronted the social and political issues of their time.

Abramovitsh brings together the orality of his fictional Yiddish speakers with parodic features, serving both social criticism and narrative ends. His parodies of Hebrew liturgy balance with his appropriations of secular European literary conventions. Abramovitsh does not satirize his character Mendele, but instead grants him a potent irony that cuts against the misguided world. Parody of Hebrew and European precursors is integral to Abramovitsh's invention of the modern Yiddish novel.

Sholem Aleichem also combines oral-style narration and literary sophistication, the illusion of everyday speech and parody. His Tevye stories and other monologues show the influence of Abramovitsh's Mendele. Moreover, early in his career Sholem Aleichem staged a direct assault on popular novels, the trashy fiction of his day. His fullest satire is the mock trial of the rival novelist Shomer, in which Sholem Aleichem finds Shomer guilty of naively imitating popular European fiction. Sholem Aleichem's novels provide numerous examples of parody, as when his third-person narrator in *Sender Blank* mocks the literary conventions he assumes. His works sometimes sound like late-nineteenth-century realist novels, but Sholem Aleichem does not let the conventions stand uncontested. To write a novel he must follow European standards, but his antipathy to Shomer precludes full-fledged acceptance of novelistic norms. Hence he takes away with one hand what he gives with the other. Rather than merely copy a familiar novelistic scene, Sholem Aleichem draws attention to the fact that he is pretending to do so; he dispenses with the stereotypical plots that characterize novels by his contemporaries.

The admixture of oral-style narrative and parody is equally prominent in I. L. Peretz's Yiddish fiction. Peretz captures the rhythms of speech in a number of forms, ranging from internal monologues to first-person narratives and dialogues. Most characteristic are the understated narrators of the chassidic tales. They do not have the variety of Sholem Aleichem's monologists, but they do imply highly charged scenes of narration. At the same time, they parody their chassidic, folkloristic prototypes. Peretz's early satires are social critiques, but his later chassidic stories move away from realism toward ironic retellings of folktales.

In 1890 the Hebrew Language Council (*Va'ad ha-leshon ha-'ivrit*) was formed in Palestine, signaling the extraordinary rebirth of Hebrew, "the Holy tongue" (*leshon ha-kodesh*), after nearly two millennia of the Jews' persecution and exile. During the past century, a rich literature in Hebrew has produced fiction, poetry, and drama at a level comparable to that in the European languages. This linguistic miracle had been made possible by the continuous use of Hebrew in study and prayer. In addition, modern Hebrew drew sustenance from centuries of Yiddish speech and writing, borrowing vocabulary, syntax, and literary models. Many important Hebrew writers, such as Abramovitsh and Peretz, were native Yiddish speakers. Like them, H. N. Bialik, Y. H. Brenner, and Uri Zvi Gnessin wrote both in Yiddish and Hebrew; Nobel-Prize winner S. Y. Agnon produced Yiddish stories before shifting to Hebrew.

The Chernovitz Conference of 1908, in which Peretz was the most outspoken participant, proclaimed Yiddish "a Jewish national language," having failed to gain a majority favoring use of the definite article. Later, after disputes arose in Yafo and Jerusalem over the language that Jews should speak in Palestine, Yiddish gradually succumbed to Hebrew. Formation of the State of Israel in 1948 consolidated the position of the Hebraists, and today only a few Orthodox communities of Israel and America have retained Yiddish as their everyday language.

Simon Dubnov and other authors of the late nineteenth and early twentieth century espoused a "diaspora nationalism," signifying that they identified with a Jewish selfhood that did not require return to Zion. Instead of placing their hopes in a modern state, they worked toward stronger cultural ties that would make political nationhood unnecessary. But no literary culture can thrive without readers, and the fate of Yiddish in Europe and America has illustrated the difficulty of maintaining it in a hostile environment or in a secular melting pot.

When Abramovitsh began writing in Yiddish, he encountered a peculiarly desolate landscape. Chassidic literature and anti-chassidic satire provided meager foundation for a new literary edifice. While nineteenth-century English, French, and German authors could build upon centuries of prior texts, Yiddish writers had few notable antecedents of their own. In a short span of years, Yiddish authors recapitulated developments that had characterized European formal experimentation. Yiddish fiction, as a latecomer lacking progenitors, took European realism as its starting point. Russian, Polish, French, German, and English authors led the way.

This process of emulation sometimes gave rise to trivial imitations, exemplified by Shomer's light romances. But even such uncritical mimicry provided material for more sophisticated reworkings.

In a number of ways, too, Yiddish fiction followed the lead of ancient and medieval Hebrew writing. Abramovitsh, Sholem Aleichem, and Peretz all relied heavily upon biblical, talmudic, and midrashic associations. Moreover, they learned from the steps Hebrew authors had already taken toward appropriating the conventions of European writing. But as modern Hebrew and Yiddish literature evolved together, in certain respects their development responded to contrary influences.

Yiddish was the common language of most Eastern European Jews; Hebrew was the language of scholarship and prayer. Rabbi Nachman of Bratslav told his tales in Yiddish and published his writings in Hebrew. Posthumously, his scribe Nathan Sternharz printed the tales in a bilingual edition. The Hebrew version placed Nachman's allegories in relation to Scripture, while the Yiddish text echoed the orality of Nachman's original storytelling. Nineteenth-century Hebrew and Yiddish fiction struggled with the dichotomy between written and spoken language, since both registers are necessary to narrative.

Hebrew had access to a wealth of turns of phrase and intertextual models whereas Yiddish possessed the stock of oral locutions and idioms. Daily prayer and study gave rise to the most obvious bridge between these disparate realms: the embedding of Hebrew words in the Yiddish lexicon. Yet this linguistic feature in itself was not enough to generate a literary style or genre in Yiddish. The formulae of Hebrew prayers and Yiddish supplications (*tekhines*) served Abramovitsh well as a resource for his parodies. Another significant Yiddish literary genre that Abramovitsh parodied is that of Yiddish translations from the Hebrew Bible (*taytsh-khumesh*). His political allegory, *The Nag*, may also respond to Nachman's pious allegories.

Classic Yiddish satire stands at the intersection of narrative in an oral mode and intertextual parody. On one level, satire draws from the spoken discourse of daily life, and on another level it frames this oral domain within novelistic conventions. Parody should not be equated with mockery; nor can it be subsumed under intertextuality, for parody involves appropriations of—rather than just allusions to—prior forms.

As European realism developed conventions that enabled it to succeed, Yiddish fiction required the structuring principles afforded by parody. Thus the critique of outmoded social forms in works by Abramovitsh, Sholem Aleichem, and Peretz goes hand in hand with parodies of competing literary forms. Oral-style narrative and parody are not absolute antitheses, but represent two strands of Yiddish satire: the oral mode links Yiddish fiction to everyday life, while parody sets mimetic representation in its intertextual framework. In other words, moving beyond this dialectic, Yiddish writers in the nineteenth century negotiated between oral intonations, Western literary forms, and Hebraic antecedents. The rise of Yiddish literature was rendered possible, in part, by such parodic relationships to its precursors. Thus Israel Davidson commented in 1907, as classic Yiddish fiction neared its end, that "the Jewish parodist has invaded every department of literature and every walk of life. He has drawn upon the various phases of Jewish life for his subject matter and upon the various forms of Jewish literature for his models. It is no exaggeration to say that Jewish parody contains the entire Jewish literature in miniature."

This tour of the lost continent of classic Yiddish fiction leaves vast territories unexplored. English speakers could benefit from an overview of pre-classical Yiddish writing, as well as from monographs on major twentieth-century authors in the areas of Yiddish fiction, poetry, and drama. Currently, scholars versed in comparative literature are examining the interactions between Yiddish and Hebrew in the broader context of world literature, while feminist critics are reinterpreting the image of women in Yiddish fiction and Yiddish writing by women. Another pathway for future travelers leads through the realm of neo-chassidic or pseudo-chassidic storytelling, where piety and parody meet on unstable ground. Still another route that could lead to further explorations of Yiddish culture is the study of Yiddish films from the 1930s. Postmodern theory provides a link to contemporary architecture, for parody in classic Yiddish fiction uses irony and satire to appropriate multiple traditions and amalgamate disparate styles.

ABBREVIATIONS

AP   Peretz-Laks, R. *Arum Peretzn (zikhroynes un batrakh-tungen)*. Warsaw: Literarishe bleter, 1935.

CYCO   Peretz, I. L. *Ale verk*. Vols. 1–11. New York: CYCO, 1947.

CYL   Binshtok, Lev. "A Celebration of Yiddish Literature: Solomon Moiseevitsh Abramovitsh and His Twenty-Fifth Year of Literary Activity." Unpublished translation from the Russian by Jack Blanshei. From *Voskhod* 12 (1884), 1–32.

FY   *Funem yarid: lebensbashraybung*. In *Ale verk fun Sholem Aleichem*. Vols. 26–27. New York: Folksfond Edition, 1917–23.

FZ   Dubnov, Simon. *Fun "zhargon" tsu yidish un andere artiklen: literarishe zikhroynes*. Vilna: Kletzkin, 1929.

GYL   Viner, Meir. *Tsu der geshikhte fun der yidisher literatur in 19-tn yorhundert (etyudn un materialn)*. Vols. 1–2. New York: YKUF, 1946.

H   Hebrew versions: Peretz, I. L. "Mishnat chasidim," in *Ha-chetz: yalkut sifruti*. Ed. I. L. Peretz. Warsaw: Shvartsberg, 1894; Peretz, I. L. "Ha-mekubbalim (sippur)." *Gan perakhim* 3 (1891).

ILP   *Ale verk fun I. L. Peretz*. Vols. 1–11. Ed. Shmuel Niger [Shmuel Charney]. New York: CYCO, 1948.

KK   Letters of I. L. Peretz. In *Kol kitvei I. L. Peretz*. Vol. 10. Book 2. Tel Aviv: Dvir, 1962.

MB   *Dos Mendele bukh*. Ed. Nachman Mayzel. New York: YKUF, 1959.

MBSA   Rabinovitsh, Volf (Vevik). *Mayn bruder Sholem Aleichem: zikhroynes*. Kiev: Melukhe-farlag far di natsionale minderheytn in USSR, 1939.

MF   Waife-Goldberg, Marie. *My Father, Sholom Aleichem.* New York: Schocken, 1971.

MMS   *Ale verk fun Mendele Moykher Sforim (S. Y. Abramovitsh).* Jubilee Edition. Vols. 1–17. Cracow: Farlag Mendele, 1911–13. Supplemented by additional volumes in the later edition: Warsaw: Farlag Mendele, 1928.

MZ   Peretz, I. L. *Mayne zikhroynes.* In *Ale verk fun I. L. Peretz.* Vol. 11. New York: CYCO, 1948.

R   Berkovitsh, Y. D. *Ha-rish'onim ki-vnei-adam: sippurei zikharonot 'al Sholem-Aleichem u-vnei-doro.* 3d ed. Tel Aviv: Dvir, 1976.

SA   *Ale verk fun Sholem Aleichem.* Vols. 1–28. New York: Folksfond Edition, 1917–23.

SAB   *Dos Sholem-Aleichem bukh.* Ed. Y. D. Berkovitsh. New York: Sholem-Aleichem bukh komitet, 1926.

SAP   *Sholem Aleichem Panorama.* Ed. Melech Grafstein. London, Ontario: The Jewish Observer, 1948.

SRK   *Shloyme reb Khaim's.* In *Ale verk fun Mendele Moykher Sforim (S. Y. Abramovitsh).* Vol. 2. Cracow: Farlag Mendele, 1911.

SZ   [Abramovitsh's Autobiographical Essay]. In *Sefer zikharon le-sofrei yisra'el ha-chaim 'itanu ka-yom.* Ed. Nachum Sokolov. Warsaw: Halter, 1889, pp. 117–26.

TD   Miron, Dan. *A Traveler Disguised: A Study in the Rise of Modern Yiddish Fiction in the Nineteenth Century.* New York: Schocken, 1973.

Y   Yiddish versions: Peretz, I. L. "Mishnas khasidim." In *Der yud* 4 (1902), number 19; Peretz, I. L. "Mekubolim." In *Ale verk fun I. L. Peretz.* Vol. 4. Ed. Shmuel Niger. New York: CYCO, 1947.

YL   Niger, Shmuel [Shmuel Charney]. "Yidishe literatur fun mitn 18-tn yorhundert biz 1942." In the *Algemeyne entsiklopedie.* Vol. 3: *Yidn.* New York: CYCO, 1942, pp. 65–174.

SELECTED BIBLIOGRAPHY

A. GENERAL REFERENCE WORKS

Algemeyne entsiklopedie. Volume "*Yidn,*" part 3. New York: Dubnov-fond and CYCO, 1942.

Alter, Robert. *The Invention of Hebrew Prose: Modern Fiction and the Language of Realism.* Seattle: University of Washington Press, 1988.

American Yiddish Poetry: A Bilingual Anthology. Ed. Benjamin and Barbara Harshav. Trans. Benjamin and Barbara Harshav, Kathryn Hellerstein, Brian McHale, and Anita Norich. Berkeley: University of California Press, 1986.

Bakhtin, M. M. *The Dialogic Imagination: Four Essays.* Ed. Michael Holquist. Trans. Caryl Emerson and Michael Holquist. Austin: University of Texas Press, 1981.

_____. *Problems of Dostoevsky's Poetics.* Ed. and trans. Caryl Emerson. Minneapolis: University of Minnesota Press, 1984.

Bal Makhshoves [Isidor Eliashev]. *Geklibene shriftn.* Vols. 1–5. Warsaw: Kletzkin, 1929.

_____. *Geklibene verk.* New York: CYCO, 1953.

Ben-'Or, Aharon. *Toldot ha-sifrut ha-'ivrit ha-chadashah.* Vol. 2. Tel Aviv: Izreel, 1951.

Bloom, Harold. *The Anxiety of Influence: A Theory of Poetry.* New York: Oxford University Press, 1973.

Booth, Wayne C. *The Rhetoric of Fiction.* Chicago: University of Chicago Press, 1961.

Borokhov, Ber. *Shprakh-forshung un literatur-geshikhte.* Ed. Nachman Mayzel. Tel Aviv: Peretz farlag, 1966.

_____. *Geklibene verk.* New York: CYCO, 1953.

Chajes, Saul. *Otsar biduyei ha-shem. Thesaurus pseudonymorum quae in litteratura hebraica et judaeo-germanica inveniuntur. Pseudonymen-Lexikon der hebräischen und jiddischen Literatur.* 2d ed. Hildesheim: Georg Olms, 1967.

Chew, Allen F. *An Atlas of Russian History: Eleven Centuries of Changing Borders.* Revised ed. New Haven: Yale University Press, 1970.

Cohen, Chester G. *Shtetl Finder: Jewish Communities in the 19th and Early 20th Centuries in the Pale of Settlement of Russia and Poland, and in Lithuania, Latvia, Galicia, and Bukovina, with Names of Residents.* Bowie, Maryland: Heritage, 1989.

Davidson, Israel. *Parody in Jewish Literature.* New York: Columbia University Press, 1907.

De Lange, Nicholas. *Atlas of the Jewish World*. New York: Facts on File, 1988.

Dubnov, Simon. *Fun "zhargon" tsu yidish un andere artiklen: literarishe zikhroynes*. Vilna: Kletzkin, 1929.

Dubnov-Erlich, Sophie. *The Life and Work of S. M. Dubnov: Diaspora Nationalism and Jewish History*. Trans. Judith Vowles. Ed. Jeffrey Shandler. Bloomington: Indiana University Press, 1991.

Encyclopaedia Judaica. Vols. 1–16. Ed. Cecil Roth. Jerusalem: Macmillan, 1971–72.

Entin, Yoel. *Di zaylen fun der nayer yidisher literatur (nayn lektsies vegn Mendele Moykher-Sforim, Sholem Aleichem, un I. L. Peretz*. New York: Yidish-natsionaln arbeter farband, 1923.

Even-Shoshan, Avraham. *Ha-milon he-chadash*. Vols. 1–4. Jerusalem: Kiryat-sefer, 1985.

The Field of Yiddish: Studies in Yiddish Language, Folklore, and Literature. Ed. Uriel Weinreich. New York: Linguistic Circle of New York, 1954.

Fremd-verter-bukh. Ed. A. B. Rozenshtayn. Warsaw: Bikher-far-ale, 1919.

Friesel, Evyatar. *Atlas of Modern Jewish History*. Revised ed. New York: Oxford University Press, 1990.

Gogol from the Twentieth Century: Eleven Essays. Ed. and trans. Robert A. Maguire. Princeton: Princeton University Press, 1974.

Goldberg, Abraham. *Pioneers and Builders: Biographical Studies and Essays*. New York: A. G. Publication Committee, 1943.

Greenberg, Louis. *The Jews in Russia: The Struggle for Emancipation*. 2d ed. Ed. Mark Wischnitzer. New York: Schocken, 1976.

Groyser verterbukh fun der yidisher shprakh. Vols. 1–4 (Aleph). New York: Yiddish Dictionary Committee, 1961–80.

Guide to Yiddish Classics on Microfiche [Di yidishe klasikers oyf mikrofish]. Ed. Chone Shmeruk. New York: Clearwater, 1980. [The microfiche set contains 152 rare titles by the three classic authors.]

Halkin, Simon. *Modern Hebrew Literature: From the Enlightenment to the Birth of the State of Israel: Trends and Values*. 2d ed. New York: Schocken, 1970.

Halpern, Moyshe-Leyb. *In New York: A Selection*. Trans. and ed. Kathryn Hellerstein. Philadelphia: Jewish Publication Society, 1982.

Harkavy, Alexander. *Yiddish-English-Hebrew Dictionary*. 2d ed. New York: Hebrew Publishing Company, 1928. Reprint, with introduction by Dovid Katz. New York: YIVO and Schocken, 1988.

Harshav, Benjamin. *The Meaning of Yiddish*. Berkeley: University of California Press, 1990.

Hoberman, J. *Bridge of Light: Yiddish Film Between Two Worlds*. New York: Schocken, 1991.

Hutcheon, Linda. *A Poetics of Postmodernism: History, Theory, Fiction*. New York: Routledge, 1988.

_____. *A Theory of Parody: The Teachings of Twentieth-Century Art Forms*. New York: Methuen, 1985.

The Illustrated Atlas of Jewish Civilization: 4,000 Years of Jewish History. Ed. Martin Gilbert. New York: Macmillan, 1990.

The Jewish Encyclopedia. Vols. 1–12. Ed. Isidore Singer. New York: Funk and Wagnalls, 1901–07.

Kagan, Berl. *Leksikon fun yidish-shraybers*. New York: Raʿaya Elman-Cohen, 1986.

Klauzner, Joseph. *A History of Modern Hebrew Literature*. Trans. Herbert Danby. Ed. Leon Simon. Reprint. Westport, Conn.: Greenwood Press, 1974.

Lachower, Fishel. *Rishʾonim ve-ʾacharonim: Masot u-maʾamarim*. Vol. 1. Tel Aviv: Dvir, 1934.

_____. *Toldot ha-sifrut ha-ʿivrit ha-chadashah*. Book 3. Part 2. Tel Aviv: Dvir, 1951.

Leksikon fun der nayer yidisher literatur. Vols. 1–8. New York: CYCO, 1956–81.

Levin, Yankev. *Verterbikhl fun hebreish-yidishe verter*. New York: CYCO, 1958.

Liptzin, Sol. *The Flowering of Yiddish Literature*. New York: Thomas Yoseloff, 1963.

Madison, Charles A. *Yiddish Literature: Its Scope and Major Writers*. New York: Schocken, 1971.

Mendelsohn, Ezra. *Class Struggle in the Pale: The Formative Years of the Jewish Workers' Movement in Tsarist Russia*. Cambridge: Cambridge University Press, 1970.

Miron, Dan. *Der imazh fun shtetl: dray literarishe shtudies*. Tel Aviv: Peretz farlag, 1981.

_____. *Bodedim be-moʿedam: le-diukna shel ha-republika ha-sifrutit ha-ʿivrit be-techilat ha-meʾa ha-ʿesrim*. Tel Aviv: ʿAm ʿoved, 1987.

The New Standard Jewish Encyclopedia. 2d ed. Ed. Cecil Roth and Geoffrey Wigoder. New York: Doubleday, 1970.

Niger, Shmuel [Shmuel Charney]. *Dertseylers un romanistn*. Vol. 1. New York: CYCO, 1946.

_____. *Vegn yidishe shrayber: kritishe artiklen*. Warsaw: Sreberk, 1927.

Oyslender, N. *Grunt-shtrikhn fun yidishn realizm*. 2d ed. Vilna: Kletzkin, 1928.

The Penguin Book of Modern Yiddish Verse. Ed. Irving Howe, Ruth R. Wisse, and Khone Shmeruk. New York: Viking, 1987.

Pines, M. *Di geshikhte fun der yidisher literatur*. Vols. 1–2. Warsaw: Shimin, 1911.

Pirsumim yehudiim be-vrit ha-moʿatzot. Ed. Chone Shmeruk. Jerusalem: Ha-chevrah ha-historit ha-yisraʾelit, 1961.

Reyzen, Zalman. *Leksikon fun der yidisher literatur un presse.* Ed. Shmuel Niger. Warsaw: "Tsentral," 1914.

———. *Leksikon fun der yidisher literatur, presse un filologie.* 2d ed. Vols. 1–4. Vilna: Kletzkin, 1926–29.

———. Review of Saul Chajes' *Otsar biduyei ha-shem.* [Provides corrections and a supplement of pseudonyms in Yiddish literature.] *YIVO bleter* 12 (1938), 585–618.

———. *Yidishe literatur un yidishe sprakh.* Ed. Shmuel Rozhanski. Buenos Aires: Yoysef Lifshitz-fond, 1965.

Readings in Russian Poetics: Formalist and Structuralist Views. Ed. Ladislav Matejka and Krystyna Pomorska. Ann Arbor: University of Michigan Press, 1978.

Roback, A. A. *The Story of Yiddish Literature.* New York: YIVO, 1940.

Robin, Régine. *L'amour du yiddish: écriture juive et sentiment de la langue (1830–1930).* Paris: Éditions du Sorbier, 1984.

Roskies, Dovid-Hirsh [David]. "Hoyptshtromen fun der hayntiker yidisher literatur-forshung." *Di goldene keyt* 94 (1977), 145–60.

Rusish-yidisher verterbukh. Ed. M Shapiro, E. Spivak, and M. Shulman. Moscow: Ruski yazik, 1984.

Sadan, Dov. *Tsvishn vayt un noent: eseyen, shtudies, briv.* Tel Aviv: Farlag Israel-bukh, 1982.

Shatsky, Yankev. *Geshikhte fun yidn in varshe.* Vol. 3. *Fun 1863 biz 1896.* New York: YIVO, 1953.

Shmeruk, Chone. *Sifrut yidish: perakim le-toldoteha.* Tel Aviv: Porter Institute, 1978.

Striedter, Jurij. *Russischer Formalismus: Texte zur allgemeinen Literaturtheorie und zur Theorie der Prosa.* Munich: W. Fink, 1971.

Stutchkoff, Nahum. *Der oytser fun der yidisher shprakh.* Ed. Max Weinreich. New York: YIVO, 1950.

Tobias, Henry J. *The Jewish Bund in Russia: From Its Origins to 1905.* Stanford: Stanford University Press, 1972.

A Treasury of Yiddish Stories. 2d ed. Ed. Irving Howe and Eliezer Greenberg. New York: Penguin, 1990.

Trunk, Y. Y. *Idealizm un naturalizm in der yidisher literatur (tendentsn un vegn fun unzere moderne shriftshteller).* Warsaw: Kultur-lige, 1927.

Verses, Shmuel. *Bikoret ha-bikoret.* Tel Aviv: Yachdav, 1982.

Waxman, Meyer. *A History of Jewish Literature.* Vols. 1–5. New York: Thomas Yoseloff, 1960.

Weinreich, Max. *Bilder fun der yidisher literaturgeshikhte: Fun di onheybn biz Mendele Moykher Sforim.* Vilna: Tomor, 1928.

Weinreich, Uriel. *Modern English-Yiddish Yiddish-English Dictionary.* New York: YIVO, 1968.

Wiener, Leo. *The History of Yiddish Literature in the 19th Century* [1899]. 2d ed. New York: Hermon Press, 1972.

Wisse, Ruth R. *The Schlemiel as Modern Hero*. Chicago: University of Chicago Press, 1971.

Yeshurun, Yefim [Ephim H. Jeshurin]. *100 yor moderne yidishe literatur*. New York: Workmen's Circle Educational Committee, 1965.

Yiddish Literature in English Translation: Books Published 1945–1967. Ed. Dina Abramowicz. New York: YIVO, 1967.

Yidishe folks-entsiklopedie. Vols. 1–2. Ed. Symcha Pietruszka. Montreal: Eagle, 1943.

Di yidishe literatur in nayntsetn yorhundert: zamlung fun yidisher literatur-forshung un kritik in ratn-farband. Ed. Chone Shmeruk and Chava Turniansky. Jerusalem: Magnes, 1993.

Yidish verterbukh: ale hebreishe (un khaldeishe) verter. Ed. Chaim Spivak and Yehoash [Solomon Bloomgarden]. New York: Farlag Yehoash, 1911.

Zinberg, Israel. *A History of Jewish Literature*. Vols. 1–12. Trans. and ed. Bernard Martin. Cleveland and New York: Case Western Reserve University and Ktav, 1972–78.

B. LITERARY WORKS, EDITIONS, AND LETTERS

1. Sholem Yankev Abramovitsh

"Aderabe, ver iz meshuge?" In *Mendele un zayn tsayt: materialn tsu der geshikhte fun der yidisher literatur in XIX yorhundert*. Moscow: Der emes, 1940, 5–11.

Ale ksovim fun Mendele Moykher Sforim. Vols. 1–2. Odessa: Varshaver, 1888.

Ale verk fun Mendele Moykher Sforim (S. Y. Abramovitsh). Jubilee Edition. Vols. 1–17. Cracow: Farlag Mendele, 1911–13.

Ale verk fun Mendele Moykher Sforim. Revised "Stereotyp" Edition. Vols. 1–22. Warsaw: Farlag Mendele, 1928.

"Arbaʿa mikhtavim meʾet S. Y. Abramovitsh le-Y. H. Ravnitzky." *Reshumot* 2 (1927), 427–31.

[Autobiographical Essay.] In *Sefer zikharon le-sofrei yisraʾel ha-chaim ʿitanu ka-yom*. Ed. Nakhum Sokolov. Warsaw: Halter, 1889, pp. 117–26.

Ha-ʾavot ve-ha-banim. Odessa: Belinton, 1868.

"Ba-yamim ha-hem: petikhta deMendele Moykher Sforim." *Pardes* 2 (1894), 173–88.

"Der baybak." *Shtern* 1 (1936), 6–12.

"Be-seter ra'am." *Ben-'ami* (April-May 1887), 1–25.

"Beshas der mehume." *Fun noentn over* 1 (1937), books 1–4, 40–45.

"Bi-ymei ha-ra'ash." *Pardes* 2 (1894), 31–59.

Chalifat 'iggrot bein S. Y. Abramovitsh u-vein H. N. Bialik ve-Y. H. Ravnitzky ba-shanim 1905–1908. Ed. Chone Shmeruk. Jerusalem: Ha-akademya ha-le'umit ha-yisra'elit le-meda'im, 1976.

Dray ertseylungen. Warsaw: Hoyz-fraynd, 1908.

'Ein mishpat. Zhitomir: Shadov, 1867.

Fishke der krumer. Zhitomir: Shadov, 1869.

Fishke der krumer. 2d ed. In *Ale verk fun Mendele Moykher Sforim.* Vol. 1. Odessa: Varshaver, 1888.

Gezamlte verk. Vols. 3–6. Moscow: Der emes, 1935–40.

"'Iggrot Mendele Moykher Sforim (reshimah kronologit)." In *Mendele Moykher Sforim: reshimat ketavav ve-'iggrotav le-hatkanat mahaduratam ha-akademit.* Jerusalem: Magnes, 1965.

"In yener tsayt." Trans. by Sh. In *Dray ertseylungen.* Warsaw: Hoyz-fraynd, 1908.

Ha-'ishon ha-katan: Dos kleyne mentshele. [Bilingual edition.] Trans. and ed. Shalom Luria. Haifa: Haifa University Press, 1984.

Kitser masoes Binyomin hashlishi. Vilna: Rom, 1878.

Kitzur masa'ot Binyamin ha-shlishi. Odessa: Belinson, 1896.

Dos kleyne mentshele oder a lebensbashraybung fun Yitskhok Avrom takif. Odessa: Nitzshe and Tsederboym, 1865.

Dos kleyne mentshele. 2d ed. Vilna: Rom, 1979.

Di klyatshe. Vilna: Rom, 1873.

Di klyatshe. 2d ed. In *Ale verk fun Mendele Moykher Sforim.* Vol. 2. Odessa: Varshaver, 1889.

Kol kitvei Mendele Moykher-Sforim (S. Y. Abramovitsh). Vols. 1–3. Odessa: "Va'ad ha-yovel," 1909–12.

Kol kitvei Mendele Moykher Sforim. 3d ed. Berlin: Moriah, 1922.

Kol kitvei Mendele Moykher Sforim. 5th ed. Vols. 1–6. Tel Aviv: Dvir, 1935–36.

Kol kitvei Mendele Moykher Sforim. Tel Aviv: Dvir, 1947.

[Letter to Sholem Aleichem.] "Mendele's letster briv tsu Sholem-Aleichemen." *Yidishe kultur* (Nov.–Dec. 1991), 31.

Limdu heitev. Warsaw: Lebenson, 1862.

Limdu heitev. Reprint. Ed. Dan Miron. New York: YIVO, 1969.

"Lo nachat be-Ya'akov." *Pardes* 1 (1892), 37–56.

Masoes Binyomin ha-shlishi; Fishke der krumer. Ed. L. Yudkevitsh. Moscow: Melukhe-farlag fun kinstlerisher literatur, 1959.

Mendele un zayn tsayt: materialn tsu der geshikhte fun der yidisher literatur in XIX yorhundert. Moscow: Der emes, 1940.

Mishpat shalom. Vilna: Rom, 1860.

"A nakht in tsores." *Der hoyz-fraynd* 3 (1894), 1–9.

"Ha-nisrafim." *Pardes* 3 (1896), 37–45.

Der nitslekher kalendar far di rusishe yidn. Zhitomir: Abramovitsh, Baksht, Rom, and Bletnitsky, 1876–84.

"Opgebrente." *Yidisher folks-kalender* 5 (1899–1900), 51–60.

"Di oysgenarte bekhoyre." In *Mendele un zayn tsayt: materialn tsu der geshikhte fun der yidisher literatur in XIX yorhundert*. Moscow: Der emes, 1940.

"Sefer ha-beheymes." *Der yud* 4 (1902), number 26, 13–15.

Sefer toldot ha-tevaʿ. Vols. 1–3. Leipzig: Yelin, 1862; Zhitomir: Shadov, 1866; Vilna: Rom, 1872.

A segule tsu di yudishe tsores. Translation of I. L. Pinsker's *Auto-Emancipation*. Odessa: A. Shultze, 1884.

"Shem ve-Yefet ba-ʿagala." In *Kaveret* (Odessa: Aba Duchna, 1890), pp. 45–59.

"A shlistsetl." *Der hoyz-fraynd*, new series, 3 (1898), 1–3.

Shloyme reb Khaim's. In *Ale verk fun Mendele Moykher Sforim (S. Y. Abramovitsh)*. Vol. 2. Cracow: Farlag Mendele, 1911.

Sippurim. Ed. Y. H. Ravnitzki. Odessa: Isakovitsh and Belinson, 1900.

Di takse: oder die bande shtot-bale toyves. 2d ed. Vilna: Fin and Rozen-krantz, 1872.

Dos vintshfingerl. Warsaw: Lebenzon, 1865.

Dos vintshfingerl. [Expanded edition.] Book One. In *Di yudishe folks-bibliotek* 1 (1888).

2. Sholem Aleichem (Sholem Rabinovitsh)

Ale verk. Jubilee Edition. Vols. 1–16. Warsaw: Progress, 1909–15.

Ale verk. Vols. 1–3. Ed. N. Oyslender and A. Frumkin. Moscow: Der emes, 1948.

Ale verk fun Sholem Aleichem. Vols. 1–28. New York: Folksfond Edition, 1917–23.

Ale verk fun Sholem Aleichem. Vols. 1–5. New York: Forverts, 1942.

Ayzenban-geshikhtes. In *Ale verk fun Sholem Aleichem*. New York: Folksfond Edition, 1917–23, vol. 28.

Berditchever sreyfes. Warsaw: Boymriter, 1909.

Berditchever teater un andere ertseylungen. New York: Reznick and Kap-lan, 1908.

A bletl shir hashirim. Warsaw: Familien-bibliotek, 1911.

Blondzhende shtern. New York: Jewish Press, 1912.

"A boydem." *Der yud* 1 (1899), number 1, 11–14 and number 3, 8–11.

"A briv tsu a gutn fraynt." In *Di yudishe folks-bibliotek* 2 (1889), 304–310.

"Chava." *Dos yudishe folk* 1 (1906), numbers 2–3 (24–31 May).

Chava: Tevye dem milkhiker's. Warsaw: Familien-bibliotek, 1909.

"Don Quixote fun Mazepevke un zayn khaver Simcha-Pinchas." [Translator not indicated.] In *Fargesene bletlekh.* Ed. Y. Mitlman and Kh. Nadel. Kiev: Melukhe-farlag far di natsionale minderheytn, 1939.

"Don Quixote mi-Mazepevke ve-Simkhe-Pinkhes reʿehu." In *Pardes* 1 (1892), 267–73.

"ʾEl yedidi ha-korʾei." Preface to *Kitvei Sholem-Aleichem.* Vol. 1. Warsaw: Ha-shachar, 1911, i–iv.

An eytse: an emese mayse, vos iz kimat shver tsu gloybn s'zol zayn an emese. Warsaw: Bikher-far-ale, 1905.

Fargesene bletlekh. Ed. Y. Mitlman and Kh. Nadel. Kiev: Melukhe-farlag far di natsionale minderheytn, 1939.

"A farshpilter lag baoymer (a mayse fun cheder)." Warsaw: Bikher-far-ale, 1905.

Gants Berditchev: a rikhtige bashraybung fun der shtot Berditchev mit ale ire antiklekh. New York: Reznik and Kaplan, 1908.

Gants Tevye der milkhiker. In *Ale verk fun Sholem Aleichem.* New York: Folksfond Edition, 1917–23, vol. 5.

"Hayntike kinder." *Der yud* (1899), number 10, 6–8, number 11, 5–7, and number 12, 5–7.

[Shulames, pseud.] "Heine un Börne un zeyere gedanken iber yudn." In *Di yudishe folks-bibliotek* 1 (1888), 435–44.

"Hodel." *Der fraynd* 2 (1904), numbers 193–96 (2–6 September).

Hodl (a mayse fun Tevye dem milkhiger, vos hot zikh farlofn mit im nor in der letster tsayt). Warsaw: Bikher-far-ale, 1905.

"In sforim-kleytl." *Der yud* 1 (1899), number 17, 14–17. Reprinted in *Fargesene bletlekh.* Ed. Y. Mitlman and Kh. Nadel. Kiev: Melukhe-farlag far di natsionale minderheytn, 1939.

Ketavim. Vols. 1–2. Trans. Y. D. Berkovitsh. Odessa: Moriah, 1913–14.

Ketavim ʿivriim. Ed. Chone Shmeruk. Jerusalem: Bialik Institute, 1976.

Kitvei Sholem Aleichem. Vols. 1–3. Warsaw: Ha-shachar, 1911.

Kol mevasser tsu der yudisher folks-bibliotek (1892).

Ksovim fun a komi-voyasher (ayznban-geshiktn). In *Ale verk.* Vol. 8. Warsaw: Progress, 1911.

[Letters to S. Y. Abramovitsh.] In *Tsum ondenk fun Sholem Aleichem: zamlbukh.* Ed. I. Zinberg and S. Niger. Petersburg: I. L. Peretz-fond, 1917, pp. 83–90.

[Letters to Yankev Dinezon.] *YIVO bleter* 1 (1931), 385–403, *YIVO bleter* 2 (1931), 13–31, and *YIVO bleter* 3 (1932), 337–53.

[Letters to Simon Dubnov.] *Literarishe bleter* 3 (April 1926), pp. 289–90.

[Letters to Simon Dubnov.] In *Fun "zhargon" tsu yidish un andere artiklen: literarishe zikhroynes.* Vilna: Kletzkin, 1929, pp. 64–96.

[Letters to Bertha Flekser.] *Tsaytshrift far yidisher geshikhte, demografie un ekonomik, literatur-forshung, shprakh-visnshaft un etnografie* 1 (1926), 250–52.

[Letters to his son Misha and to Natasha Mazor.] "Almost a Family Chronicle: Several Packets of Unpublished Letters by Sholem Aleichem" ("Pochti semeynaya khronika: o neskol'kikh pachkakh neopublikovannykh pisem Sholem-Aleichema"). *Vestnik evreiskogo universiteta v Moskve* 2 (1992), 190–215, and 3 (1993), 228–56.

[Letter to Y. Y. Propus.] *Literarishe bleter* 3 (1926), 290.

[Letters to Y. H. Ravnitsky.] In *Tsum ondenk fun Sholem Aleichem: zamlbukh*. Ed. I. Zinberg and S. Niger. Petersburg: I. L. Peretz-fond, 1917, pp. 91–98.

[Letters to Shmuel Shariro.] In *Tsum ondenk fun Sholem Aleichem: zamlbukh*. Ed. I. Zinberg and S. Niger. Petersburg: I. L. Peretz-fond, 1917, pp. 101–7.

[Letters to Mordechai Spektor.] "Der onheyb fun *Tevye der milkhiker*." Ed. Y. D. Berkovitsh. With a facsimile of Sholem Aleichem's letter to the printer of *Der hoyz-fraynd. Di goldene keyt* 56 (1966), 16–21.

[Letters.] *Bikher velt* 1 (1922), number 3, 325–27 and numbers 4–5, 463–66.

[Letters.] "Briv fun Sholem-Aleichem." Ed. Itche Goldberg. *Yidishe kultur* (Nov.-Dec. 1991), 9–13.

[Letters.] "Draysik nit-publikirte briv fun Sholem-Aleichemen." *Filologishe shriftn [fun YIVO]* 3 (1929), 153–72.

[Letters.] "Fun Sholem-Aleichems nit-farefntlekhte briv." *Sovetishe literatur* 3–4 (March-April 1939), 269–78.

[Letters.] "Sholem-Aleichem's arkhiv." *Der tog* (1923–24). In the archives of the Beit Sholem Aleichem in Tel Aviv.

Mayses un monologn. In *Ale verk*. Vol. 13. Warsaw: Progress, 1913.

Menakhem-Mendl. In *Ale verk fun Sholem Aleichem*. New York: Folksfond Edition, 1917–23, vol. 10.

Monologn. In *Ale verk fun Sholem Aleichem*. New York: Folksfond Edition, 1917–23, vol. 21.

Motl peysi dem khazn's. In *Ale verk fun Sholem Aleichem*. New York: Folksfond Edition, 1917–23, vol. 18.

Di nayste verk fun Sholem Aleichem. Vols. 1–3. Warsaw: Progress, 1909.

Oyf vos badarfn yudn a land? Etlekhe ernste verter far'n folk. Warsaw: Shuldberg, 1898.

Oysgeveylte briv. In *Oysgeveylte verk*. Vol. 16. Moscow: Der emes, 1941.

Oysgeveylte verk. Ed. Abraham Frumkin. Vols. 1–16. Moscow: Der emes, 1935–41.

Oysgeveylte verk. Ed. Aron Vergelis. Moscow: Melukhe farlag fun kinstlerisher literatur, 1959.

Reb Sender Blank un zayn fulgeshetste familie: a roman on a libe. St. Petersburg: Israel Levi, 1888.

[Esther, pseud.] "Di rusishe kritik vegn dem yudishn zhargon." In *Di yudishe folks-bibliotek* 1 (1888), 454–58.

Sender Blank un zayn gezindl, in *Ale verk fun Sholem Aleichem.* New York: Folksfond Edition, 1917–23, vol. 11.

"Shimele." *Ha-'asif* 5 (1889), 47–61.

Sholem Aleichem's ale verk. Vols. 1–4. Warsaw: Folksbildung, 1903.

Shomers mishpet, oder der sud prisyazhnykh oyf ale romanen fun Shomer. Berditchev: Jacob Sheftil, 1888.

"Stantsie Mazepevke! (felyeton)." *Der hoyz-fraynd* 3 (1894), 321–26.

Stempenyu. In *Ale verk fun Sholem Aleichem.* New York: Folksfond Edition, 1917–23, vol. 11.

"Dos tepl (monolog)." Warsaw: Bikher-far-ale, 1905.

"Tevye der milkhiker." *Der hoyz-fraynd* 4 (1895), 63–80.

"Tsu unzere shvester in Zion." Warsaw: Shuldberg, 1898.

Tuvia ha-cholev. In *Kitvei Sholem-Aleichem.* Warsaw: Ha-shachar, 1911, vol. 1.

Yaknehoz. Kiev: Sheftil, 1894

Yosele solovey. In *Ale verk fun Sholem Aleichem.* New York: Folksfond Edition, 1917–23, vol. 14.

Di yudishe folks-bibliotek 1–2 (1888–89).

Der yudisher kongres in Basel. Warsaw: Shuldberg, 1897.

3. Isaac Leybush Peretz

"'Af 'al pi she-chatta yisra'el hu." *Ha-'asif* 3 (1886), 620–27.

Ale verk. Vols. 1–11. New York: CYCO, 1947–48.

Ale verk. Vols. 1–10. Warsaw: Progress, 1909–13.

Ale verk fun I. L. Peretz. Vols. 1–18. Vilna: Kletzkin, 1925–29.

"Der alter reb Shimon." *Der yud* 4 (1902), numbers 42–43, 4–6.

"Az men zogt meshuge—gleyb!" *Yontev bletlekh: Tammuz* (1895–96), 38–54. In *Ale verk fun I. L. Peretz* (CYCO). Vol. 4.

Baynakht oyfn altn mark. Warsaw: Bikher-far-ale, 1907.

"Be-'agaf ha-meshuga'im." *Ha-tzefirah* (1896), 948, 952, 962–63.

"Be-ma'on kayitz (tziur)." *Achiasaf* 1 (1893), 39–42.

Bilder fun a provints-rayze. In *Ale verk fun I. L. Peretz* (CYCO). Vol. 2.

Bletlekh: zhurnal far literatur, gezelshaft, un ekonomiye. Reprint of *Yontev bletlekh* [1894–96]. Warsaw: Progress, 1913.

"Bontshe shvayg." In *Ale verk fun I. L. Peretz* (CYCO). Vol. 2.

Briv un redes fun I. L. Peretz. 2d ed. Ed. Nachman Mayzel. New York: YKUF, 1944.

Ha-chetz: yalkut sifruti. Warsaw: Shvartsberg, 1894.

"Ha-dibuk ve-ha-meshuga'." *Ha-'asif* 3 (1886), 627–33.

"Der feter Shakhne un di mume Yakhne." *Di yudishe bibliotek* 3 (1895), 42–50.

"Hitztadkut ha-ne'esham." *Ha-'asif* 3 (1886), 633–36.

In keler-shtub: dertseylungen. Ed. Rivke Rubin. Moscow: Melukhe-farlag, 1959.

"Ha-kadish." *Ha-yom* 1 (1886), number 14, 2–3.

"A kas fun a yidene." *Di yudishe bibliotek* 3 (1895), 35–41.

Ketavim. Vols. 1–4. Warsaw: Toshia, 1899–1901.

Ketavim chadashim. Warsaw: Aviv, 1909.

Khasidish. Vilna: Kletzkin, 1925.

"Der khelmer melamed." *Di yudishe folks-bibliotek* 2 (1889), 126–29.

Kitvei I. L. Peretz. Vols. 1–10. Tel Aviv: Dvir, 1924–27. [Vols. 1–2 published in Berlin and Jerusalem.]

Kitvei I. L. Peretz. 2d. ed. Vols. 1–10. Tel Aviv: Dvir, 1934.

Kleyne ertseylungen: tsvey bilder. Ed. Isaac Guido. Vilna: Guido, 1894.

Kleyne mayses far groyse mentshn. Warsaw: Halter, 1894.

"A klezmer toyt." *Di yudishe bibliotek* 2 (1892), 41–44.

Kol kitvei I. L. Peretz. Vols 1–10. Ed. and trans. Shimshon Meltzer. Tel Aviv: Dvir, 1947–62.

"Dos kranke yingl." In *Ale verk fun I. L. Peretz* (CYCO). Vol. 2.

"Leil zeva'ah." *Ha-'asif* 6 (1893), 136–46.

Literatur un lebn: a zaml-bukh far literatur un gezelshaft. Warsaw: Funk, 1894.

"Manginot ha-zman." *Ha-'asif* 3 (1886), 718–31.

"Ha-machshavah ve-ha-kinor (hagadah 'aravit)." In *Ha-chetz: yalkut sifruti.* Ed. I. L. Peretz. Warsaw: Shvartsberg, 1894, pp. 16–29.

Mayne zikhroynes. Vilna: Kletzkin, ca. 1913.

"Mayse'lekh fun dulhoyz." *Yontev bletlekh,* second series (1895), number 3, 7–23. In *Ale verk fun I. L. Peretz* (CYCO). Vol. 2.

"Ha-mekubbalim (sippur)," *Gan perachim* 3 (1891), 83–85.

"Mekubolim." *Yontev bletlekh,* first series (1894), number 4, 3–14. In *Ale verk fun I. L. Peretz* (CYCO). Vol. 4.

"Mendl Braynes." *Di yudishe bibliotek* 2 (1892), 26–34.

"Meshiekh's tsaytn." *Yidisher folkskalender.* Vol. 6. Ed. Gershom Bader. Lemberg: Zupnik, 1900–1901.

"Der meshugener batlen." In *Bakante bilder.* Ed. Yankev Dinezon. Warsaw: Boymriter, 1890. Reprinted in *Ale verk fun I. L. Peretz* (CYCO). Vol. 2.

"Meshugoyim." In *Ale verk fun I. L. Peretz* (CYCO). Vol. 4.

"Der meshulekh." In *Bakante bilder.* Ed. Yankev Dinezon. Warsaw: Boymriter, 1890. Reprinted in *Ale verk fun I. L. Peretz* (CYCO). Vol. 2.

"Mikhtavim le-Mikha Yosef Berdichevsky." *Moznaim* 8 (1939), 93–95.

"Mishnas khasidim." In *Der yud* 4 (1902), number 19, 11–14.

"Mishnat chasidim." In *Ha-chetz: yalkut sifruti*. Ed. I. L. Peretz. Warsaw: Shvartsberg, 1894, pp. 35–41.
"Neila." *Der hoyz-fraynd* 3 (1894), 101–10.
"Oyb nisht nokh hekher." *Der yud* 2 (1900), number 1, 12–13.
"Oyb nisht nokh hekher." In *Ale verk fun I. L. Peretz* (CYCO). Vol. 4.
Oysgeveylte verk. Vols. 1–2. Ed. Rivka Rubin. Moscow: Der emes, 1941.
Poezie. Vols. 1–2. Warwaw: Shuldberg, 1892.
"A shnayderisher purim." *Der yud* 3 (1901), number 9, 5–11.
Shriftn. Vols. 1–2. Warsaw: Halter, 1901.
"Dos shtrayml." In *Literatur un lebn: a zaml-bukh far literatur un gezelshaft*. Ed. I. L. Peretz. Warsaw: Funk, 1894. Reprinted in *Ale verk fun I. L. Peretz* (CYCO). Vol. 2.
Dos shtrayml. Warsaw: Halter, 1896.
"Di toyte shtot." In *Ale verk fun I. L. Peretz* (CYCO). Vol. 2.
"Tsvishn tsvey berg." In *Ale verk fun I. L. Peretz* (CYCO). Vol. 4.
"Venus un Shulames." *Di yudishe folks-bibliotek* 2 (1889), 142–47.
"Venus ve-Shulamit (zeh le-'umat zeh)." *Gan perachim* 2 (1890), 122–27.
"Vos hert zikh." *Di yudishe bibliotek* 2 (1892), 5–10.
"Vos heyst 'neshome.'" In *Bakante bilder*. Ed. Yankev Dinezon. Warsaw: Boymriter, 1890. Reprinted in *Ale verk fun I. L. Peretz* (CYCO). Vol. 2.
"Yenkl pesimist." *Di yudishe folks-bibliotek* 2 (1889), 136–38.
"Yitskhok'l shoykhet." *Der yud* 1 (1899), number 1, 10–11.
"Yokhanan Melamed's mayselekh." In *Ale verk fun I. L. Peretz* (CYCO). Vol. 4.
Yontev bletlekh. Two series (1894–95, 1895–96).
Yudish: a zamelbukh. Vols. 1–2. Warsaw: Progress, 1910–13.
Di yudishe bibliotek 1–3 (1891–95).
Di yudishe bibliotek. New series, 1 (1904).

C. ENGLISH TRANSLATIONS

1. S. Y. Abramovitsh

"Burned Out." Trans. Jeffrey M. Green. In *The Literature of Destruction: Jewish Responses to Catastrophe*. Ed. David. G. Roskies. Philadelphia: The Jewish Publication Society, 1988, pp. 136–44.
"The Calf." Trans. Jacob Sloan. In *A Treasury of Yiddish Stories*. 2d ed. Ed. Irving Howe and Eliezer Greenberg. New York: Penguin, 1990, pp. 97–111.
Fishke the Lame. Trans. Gerald Stillman. New York: Thomas Yoseloff, 1960. Reprinted in *Selected Works of Mendele Moykher-Sforim*. Ed.

Marvin Zuckerman, Gerald Stillman, Marion Herbst. Malibu, Calif.: Joseph Simon/Pangloss Press, 1991, pp. 171–312.

The Little Man. Trans. Gerald Stillman. In *Selected Works of Mendele Moykher-Sforim.* Ed. Marvin Zuckerman, Gerald Stillman, Marion Herbst. Malibu, Calif.: Joseph Simon/Pangloss Press, 1991, pp. 53–167.

The Mare. Trans. Joachim Neugroschel. In *The Great Works of Jewish Fantasy and Occult.* Woodstock, N.Y.: Overlook Press, 1987, pp. 545–663.

The Nag. Trans. Moshe Spiegel. New York: Beechhurst Press, 1955.

"Notes for My Biography." Trans. Gerald Stillman. In *Selected Works of Mendele Moykher-Sforim.* Ed. Marvin Zuckerman, Gerald Stillman, Marion Herbst. Malibu, Calif.: Joseph Simon/Pangloss Press, 1991.

Of Bygone Days. Trans. Raymond P. Sheindlin. In *A Shtetl and Other Yiddish Novellas.* 2d ed. Ed. Ruth R. Wisse. Detroit: Wayne State University Press, 1986.

The Parasite. [*The Little Man.*] Trans. Gerald Stillman. New York: Thomas Yoseloff, 1956.

Selected Works of Mendele Moykher-Sforim. In *The Three Great Classic Writers of Modern Yiddish Literature.* Vol. 1. Ed. Marvin Zuckerman, Gerald Stillman, Marion Herbst. Trans. Gerald Stillman et al. Malibu, Calif.: Joseph Simon/Pangloss Press, 1991.

"Shem and Japheth on the Train." Trans. Walter Lever. In *Modern Hebrew Literature.* Ed. Robert Alter. New York: Behrman, 1975, pp. 19–38.

The Travels and Adventures of Benjamin the Third. Trans. Moshe Spiegel. New York: Schocken, 1968.

The Travels of Benjamin the Third. Trans. Joachim Neugroschel. In *The Shtetl.* Woodstock, N.Y.: Overlook Press, 1989, pp. 179–264.

"The Wandering of a Soul." Trans. Joachim Neugroschel. In *The Great Works of Jewish Fantasy and Occult.* Woodstock, N.Y.: Overlook Press, 1987, pp. 21–30.

2. Sholem Aleichem

The Adventures of Mottel: The Cantor's Son. Trans. Tamara Kahana. New York: Collier, 1961.

The Adventures of Menahem-Mendl. Trans. Tamara Kahana. New York: Paragon, 1979.

The Best of Sholem Aleichem. Ed. Irving Howe and Ruth R. Wisse. Washington, D.C.: New Republic Books, 1979.

The Bewitched Tailor. Trans. Bernard Isaacs. Moscow: Foreign Languages Publishing House, 1958.

"Chava." Trans. Frances Butwin. In *The Best of Sholem Aleichem.* Ed.

Irving Howe and Ruth R. Wisse. Washington, D.C.: New Republic Books, 1979, pp. 165–78.

Collected Stories of Sholom Aleichem. Trans. Julius and Frances Butwin. Vols. 1–2. New York: Crown, 1965.

"A Consultation." Trans. Moshe Spiegel. In *Sholem Aleichem Panorama.* Ed. M. W. Grafstein. London: Jewish Observer, 1948.

"Eternal Life." Trans. Saul Bellow. In *A Treasury of Yiddish Stories.* 2d ed. Ed. Irving Howe and Eliezer Greenberg. New York: Penguin, 1990, pp. 151–68.

Favorite Tales of Sholom Aleichem. Trans. Julius and Frances Butwin. New York: Avenel, 1983.

From the Fair: The Autobiography of Sholem Aleichem. Trans. Curt Leviant. New York: Viking, 1985.

The Great Fair: Scenes from My Childhood. Trans. Tamara Kahana. New York: Collier, 1970.

"Hodel." Trans. Julius and Frances Butwin. In *A Treasury of Yiddish Stories.* 2d ed. Ed. Irving Howe and Eliezer Greenberg. New York: Penguin, 1990, pp. 168–82.

Inside Kasrilevke. Trans. Isidore Goldstick. New York: Schocken, 1965.

The Jackpot. Trans. Kobi Weitzner and Barnett Zumoff. New York: Workmen's Circle Education Department, 1989.

Jewish Children. Trans. Hannah Berman. New York: Bloch, 1937.

"Joseph." Trans. and ed. Golda Werman. *Fiction* 11 (1992), 137–48.

"The Little Pot." Trans. Frances Butwin. In *Tevye's Daughters.* Trans. Julius and Frances Butwin. New York: Crown, 1949.

The Nightingale: Or, The Saga of Yosele Solovey the Cantor. Trans. Aliza Shevrin. New York: New American Library, 1987.

The Old Country. Trans. Julius and Frances Butwin. New York: Crown, 1946.

Old Country Tales. Trans. Curt Leviant. New York: G. P. Putnam's Sons, 1966.

"On Account of a Hat." Trans. Isaac Rosenfeld. In *A Treasury of Yiddish Stories.* 2d ed. Ed. Irving Howe and Eliezer Greenberg. New York: Penguin, 1990, pp. 111–18.

Selected Stories of Sholom Aleichem. Trans. Julius and Frances Butwin, Isaac Rosenfeld, and Shlomo Katz. New York: Modern Library, 1956.

Sholem Aleichem Panorama. Ed. M. W. Grafstein. London, Ontario: Jewish Observer, 1948.

Some Laughter, Some Tears: Tales from the Old World and the New. Trans. Curt Leviant. New York: Paragon, 1979.

Stempeniu: A Jewish Romance. Trans. Joachim Neugroschel. In *The Shtetl.* Woodstock, N.Y.: Overlook Press, 1989, pp. 287–375.

Stempenyu. Trans. Hannah Berman. London: Methuen, 1913.

Stories and Satires. Trans. Curt Leviant. New York: Thomas Yoseloff, 1959.

Tevye the Dairyman and Other Stories. Trans. Miriam Katz. Moscow: Raduga, 1988.

Tevye the Dairyman and the Railroad Stories. Trans. Hillel Halkin. New York: Schocken Books, 1987.

The Tevye Stories and Others. Trans. Julius and Frances Butwin. New York: Pocket Books, 1965.

Tevye's Daughters. Trans. Frances Butwin. New York: Crown, 1949.

"Three Widows." Trans. Curt Leviant. In *Stories and Satires.* New York: Thomas Yoseloff, 1963, pp. 182–213.

Wandering Stars. Trans. Frances Butwin. New York: Crown, 1952.

Why Do the Jews Need a Land of Their Own? Trans. Joseph Leftwich and Mordecai S. Chertoff. New York: Cornwall Books, 1984.

"Yosif." Trans. Miriam Katz. In *Tevye the Dairyman and Other Stories.* Moscow: Raduga, 1988, pp. 374–96.

3. I. L. Peretz

"Advice to the Estranged." Trans. Nathan Halper. In *Voices from the Yiddish: Essays, Memoirs, Diaries.* Ed. Irving Howe and Eliezer Greenberg. New York: Schocken, 1975, pp. 19–21.

"And Maybe Even Higher" in *Selected Stories: Bilingual Edition.* Selected and ed. Itche Goldberg and Eli Katz. Trans. Eli Katz. New York: Zhitlowsky Foundation for Jewish Culture, 1991, pp. 270–81.

As Once We Were: Selections from the Works of I. L. Peretz. Trans. Elly T. Margolis. Los Angeles: Peretz Translations Committee, 1951.

"Between Two Mountains." Trans. Goldie Morgentaler. In *The I. L. Peretz Reader.* Ed. Ruth R. Wisse. New York: Schocken, 1990, pp. 184–95.

"Between Two Mountains (Between the Rabbi of Brisk and the Rebbe of Byàle): A Simchas Torah Tale Told by an Old Teacher." Trans. Helena Frank. In Isaac Loeb Perez, *Stories and Pictures.* Philadelphia: Jewish Publication Society, 1906, pp. 429–46.

"Between Two Peaks." Trans. Nathan Halper. In *Selected Stories.* Ed. Irving Howe and Ruth Wisse. New York: Schocken, 1975, pp. 83–95.

Bontshe the Silent [and other stories]. Trans. A. S. Rappoport. Reprint of 1927 ed. Freeport, New York: Books for Libraries, 1971.

"Bontsha the Silent." Trans. Hilde Abel. In *A Treasury of Yiddish Stories.* 2d ed. Ed. Irving Howe and Eliezer Greenberg. New York: Penguin, 1990, pp. 223–30.

"Bontshe Shvayg." Trans. Hillel Halkin. In *The I. L. Peretz Reader.* Ed. Ruth R. Wisse. New York: Schocken, 1990, pp. 146–52.

"Bontshe Shvayg." Trans. Eli Katz. In *Selected Stories: Bilingual Edition.*

Selected and ed. Itche Goldberg and Eli Katz. Trans. Eli Katz. New York: Zhitlowsky Foundation for Jewish Culture, 1991, pp. 192–213.

"Bontzye Shweig." Trans. Helena Frank. In Isaac Loeb Perez, *Stories and Pictures*. Philadelphia: Jewish Publication Society, 1906, pp. 171–81.

The Book of Fire. Trans. Joseph Leftwich. New York: Thomas Yoseloff, 1960.

"Buntcheh the Silent." In *In This World and the Next: Selected Writings*. Trans. Moshe Spiegel. New York: Thomas Yoseloff, 1958, pp. 58–65.

"The Cabalists." In *In This World and the Next: Selected Writings*. Trans. Moshe Spiegel. New York: Thomas Yoseloff, 1958, pp. 171–75.

"Cabalists." Trans. Shlomo Katz. In *A Treasury of Yiddish Stories*. 2d ed. Ed. Irving Howe and Eliezer Greenberg. New York: Penguin, 1990, pp. 219–23.

"Cabbalists." In *Peretz*. Trans. and ed. Sol Liptzin. New York: YIVO, 1947, 224–33.

"Concerning History." Trans. Joseph Leftwich. In *The Way We Think: A Collection of Essays from the Yiddish*. Vol. 1. New York: Thomas Yoseloff, 1969, pp. 46–51.

"Devotion Without End." Trans. Irving Howe and Eliezer Greenberg. In *A Treasury of Yiddish Stories*. 2d ed. Ed. Irving Howe and Eliezer Greenberg. New York: Penguin, 1990, pp. 118–48.

"Hope and Fear." Trans. Nathan Halper. In *Voices from the Yiddish: Essays, Memoirs, Diaries*. Ed. Irving Howe and Eliezer Greenberg. New York: Schocken, 1975, pp. 22–24.

"If Not Higher." Trans. Helena Frank. In Isaac Loeb Perez, *Stories and Pictures*. Philadelphia: Jewish Publication Society, 1906, pp. 13–18.

"If Not Higher." In *Peretz*. Trans. and ed. Sol Liptzin. New York: YIVO, 1947, pp. 174–81.

"If Not Higher." Trans. Marie Syrkin. In *A Treasury of Yiddish Stories*. 2d ed. Ed. Irving Howe and Eliezer Greenberg. New York: Penguin, 1990, pp. 231–33.

"If Not Higher. . . ." In *In This World and the Next: Selected Writings*. Trans. Moshe Spiegel. New York: Thomas Yoseloff, 1958, pp. 76–79.

The I. L. Peretz Reader. Ed. Ruth R. Wisse. New York: Schocken, 1990.

"Impressions of a Journey Through the Tomaszow Region." Trans. Milton Himmelfarb. In *The I. L. Peretz Reader*. Ed. Ruth R. Wisse. New York: Schocken, 1990.

In This World and the Next: Selected Writings. Trans. Moshe Spiegel. New York: Thomas Yoseloff, 1958.

"Kabbalists." Trans. Helena Frank. In Isaac Loeb Perez, *Stories and Pictures*. Philadelphia: Jewish Publication Society, 1906, pp. 213–19.

"The Mad Talmudist." Trans. Irving Howe and Eliezer Greenberg. In *A Treasury of Yiddish Stories*. 2d ed. Ed. Irving Howe and Eliezer Greenberg. New York: Penguin, 1990, pp. 234–42.

"The Messenger." Trans. Helena Frank. In Isaac Loeb Perez, *Stories and Pictures*. Philadelphia: Jewish Publication Society, 1906, pp. 101–13.

"The Messenger." In *In This World and the Next: Selected Writings*. Trans. Moshe Spiegel. New York: Thomas Yoseloff, 1958, pp. 176–85.

"Monish." Trans. Seymour Levitan. In *The Penguin Book of Modern Yiddish Verse*. Ed. Irving Howe, Ruth R. Wisse, and Khone Shmeruk. New York: Viking, 1987, pp. 52–81.

My Memoirs. Trans. Fred Goldberg. New York: Citadel, 1964.

Peretz. [Bilingual edition.] Trans. and ed. Sol Liptzin. New York: YIVO, 1947.

"Roads That Lead Away from Jewishness." Trans. Joseph Leftwich. In *The Way We Think: A Collection of Essays from the Yiddish*. Vol. 1. New York: Thomas Yoseloff, 1969, pp. 36–46.

Selected Stories. Ed. Irving Howe and Eliezer Greenberg. New York: Schocken, 1975.

Selected Stories: Bilingual Edition. Selected and ed. Itche Goldberg and Eli Katz. Trans. Eli Katz. New York: Zhitlowsky Foundation for Jewish Culture, 1991.

Stories and Pictures. Trans. Helena Frank. Philadelphia: Jewish Publication Society, 1906. Reprint. New York: Gordon Press, n.d.

The Three Canopies. Trans. Tehilla Feinerman. New York: Shoulson Press, 1948.

"Three Gifts." Trans. Hillel Halkin. In *The I. L. Peretz Reader*. Ed. Ruth R. Wisse. New York: Schocken, 1990, pp. 222–30.

Three Gifts and Other Stories. Trans. Henry Goodman. New York: Book League of the Jewish Peoples Fraternal Order, 1947.

"What Is Missing in Our Literature." Trans. Joseph Leftwich. In *The Way We Think: A Collection of Essays from the Yiddish*. Vol. 1. New York: Thomas Yoseloff, 1969, pp. 31–36.

"What Is the Soul?" Trans. Helena Frank. In Isaac Loeb Perez, *Stories and Pictures*. Philadelphia: Jewish Publication Society, 1906, pp. 117–32.

"What Is the Soul? The Story of a Young Man." Trans. Michael Stern. In *The I. L. Peretz Reader*. Ed. Ruth R. Wisse. New York: Schocken, 1990, pp. 93–104.

"What Our Literature Needs." Trans. Nathan Halper. In *Voices from the Yiddish: Essays, Memoirs, Diaries*. Ed. Irving Howe and Eliezer Greenberg. New York: Schocken, 1975, pp. 25–31.

D. SECONDARY LITERATURE

1. S. Y. Abramovitsh

Abramovitsh, Nadiezhda. "Sholem-Aleichem un Mendele Moykher Sforim (zikhroynes fun Mendeles tokhter)." *Sovetish* 12 (1941), 264–71.

――――. *Der zeyde tsvishn eygene un fremde.* Warsaw: Kultur-lige, 1928.

Abtshuk, A. *Mendele Moykher Sforim.* Kiev: Kultur-lige, 1927.

Bal Makhshoves [Isidor Eliashev]. "Mendele, Grandfather of Yiddish Literature." [Excerpt.] Trans. Ronald Sanders. In *Voices from the Yiddish: Essays, Memoirs, Diaries.* Ed. Irving Howe and Eliezer Greenberg. New York: Schocken, 1975, pp. 32–40.

Ger Tsedek [Bal Makhshoves]. "Sholem Yankev Abramovitsh (Mendele Moykher Sforim)." In Bal Makhshoves [Isidor Eliashev], *Geklibene shriftn.* Vol. 1. Warsaw: Kletzkin, 1929, pp. 34–69. Originally published in *Di yudishe familie* 2 (1902), 103–15, 164–73, 207–11.

Bartana, Ortzion. *Mendele Moykher Sforim: ʿiyyun bikorti be-mikhlol yetzirato shel Abramovitsh.* Tel Aviv: Dekel Academic Press, 1979.

Ben-Yeshurun, Y. "Hashpaʿat ha-proza ha-rusit ʿal Mendele." *ʿOrlogin* 7 (January 1953), 216–19.

Bialik, H. N. "Mendele's *nusach.*" In *Ale verk Mendele Moykher Sforim (S. Y. Abramovitsh).* Vol. 17: *Kritik iber Mendele Moykher Sforim* (Cracow: Farlag Mendele, 1911), pp. 151–55.

Binshtok, Leon. "A Celebration of Yiddish Literature: Solomon Moiseevitsh Abramovitsh and His Twenty-Fifth Year of Literary Activity" [Russian]. *Voskhod* 12 (1884), 1–32. Unpublished translation by Jack Blanshei.

Blum, Ze'ev [Binyamin Makhlin]. *Dem zeydns kroyn.* Tel Aviv: Peretz farlag, 1978.

Dubilet, M. "Viazoy hot gearbet Mendele Moykher-Sforim." *Farmest* 1 (January 1936), 149–71.

[Essays on Abramovitsh.] In *Kol kitvei Mendele Moykher Sforim.* Vol. 7. Berlin: Moriah, 1922.

Eynhorn, David. "Mendele bay der arbet." In *Zikhroynes vegn Mendelen.* In *Ale verk fun Mendele Moykher-Sforim.* Vol. 20. Ed. Nachman Mayzel. Warsaw: Farlag Mendele, 1928, pp. 55–86.

Frishman, David. "Mendele Moykher-Sforim (Sholem Yankev Abramovitsh): toldotav, ʿarkho ve-sfarav." In *Kol kitvei Mendele Moykher-Sforim*. Odessa: Vaʿad ha-yovel, 1911, vol. 2, pp. iii–xxix.

Gottlober, A. B. "Zikhroynes (erinerungen iber yidishe shrayber un sforim)." In *Di yudishe folks-bibliotek* 1 (1888), 250–55.

Gross, Moyshe. *Mendele Moykher Sforim*. Vienna: Der Kval, 1920.

Gurshteyn, A. "Sakhaklen fun der Mendele-forshung." In *Tsaytshrift* 2–3 (1928), 485–524.

———. "Vegn ʿShloyme reb Khaims.'" In Abramovitsh's *Gezamlte verk*. Vol. 6. Moscow: Der emes, 1935.

———. "Der yunger Mendele in kontekst fun di 60er yorn (shtrikhn)." In *Shriftn* 1 (1928), 180–98. Reprinted in *Di yidishe literatur in nayntsetn yorhundert: zamlung fun yidisher literatur-forshung un kritik in ratn-farband*. Ed. Chone Shmeruk and Chava Turniansky. Jerusalem: Magnes, 1993, pp. 485–510.

Hrushavski [Harshav], Benjamin. "50 shana le-moto shel Mendele Moykher Sforim." With a facsimile of Abramovitsh's revisions of *The Travels of Benjamin the Third*. *Ha-sifrut* 1 (1968), 63–65.

Kaufman, Dalia. "Mendele Moykher Sforim be-vrit ha-moʿatzot (1917–1948): bibliografia." *Kiryath sefer* 50, number 3 (June 1975), 497–516.

Klauzner, Joseph. *Historia shel ha-sifrut ha-ʿivrit ha-chadashah: shiʿurim*. Vol. 6. *Mendele Moykher-Sforim*. Jerusalem: Achiasaf, 1958.

———. "Pirkei-Mendele." *Metsudah* 7 (1954), 347–56.

Kritik iber Mendele Moykher Sforim. In *Ale verk fun Mendele Moykher Sforim (S. Y. Abramovitsh)*. Jubilee edition. Vol. 17. Cracow: Farlag Mendele, 1911.

Kurzweil, Baruch. "ʿOlamo ha-epi shel Mendele." In *Sifrutenu ha-chadashah—hemshekh 'o mahapekha?* Tel Aviv: Schocken, 1959.

Lansky, Aaron. "Artistic Voice and Implicit Social Theory in the Early Yiddish Fiction of Mendele Moykher Sforim." M.A. thesis, McGill University, 1980.

[Letters of S. Y. Abramovitsh.] In *Shriftn* 1 (1928). Reprinted in *Dos Mendele bukh*. Ed. Nachman Mayzel. New York: YKUF, 1959.

Litvak, A. *Literatur un kamf*. New York, 1933.

Luria, Shalom. "Ha-lashon ha-figurativit bi-yetzirato ha-du-leshonit shel Mendele Moykher Sforim." Ph.D. diss., Hebrew University of Jerusalem, 1977.

———. "Sippuro ha-rish'on shel Mendele Moykher Sforim," in Mendele Moykher Sforim, *Ha-'ishon ha-katan*. Haifa: Haifa University Press, 1984.

Mani-Leyb. *Mendele Moykher Sforim (S. Y. Abramovitsh): biografie*. New York: Mendele Jubilee Committee, 1936.

Mayzel, Nachman. *Doyres un tekufes fun der yidisher literatur.* New York, 1942.

_____. "Di grenetsn tsvishn S. Y. Abramovitsh un Mendele Moykher Sforim." In *Dos Mendele bukh.* Ed. Nachman Mayzel. New York: YKUF, 1959, pp. 294–325.

_____. *Noente un vayte.* 2d ed. Vilna: Kletzkin, 1927–29.

Dos Mendele bukh. Ed. Nachman Mayzel. New York: YKUF, 1959

Mendele Moykher Sforim: reshimat ketavav ve-'iggrotav le-hatkanat mahaduratam ha-akademit. Jerusalem: Magnes, 1965.

Mendele un zayn tsayt: materialn tsu der geshikhte fun der yidisher literatur in XIX yorhundert. Moscow: Der emes, 1940.

Mezheritski, Z. "'Fishke der krumer' (shtil un kompozitsie)." *Di royte velt* 4 (1927), number 12, 104–28.

Miron, Dan. "'Arbaʿ heʿarot le-te'urei ha-tevaʿ be-ha-'avot ve-ha-banim le-Abramovitsh." *Moznayim,* new series, 28 (1969), 255–65.

_____. "'Ha-chinukh ha-sentimentali' shel Mendele Moykher Sforim," in Mendele Moykher Sforim [S. Y. Abramovitsh], *Sefer ha-kabtsanim* (Tel Aviv: Dvir, 1988).

_____. "Pirkei mavo' le-'Susati' le-Abramovitsh." *Ha-do'ar* (1972), number 36, 606–08. Continued as "'Sifriya li-meturafim'—ha-rekaʿ li-yetzirat 'Susati' le-Abramovitsh." *Ha-do'ar,* number 38, 682–83 and number 39, 698–99.

_____. *A Traveler Disguised: A Study in the Rise of Modern Yiddish Fiction in the Nineteenth Century.* New York: Schocken, 1973.

Miron, Dan, and Anita Norich. "The Politics of Benjamin III: Intellectual Significance and Its Formal Correlatives in Sh. Y. Abramovitsh's *Masoes Benyomin Hashlishi.*" In *The Field of Yiddish: Studies in Language, Folklore, and Literature.* Fourth Collection. Ed. Marvin I. Herzog, Barbara Kirshenblatt-Gimblett, Dan Miron, and Ruth Wisse. Philadelphia: Institute for the Study of Human Issues, 1980.

Mirski, M. *Problemen fun literatur un kritik.* Warsaw: Yidish bukh, 1953.

Niger, Shmuel. *Mendele Moykher Sforim: zayn lebn, zayne gezelshaftlekhe un literarishe oyftuungen.* Chicago:L. M. Stein, 1936.

_____. *Mendele Moykher Sforim.* New York: I. L. Peretz shrayber farayn, 1928.

Y. Nusinov. "Di ershte oysgabe fun 'Vintshfingerl.'" In *Shriftn* 1 (1928), 199–218. Reprinted in *Di yidishe literatur in nayntsetn yorhundert: zamlung fun yidisher literatur-forshung un kritik in ratn-farband.* Ed. Chone Shmeruk and Chava Turniansky. Jerusalem: Magnes, 1993, pp. 511–38.

_____. "Fun bukh tsu bukh (tsu der geshikhte fun di Mendele-variantn." *Tsaytshrift* 2–3 (1928), 424–85.

Oyslender, Nakhum. "Mendeles mitgeyer in di 60er–70er yorn." In *Mendele un zayn tsayt: materialn tsu der geshikhte fun der yidisher literatur in XIX yorhundert*. Moscow: Der emes, 1940, pp. 92–171. Reprinted in *Di yidishe literatur in nayntsetn yorhundert: zamlung fun yidisher literatur-forshung un kritik in ratn-farband*. Ed. Chone Shmeruk and Chava Turniansky. Jerusalem: Magnes, 1993, pp. 391–455.

Perry, Menachem. "Ha-analogia ve-mekoma be-mivne ha-roman shel Mendele Moykher Sforim." *Ha-sifrut* 1 (1968), 65–100.

Pines, M. "S. Y. Abramovitsh (Mendele Moykher Sforim)." In *Di geshikhte fun der yudisher literatur biz'n yor 1890*. Ed. Bal Makhshoves. Vol. 1. Warsaw: Shimin, 1911.

Pinsker, S. "Mendele: Hasidic Tradition and the Individual Artist." *Modern Language Quarterly* 30 (1969), 234–47.

Prilutsky, Noah. *Sholem-Yankev Abramovitsh*. Warsaw: Nayer farlag, 1920.

Reyzen, Zalman. *Dos lebn fun Mendele*. Vilna, 1918.

_____. *Fun Mendelssohn biz Mendele*. Warsaw: Kultur-lige, 1923.

Roskies, David G. "Broken Tablets and Flying Letters." In *Against the Apocalypse: Responses to Catastrophe in Modern Jewish Culture*. Cambridge, Mass.: Harvard University Press, 1984.

Shaked, Gershon. *Bein tzechok le-demaʿ: ʿiyyunim bi-yitzirato shel Mendele Moykher-Sforim*. Tel Aviv: Massada, 1965.

Shatzki, Yakov. *Geshikhte fun der yidn in Varshe*. Vol. 3. New York, 1953.

Shmeruk, Chone. "Baʿayot be-cheker ha-tekstim shel Mendele be-yidish (yetzirato shel Mendele min ha-machatzit ha-rish'onah shel shnot ha-shivʿim." *Divrei ha-kongres ha-ʿolami ha-reviʿi le-m'daʿei ha-yahedut* (1969). Vol. 2, 25–30.

_____. "Mendele's tilim-iberzetsungen." *Di goldene keyt* 62/63 (1968), 290–312.

Shneour, Zalman. *Fun dem "zeydns" kval*. Berlin: Klal farlag, 1922.

Sholem Aleichem. "Fir zenen mir gezesn." In SA 15: 111–86.

_____. "Oyto-da-fe." In SA 15: 31–40.

_____. "Vi sheyn iz der boym!" In SA 15: 21–28.

Szeintuch, Yechiel. "Sippurav ha-ketzarim shel Mendele Moykher Sforim ʿal nuscha'otehem: berur bibliografi ve-tekstologi." *Ha-sifrut* 1 (1968), 391–409.

Taʿarukhat Mendele Moykher Sforim (Sholem Yankev Abramovitsh) be-mele'at chamishim shana le-petirato: katalog. Jerusalem: Beit ha-sefarim ha-le'umi ve-ha-universita'i, 1967.

Tsitron, Sh. L. "Mendele der sprakhkinstler." In *Dray literarishe doyres: zikhroynes vegn yidishe shriftshteler*. Vol. 4. Warsaw: Achiasefer, 1928, pp. 35–45.

———. "Sholem Yankev Abramovitsh (Mendele Moykher-Sforim)." In *Dray literarishe doyres: zikhroynes vegn yidishe shriftshteler*. Vol. 2. Warsaw: Sreberk, 1921, pp. 105–26.

Verses, Shmuel. "Mendele Mokher-Seforim." In *Encyclopaedia Judaica*. Vol. 11, pp. 1317–23.

———. *Mi-Mendele ʿad Hazaz: sugiot be-hitpatchut ha-siporet ha-ʿivrit*. Jerusalem: Magnes Press, 1987.

"Di vikhtikste faktn un dates fun Mendeles lebn un shafn." New York: YIVO, 1936.

Viner, Meir. *Etyudn vegn Mendelen in di zekhtsiker un zibetsiker yorn*. Moscow: Der emes, 1935.

———. "Mendele Moykher-Sforim (tsum hundertstn yortog fun zayn geboyrn)." *Farmest* 1 (January 1936), 114–48.

———. *Tsu der geshikhte fun der yidisher literatur in 19-tn yorhundert (etyudn un materialn)*. Vol. 2. *Mendele Moykher Sforim, Sholem-Aleichem*. New York: YKUF, 1946.

Weinreich, Max. "Mendele-dokumentn." Compiled by Max Weinreich. *YIVO bleter* 10 (1936), 364–75.

———. "Mendeles ershte 25 yor." *YIVO bleter* 10 (1936), 167–80.

———. "Mendeles onheyb." In *Bilder fun der yidisher literaturgeshikhte: fun di onheybn biz Mendele Moykher Sforim*. Vilna: Tomor, 1928, pp. 330–51.

Wisse, Ruth R. *The Schlemiel as Modern Hero*. Chicago: University of Chicago Press, 1971.

Zikhroynes vegn Mendelen. In *Ale verk fun Mendele Moykher-Sforim*. Vol. 20. Ed. Nachman Mayzel. Warsaw: Farlag Mendele, 1928.

2. Sholem Aleichem

Abramovitsh, Nadiezhda. "Sholem-Aleichem un Mendele Moykher-Sforim (zikhroynes fun Mendeles tokhter)." *Sovetish* 12 (1941), 264–71.

Astro, Alan. "La Langue comme patchwork: *Le Tailleur ensorcelé* de Sholem-Aleichem." *Cahiers Confrontation* 16 (1986), 137–45.

Bechtel, Delphine. "America and the *Shtetl* in Sholem Aleichem's *Di goldgreber* [The golddiggers]." *Melus* 17, number 3 (Fall 1991–92), 69–84.

———. "Le chapeau fait-il le juif? Aspects de la poétique de Sholem Aleykhem." *Yod: Revue des études hébraïques et juives modernes et contemporaines*. Numbers 31–32: *Domaine Yiddish* (1990), 67–79.

Beilin, Osher. *Sholem-Aleichem*. Merchavia: Ha-kibbutz ha-ʾartzi ha-shomer ha-tzaʿir, 1945.

Bergelson, David. "Sholem Aleichem (tsum akhtsikstn yor fun zayn geboyrn." *Sovetishe literatur* 3–4 (March-April 1939), 65–78.

Berkovitsh, Y. D. *Ha-rishʾonim ki-vnei-adam: sippurei zikharonot ʿal Sholem-Aleichem u-vnei-doro*. 3d ed. Tel Aviv: Dvir, 1976.

Bilik, Dorothy. "Love in Sholem Aleykhem's Early Novels." *Working Papers in Yiddish and East European Jewish Studies* 10 (1975), pp. 1–20.

Borokhov, Ber. "Di bibliografie fun Sholem Aleichem." *Di tsukunft* 21 (1916), 721–23, 801–03, 893–95, 1062–64. Reprinted in Ber Borokhov's *Shprakh-forshung un literatur-geshikhte*. Ed. Nachman Mayzel. Tel Aviv: Peretz farlag, 1966.

Dimerman, Liubov. "Literary Functions of Slavicisms in the Works of Sholom Aleichem." M.A. thesis, University of Manitoba, 1968.

Dobin, S. "Sholem-Aleichem, vi ikh hob im gekent." *Sovetish* 12 (1941), 272–90.

Dobrushin, Y. "Sholem-Aleichem der humorist." *Tsum ondenk fun Sholem Aleichem: zamlbukh*. Ed. I. Zinberg and S. Niger. Petersburg: I. L. Peretz-fond, 1917, pp. 167–73.

Druker, I. *Sholem-Aleichem (kritishe etyudn)*. Kiev: Melukhe-farlag far di natsionale minderheytn in USSR, 1939.

Eilat, Eliahu. "Beit Sholem Aleichem: rede fun prezident fun yerushalaymer universitet oyf dem khanekes-habays." *Di goldene keyt* 56 (1966), 5–7.

Erik, M. "Vegn Sholem Aleichem's 'Ksovim fun a komivoyasher.'" *Visnshaft un revoliutsie* 3–4 (1935), 161–72.

Erlich, Victor. "A Note on the Monologue as a Literary Form: Sholem Aleichem's 'Monologn'—A Test Case." In *For Max Weinreich on his Seventieth Birthday*. The Hague: Mouton, 1964, pp. 44–50.

Finkl, Uri. *Sholem-Aleichem (monografie)*. Warsaw: Yidish bukh, 1959.

Frieden, Ken. "A Century in the Life of Sholem Aleichem's *Tevye*." *B. G. Rudolph Lectures in Judaic Studies*. Syracuse: Syracuse University Press, forthcoming.

———. "Sholem Aleichem: Monologues of Mastery." *Modern Language Studies* 19 (1989), 25–37.

Gurshteyn, A. "Sholem-Aleichems lebn un shafn." *Sovetishe literatur* 3–4 (March–April 1939), 187–217. Reprinted as *Sholem-Aleichem*. Moscow: Der emes, 1946.

Halberstam-Rubin, Anna. *Sholem Aleichem: The Writer as Social Historian*. New York: Peter Lang, 1989.

Hrushavski [Harshav], Benjamin. "Dekonstruktsia shel dibbur: Sholem-Aleichem ve-ha-semantika shel ha-folklor ha-yehudi." In Sholem Aleichem's *Tevye ha-chalban ve-monologim*. Trans. H. Benjamin [Harshav]. Tel Aviv: Siman kri'ah, 1983, pp. 195–212.

———. Forward to his trans. of Sholem Aleichem's "Shlosha monologim," "Perakim metokh Tevye ha-chalvan," and "Menachem-Mendl." *Ha-sifrut* 10 (1980), 188–89.

Klauzner, Israel. "Sholem-Aleichem der Hovev-Zion." *Di goldene keyt* 6 (Spring 1950), 198–208.

Kressel, G. *Sholem Aleichem: chayav u-yetzirato.* Tel Aviv: Dvir, 1959.

Mayzel, Nachman. "Peretz un Sholem-Aleichem in zeyere perzenlekhe batsiungen." *Filologishe shriftn [fun YIVO]* 1 (1926), 263–84.

_____. "Sholem-Aleichems briv tsu Yankev Dinezon." *YIVO bleter* 1 (1931), 385–403; *YIVO bleter* 2 (1931), 13–31; and *YIVO bleter* 3 (1932), 337–53.

_____. *Sholem Aleichem (tsu zayn 80stn geburtstog).* New York: Yiddish Cooperative Book League, 1939.

_____. *Undzer Sholem-Aleichem.* Warsaw: Yidish bukh, 1959.

Mendele un zayn tsayt: materialn tsu der geshikte fun der yidisher literatur in XIX yorhundert (Moscow: Der emes, 1940).

Miller, David Neal. "'Don't Force Me to Tell You the Ending': Closure in the Short Fiction of Sh. Rabinovitsh (Sholem-Aleykhem)." *Neophilologus* 66 (1982), 102–10.

_____. "Sholem Aleichem in English: The Most Accessible Translations." *Yiddish* 2 (Summer 1977), 61–70.

Miron, Dan. "Masaʿ beʾezor ha-dimdumim." Afterword to his trans. of Sholem Aleichem's *Sippurei rakevet.* Tel Aviv: Dvir, 1989, pp. 225–99.

_____. "Shalom Aleichem." In *Encyclopaedia Judaica.* Vol. 14. Jerusalem: Keter, 1971, pp. 1272–86.

_____. *Sholem Aleichem: pirkei masah.* Ramat-Gan: Massada, 1970. Reprinted as *Sholem Aleichem: masot meshulavot.* Ramat Gan: Massada, 1976.

_____. "Sholem Aleykhem: Person, Persona, Presence." *The Uriel Weinreich Memorial Lecture* 1. New York: YIVO Institute for Jewish Research, 1972.

Niger, Shmuel. "The Humor of Sholem Aleichem." In *Voices from the Yiddish: Essays, Memoirs, Diaries.* Ed. Irving Howe and Eliezer Greenberg. New York: Schocken, 1975.

_____. "Polemik un visnshaft." *Di yidishe velt* 7 (October 1928), 137–43.

_____. *Sholem Aleichem: zayne vikhtikste verk, zayn humor un zayn ort in der yidisher literatur.* New York: YKUF, 1928.

Norich, Anita. "Portraits of the Artist in Three Novels by Sholem Aleichem." *Prooftexts* 4 (1984), 237–51.

Novershtern, Avrom. "'Menakhem-Mendel' le-Sholem Aleichem: bein toldot ha-tekst le-mivne ha-yetzirah," *Tarbitz* 54 (1984), 105–46.

_____. "Sholem-Aleichem un zayn shtelung tsu der shprakhn-frage." *Di goldene keyt* 74 (1971), 164–88.

Oyslender, N. "Der yunger Sholem Aleichem un zayn roman 'Stempenyu.'" *Shriftn* 1 (1928), 1–72.

Ozick, Cynthia. "A Critic at Large: Sholem Aleichem's Revolution." *The New Yorker* (28 March 1988), 99–108.

Prilutsky, Noah. "Mekoyekh di kvaln fun Sholem-Aleichems humor." *Di yidishe velt* 4 (July 1928), 138–47.

Prooftexts 6 (1986), number 1. [Special Issue on "Sholem Aleichem: The Critical Tradition."]

Rabinovitsh, Volf (Vevik). *Mayn bruder Sholem Aleichem: zikhroynes.* Kiev: Melukhe-farlag far di natsionale minderheytn in USSR, 1939.

Raskin, Orn. "Der hebreisher variant fun 'Tevye dem milkhikn.'" *Sovetish heymland* 11 (1973), 155–62.

Ravnitsky, Y. H. "Di ershte yorn fun mayn bakantshaft mit Sholem Aleichem'en." In *Tsum ondenk fun Sholem Aleichem: zamlbukh.* Ed. I. Zinberg and S. Niger. Petersburg: I. L. Peretz-fond, 1917, 43–56.

Reminik, H. "Linetski un Sholem-Aleichem." *Shtern* 15 (1939), number 9, 80–90.

_____. "Sholem Aleichems literarish-kritishe tetikayt," *Sovetish* 12 (1941), 155–83.

Reminik, Y. "Sholem-Aleichem der novelist." *Sovetishe literatur* 3–4 (March-April 1939), 218–50.

Roskies, David G. "Laughing Off the Trauma of History." In *Against the Apocalypse: Responses to Catastrophe in Modern Jewish Culture.* Cambridge, Mass.: Harvard University Press, 1984, pp. 163–95.

_____. "Sholem Aleichem: Mythologist of the Mundane." *AJS Review: The Journal of the Association for Jewish Studies* 13 (1988), 27–46.

_____. "Sholem-Aleichems veg tsu zikh (tsu zayn finf un zibetsikstn yortsayt)," *Di goldene keyt* 132 (1991), 6–22.

_____. "Unfinished Business: Sholem Aleichem's *From the Fair,*" *Prooftexts* 6 (1986), 65–78.

Sadan, Dov. "Dray yesoydes." In *Heymishe ksovim: shrayber, bikher, problemen.* Tel Aviv: Ha-menorah, 1972, vol. 1, pp. 15–27.

_____. "K'mo she-katuv: araynfir-bamerkn tsu Tevye dem milkhiker's toyre." In *Tsvishn vayt un noent: eseyen, shtudies, briv.* Tel Aviv: Israel-bukh, 1982.

Samuel, Maurice. *The World of Sholem Aleichem.* New York: A. A. Knopf, 1943.

Shmeruk, Chone. Entry under "Sholem-Aleichem." In *Leksikon fun der nayer yidisher literatur.* Vol. 8. New York: CYCO, 1981, pp. 677–720.

_____. "Sholem-Aleichem in Amerike." *Di goldene keyt* 121 (1987), 56–77.

_____. *Sholem Aleichem: madrikh le-chayav u-li-yitzirato.* Tel Aviv: Ha-kibutz ha-me'uchad, 1980.

_____. "'Tevye der milkhiker'—le-toldoteha shel yetzira." *Ha-sifrut* 26 (April 1978), 26–38.

Shneour, Zalman. *Sholem-Aleichems ondenken.* Berlin: Klal farlag, 1922.

Dos Sholem-Aleichem bukh. Ed. Y. D. Berkovitsh. New York: Sholem-Aleichem bukh komitet, 1926.

Sholem-Aleichem: chayav be-temunot/zayn lebn in bild. Ed. Abraham Lis. Tel Aviv: Dvir, 1988.

Sholem Aleichem: me'a shana le-huledeto. Jerusalem: Keren kayemet, 1959.

Sholem Aleichem Panorama. Ed. Melech Grafstein. London, Ontario: The Jewish Observer, 1948.

Sholem Aleichem: A Source Book for Programming. Ed. Philip Goodman. New York: National Jewish Welfare Board, 1966.

Sovetish 12 (1941). [Sholem Aleichem volume.]

Sovetishe literatur 3–4 (March–April 1939). [Sholem Aleichem volume.]

Spivak, E. "Notitsn vegn Sholem-Aleichems sintaks." *Sovetishe literatur* 1 (January 1939), 150–64.

———. *Sholem-Aleichems shprakh un shtil: etyudn.* Kiev: Melukhe-farlag far di natsionale minderheytn in USSR, 1940.

Stern, Michael. "Quotations from Jewish Sources in Sholem Aleykhem's *Tevye der milkhiker.*" Unpublished manuscript, pp. 1–51.

———. "Tevye's Art of Quotation." *Prooftexts* 6 (1986), 79–96.

Trunk, Y. Y. *Sholem-Aleichem (zayn vezn un zayne verk).* Warsaw: Kultur-lige, 1937.

———. *"Tevye der milkhiker": shikzal un bitokhn.* Vilna: Tomor, 1939.

———. *Tevye un Menakhm-Mendl in yidishn velt goyrl.* New York: CYCO, 1944.

———. *Di yidishe proze in Poyln.* 1949.

Tsum ondenk fun Sholem Aleichem: zamlbukh. Ed. I. Zinberg and S. Niger. Petersburg: I. L. Peretz-fond, 1917.

Venrop, Z. "Etlekhe teg mit Sholem-Aleichemen (fragmentarishe zikhroynes)." *Sovetish* 12 (1941), 300–05.

Verses, Shmuel. "Sholem Aleichem." *Molad* (Sept.–Oct. 1959), 133–34, 404–21.

Viner, Meir. *Tsu der geshikhte fun der yidisher literatur in 19-tn yorhundert (etyudn un materialn).* Vol. 2. *Mendele Moykher Sforim, Sholem-Aleichem.* New York: YKUF, 1946.

Waife-Goldberg, Marie. *My Father, Sholem Aleichem.* New York: Schocken, 1971.

Weinreich, Uriel. "Literary Bibliographies." [Sholem Aleichem.] In *The Field of Yiddish: Studies in Yiddish Language, Folklore, and Literature.* Ed. Uriel Weinreich. New York: Linguistic Circle of New York, 1954, pp. 278–91.

Weitzner, Kobi. *Sholem Aleichem in the Theater.* Forthcoming.

Wirth-Nesher, Hana. "Voices of Ambivalence in Sholem Aleichem's Monologues." *Prooftexts* 1 (1981), 158–71.

Wisse, Ruth R. "Sholem Aleichem and the Art of Communication." *The B. G. Rudolph Lectures in Judaic Studies*. Syracuse: Syracuse University, 1980.

Wolitz, Seth. "The Americanization of Tevye or Boarding the Jewish *Mayflower*." *American Quarterly* 40 (1988), 514–36.

Yidishe kultur 5 (May 1946). [Issue on Sholem Aleichem.]

3. I. L. Peretz

'Al I. L. Peretz: divrei sofrim 'ivriim. Ed. S. Meltzer. Tel Aviv: Dvir, n.d.

An-ski, S. [Solomon Rapoport]. "Isaac Leybush Peretz (erinerungen)," *Di yidishe velt* 4 (1915), vol. 2, books 1–2 (April–May), 17–30.

Ash, Sholem. "I. L. Peretz." In *Di goldene keyt* 10 (1951), 48–54.

———. "Mayn ershte bakantshaft mit Peretz'n." *Di tsukunft* 20 (1915), number 5, 458–63.

———. "My First Meeting with Peretz." Trans. Moshe Spiegel. In *In This World and the Next: Selected Writings*. New York: Thomas Yoseloff, 1958, pp. 343–51.

Bal Makhshoves [Isidor Eliashev]. "I. L. Peretz." *Di yidishe velt* 4 (1915), vol. 2, books 1–2 (April–May), 31–42.

——— [Listed as J. Eliaschoff]. "Leon Perez: Ein moderner jüdischer Volksdichter." In *Ost und West* 1 (1901), 299–306.

Borokhov, Ber. "Di Peretz-bibliografie." In *I. L. Peretz: a zamlbukh tsu zayn ondenkn*. New York: Literarisher farlag, 1915, pp. 103–21.

Bergelson, David. "I. L. Peretz un di khasidishe ideologie." *Literarishe bleter* 2 (1925), numbers 49–50 (April), 3.

Bialeshtotski, B. *I. L. Peretz*. New York, 1940.

Bikls-Shpitser, Tsvi. "Di heroishe motivn in Peretz's shafn." *Di goldene keyt* 10 (1951), 66–82.

Briv un redes fun I. L. Peretz. Ed. Nachman Mayzel. New York: YKUF, 1944.

Buber, Martin. "I. L. Perez (Ein Wort zu seinem fünfundzwanzigjährigen Schriftsteller-Jubiläum)." *Die Welt* 5 (1901), number 18, 9.

Diner, P. *Di vortseln fun Peretz's shafn*. Warsaw: n.p., 1934.

Epelboym, B. "Unzerer (tsum finfyorikn yortsayt fun I. L. Peretz)." In *Tsum ondenk fun I. L. Peretz*. Odessa: Yidishe sektsye bam "gubnarobraz," 1920, pp. 7–11.

Epstein, Shakhne. *I. L. Peretz als sotsialer dikhter*. New York: M. N. Mayzel, 1916.

———. "I. L. Peretz un di yidishe arbeter." *Di tsukunft* 20 (1915), number 6, 539–43; continued as "Arbeter tipn bay I. L. Peretz." *Di tsukunft* 20 (1915), number 7, 655–58.

Frieden, Ken. "Psychological Depth in I. L. Peretz' *Familiar Scenes*." *Jewish Book Annual* 47 (1989–90), 145–51.

Glatstein, Jacob. "Peretz and the Jewish Nineteenth Century." In *Voices from the Yiddish: Essays, Memoirs, Diaries*. Ed. Irving Howe and Eliezer Greenberg. New York: Schocken, 1975, 51–63.

Goldberg, Avrom [David Frishman]. *A floy fun Tish'a b'Av: a shvarts, shpringendik, lebedik, baysendik bletl*. Warsaw: Shuldberg, 1894. *Di goldene keyt* 10 (1951). [Peretz volume.]

Goldsmith, Emanuel S. "Yitzkhok Leybush Peretz." In *Modern Yiddish Culture: The Story of the Yiddish Language Movement*. New York: Shapolsky, 1987, chapter 5.

Golomb, A. "I. L. Peretz un undzer kultur-gantskeyt." In *Di goldene keyt* 10 (1951), 86–90.

Gorin, B. [Isaac Guido]. "Isaac Leybush Peretz," *Di tsukunft* 16 (1911), number 7, 389–95.

———. "Warsaw and Odessa (Peretz un zayne ershte kritiker)." *Di tsukunft* 20 (1915), number 6, 548–52.

Grafstein, Melekh, ed. *I. L. Peretz*. Peretz Memorial Issue: Thirtieth Anniversary. *Jewish Observer* 4 (December 1945).

Gurshteyn, A. "Der itstiker tsushtand fun Peretzes biografie (vegn di farefntlekhte materialn far Peretzes biografie)." *Tsaytshrift* 1 (1926), 73–86.

I. L. Peretz: a zamelbukh tsu zayn ondenken. New York: Literarisher farlag, 1915.

I. L. Peretz in likht fun yidisher kritik. Parts 1–4. Vilna: Tsisho, 1940.

Jacobson, David Cortell. "The Recovery of Myth: A Study of Rewritten Hasidic Stories in Hebrew and Yiddish 1890–1910." Ph.D. diss., University of California, Los Angeles, 1977.

Jewish Observer 4 (1945). [Peretz Memorial Issue.]

Levin, Gershon. *Peretz: a bisl zikhroynes*. Warsaw: Yehudia, 1919.

Literarishe bleter 2 (10 April 1925), numbers 49–50. [Issue on I. L. Peretz.]

Mark, Yudel. *I. L. Peretz (1852–1915): His Life and Works*. Trans. J. Noskowitz. New York: Workmen's Circle, 1952.

———. "The Language of Y. L. Peretz." *YIVO Annual of Jewish Social Science* 4 (1949), 64–79.

Mayzel, Nachman. "Peretz un Sholem-Aleichem in zeyere perzenlekhe batsiungen." *Filologishe shriftn [fun YIVO]* 1 (1926), 263–84.

———. *Yitskhok Leybush Peretz un zayn dor shrayber*. New York: YKUF, 1951.

———. *I. L. Peretz: zayn lebn un shafn*. New York: YKUF, 1945.

Medem, V. "Peretz un mir." In *I. L. Peretz in likht fun yidisher kritik*. Part 4. Vilna: Tsisho, 1940, pp. 19–31.

Menachem [Goldberg]. "Mit Peretz'n (erinerungen)." In *I. L. Peretz: a zamlbukh tsu zayn ondenken.* New York: Literarisher farlag, 1915, pp. 21–37.

Mikhelzon, M. [Mikhl Rubinshteyn]. "Fun I. L. Peretz's radikal-sotsialistishe yorn." In *I. L. Peretz: a zamelbukh tsu zayn ondenken.* New York: Literarisher farlag, 1915, pp. 38–42.

Mukdoyni, A. [A. D. Kapel.] "How I. L. Peretz Wrote His Folk Tales." Trans. Moshe Spiegel. In *In This World and the Next: Selected Writings.* New York: Thomas Yoseloff, 1958, pp. 352–59.

———. *I. L. Peretz un dos yidishe teater.* New York: YKUF, 1949.

Niger, Shmuel. *I. L. Peretz: zayn lebn, zayn firndike perzenlekhkayt, zayne hebreishe un yidishe shriftn, zayn virkung.* Buenos Aires: Alveltlekher yidisher kultur-kongres, 1952.

———. "I. L. Peretz's lebn nokhn toyt." In *Di goldene keyt* 10 (1951), 34–47.

———. "The Legacy of I. L. Peretz." In *In This World and the Next: Selected Writings.* New York: Thomas Yoseloff, 1958, pp. 371–77.

———. "Vegn I. L. Peretz." *Literarishe monatsshriftn* 1 (February 1908), 81–106.

———. "Vegn Peretz's Yiddish." *Di yidishe velt* 4 (1915), book 2, vols. 1– 2 (April–May), 71–94.

Nomberg, H. D. *Dos bukh felyetonen.* Warsaw: S. Jaczkowski, 1924.

———. *I. L. Peretz.* Buenos Aires: Tsentral-farband fun poylishe yidn in Argentina, 1946.

———. "I. L. Peretz: der foter fun der literarisher mishpokhe." In *Tsum yortsayt.* Vilna: Kletzkin, 1916, pp. 35–40.

———. "I. L. Peretz (tsu zayn zibetn yortsayt)." *Bikher velt* 1 (1922), number 2, 115–18

———. "Di simfonie—I. L. Peretz." In *I. L. Peretz in likht fun yidisher kritik.* Part 2. Vilna: Tsisho, 1940, pp. 15–25.

Nusinov, Y. "Peretzes publitsistishe yerushe." *Di royte velt* 7 (April 1925), 23–28.

Oyslender, N. "Peretzes 'Shtet un shtetlekh.' " *Tsaytshrift* 1 (1926), 61– 72.

———. "Peretzes veg." *Di royte velt* 7 (April 1925), 29–32.

———. "Vegn tsvey shtromen in Peretzes kinstlerisher shprakh fun di 90-er yorn." *Di yidishe shprakh* 4 (1930), numbers 1–2, 15–30; continued in *Afn shprakhfront* 5: 1–2 (26–27) (January–April 1931), 55– 70.

Peretz-Laks, R. *Arum Peretzn (zikhroynes un batrakhtungen).* Warsaw: Literarishe bleter, 1935.

Pinsky, David. "Dray yor mit I. L. Peretz." In *Di goldene keyt* 10 (1951), 5–31.

———, and Melech Grafstein. "I. L. Peretz—the Man and Writer." Trans. Moshe Spiegel. In *In This World and the Next: Selected Writings.* New York: Thomas Yoseloff, 1958, pp. 367–70.

———. Introduction to *Di verk fun Isaac Leybush Peretz.* Vol. 1. New York: Farlag Yiddish, 1920.

Reyzen, Avrom. "Mayn bakantshaft mit I. L. Peretz (brivlekh un perzenlekh)." *Di tsukunft* 20 (1915), number 7, 647–54.

———. "Tsvey momentn mit I. L. Peretz." *I. L. Peretz in likht fun yidisher kritik.* Part 4. Vilna: Tsisho, 1940, pp. 11–18.

Roback, A. A. *I. L. Peretz: Psychologist of Literature.* Cambridge, Mass.: Sci-Art Publishers, 1935.

———. "A Psychologist Evaluates Peretz." Trans. Moshe Spiegel. In *In This World and the Next: Selected Writings.* New York: Thomas Yoseloff, 1958, pp. 360–66.

Roskies, Dovid-Hirsh [David]. "A shlisl tsu Peretz's zikhroynes." *Di goldene keyt* 99 (1979), 132–59.

Rozentsvayg, Isaac. *Der radikaler period fun Peretz's shafn (di "Yontev bletlekh").* Kiev: Melukhe farlag far di natsionale minderheytn, 1934.

Samuel, Maurice. *Prince of the Ghetto.* Philadephia: A. A. Knopf, 1948.

Schweid, Mark. *Treyst mayn folk: dos lebn fun I. L. Peretz.* New York: Farlag Peretz, 1955.

Shaked, Gershon. "I. L. Peretz." In *Ha-sifrut ha-'ivrit 1880–1980.* Vol. 1: *Ba-gola.* Tel Aviv: Keter, 1977.

Shalit, Moyshe. "Peretz in Vilna." *Literarishe bleter* (1925), numbers 49–50, 9.

Shmeruk, Chone. *Peretz's yiesh vizie.* New York: YIVO, 1971.

Shofman, G. "I. L. Peretz." In *Di goldene keyt* 10 (1951), 115–16.

Sholem Aleichem. "A vokh mit I. L. Peretz." In SA 15: 71–78.

Spektor, Mordechai. "In tseyntn pavilyon (fun mayne zikhroynes)." In *Tsum ondenk fun I. L. Peretz.* Odessa: Yidishe sektsye bam "gubnarobraz," 1920, pp. 22–24.

———. *Mit I. L. Peretz in festung.* Odessa: Farlag literatur, 1919.

Trunk, Y. Y. "I. L. Peretz der romantiker (esey)." In *I. L. Peretz in likht fun yidisher kritik.* Part 3. Vilna: Tsisho, 1940, pp. 14–26.

———. *Poyln: zikhroynes un bilder.* Vol. 5: *Peretz.* New York: Farlag unzer tsayt, 1949.

Tsitron, S. L. *Dray literarishe doyres: zikhroynes vegn yidishe shriftshteler.* Vols. 1–4. Warsaw: Sreberk and Achiasefer, 1920–28.

———. "Fun mayne zikhroynes: Peretz's ershtn arayntrit in der yidisher literatur." *Literarishe bleter* 2 (10 April 1925), 7.

———. "I. L. Peretz (erinerungen)," *Di yidishe velt* 4 (1915), vol. 2, books 1–2 (April–May), 95–103.

Di tsukunft 20 (1915), numbers 5–6. [Issues on I. L. Peretz.]

Tsum ondenk fun I. L. Peretz. Odessa: Yidisher sektsye bam "gub-narobraz," 1920.

Tsum yortsayt. Vilna: Kletzkin, 1916.

Weinreich, Uriel. "Literary Bibliographies." [I. L. Peretz.] In *The Field of Yiddish: Studies in Yiddish Language, Folklore, and Literature.* Ed. Uriel Weinreich. New York: Linguistic Circle of New York, 1954, pp. 292–99.

Wisse, Ruth R. *I. L. Peretz and the Making of Modern Jewish Culture.* Seattle: University of Washington Press, 1991.

Yeshurun, Y. "Isaac Leybush Peretz-bibliografie." In *I. L. Peretz in 19tn yorhundert.* Buenos Aires: Musterverk Series, 1962.

———. "Zikhroynes vegn Peretzn: a bibliografie." *YIVO bleter* 28 (Fall 1946), 165–70.

Di yidishe velt 4 (1915), vol. 2, books 1–2 (April–May): *Tsum ondenk fun I. L. Peretz.*

YIVO bleter [Peretz issue] 28 (1946).

Zagorodski, Y. H. "Isaac Leybush Peretz," *Achiasaf* 9 (1901), 356–60.

Zakuski, A.Y. *I. L. Peretz.* Buenos Aires: Bukh-gemeynshaft bay der yidisher ratsionalistisher gezelshaft, 1942.

Zhitlovski, Haim. "I. L. Peretz's kinstlerisher tekhnik." In *I. L. Peretz in likht fun yidisher kritik.* Part 4. Vilna: Tsisho, 1940, pp. 3–10.

———. *Isaac Leybush Peretz (artiklen un redes).* New York: YKUF, 1951.

———. *I. L. Peretz's natsionale badaytung.* New York: YKUF, 1951.

Zhitnitzki, L. *I. L. Peretz.* Buenos Aires: Yidisher literatn- un zhurnalistn-fareyn "H. D. Nomberg," 1950.

INDEX OF AUTHORS
AND WORKS